"It is not often that we find a comprehensive and down to earth book on the topic of tentmaking. Patrick Lai has done a great service to the global mission community by writing *Tentmaking*. As one reads the book, one will quickly find that this book is not crafted from a desk only. Rather it comes out of a personal and corporate experience of many tentmakers who have been actively practicing what he has written."

DAVID LEE TAI-WOONG, DIRECTOR OF GLOBAL MISSIONARY
TRAINING CENTER, SEOUL

"Patrick is no armchair theorist. Having watched him in action for nearly two decades, I am impressed with his abilities and expertise in tentmaking. His book is an excellent tool of practicality for anyone interested in serving the Lord through the professional, 'secular' route."

PHIL PARSHALL, SIM, PHILIPPINES

"Finally a book on tentmaking in a pioneer context that causes us to 'love God with our minds.' No glittering generalities here. Patrick is one who has planted churches, started businesses, and now thoroughly researched those who are living overseas doing ministry via secular jobs. We must be grateful for both the demythologizing and for the practical guidance herein. Don't go overseas without it!"

GREG LIVINGSTON, DIRECTOR EMERITUS, FRONTIERS

"Patrick and his wife are two of the most experienced and effective tentmakers today. This long-awaited book is the clearest and most comprehensive treatment of the subject to date. It will no doubt be a tremendously useful resource for tentmaking novices and veterans alike."

STEVE RUNDLE, ASSOCIATE PROFESSOR OF BUSINESS AT BIOLA UNIVERSITY,
CALIFORNIA AND CO-AUTHOR OF *GREAT COMMISSION COMPANIES*

"Patrick Lai has done an outstanding job! The combination of his own successful tentmaking work, both as a businessman and church planter in the 10/40 Window, makes this book relevant and to the point. Patrick's meticulous research, upon which much of the book is based, also gives added credibility to everything he says. *Tentmaking* is a 'must read' for all current and future tentmakers worldwide."

LARRY W. CALDWELL, DIRECTOR DOCTOR OF MISSOLOGY, PROGRAM DIRECTOR, ASIA GRADUATE SCHOOL OF THEOLOGY, MANILA

"This book is the definitive work for contemporary tentmaking. Patrick Lai has composed a very extensive and highly-practical resource birthed from many years of personal experience and interviews from over 450 tentmakers serving in the 10/40 Window. The breadth and depth of Lai's book makes it the most comprehensive piece of literature on the topic to date."

EVANGELICAL MISSIONS QUARTERLY

TENTMAKING

TENTMAKING

The
Life and Work
of Business as Missions

PATRICK LAI

IVP Books

An imprint of InterVarsity Press
Downers Grove, Illinois

InterVarsity Press
P.O. Box 1400, Downers Grove, IL 60515-1426
World Wide Web: www.ivpress.com
E-mail: email@ivpress.com

InterVarsity Press® is the book-publishing division of InterVarsity Christian Fellowship/USA®, a movement of students and faculty active on campus at hundreds of universities, colleges and schools of nursing in the United States of America, and a member movement of the International Fellowship of Evangelical Students. For information about local and regional activities, write Public Relations Dept., InterVarsity Christian Fellowship/ USA, 6400 Schroeder Rd., P.O. Box 7895, Madison, WI 53707-7895, or visit the IVCF website at <www .intervarsity.org>.

All Scripture quotations, unless otherwise indicated, are taken from the The Holy Bible, New International Version®, NIV.® *Copyright © 1973, 1978, 1984 by Biblica, Inc.™. Used by permission of Zondervan. All rights reserved worldwide.*

Originally published by Biblica.

ISBN 978-0-8308-5766-1

Printed in the United States of America ∞

 InterVarsity Press is committed to protecting the environment and to the responsible use of natural resources. As a member of Green Press Initiative we use recycled paper whenever possible. To learn more about the Green Press Initiative, visit <www.greenpressinitiative.org>.

Cataloging-in-Publication Data is available through the Library of Congress.

P	20	19	18	17	16	15	14	13	12	11	10	9	8	7	6
Y	28	27	26	25	24	23	22	21	20	19	18				

CONTENTS

ACKNOWLEDGMENTS

Today, it became clear. Driving home from the office, I caught the movement of something out of the corner of my eye. It was the blowing of a blanket. It drew my attention. Three scrawny little boys were building a tent. In the steppes of Central Asia, this is not a shiny, nylon, Sears store-bought tent, but a "blankets and sheets borrowed from Mom" tent. The best kind. The children looked so cute, I stopped to watch. They saw me and waved. I waved back. The tent was tight and strong.

"Wow! I used to do that," I said to myself. Then it hit me. I am still doing that! I get to build any tent business I want, and it never stops. God's grace, a talented wife, helpful friends, and this tent interest have enabled us to build several tentmaking businesses. The businesses have allowed us to employ wonderful, responsible, and fun-to-work with nationals and expatriates who, as one like-minded team, have been used by our Master to bring His good news to an unreached people group. Yes, there have been hard times, but we have lacked nothing. We have watched our children grow and move on. We have made dear friends who have helped us in our quest to love the Lord our God with all our heart, soul, mind, and strength.

I wish to thank Jesus for the wonderful life He has given me. This book and all that I am and do is dedicated to Him. I wish to thank the many team members I have worked with over the years for your part in God's transformation in my life. To my current co-workers, thank you for your patience, help, wisdom, and perseverance as we struggled to start businesses and plant the church. Thank you too for enabling me to have the time to finish this assignment. *You are the best!* I also wish to thank the hundreds who participated in the survey and interviews, which provided the data for my research. In addition, I want to thank the many unnamed others who helped edit this book. And finally, I wish to thank my wife of twenty-five years who continues to put up with my propensity to start and be consumed with projects such as this book. She is my keenest critic and biggest help. A Proverbs 31 woman is defined by the respect she brings her husband. She has brought me so much. Without her sacrifices and tireless help, nothing I have done in life would be accomplished. She truly is a God-given helper for me.

I owe a debt of thanks to Phil and Julie Parshall for their challenges and guidance, forcing me to substantiate what is and is not effective in the areas of evangelism and church planting among those serving in the 10/40 Window. I also owe a huge debt of gratitude to Greg and Sally Livingstone, our mentors, who have kept us on task and guided us in ministry. It is my prayer that this book will encourage and assist in adequately equipping those going to or already serving in the 10/40 Window.

As we move into our twenty-second year overseas, organizations we once begged for help are now contacting us for "how-to" information. We are thankful to our Master for our businesses, our team, and our lives, which He uses to transform us into His image. We keep three simple standards for our businesses: strive for quality, be profitable, and create witnessing opportunities for Christ. We know we are blessed to do what we do, and we know that if we keep doing the best work of which we are capable, we can always be as joyful as those little people building their remarkable blanket tents.

PREFACE

In 2 Samuel 18, we are told the story of Ahimaaz and the Cushite, messengers of General Joab. The Cushite fought in the battle. He had experienced first hand the results of close combat. In need of a messenger, Joab chose him to go and report what he had seen to King David. Ahimaaz was standing there when the Cushite was sent out. Ahimaaz wanted to run and take the good news to the King, too. As Joab's assistant, Ahimaaz had not been in the battle, yet he felt a desire to share what he heard with the King. Not weary from the battle and knowing a short cut, Ahimaaz outran the Cushite. David was waiting at his headquarters for news of the battle. He wanted specific information about the battle and especially his son, Absalom. When Ahimaaz reported to King David, he did not know the details. He had not experienced the battle nor seen what happened. As a result of his second hand information, he was told to "stand aside" while the Cushite was ushered into the presence of the King. The Cushite had fought in the battle; he had accurate, first-hand information. Ahimaaz was eager to serve, but he did not share from his own life's experiences.

What little has been written on tentmaking has been given us largely by observers who have not fought in the battle. This book is a report from those who are still in the battle. It has been in formation for years, simply because there has been little free time for anything but fighting the battle.

Antonia Van der Meer trains tentmakers at the Brazilian Evangelical Center for Missions. In a recent discussion about tentmaking, she asked me, "How can I give the answers, if I do not know the questions?" This book is written to both ask and answer the questions faced daily by soldiers fighting the battle in the 10/40 Window. A second book, which is in progress, will discuss issues tentmakers face in setting up and operating businesses among the least reached. Truly, each person's journey with God is unique, yet the stories and experiences of others who have gone before may serve to direct us, as well as provide warnings about how to proceed.

This book is written for missionaries, tentmakers, and Christians who are focused on reaching the unreached. The book is an accumulation of nearly thirty years of service to our Master, Jesus Christ. My wife and I have served as regular missionaries, as well as T-5 and T-3 tentmakers. We have started several businesses and schools and an NGO (Non-Governmental Organization). We have team members who worked as T-2 and T-4 tentmakers. I first started this book in 1989, after attending the Tentmaking Task Force of the Lausanne II Congress in Manila. As part of my doctoral studies on the effectiveness of tentmakers, I have visited and interviewed/surveyed 450 workers who are living, working, and ministering around the 10/40 Window. The data given here comes from my research.

In this book, there are many practical stories and quotes given by real people, who are presently serving in the uttermost parts of the earth. When possible, I took notes, but some workers did not want me to write anything down. Consequently, my memory of events may differ occasionally from that of others, yet the best I can do is write the events as I recall them. For obvious reasons, most of the names have been changed, along with many of the locations. Names of real locations are often used simply for the sake of interest. The few real names which are given have been used with permission or are quotes from published sources. This book attempts to deal with the issues which separate tentmakers from more conventional missionaries (whom I refer to as "regular missionaries") in their daily ministry, family life, and work. It provides a different viewpoint, sharing proven, workable alternatives to conventional missionary life.

After reading hundreds of articles on ministry, missions, the marketplace, and work, I believe tentmaking is a subset of mission work. Thus, I have chosen to use the terms *worker*, *missionary*, and *tentmaker* interchangeably. The term *tentmaker* is used because of its historical and biblical implications.

The working world knows that *business* is a broad term that reflects the many varied ways of making money. In this book, the term business is used in the broadest sense, incorporating any profit-making enterprise, such as schools, travel agencies, clinics, stores, restaurants, consulting firms, import-export, computer businesses, etc. Those businesses operated "not for profit," like clinics, schools, and even some commercial businesses are referred to as NGOs. In many of the stories and examples I cite, my use of the term *business* has application for NGO workers as well.

This book is designed to be a manual of the key issues today's tentmakers face. There are so many stories, each of which would be helpful, but space requires me to select the most meaningful. Many of these stories are written in the first person by my friends or me. There is no pride intended, but like the Cushite, just an honest effort to report from the front lines, what we have experienced.

Here is Edward Bear, coming downstairs now, bump, bump, bump, on the back of his head, behind Christopher Robin. It is, as far as he knows, the only way of coming down stairs, but sometimes he feels there really is another way, if only he could stop bumping for a moment and think of it.

WINNIE THE POOH

Intelligent people are always open to new ideas. In fact, they look for them.

PROVERBS 18:15 LB

chapter 1
BREAKING BOXES

What do you do when the Master has called you to preach, but having an unconventional style gets you barred from reaching the very people you are called to preach to? John Wesley faced this very problem. The leaders of his day felt biblical preaching should be done in a church behind a pulpit. Their limited view of doing outreach was based on their own experiences. They were living in a box, unable to see beyond what they already knew. John Wesley stepped outside of this box. Barred from his city's pulpits, he bought a horse and rode out to the countryside where he began open air preaching. Wesley fulfilled his calling without worrying about the traditions and structures of the church. He did not live boxed in by the inhibitions of others. He did not allow the narrow mindedness of others to hinder his ministry of evangelism and church planting. He stepped out of the box, believing the Spirit of God could manifest Himself in unexplored ways, reaching beyond structured and controlled institutions and their liturgies. Wesley appreciated the church, but he did not have a need to reform it. He understood the limitations of traditional methods of outreach and climbed outside the box to reach the less reached. He focused his efforts and resources on implementing new strategies for reaching those who were beyond the reach of the gospel.

Mission agencies now have over two hundred years of traditions, values, policies, and practices. During the nineteenth and twentieth centuries, mission organizations enjoyed the protection of western governments and the donations of wealthy western churches. Having been built on such a foundation, mission agencies are finding it hard to remodel themselves to fit today's world. Many agencies embrace strategies and methods that contrast with those of the world around them. The ways of bringing missions and business together are difficult. A paradigm shift is needed. We must break out of our boxes.

It is a waste of time and resources to train people to learn more and better things, when the context in which the learner thinks has not shifted. It is like trying to add ten new storeys to a building without making adjustments to the foundation. Shifting paradigms cannot be done simply via the imparting of knowledge. Presenting facts and telling stories may or may not help. If leaders are going to look at things differently, we must willingly choose to re-look at the same situation from a totally different point of view. Old foundations need to be put aside so new structures may be built. Revamping former strategies and methodologies will not work. "We need to wake up to the fact that we can not rely on the 'tried and true' because what was tried yesterday is no longer true today."[1] Mission organizations need to retool. We need to attempt new models of sending workers. Like John Wesley, we need to pray and think and then be ready to step outside the box.

Jesus says, "Come follow me and I will make you fishers of men."[2] Jesus is still seeking fishers of men; some are to leave their nets, and others are to bring their nets with them. But how are we to reach those living in countries which restrict missionary access? How are we to evangelize neighborhoods and nearby classes of society that are still largely untouched by churches just around the corner?

Encouraging changes are beginning to occur, both in churches and mission agencies. Some leaders are assessing the successes and failures of current tentmaker-missionaries. New insights are being gleaned from the lives of many scriptural heroes, like Abraham, Joseph, Daniel, Paul, Aquilla, and Priscilla. We are beginning to grasp the importance of holistic believers who go about their "business" while being agents of a much higher calling. We are being forced to recognize that the Great Commission does not end when missionary visas are withdrawn. We are accepting, even encouraging, new workers to take their nets with them.

IT'S A NEW WORLD

After World War II, there was a shift among the nations from colonialism to nationalism and independence. To demonstrate their newly gained freedom, many former colonies closed their doors to missionaries. As a result, some Christian leaders began to consider that the end of the era of sending missionaries was near. In the 1970s, such thinking was modified, with Ralph Winter drawing the attention of mission leaders to the priority of unreached peoples. But the question quickly arose, "How can missionaries serve in countries that do not grant missionary visas?" Churches and missions were told they needed to study the situation, to develop new strategies, and to pursue a higher order of performance. During the past thirty years, the discussions have evolved from "how to do tentmaking," to the "ethics of tentmaking," to the "biblical basis of tentmaking," to the "historical basis of tentmaking," to "evaluating the successes and failures of those who are doing tentmaking." Though these foundational issues needed to be discussed, progress has been slow in convincing decision makers to change their positions. Only since the turn of the century have mission leaders begun to formulate creative tentmaking strategies.

In reality, many leaders and missiologists are scarcely aware of the conceptual re-tooling needed for directing change on the mission field of the 21st century. In attempting to initiate changes, most mission organizations fail to realize that, though tentmakers are missionaries, the scope of their assignment creates problems and stresses which are unique and different from those experienced by regular missionaries. As a result, tentmakers who are teamed with regular missionaries often find they are unable to relate to one another. Though the tentmaker's approach to solving problems and relieving stresses will in some ways parallel that of the regular missionary, the differences are significant and need to be addressed. Missiologists need to come to a point where we admit that long-held perspectives are inapplicable and irrelevant to a tentmaker's life and work.

We live in a new and unpredictable world. Governments, the marketplace, and life in general are changing at speeds never heard of before. The way of life and the values that were the norm in our grandparents' childhood are in many ways completely out of date. Any resemblance between today and the 1950s is purely coincidental. Nonetheless, the Word of God is constant. We know that "Jesus Christ is the same yesterday and today and forever."[3] As Paul was a Jew to the Jews and a Greek to the Greeks, so we must adapt the delivery, not the content, of our message to the changing world around us. We have not played in this arena before. The rules are different. Everything is moving faster. What we need to know and how we need to act in order to win the world to Jesus has changed as well.

TENTMAKING

What is tentmaking? Tentmaking is often understood to refer to an economic factor: "a missionary being financially self-supporting." A handful of missiologists stubbornly stress this narrow point of view, relating tentmaking to money. However, tentmaking is not about money; it is about God. Tentmaking is about a way of revealing God's glory to the ends of the earth. Jesus makes it clear: "You cannot serve both God and Money . . . Is not life more important than food, and the body more important than clothes?"[4] Tentmakers know that tentmaking is not about money, visas, entry strategies, or all the other issues missiologists love to debate. The objective of tentmaking is to put Jesus in front of those who have never had an opportunity to hear the truth about Him, or who have turned their backs on Him because of an encounter with some form of "Christian religion." Tentmaking provides many advantages, but the most important aspect of tentmaking is giving the lost a good look, and often a first look, at who Jesus really is. Tentmaking is using daily-life strategies to tell people about Jesus. The models and methods vary, but the goal is to glorify Jesus among the unreached.

When we stop and consider the world, we realize that money is the primary motivation behind most activities. Buying, selling, and creating material wealth—that's where people are; that's what they think about; that's what they strive for. The world revolves around the marketplace. That is where people learn values and methods. That is where people function and gain satisfaction. It is crucial that we meet people in their comfort zones and impart godly values, methods, and satisfaction. People need to see the Christian life lived right before their eyes. Our faith in Jesus needs to be made real; it is to be lived where the people live. George MacLeod urges:

> "I simply argue that the cross must be raised again at the center of the marketplace as well as on the steeple of the church. I am recovering the claim that Christ was not crucified in a cathedral between two candles, but on a cross between two thieves; on the town garbage-heap; at a crossroad so cosmopolitan that they had to write His title in Hebrew, Latin, and Greek; at the kind of place where cynics talked smut, and thieves cursed, and soldiers gambled. Because that is where He died and that is what He died about, that is where the churchmen should be and what the churchmen should be about."[5]

Whether it is in New York or New Delhi, San Jose or Shanghai, we need to live out our faith in ways that are both understandable and genuine.

As missiologists debated the tentmaking issues, a few thousand workers who could not wait while millions perished into a Christ-less eternity stepped out of the box. They picked up their nets and went without missionary visas into countries which restrict the spread of the gospel. This first wave of 20th century tentmakers worked primarily as professionals with multi-national corporations and as English teachers in local schools and universities. Some set up Non-Government Organizations (NGOs), which for all intents and purposes, operate like a mission organization providing social services without the Christian label. Others went as students. The successes and failures of these early pioneers were duly noted. Both sides of the argument had illustrations to prove their points for or against tentmaking. As more and more young people accepted this new approach, missiologists became more informed about the how to's of tentmaking. In 1983, Frontiers, a new mission agency, was created for the purpose of facilitating the efforts of tentmakers in closed countries. Their willingness to think and live outside the box eventually led to the spawning of many similar missions and is bringing changes to the more established sending agencies.

Change—it is all around us. Our Creator is a God of change. To thrive in the 21st century, we must love change—not just endure it, but love it. Globalization and the internet, along with the rise of fundamentalist branches of the world's religions, have shaken many mission organizations, forcing them to look outside the box. This new viewpoint is leading more and more organizations to embrace entrepreneurial tentmaking as a legitimate strategy. Today, nearly every large mission organization has developed a tentmaking arm. Yet, as traditional missions cease their criticisms and embrace tentmaking, many still fail to grasp the fundamentals. The methods mission agencies use to recruit and train tentmakers and the way mission executives counsel and lead their tentmakers once they are out on the field shows little understanding of the differences tentmakers encounter in their daily life and work. My research reflects two divergent approaches mission agencies take toward tentmaking. The first is a paternalistic view, requiring tentmakers to live, work, and perform much as traditional missionaries do. The second is a hands-off approach, allowing tentmakers to write their own agenda with little, if any, care and accountability provided by the mission agency.

Rather than add to the already challenging rhetoric, this book is a manual of key issues today's tentmakers are facing, presenting both illustrations and practical suggestions for the re-examination of tentmaking life and work. I wish to encourage both leaders and workers to look beyond the box.

SUMMARY

If the church is to take the gospel to every tribe, nation, tongue and people group, it must step outside the box. Tentmakers are determined to build roads through or around the walls which have blocked the spread of cross-cultural discipleship and church planting in the least-reached corners of the world. If the church is to see new churches planted in hostile environments, it must break new ground and build new foundations. Business as usual won't do. And that's the point. Tentmaking is *ministry* outside the box AND *business* outside the box. We want to ask Christopher Robin to pause for a moment so that Edward Bear can consider other, perhaps better, options for descending the stairs.

ACTION STEPS

- What boxes do you need to break out of?
- Are there any boxes your church needs to break out of?
- In what ways does Edward Bear's problem relate to missions today?

"Dad," a polar-bear cub asked his father, "Am I 100 percent polar bear?" "Of course you are," answered his father. "My parents are 100 percent polar bear which makes me 100 percent polar bear and your mother's parents are all polar bear so she's 100 percent polar bear. So that makes you 100 percent polar bear too. Why?" The cub replied, "Because Dad, I'm freezing."

We know that we all possess knowledge. Knowledge puffs up, but love builds up. The man who thinks he knows something does not yet know as he ought to know.

1 CORINTHIANS 8:1-2

chapter 2
WHO AM I, ANYWAY?

I hate being the bearer of bad news. I was in China visiting a dear friend, Karl. As requested, I had picked up his mail in Hong Kong to deliver to him. As he sat down to read the bundle, I left to scout out the area. I hadn't made it to the stairwell when I heard shouting. I rushed back and opened the door find Karl standing there with a letter in his hand, half shouting, half questioning his roommate, "Who am I, anyway? What am I doing here? How do I explain to my church what I am doing here? Can you believe it? They do not want to fund a student!" Karl had just received a letter from his home church telling him they would no longer be supporting him, as it was the policy of the church not to support students while they pursued their education. The letter went on to state that once he finished his studies, the church would gladly consider supporting him again. Yes, Karl had become a student, studying for an MA in the music of the local people. However, music, though an interest, was hardly a priority for Karl. Unable to get a missionary visa, he became a student to obtain a legal residence that provided him natural opportunities among his focus people to build friendships and share his faith.

TENTMAKING IN THE 10/40 WINDOW

The status of tentmaking as a tool for world missions is not well grasped, even by the handful of missions-minded churches that helped make it popular. Few are aware of the practical implications involved with mission efforts into "creative access nations" (CANs). Yet, virtually all Buddhist, Hindu, and Muslim countries fall into this category. It surprises many to learn that there are no churches or Christian nationals in or near half of the distinct language and cultural groups of the world. The Gospel's initial presence must be established by expatriate missionaries who step across cultural barriers from places where the church is thriving and the Great Commission has been heeded. Particularly in the case of nations where missionary visas are not issued, other means must be employed to establish a witness—thus, the need for tentmakers.

Estimates vary widely concerning the number of tentmakers in the world, all the way from ten thousand to a hundred thousand. Missiologists decline to even give a ball park guestimate of the number of tentmakers serving in the 10/40 Window. Because many tentmakers have very real security concerns, the actual number may never be known. But numbers are not as important as productivity. The effectiveness of tentmakers working in the 10/40 Window has been researched. We know that within the past decade tentmakers have gathered over two hundred fellowships of new believers, and started at least 157 new churches among the least-reached peoples of the world. Though not as effective in planting churches as regular missionaries, tentmakers have proven they are a valuable force and a good investment of church resources.

WHAT IS A TENTMAKER?

Tentmaking is not a new idea. It is as old as the Scriptures. There is no need to argue about it being a better or worse method of sending Christian missionaries than other approaches. Both regular missionaries and tentmakers are biblical models and are urgently needed if the task of world evangelization is to be completed. The extent of the unfinished task is enormous. Thanks to the research efforts of many, we now have a clear picture of what remains to be done to finish Christ's task of evangelizing the world. The great number of workers required, the difficulty of financially supporting these workers, and the increasing amount of countries that restrict the entry of regular missionaries are three important reasons tentmakers are needed for completing the Great Commission. Until the name of Jesus is lifted up amongst all peoples, we must use every means possible to declare His glory among the unreached.

Oswald Chambers said, "Looking for opportunities to serve God is impertinence; every time and all the time is our opportunity to serve God. God does not expect us to work for Him, but with Him." Christians believe that "whatever anyone does in word or deed, it should all be done in the name of the Lord Jesus."[6] It is important to understand there is no dichotomy between work and ministry. Work and ministry are to be one. However, as an experienced tentmaker knows, there are times when I must defer going to the office so I can meet with Abdullah to study the Bible. I cannot be two places at once. Sometimes I can do evangelism or discipleship at work, but often I cannot. In this sense, work and ministry do conflict. Thus, in real life there are times when we must choose between our vocational work and our ministry outreach.

In Acts 18, we read that Paul made tents. In all probability, he did this for one of two reasons. First, he sometimes worked to supplement his income so as not to burden those to whom he was ministering (1 Corinthians 9:12; 1 Thessalonians 2:9). Second, he worked to identify with people and make friendships through which he could share his faith (Acts 18:2–3). In considering tentmaking, it is important to evaluate one's true motives for pursuing it. We need to honestly ask ourselves, "Is this God's leading or my own desire?"

The term *tentmaker* has it proponents and opponents. No term is perfect. The word may be misleading as it already has varying applications. But the word *tentmaker* is a biblical term, and it does point us in the right direction. First, it communicates that our vocation should be seen as a means of serving God. As I tell my employees and friends, "I am here because God told me to come here." Second, it stresses the intentionality of my work choices. Tentmakers are missionaries. We are called, prepared, sent out by a church, and held accountable, just as any other missionary. I do not live and work in the 10/40 Window because I make a lot of money, but because there is so little witness here. Tentmakers are on God's assignment and He has assigned us to be where we are.

There are many missiological terms which express tentmaking. Possibly the other most commonly used term is *bi-vocational worker*. This emphasizes the point that tentmakers are "professional missionaries" fulfilling two callings. We are career business people *and* career missionaries. Yet the term does not reflect the cross-cultural component of tentmaking. The Koreans coined the term *bussionaries*, combining the words business and missionary, but it has not caught on anywhere else. Most Christians wrongly perceive all tentmakers to be fully self-supported, cross-cultural workers. We know the Apostle Paul received some support from churches (2 Corinthians 11:8 and Philippians 4:15), so limiting the term to being fully self-supported is unnecessarily narrow, if not divisive.

In her book, *From Jerusalem To Irian Jaya*, Ruth Tucker shares the stories of ninety-nine influential missionaries who contributed to the development and spread of the church and world missions. Tucker documents that twenty-three of these workers were tentmakers. Thus, nearly one quarter of the key missionary leaders in history were tentmakers. For example, William Carey, the founder of the modern missions movement, was both a cobbler and a factory manager. Hudson Taylor, the founder of the China Inland Mission (today's Overseas Missionary Fellowship), was a medical doctor. These early tentmakers were often sent to unreached areas to initiate missionary work and plant churches. In an effort to win the trust of officials and the hearts of the people, these pioneer workers would serve the physical needs of people to gain an opportunity to meet their spiritual needs. Their evangelistic efforts were often promoted by the healing and education offered in their hospitals or schools. The strategy worked well, but today some countries are even restricting the entry of medical people for fear they are undercover missionaries. Today's tentmaker may not be as easily identified. Some are not openly related to any missionary institution and do not live and act as regular missionaries. Rather, they have entered a country as professionals—teachers, businessmen, engineers, social workers, etc.—all secular professions. None of these suggest an obvious connection with missionary work.

TENTMAKING TERMS

In coming to terms with tentmaking, it is important to understand what tentmaking is. The word *tentmaking* is related to Paul's work. The Apostle Paul is most frequently upheld as the biblical model of tentmaking. Acts 18 tells us that the Apostle Paul and his friends, Aquilla and Priscilla, were tentmakers. They made tents while doing missionary work in Corinth. During the week, they could be found in the central marketplace making tents, trading, and interacting with the people of the area. But on Saturdays they closed shop to spend time in the synagogue, striving to convince both Jews and Greeks that Jesus was the Christ. Paul, Aquilla, and Priscilla were tentmakers by trade, but missionaries by calling. Like a regular missionary, Paul was sent out by his home church (Acts 13:3) and reported back to them (Acts 15:4; 21:17). During his travels, he was identified as both a religious worker and a tentmaker businessman (Acts 16:17; 18:3). He received personal income from both churches and his business (2 Corinthians 11: 8; 1 Corinthians 9:6, 12). Calling, identity, source of income, and having a measurable ministry are each part of defining a tentmaker. One mission leader told me, "The Muslim world requires the finest type of missionary to bear witness to them. We desire the best people and the best training for those who work with Muslims. Where does tentmaking fit into all this? Simple—there are few or no Muslim countries today that grant missionary visas. Tentmaking is a means of getting into these countries." Serving where access is difficult, providing a legal, long-term entry strategy, intentionality and preparation are all important factors in defining a tentmaker.

MISSIOLOGISTS' DEFINITIONS

Greg Livingstone, the director emeritus of Frontiers, suggests there are three types of tentmakers: *job takers, job makers,* and *job fakers. Job takers* work for national or international companies. As these tentmakers hold jobs that nationals might have had, they are viewed as workers who take jobs. *Job makers* are workers who set up their own businesses, offer social services for nationals, or open schools. All of these strategies may employ nationals or enhance educational opportunities for nationals, thus creating new jobs. *Job fakers* find some legal way to get a resident visa that keeps them free enough to be fully involved in proclamation and discipleship of new believers. *Job fakers,* like regular missionaries, are supported by their home churches. Livingstone's nomenclature is descriptive and easy to remember, but it fails to cover several key concerns.

Ed Van Baak, missions director of the Dutch Reformed Church, gives the most common definition of a tentmaker when he writes, "A tentmaker is a missionary in terms of commitment, but is fully self-supporting." Don Hamilton, in his book *Tentmakers Speak*, defines a tentmaker as "a Christian who works in a cross-cultural situation, is recognized by members of the host culture as something other than a *religious professional*, and yet, in terms of his or her commitment, calling, motivation, and training, is a *missionary* in every way." (italics mine) Each of these definitions is helpful, but still inadequate. For example, the Apostle Paul would not qualify as a tentmaker according to these definitions. In several places in Scripture, Paul is recognized as a religious worker (Acts 14:11,15; 16:17; 17:18). Paul also received some support from churches (2 Corinthians 11:7–9; Philippians 4:15).

Richard Chia puts forward one of the more concise definitions befitting those working in restricted access nations. He sees a tentmaker as, "One who has a calling for full-time missionary service but is unable to enter a country of choice because of restrictions. One whose primary purpose is to do full-time missionary work but because of restrictions has to modify his mode of service." Ruth Siemens adds clarity to our understanding in pointing out that "tentmaking cannot be equated with lay ministry because it is a missionary mode, a missions strategy. But some of Paul's principles are equally applicable to lay ministry."

I was attending a local church mission conference in Singapore. The speaker was a well-known mission director of one of the largest "faith" missions. During a question and answer session, he responded sharply to a question about tentmaking, saying, "Tentmakers are not missionaries.

. . . Paul is the only example of tentmaking in the New Testament." That evening, this same speaker, as he was preaching from the book of Acts stated, "Paul was the greatest missionary who ever lived." Are tentmakers missionaries or not? It seems tentmakers have an identity crisis. It is no wonder we find workers around the world throwing up their hands and shouting, "Who am I, anyway?"

CONSIDERATIONS AFFECTING THE DEFINITION OF A TENTMAKER

There are a number of factors to consider when defining a tentmaker. Some of these factors are obvious, some more complex. In discussing the various roles and types of tentmakers, the Tentmaking Task Force of the Lausanne II Congress outlined nine considerations which affect the definition of a tentmaker. They are:

1. Called to minister
2. Religious ministry
3. Secular identity
4. Intentionality
5. Training
6. Cross-cultural
7. Closed country—RAN, CAN
8. Resident visa
9. Source of salary

Called to Minister

William Carey, the father of the modern missionary movement, was a tentmaker. When the British East India Company would not allow Carey to work as a missionary, he took employment in a location outside of their control. When he or his co-workers' funds ran low, he found employment to supplement their needs. During his career in India, Carey worked as a translator, cobbler, factory manager, educator, and journalist. Even so, Carey had a very productive ministry. In addition to planting a church, he translated portions of the Bible into more than forty languages. He founded both a college and a daily newspaper. He said, "My business is to witness for Christ, I make shoes just to pay my expenses."

All tentmakers have a calling to minister for Jesus. Work is ministry; ministry is work. To separate our work from our ministry is to separate who we are. As ambassadors of Jesus Christ, our primary desire is to please Him and fulfill His purposes for our lives. Like Carey, we do whatever it takes to get the gospel out among the people. Our motivation for going overseas is to be witnesses for Christ. We are living abroad in obedience to His calling.

Many people struggle with the word *calling*. How do I know I have been called? What is a calling? In the book of Acts, we find four types of callings. The first example is found in Acts 10:3–16 and again in 16:9. In both places, the Lord uses a vision or a dream to direct or call His servant. Second, in Acts 13:1–4 God speaks directly to the church leaders to appoint Paul and Barnabas to go forth with His message. Third, in Acts 15:40 we read that the missionary Paul "chose Silas." Silas' calling was nothing other than Paul recognizing a man with gifts that were needed on his team and Paul extending an invitation to join him. Fourth, Acts 18:27 says, "Apollos wanted to go to Achaia" and "the brothers encouraged him and wrote to the disciples there to welcome him." You could say Apollos had a burden for the people of Achaia.

A dream or vision, being singled out by church leaders, being invited by a missionary worker, or having a burden for a group of people, are all biblical examples of ways God calls people. It is important to note that though callings are initiated differently, the local church is involved with each. It is God's plan to use the local church to confirm His guidance and ensure accountability in the life of each worker. This measure of accountability keeps some of us from running off with our hearts aimed at the ends of the earth and our heads in the clouds. Tentmakers have a calling to ministry.

Religious Ministry

I first met Bill when he passed through our city. We had lunch together. He was sharp, young, Navigator trained; I was impressed. He soon found a job in a nearby country teaching English. The next year when I was in his area on business, I decided to visit him. When I arrived at his home, he was in class, teaching. Knowing the local language, I struck up a conversation with his neighbor, Mr. Ahmad. Ahmad told me he had known Bill for nearly a year. I asked Ahmad what he thought of Bill. He replied, "Bill's a wonderful guy. He helps me with my garden, brings my children toys when he comes back from trips, he is very polite and kind, and an excellent neighbor." I asked Ahmad if there was anything else he knew about Bill. When he replied, "No," I pressed, "Do you know Bill is a Christian?" He replied, "Well, all Americans are Christians." Later, I asked Bill, "Have you ever shared the gospel with Ahmad?" "No," was Bill's reply, "I am here to be a light for the gospel. I don't want to tell people about my faith unless they ask; otherwise, I might jeopardize my visa."

Bill is not tentmaking. Tentmakers are involved in ministry. Whether we are doing medical work, helping the poor, or running computers, tentmakers have a duty to give glory to our Father in heaven. If God is not receiving the credit, then no ministry is taking place. As the Apostle Paul put it, "Woe to me if I do not preach the gospel!"[7]

This is not to say that verbal witnessing is the only way to witness. Clearly, there are many ways to communicate an idea. Words are just one way. Our message is founded in our lives. Our words and our actions reflect who we are, for in truth, we are the message. When we limit Christ's message to spoken words or actions, we are not only limiting what He might do through us, but we are handicapping our efforts to witness for Him. However, I know several supposed tentmakers who after serving overseas, confessed that due to fears of persecution, they never shared the gospel with anyone. They did not even tell people they were Christians. We are to place God's light on a stand, not under a bowl. Tentmakers are intentional about their religious ministry. As ambassadors, we are to both represent and speak out for our King.

Secular Identity

When I first went overseas, I worked with a large faith mission. I was assigned to a local Baptist church in an open country where my wife and I trained leaders and did evangelism. Though my education and background was in business, I never called myself a tentmaker. Why? Because I *was* a missionary. My visa said I was a missionary; the church I served and even my non-Christian neighbors called me a missionary. The primary difference between a missionary and a tentmaker is having a secular job. Many times these jobs are in fact, *faker* jobs. Some workers create companies or find positions with a company in order to gain access into a country. However, they do not actually work for or receive payment from the company. These tentmakers obtain a secular identity but are basically living and functioning as missionaries. Whether employed in a paid or unpaid position, serving in an NGO, or otherwise working for a company, tentmakers are not identified in their host community as missionaries.

Intentionality

Brian felt God's leading to work among the Berbers of North Africa. He had a university degree in electrical engineering. He heard that the British Council English School in Melilla was looking for English teachers. He immediately enrolled in a five-week Teaching English as a Second Language course, and he also applied for the job. Upon receiving his TESL certificate, Brian was hired to teach English. Brian is an example of how intentionality works; he set aside his training to get a job among the people the Lord wanted him to serve. Tentmakers are intentional about their life and work. We set goals which will bring glory to God. Most tentmakers set long-range objectives such as evangelism and church planting, before heading overseas. Setting goals and asking someone to hold us accountable keeps us focused in the midst of many distractions and aids us in keeping our priorities right. Whatever we do, wherever we are, tentmakers intend to be, first and foremost, witnesses to the glory of God.

Training

To the uninformed, spring training in baseball is a little odd. It is a period when, in addition to getting into shape to play after the winter lay-off, teams spend a huge amount of time going through drills that stress the basics. It is curious that these men who have been playing baseball passionately since they were little boys and are now highly paid professionals would need to spend weeks reviewing the basics. However, a closer look reveals it is not that they do not know what to do; rather it is a matter of being able to perform these basic skills without hesitation or error when the pressure is on. The drills are designed to reinforce good habits until the players' actions become natural reflexes. Coaches use diagrams, videos, repetitive drills, chalk talks, and games: as many methods as possible to make the point—practice makes perfect.

As tentmakers, we need to train and retrain. Like spring training, our desire should be to drill the basic values and practices into our thoughts and actions until they become natural habits. This takes more than classroom lectures and reading a few books. We need to practice and participate in both ministry and job situations before moving overseas. We need to master the basics in preparation for becoming champions, not of a game, but of life itself. Leroy Eims of the Navigators once told me, "If the Lord told me to do a job and that I had three years to live to do it, I would invest two years preparing and one year doing it."

Some tentmakers think that as they are not regular missionaries, they may go to the field with little or no training. They believe they can witness at work overseas in the same fashion they do at home. However, though many similarities exist, there are many important differences, too. Moreover, career missionaries usually have a good support system on the field, whereas many tentmakers have to depend on their own resources. It is essential that tentmakers receive both adequate and appropriate training before going abroad.

Tentmakers are both fully missionary and fully business people. Thus, we must be trained in our job skill and again as regular missionaries. Studying adequately and gaining practical experience can sometimes take years. Ted Yamamori states training objectives well:

"These ambassadors must be:

1. physically, emotionally, and spiritually self-reliant;
2. adaptable;
3. biblically literate;
4. alert to the emerging mission context;
5. trained in meeting needs vital to the people group they seek to penetrate;
6. trained in long-term and low-profile evangelistic skills;
7. equipped with broad new strategic thinking; and prepared with a special strategy for responding to opportunities presented by need."[8]

It is not uncommon for tentmakers to invest four to six years in preparation after graduating from university. Wise tentmakers invest the time and effort to be adequately equipped for every good work.

Cross-Cultural

Jack has been serving as a pastor in the church he grew up in, but as funds are low, he also works as an assistant manager of a local Burger King. Although Jack is called to ministry, has a secular job, is intentional about sharing his faith at work, and has been trained to do ministry, he is not a tentmaker. Why not? Webster defines a missionary as "a person sent out by his church to preach, teach and proselytize, as in a foreign country." Tentmakers are missionaries whose assignments prevent them from being identified as such, and by definition, a missionary is one who serves in a foreign country.

The growth of lay ministries is exciting. Around the world, God is taking His presence into the marketplace. However, marketplace ministry is not tentmaking unless it is done cross-culturally. Stephen Neil once observed that "when everything is mission, nothing is mission." Similarly, if we call every expatriate Christian worker who lives abroad a tentmaker, we muddy, rather than clarify, our understanding of tentmaking and harm the potential possibilities of churches and missions cooperating to assist and send aspiring tentmakers.

If we hold to the premise that apostolic mission is evangelism, discipleship, and church planting among those who are not being ministered to by a church, then our intent is cross-cultural ministry. For the church to reach out where there are no believers requires a worker to cross over into another culture. The missionary/tentmaker may carry the same passport as the people he is seeking to reach, but he must be cross-cultural, meaning he comes from another segment of society (usually another ethnic group) and possibly a different socio-economic level. Therefore, a way must be found to cross cultural barriers and become a trusted significant-other—an insider—who can present the gospel in understandable ways.

Every people group in the world today where a church exists was at one time the recipient of foreign or cross-cultural workers. Rick Love, the international director of Frontiers, said, "The peoples of the world without a church still need, first of all, apostles—someone who is going to start the church where it does not exist." Tentmakers are workers who have entered another culture and are serving the Lord among a people group other than their own.

Closed Country—CAN, RAN

Over 80 percent of unreached peoples, those people groups without a church, are living in countries that do not grant missionary visas. Yes, there are tentmakers in many countries, including Korea, Kenya, and Brazil, which have robust churches and are becoming major sending countries in their own right. However, our priority is to work where there is no church. Paul made it clear when he wrote, "It has always been my ambition to preach the gospel where Christ was not known, so that I would not be building on someone else's foundation." The research shows that regular missionaries are more effective in evangelism, discipleship, and church planting, so where visas are granted for missionary work, this option should be seriously considered. Yes, the Master will lead some tentmakers to serve in reached areas. As tentmakers, we often have access to people who would never come near a church or Christian worker. We also have an identity and business network which leads us into natural relationships for sharing our faith. Nonetheless, we wish to keep our focus on bringing the gospel to the whole world.

In many countries that restrict missionary visas, the unreached people groups live under the watchful eye of governments that are openly hostile to the gospel. Often the country has a national religion to which the people are expected to adhere. These governments see no reason to encourage defection from Buddhism, Hinduism, Islam, and others. Some governments, wanting to appease the clergy and fundamental sects, will take overt actions to prevent people from becoming Christians. For example, more Muslim countries are seeking to install portions of shari'ah law into their legal code—if not adopt it altogether. However, countries that are closed to regular missionaries are still open for business. These countries require some creativity to enter, stay, and share the gospel. We often refer to these countries as *creative access nations,* or CANs. Countries which restrict missionary visas are also referred to as *restricted access nations*, or RANs. The terms have the same meaning and are interchangeable.

Mission work in such places is risky business, but it is still biblical business. George Verwer, the founder of Operation Mobilization, has said, "There are no closed countries as long as you are willing to not leave once you get in." If regular missionaries cannot get into a country to do the Lord's work, then tentmakers must. There are workers in every 10/40 Window country of the world. If we think and are willing to act outside the box, there are no closed doors. Where the church already exists among a people group, missionaries are more effective workers. Tentmakers are best suited for serving where regular missionaries cannot.

Resident Visa

Lee, a Singaporean, lives at home but travels regularly to nearby CANs to do both business and ministry. However, he is not a tentmaker since he does not reside with the people he is seeking to reach.

Non-residential missionaries (NRMs) are not tentmakers either, for two reasons. One, most NRMs being non-residential, live outside their area of ministry. Two, NRMs have their own special identity and service, thus they do not need another defining term.

The two best points of contact for making friends and sharing the gospel are in the work place and among our neighbors. Tentmakers find creative avenues to reside in the country and live among the people they are trying to reach.

Source of Salary

The Lausanne Tentmaking Task Force failed in its assignment to define what a tentmaker is, as the committee could not agree on the tentmaker's source of salary. The divisive issue is, "Must tentmakers be fully self-supporting?" Or may they be partially supported by churches? Or may they be fully supported by churches and simply have a non-missionary identity?

I remember the first time I went to a 31 Flavors Ice Cream store in Singapore. I was with a close college buddy who I had discipled and not seen for several years. I ordered a double scoop Rocky Road (my favorite) and paid the attendant. After I had paid and started to walk away, my friend told the attendant that I did not live there and was his guest. Without saying another word, the attendant promptly dug my money out of the cash register and placed it on the counter for me to take back. My friend then paid for me.

The Apostle Paul did not wish to be a burden to the people he was sent to witness to. The custom in Paul's day, which still holds true in Asia today, is for the host to pay all the expenses of the guest. This is all the more important if the guest is a teacher or a leader. Paul broke with tradition when he would not allow the churches he was serving to financially support him. He did not have a problem accepting financial assistance from his sending churches. Rather, he wanted it to be clear to those he was proclaiming the good news that his motive for evangelism and church planting was not to make a living. Paul took pains to have a clear conscience before God and men (Acts 24:16).

Many people think tentmakers do their job or work first and then minister on the side. This is true of some tentmakers, but not most. Over 80 percent of all workers ministering in the 10/40 Window have a tentmaker job and/or identity. Yet, most of us (94 percent) receive some income from churches or friends. This income enables us to limit the number of hours we are involved in business and provides time for language and cultural studies. Money was not an issue for Paul. God supplied his needs, sometimes through churches and friends and sometimes from the income he earned through making and repairing tents. Paul's primary desire was to preach the gospel. It was inconsequential to Paul whether his source of income was from his sending churches or his tentmaking business.

Tentmakers, as missionaries, are called to minister the gospel of Jesus cross-culturally. Tentmakers are intentional in serving God. To that end, tentmakers pursue appropriate training, which equips them for a measurable religious ministry while living among the people they are called to reach. Tentmakers have a non-missionary identity. Some tentmakers are supported wholly by their job, while others receive support from churches and Christian friends.

FIVE TYPES OF TENTMAKERS

When you meet someone, one of the first questions you ask is, "What do you do?" or "Where do you work?" It is from a person's role in the community that we begin to understand them and formulate opinions of who they really are. It is the same with our biblical heroes. We learn about the lives and faith of Isaac and Jacob, the shepherds; Joseph, David, Solomon, and Daniel, the government officials; Amos, the herdsman; and Nehemiah, the city developer. The majority of Jesus' disciples were fisherman, with a tax collector thrown in to keep the books. I asked a dozen Christians, "Did Jesus and Paul have a job?" and "What did they do?" All answered the same, "Yes, Jesus was a carpenter, and Paul was a tentmaker." The men we revere as the fathers of the faith were known by their contemporaries for their livelihoods, even as we are known today.

In seeking to grasp the scope of tentmaking, I surveyed or interviewed 450 tentmakers and regular missionaries serving in the 10/40 Window. Taking the basic characteristics of the tentmakers and breaking them down into categories, I discovered common denominators of five common groupings. People like clear-cut definitions. However, these are categories, not definitions. The intention of these categories is to help workers more readily explain their calling, role, and ministry.

T-1

Len was a deacon in the First Baptist Church of Podunk, USA. He had worked for American Express for eight years and then was asked to transfer to their office in Bangalore. Intrigued at the thought of living overseas (and the extra benefits he would receive), he moved his family to India. Soon after arriving, Len was surrounded by both Hindu and Muslim co-workers. Back home, Len loved to share about Jesus. However, at the office, his boss often hindered him from witnessing. Now he was the head of the office. Many of his employees wanted to improve their English. Not wishing his employees to convert for the sake of their jobs, he invited a missionary working in the city to come and teach them English classes in the evenings. He encouraged this Christian worker to share his faith boldly. Several employees came to know Christ through this ministry. Len assisted the missionary in discipling two of the men. Though he went overseas in obedience to his company, Len saw this as an opportunity to bless the Lord and made the most of it.

T-1 tentmakers are Christians who are employed abroad in the course of their careers without any initial commitment to cross-cultural evangelism or church planting. Most T-1 tentmakers are hired by a company in their home country to do a job they are uniquely qualified for in another country. The company pays a salary and often provides numerous other benefits to entice the employee to work overseas. T-1 tentmakers are sincere Christians who are active witnesses for the Lord at home, as well as abroad. However, they are overseas because they have been sent there by their company, not out of any special calling. In other words, their primary motivation for being overseas is their job, not to be a witness. Usually T-1s have no full-time ministry experience and have not thought through how they will witness, disciple, or plant a church in their new country. T-1s take things as they come. They may work forty to eighty-four hours a week and minister as opportunities arise. In other words, their life and outreach is much the same as it is in their home country. There is no evidence of T-1 tentmakers having planted a church, though several have been used to win people to Christ and disciple secret believers. T-1s have assisted other tentmakers in finding jobs and in setting up and gaining government approval for the establishment of other tentmaking businesses or NGOs. T-1s rarely learn the local language. They perform their job and ministry in English or their native language.

The U.S. Bureau of Consular Affairs estimates there are over 320,000 Americans living in the 10/40 Window. According to a Gallup survey, approximately one-third of American citizens are committed Christians. If one-third of America is evangelical Christian, that represents a potential 100,000 or more workers among the portion of Americans already living in the 10/40 Window! Consider the Philippines. The Philippine Mission Association estimates that there are over one million evangelical Filipinos working in the Middle East. These are also potential tentmakers who could be mobilized for an effective evangelistic role while working abroad.

Though a harsh example, Onesimus is a New Testament example of a T-1 tentmaker. Onesimus was a runaway slave who went to Rome; there he met Paul, converted and became "very useful" to Paul (Philemon 11).

There are several advantages to being a T-1 tentmaker. T-1s normally live a very comfortable life, giving them access to influential people, both in the business community and in the government. As leaders within their businesses, they have both the authority and opportunity to make decisions that may open a door for their employees to hear the gospel. T-1s are self-supporting. Most are well paid, having enough discretionary income to hire servants who do many of their daily chores. Though they may work more hours for their company, their house-help grants them the time for following up with nationals who are interested in the gospel. T-1s are all but untraceable statistically since they do not belong to any sending body or mission agency. The T-1 does not need to return home at regular intervals to secure funds or report to churches. T-1s are believed to be the least common category of tentmaking; just over 1 percent of the workers surveyed are T-1s.

T-2

The T-2 tentmaker is different in that a T-2 does have a calling from the Lord to reach out to a specific people. In addition, T-2 tentmakers are distinguished from T-1s by their evangelistic motivation, their intentionality, and their training. Knowing the country is closed to missionaries; T-2s seek out training that qualifies them to work for a foreign or national firm. Often, the needs of their selected country or the opportunities for work there will determine what type of training the T-2 completes. These focused workers then apply for positions that will permit them to reside long-term in the country. For a T-2, a job is taken primarily to facilitate residing in the country in order to minister. In their hearts and minds, ministry comes first, the job second. Many T-2s also have some practical ministry experience and cross-cultural skills. T-2 tentmakers have a plan for evangelizing and discipling nationals and often have church planting goals. T-2s are usually connected with a mission sending-agency for emotional support and guidance. T-2s are fully supported by their job. Normally, their secular work requires more than forty hours a week, leaving little time for ministry outside the work place.

Most T-2s work for non-Christians, so witnessing may be restricted at the office. In addition, most T-2s do not learn the local language well. Sometimes their jobs provide unique access to nationals, which leads to natural witnessing opportunities. However, often their jobs provide somewhat limited access to nationals.

T-1 and T-2 tentmakers serve without cost to the church. By sending T-1 or T-2 tentmakers, churches can multiply their missionary efforts with little increase to their budgets, reserving limited funds for other strategic purposes. The financial needs of the workers are met through secular, salaried positions, or their own businesses. Yet they are in full-time service for the Lord. They tactfully do evangelism and make disciples in the work place.

Aquila and Priscilla were T-2 tentmakers. They made tents with Paul in Corinth and helped him start that congregation (Acts 18:2–4). Having been discipled by Paul, they moved from Corinth to Ephesus, where they started a church in their house and discipled Apollos (Acts 18:19–28). From there, they moved to Rome and started another church in their home (Romans 16:3–5). Aquila and Priscilla made their living by making tents. There is no indication in Scripture that they received financial support from other believers. They were real makers of tents and they also planted at least two house churches in unreached areas.

There are several advantages to being a T-2 tentmaker. Their jobs create natural relationships for sharing their faith. T-2s, like T-1s, do not need to raise support, saving them the time and energy of having to traverse the home country finding donors. This also eliminates the need for regular home assignments to maintain support. T-2s have been relatively good at evangelism, and at least one T-2 worker has planted a church. Roughly 5 percent of those surveyed are T-2 tentmakers.

T-3

T-3 tentmakers differ in that a part of their income, or in some cases, all of their income, is derived from churches or friends back home. T-3s usually have control of their time, meaning they own their own businesses or work only part-time jobs. As a result, when ministry opportunities arise outside the work place, they usually have the flexibility to attend. Being one's own boss or limiting their working hours gives the T-3 more discretionary time for language learning and accomplishing other ministry related tasks. T-3s also have a strategy for evangelizing, discipling, and church planting. They have developed a professional skill desired by their chosen country, which gives them long-term access to reside in that country. T-3s are nearly always associated with a mission agency or a team of like-minded workers. Most T-3s commit to working with a team before they go overseas, though a few make such a commitment after arriving on the field. Many T-3s are part of a team that started and operates its own business. Whereas T-1s and T-2s will invest most of their time in working at their secular jobs to earn a living, T-3s view their jobs as a vehicle to enter the country, a way for reaching out to people, and a means of financial support. A T-3's job is not as demanding and often not full time. Obviously, this affects their pay. As a result, T-3s may supplement their income by raising support, as would a regular missionary. On one side of the ocean, T-3s are perceived as businessmen or teachers, et al. while back home they are considered to be missionaries. Having a dual identity has its advantages and disadvantages.

The Apostle Paul is an example of a T-3 tentmaker. He made tents so as not to burden others and to provide some income. Paul did not wish to appear to have dual motives in planting churches. He wanted to identify with others as well. On each of the three missionary journeys he made, he practiced his trade, but also spent concentrated times in the synagogue or house churches, ministering the gospel (1 Corinthians 9:6; Acts 18:3, 20:34 and Acts 14:1; 18:4; 21:8).

There are many advantages to being a T-3 tentmaker. The T-3 category provides a long-term entry strategy into a closed country, while giving the flexibility to invest time in non-work-related endeavors. Doors to individuals which are opened via the work place may easily be followed up after working hours. Having control of your time and support from churches at home reduces the pressure to earn money. Most T-3 tentmakers learn the local language well. Over 35 percent of the workers surveyed are T-3 tentmakers. Both T-3 and T-4 tentmakers proved to be more effective in evangelism and church planting than T-1, T-2, or T-5 tentmakers.

T-4

The T-4 tentmaker is not a tentmaker in the sense of working for a company; however, they are not regular missionaries either. Most T-4s work in NGOs (Non-Government Organizations). T-4 tentmakers have a non-missionary identity and are actively working in the community in a job consistent with their identity. This category includes social or health workers, medical personnel, teachers, agronomists, engineers, and others serving through an NGO, volunteer, or non-profit organization. This category also includes students and retirees who are serving full time in flexible capacities. In many ways, T-4s are ministering as regular missionaries but are known as something other than a missionary to the host people. Most T-4s have received training in both missiology and the skill or job they are using to serve the people. The T-4 entry strategy is very popular and effective for reaching into poor communities and underdeveloped countries. Like T-3s, T-4s are often connected to a mission organization through which they raise financial support and receive guidance. T-4 workers may be paid by the NGO or supported by churches back home; their source of income is not a factor. T-4s have clear ministry objectives.

The Apostle Peter is an example of a T-4 tentmaker. In today's world, Peter probably would be an NGO worker—healing the sick, helping the oppressed, and winning the lost. Peter was a witness for Jesus wherever he went and whatever he did.

There are several important advantages to being a T-4. To begin with, workers who serve in relief and development ministries are helping to meet the physical, educational, and material needs of people. Meeting the needs of people is an obligation of all Christians. By meeting physical needs, the individuals helped along with their community often become open to hearing our suggestions concerning their spiritual needs as well. T-4 jobs are often provided the flexibility needed to change their daily schedule.

The research shows T-3s and T-4s to be the most effective evangelists and church planters. T-4 tentmakers also learn the language best. For all intents and purposes, T-4s live and work as missionaries, but with a non-missionary identity. Approximately 30 percent of those surveyed are T-4 tentmakers.

T-5

The T-5 tentmaker is really a regular missionary, not a tentmaker. However, because the country they are ministering in does not grant missionary visas, T-5s have non-missionary or religious-professional identities. T-5s may have a job with a business, but by prior agreement do little or no work for the company. Some T-5s create cover or shell companies to enable them to reside in the country. The company, whether functioning or not, provides a cover visa by which the T-5 may enter and reside in the country. T-5s ordinarily raise their salary support like a regular missionary. They usually have theological and missiological training but little secular job training. T-5s are usually connected to a mission-sending organization and have clear ministry objectives.

T-5 tentmakers need to closely evaluate relationships with government officials. T-5s normally do not want officials to know much about what they are doing. Once T-5s have gathered a group of believers, it is likely the religious or government authorities will investigate them. Thus, a T-5 strategy tends not to be a good long-term model but is more effective as a stepping stone to setting up a more established NGO or business. The T-5 strategy is good for doing evangelism but is not as good a model for discipling or gathering believers.

One of the advantages of being a T-5 tentmaker is the ease of entering a new country. Visas may be acquired quickly by setting up a representative office or a shell company. T-5 tentmakers are able to function as full-time missionaries but with a credible non-missionary identity. The platform they establish facilitates a God-given ministry and provides an identity acceptable to both local authorities and religious leaders. T-5s have greater flexibility and freedom to minister as they feel led. Just over 5 percent of those surveyed are T-5 workers.

SUMMARY

Using the T-1, T-2, T-3, T-4, T-5 tentmaker categories resolves many of the questions and problems in understanding who we are. Each strategy has various advantages and disadvantages. I am not proposing that one is better than the other or more spiritual than the other. God may lead

DEFINING QUALITIES
OF THE FIVE TENTMAKER CATEGORIES

Defining Characteristic	T1	T2	T3	T4	T5
Live and work in a cross-cultural situation	•	•	•	•	•
Religious ministry	•	•	•	•	•
Live in a closed country (CAN/RAN)	•	•	•	•	•
Reside among the people	•	•	•	•	•
Have a legal resident visa	•	•	•	•	•
Secular job or identity	•	•	•	•	?
Defined ministry goals		•	•	•	•
Calling or clear leading		•	•	•	•
Intentional witness		•	•	•	•
6+ hours work a day	•	•	?	?	
1-2 hours work a day	•	•	•	•	
Job fully provides financial support	•	•			
Church/supporters fully provide financial support			?	?	•
Job & church/supporters provide some financial support			•	•	
Missiological and secular training	?	?	•	•	•
Sent out by a church and/or mission agency		?	•	•	•
Accountable to experienced field personnel		?	•	•	•
Invests time learning local language to a reasonable level	?	?	•	•	•

? = optional, may or may not be true

some people into one role and others to another. Some workers may be more comfortable in one role than another. Whatever our calling or backgrounds, every person can fill a need and have a place. These categories are tools to help us realize our identity and find our place of service.

ACTION STEPS

• Why do tentmakers have an identity crisis?

- What are four examples of how God calls people into cross-cultural work?
- What criteria are important in defining a tentmaker?
- Describe the five types of tentmakers.
- Name one person currently on the field who you know who fits each type of tentmaker.
- Of the five types of tentmakers, which category do you feel most drawn to?
- Explain the difference between a tentmaker, NRM, and traditional missionary.

"The significant problems we face cannot be solved at the level of thinking we were at when we created them."

ALBERT EINSTEIN

Wisdom is more precious than rubies; nothing you desire can compare with her.

PROVERBS 3:15 LB

chapter 3
PROS AND CONS OF SETTING UP A TENT

As a young Christian, long before the unreached were called "the unreached," I had a burden to win the lost, and the more lost the better. This burden led me to join a mission agency in preparation to go to China. In the early 1980s, China was still closed to most foreigners, Christian or non-Christian, so my wife and I moved to Hong Kong, seeing that as a stepping stone into an unreached China. As China began to open, we were encouraged to find many thriving house-churches throughout the country; even many of the Three-Self Churches had evangelical pastors. As the doors opened wider, it became clear that China housed one of the largest, most evangelical Christian populations in the world. Then, one Saturday, I was teaching in a Chinese church about missions and the need to reach the unreached. A young teenage girl innocently raised her hand and asked, "With so many churches here and so many people groups still without churches, why do you missionaries bother to come here? Can't we evangelize our own people so you can go elsewhere?" I scrambled for an answer, pointing out the minority groups (who we were not working with) and other ways our western expertise could provide for the Chinese church. I doubt my answer satisfied her, as it did not satisfy me. As a missionary, I had chosen to serve with a local church. We discipled the church's leaders and did evangelism. My wife and I loved our ministry and the people. Many had come to faith. But in truth, we were an added extra. We were like the cherry on a chocolate sundae; we added color and were wanted by the church, but we were not needed.

As we considered our ministry in Hong Kong and China, we realized that much of our work was, and would be, with Christians. However, we knew that the Master did not want us to build on another man's foundation

(Romans 15:20). As missionaries and full-time Christian workers, we knew we were doing exactly that—ministering full time to Christians. We began to feel that the term "full-time Christian worker" means one who works full time with Christians. If so, we wondered how the unreached are to be reached? Could we minister where there were no Christians in a country that did not grant missionary visas? The more we thought and prayed, the more we sensed His leading to stop being missionaries and re-enter the business world. It was time to get out of full-time Christian work so that we could get into the ministry.

During our home assignment, we sought the Lord for direction and He answered, leading us to a distant Muslim country. Upon announcing this decision, it was interesting how Christian leaders were quick to point out that we should not "throw away" our years of learning Asian culture and the Chinese language for the Muslim world. Thinking back, we did not recall anyone questioning our "throwing away" our business degrees and work experience when we began doing regular missionary work. Well-meaning co-workers unequivocally told us that tentmaking is not real missionary work and that we would be wasting our lives.

MISCONCEPTIONS ABOUT MAKING TENTS

Tentmaking has its problems and disadvantages. Yet many of the problems are not the ones being discussed in mission periodicals. It is safe to say there are misunderstandings about tentmaking in the churches and even in the mission world. In my reading on tentmaking, I consistently uncovered thirteen criticisms of tentmaking and tentmakers. These criticisms would lead us to believe that tentmakers:

1. Are mavericks, or lone rangers
2. Do not wish to raise funds—have mixed motives
3. Have little accountability
4. Lack Bible training
5. Do not learn the local language
6. Have inadequate time for ministry
7. Hold tentmaker jobs which last only two to three years
8. Do not plant churches
9. Are deceitful
10. Are hindered in witnessing by their employers
11. Have a conflict of priorities
12. Lack prayer and financial support from home churches

13. Are dreamers taking on too many responsibilities

Based on my research, here is a critique of these items:

Tentmakers are mavericks, or lone rangers

Much of this criticism seems valid on the surface. Many (29 percent) of those who were surveyed did view themselves as "entrepreneurs." An additional 58 percent said they "take calculated risks." Clearly it is not the safe and secure home-body that pursues serving the Lord overseas. Those seeking to start a business and a ministry need a good dose of creativity and the ability to risk—to step out in faith.

However, 93 percent of the workers are on teams and most of these teams are a workable size, with 71 percent of the teams having six or more adults. A large majority of the teams (81 percent) meet once a week or more. Most teams are made of expatriates only; however, almost half are a blend of workers from various sending agencies. Tentmakers are team players.

Tentmakers do not wish to raise funds—have mixed motives for becoming a tentmaker

Some people may become tentmakers because they do not wish to ask others for financial support. Is this pride? Mixed or impure motives? Some workers serve God for the "good feelings" they get from helping others. Workers motives vary from not wanting to raise financial support, to seeing the world, to impressing others. Whatever human motives are among our incentives for doing any form of Christian ministry, such motives fall short of God's mark. The right motive for doing anything is to glorify God as God has guided me to do this. Jesus tells us to seek first His kingdom, and His righteousness (Matthew 6:33).

What are tentmakers' motives for serving abroad? Of those we surveyed, 0.4 percent went overseas for the prospect of increased salary benefits and another 1 percent because their employer transferred them overseas. Not surprisingly, these are all T-1 and T-2 tentmakers. Receiving a clear call from God was the primary motivation for 95 percent of the workers. Over 70 percent of the workers reported their secondary motive for being a tentmaker is that it is a more credible, natural way to witness, rather than being a regular missionary. Desiring to be a witness, interaction with missionaries (talking with and/or reading about them), personal study, and the influence of their church were also very significant secondary motivational factors for workers leaving their homeland. Tentmakers may have congruent motives, but rarely mixed motives in the invidious sense. We are not in it "for the money."

Tentmakers have little accountability

Accountability is a critical issue. One of the major reasons we have not completed the task of world evangelization is (to borrow a soccer term) "our poor finishing." All Christians need accountability to keep us sharp, focused, and ethical (Proverbs 27:17). As individuals, we are responsible to be accountable to others. Some workers find their accountability within their mission organization and some with nearby workers of other organizations.

Personally, I was a member of a traditional mission for nearly five years and have been with a tentmaking mission for eighteen years. Though organizations will vary, missions in general are lacking in assuring accountability. I have found tentmakers to be more aware of the need for accountability than regular missionaries. All organizations provide accountability, but most are weak on their follow through. Of the workers surveyed, leaders were holding 67 percent of their workers accountable on a monthly basis or more.

Leaders indicate that they hold their workers accountable in their relationship with God, their character, and their ministry. Interestingly enough, these are also the same areas in which workers want more accountability. Less than half of all the workers (49 percent) set annual goals to which they are held accountable. Nearly half the workers (47 percent) wish they had more accountability. From my experience, I believe these numbers would be similar for regular missionaries as for tentmakers. Tentmakers are being held accountable.

Tentmakers lack Bible training

Regular missionaries point to a lack of formal Bible training in the lives of tentmakers. It is presumed that tentmakers lack pre-field preparation (theological training, ministry experience, missiology, etc.) and orientation on the field (language acquisition and culture). Some tentmaker training-literature contributes to this misconception by encouraging short-cuts to the field. As a result, some agencies see tentmakers merely as "foot soldiers" who are there to support the regular missionary ranks. Even though these agencies use tentmakers, they do not accord tentmakers full respect as participants in developing and implementing their mission strategy.

The research shows that a significant percentage of tentmakers (65 percent) had some formal training in either a mission school or Bible school or seminary. A solid majority (78 percent) had training in missiology. Fifty-seven percent of the workers checked that they had both Bible and missiological training. One quarter of the workers participated in all of the following forms of preparation: Bible school or seminary, missiological training, short-term trips, and language training. Eighty percent felt they were adequately prepared to be tentmakers. This is thorough preparation and training. It indicates that tentmakers understand the need to be thoroughly trained before going overseas. Tentmakers are adequately equipped.

Tentmakers do not learn the local language

The good news is that 97 percent of the workers are seeking to learn the language. Well under half the field workers (37 percent) said they are "fluent in the local language." However, a good measure of this is being able to read the local language newspaper. Just 18 percent of the workers said they read the local language newspaper twice a week or more. Forty-one percent of the workers minister mostly in English or their own native language. Clearly tentmakers do have a language learning problem. This is one criticism that really is a problem. Though nearly everyone is learning the language, the lack of fluency indicates language learning is not given the priority it should have. One language expert who reviewed the data was more positive noting that missionaries/tentmakers tend to underestimate their own language abilities. He also pointed out that most workers focus on speaking and not reading skills. In addition, many places do not have newspapers in the local language.

It is encouraging that most of the workers who learn the language study the people's heart language rather than the trade/national language. Only 38 percent have someone evaluate their language ability regularly. This lack of accountability could be a factor in the poor level of language proficiency. Language learning is an area in which tentmakers need upgrading. Workers need to set aside adequate time once they arrive on the field for language and cultural studies.

Tentmakers have inadequate time for ministry

One mission director asked me, "Being a missionary is a full-time job and more, so why is there value in being part-time?" The answer to that lies in a variety of areas: a definite calling, better access to people, long-term visas, modeling, viability, different avenues of assimilation, etc. Another mission leader questioned, "If tentmakers are in fact 'missionaries in every way,' why be a part-time missionary when you can serve full-time?"

A demanding job can limit the time for spiritual ministry, but being in the marketplace also creates opportunities for witnessing that regular missionaries do not have. Tentmakers need to evaluate each job offer to discern if it will hinder or facilitate their ministry calling. The T-3, T-4, and T-5 categories enable tentmakers to have greater control over their time.

A tentmaker is not a part-time missionary. Tentmakers witness while they work. We not only live out the gospel daily on the job, but we also engage in other ministries during our free time. Time is money. Our jobs do take up time, but money creates time too. One regular worker shared with me that their support was so low she spent hours undarning her children's sweaters so she could reuse the yarn to make new sweaters. Tentmakers have the funds to buy clothes, saving time. Only 20 percent of the workers found their job to take too much time from ministry. In contrast, 48 percent did most of their ministry at their work place among co-workers.

Seventy-five percent of the tentmakers work for a school, business, NGO, or they are students. In turn, three quarters of these workers are satisfied with the balance they have between work and ministry. Interestingly, 24 percent use their job as a cover to do ministry. Sixty percent work in their secular job six hours a day or less; about 50 percent of that time they are working with non-Christian nationals. Though tentmakers do work jobs, most have a significant ministry, and many are living and working where regular missionaries can not go.

Tentmaker jobs last only two to three years

Most visas, whether missionary visas or others, are granted for one or two years. Thus, this is not a viable criticism. As expected, only 25 percent of the workers were initially granted visas for two or more years. Nonetheless, 77 percent of the tentmakers are committed to long-term service among their people group. Tentmaking is not a short-term strategy. Though most job contracts are for two years or less, these jobs are often renewable.

Tentmakers do not plant churches

Tentmakers have a reputation of being generally ineffective in the larger program of planting viable church bodies and reproducing themselves in the hostile environments of restricted access nations. However, 30 percent of the workers reported they have been involved in planting a church. There are at least 157 churches that have been planted among Muslims by tentmakers in Muslim countries within the past ten years.

Tentmakers plant churches.

Tentmaking is deceitful

In nearly twenty years of tentmaking I have been arrested once, detained by authorities one other time, and questioned by officials numerous times. In all these trials I have never had to lie about my job or ministry. However, I do know workers who struggle with deceit. Five percent of the workers said they had to lie to keep their job or protect their employer. An additional 20 percent said they had to lie to hide their missionary identity. In my opinion both cases are inexcusable. We are told, "Do not lie" (Leviticus 19:11; Colossians 3:9). Most of this 20 percent are T-5 workers who do not have a real job. Too many tentmakers are not taught the ethics which govern having a dual identity nor how to answer questions. Jesus was a master at answering a question while not answering the question. Deceit is a concern and may be a problem. Later in this book, I will give suggestions on how to answer questions. Tentmakers do need training in how to have a dual identity without lying.

Tentmakers are hindered in witnessing by their employers

Working overseas means that many hours of the day are already taken and are therefore not available for "ministry." It is essential that the tentmaker view the work place, and the relationships established there, as a place of ministry. In some cases, a company will prohibit the sharing of one's faith. This was reported to be true only 7 percent of the time. In any case, relationships may be built at work, and no country has made it illegal to love or serve people. By demonstrating the reality of the Spirit of God in the work place we can meet with co-workers outside work and clarify our beliefs. In the vast majority of situations the work place is not a hindrance, but a help to shining forth God's light.

Tentmakers have a conflict of priorities

The majority of tentmakers are called to make disciples, not tents. One of the criticisms leveled against tentmaking is that we wear two hats. We have, in a sense, a divided loyalty. On the one hand we have come to our host country to share our faith in Jesus Christ, but we must also perform our job in way that is a good testimony to our employer and co-workers. This is true, but like any other Christian at home or wherever, we are to glorify God in whatever we do (Colossians 3:23). There are various options, but our job commitment is a priority and not just an excuse to be in the country. We honor God when we do our best in whatever we set our hands to. Our actions and words bear witness to our Master. He alone is our priority; there is not a conflict.

Tentmakers lack prayer and financial support from home churches

Tentmakers have a strong commitment to prayer, and 98 percent have churches or friends back home committed to praying for them. Ninety-two percent of the workers communicate with their churches regularly. However, their churches often do not adequately reciprocate; only half the churches communicate with their workers bi-monthly or more. Tentmakers who are financially independent have a greater need to raise prayer support, as supporters naturally pray for those in whom they invest. Ninety percent of the workers said they were commissioned/sent out as a missionary or tentmaker by their home church. This shows the church is filling a major role in the sending out of most workers.

Tentmakers are dreamers taking on too many responsibilities

I would agree that it is safe to say both tentmakers and regular missionaries are guilty of being idealistic, even romanticizing mission work. I do hope we all dream a bit (Acts 2:17). However, some missionaries have indicated they see tentmakers as pretenders, persons who seek to usurp an identity as missionaries. They have a sense that tentmakers either do not qualify or do not want to go overseas as career missionaries. Some others see tentmaking as a second-best option, not a primary calling. My research shows these views are incorrect. Tentmakers, as missionaries, are truly called, trained, and sent out on teams equipped to bring the saving grace of Jesus to those who have yet to hear His good news.

ADVANTAGES OF TENTMAKING

A Muslim perspective shows an appreciation of the inevitable mixture in life of material and spiritual concerns:

> "The reality, a situation where some totally turn their backs on the world while others support society through 'worldly activities' is not feasible. Even in the days of the Prophet Muhammad, those who believed staunchly in spiritual values were beset with all manner of threats. To overcome these, the Muslims of the time, including the Prophet himself, paid due attention to worldly activities. The acquisition of wealth and property, the mastery of martial arts and the establishment of a well-ordered administration were among the important activities in which all Muslims involved themselves so as to be strong enough to defend spiritual

values and the Islamic religion. Surely it would not be reasonable to suppose that worldly activities can be separated from spiritual ones in human society today when no such dichotomy was possible in the days of the Prophet. It is clear that neither spiritual values nor material ones can, on their own, nurture and bring happiness to the lives of human begins. For a human society, large or small, to be complete and wholesome, a balance between material and spiritual values is essential. The question is to find the right ratio between the two value systems for the attainment of the happiness desired."[9]

Wealthy Christian countries have many things to offer the world: culture, language, services, goods, education, in addition to faith in Jesus. Yet the bottom line is that developing countries want commerce, not Christianity, bucks not Bibles. As missionaries, as tentmakers, as disciples of Christ, with one hand we should avail ourselves of the open doors to introduce enterprises which provide what the people and the governments perceive they need, such as; schools which enhance the peoples' education, and businesses which create economic benefit. With the other hand we should be introducing what we understand them to need from God's point of view; a saving relationship with Jesus. Jesus teaches us to know our adversary (Luke 14:31–32). Buddhists, Hindus, and Muslims understand the godly value of a holistic life. Tentmakers have open doors to establish businesses, NGOs, schools, etc., that will succeed in presenting a gospel which addresses both physical and spiritual needs.

Tentmaking has many advantages for those seeking to reach the unreached. There are twenty advantages tentmakers have over other strategies for sharing the gospel:

1. Access
2. Identity
3. Longevity
4. Credibility
5. Flexibility
6. Viable evangelism
7. Natural evangelism
8. Focused evangelism
9. Community evangelism
10. Creates jobs for nationals
11. Creates jobs for missionaries

12. Provides money for mission work
13. Vast resources to draw from
14. Vast experiences to learn from
15. Modeling
16. Reproducible
17. Reduces dependency
18. Involves the laity
19. Blesses the nation
20. Biblical

Access

Tentmakers as teachers, businessmen, social workers, etc., can have access to nations which are not open to regular missionaries. Most 10/40 Window countries, where the majority of the unreached peoples live, are closed to missionaries. There are no countries which are closed to business, trade, or education.

Entry into creative access nations is a key factor for becoming a tentmaker. Unfortunately, this is the one advantage that is promoted the most. Though it is an important reason to do tentmaking, in my experience it is not the most important. Being an engineer, doctor, or businessman enables us to penetrate into people's lives naturally. The world's heart beats with the marketplace. That is where people spend most of their waking hours and gain their satisfaction. It is crucial we meet people on the frontlines of their lives with godly values and satisfaction. People need to see the Christian life lived right before their eyes. As tentmakers, we have access to do that.

Identity

Tentmaking creates great contact with people. We are not known as missionaries or religious professionals. We have a secular identity. A tentmaker, unlike a regular missionary, is free from the stigma of proselytizing. Having natural access to people creates unexpected opportunities to witness. As tentmakers, we do not wear the Christian label; we are one of the crowd. When I was a regular missionary, at times I would engage people in spiritual topics only to have them exclaim, "Well, of course you wish to share your religion. That's your job!" Scott, a worker in Turkey, writes, "Being in business has actually extended my ministry because I meet people I would never meet as a missionary. And it deepens my ministry because I see the world from the perspective of ordinary people, not only from the specialized perspective of the pastors."

Foreigners (missionaries and tentmakers included) cannot define themselves; the host people do. However, the way we are identified will yield expectations. This creates opportunities and risks. Our lives are a huge part of our witness, and being in the world, we are constantly watched. If our character is not godly, our witness will be negative rather than positive. The tentmaker has less control over how he or she is identified than the religious professional. Once you are identified as a religious professional, people expect you to be good. People understand that religious professionals are paid to be good. As a business person, people expect us to be "bad," so when we are good, they wonder why and ask. Though some people who are seeking God will seek out a religious professional, many will be afraid and prefer to talk to someone they perceive as neutral, or who is known to be "one of them."

Longevity

A business or work visa offers a security and longevity that a missionary visa cannot. Governments change leadership. When fundamentalist parties take control, often they do not renew missionary visas. Jim, a missionary, served in the same city we did. We often ministered together. One day the state government decided to appease the fundamentalists by canceling all missionary visas. Jim left the country for a few months and returned as a T-5 tentmaker. However, because he had previously been there as a missionary, people knew him as a missionary. Jim was deported after being back in the country less than a year. Workers who are doing viable business or social work and are adding value to the community are desired by local governments. Many tentmakers have been rebuked by officials for sharing their faith but have continued to work in the country as the officials valued their economic or educational input more than fearing their religious zeal.

Credibility

Tentmakers are credible witnesses. We are recognized as secular workers who are not a threat to society. One day my wife was visiting some Muslim-background believers (MBBs) we were discipling, when the police stopped her. She was escorted to the police station for questioning and the local imam happened to be there. When the sergeant asked, "What does your husband do?" she told them about our business. The imam interrupted, "He's just like me, he works and teaches his religion.

He's not a missionary, he's okay." Many people view missionaries as professional "terrorists," men and women who have come to subvert their culture, change their religion, and steal away their children. As a Christian businessman, I do not carry this stigma. I am not seen as a cultural or religious terrorist. I am adding value to the community that the community desires. Though I am known for sharing the gospel, I am seen to be like any good believer, simply obedient to the wishes of my God.

Flexibility

Tentmakers have the flexibility to respond to needs immediately. When I was a regular missionary, I was bound to mission rules and schedules. One time there was a flood, and we needed money to help some nearby villagers. Going through procedures to procure funding took six weeks, and by then the need had been met by a nearby Buddhist temple. As a tentmaker I have funds at hand. I can immediately respond to needs, big or small. Our business specifically sets aside monies in a benevolent fund for such opportunities. Timely gifts have served as tools for sharing the Word. In the same manner, when a government official has asked for help with a project, we have been able to respond. The help we give blesses the people, brings honor to the officials, and creates opportunities for us to give the glory to God.

Viable Evangelism

Tentmakers are viewed as 'contributors' to society. Many non-Christian countries look at missionaries with disdain or distrust. However, tentmakers are seen as people who invest in the community by creating services, providing education, or employing people. This viability gives us respect, which opens doors among both government and religious leaders. Most people know right from wrong. It is not unusual for our clients to remark, "There is something different about your company." This creates opportunities to explain why we are different. As Christians, we can take a stand for biblical values in the marketplace. We can maintain the good name of the gospel in a milieu of corruption and self-centeredness. This earns respect, which brings glory to the Father and enhances our witness for our Lord.

Natural Evangelism

Tentmakers do not exist in abstract; we are always incarnated. The question of identity is based on our character and our actions. We have no need to explain ourselves, nor find reasons for being here. Questions concerning our religious role or secular role are no problem. The locals see tentmakers in natural terms.

Tentmakers are full-time witnesses on the job. The work place is an open and natural setting for people to observe our habits, discern our character, and watch how we live out our priorities. Tentmakers are natural witnesses of the gospel. NGOs, schools, and businesses offer many opportunities for evangelism that might otherwise be nonexistent. Often groups such as businessmen remain unreached while much missionary work focuses on those from lower socio-economic groups. In many undeveloped or developing countries like Pakistan, India, and Indonesia, the gospel is spreading among the poor, but barely touching the upper classes. By observing us in the marketplace, people better understand the life and faith we verbally proclaim.

Focused Evangelism

Regular missionaries are often forced to live at the level of local 'religious professionals.' As professional religious workers, regular missionaries have preconceived status and have expectations placed upon them which may hinder both their desire and ability to minister. Tentmakers may choose their entry strategy to fit their ministry goals. Skills may be obtained to enable them to enter specific levels of society. Businesses, schools, or NGOs may be established to best serve the needs of the people the tentmaker is seeking to reach. Tentmaking enhances our ability to meet people's needs and reach out to people by selecting the appropriate means to enable His light to shine forth. It is a way of life that identifies with all manners of people. Tentmaking offers a better opportunity to become all things to all men, so that by all possible means we might save some (1 Corinthians 9:22).

Community Evangelism

Tentmakers create jobs, provide services, and improve the education of locals. These activities are a bridge into communities, opening doors to witness to the community at large. Victor shared how his NGO in the former Yugoslavia came under attack during one of the many uprisings. Gunmen entered his home and threatened to kill him and his workers, only to have his neighbors rush in and convince the vigilantes that they were good people. John is one of several workers I know who has been invited to lead prayers in his Muslim land at non-Christian events. There are many stories of tentmakers who have been recognized publicly because of their contributions to the community. In addition to creating opportunities to witness to individuals, tentmaking also opens doors to witness to the community and its leadership.

Jobs for Nationals

"Therefore, as we have opportunity, let us do good to all people, especially to those who belong to the family of believers."[10] Tentmaking enables us to give ungrudgingly. Paul wanted everyone to work and earn his bread (2 Thessalonians 3:10). It is not unusual for a Muslim, Hindu, or Jew who becomes a Christian to lose his job. Tentmaking creates employment for local believers. One business friend in the Middle East had several unemployed believers travel across the country to apply for work at his factory. When a believer is the bread winner for his non-Christian extended family, this gives him status and respect within the family. This has led to the conversion of more than a few families. One of the best ways of helping the poor is to create jobs for them to work, enhancing their value to their family and the community.

Jobs for Missionaries

Operating an NGO or business provides opportunities for more workers to enter the country. As a business expands, additional tentmakers may come, forming a team of workers who work both in the office and in the ministry. Many Latino and Asian workers whose churches lack the financial means to send out regular missionaries are discovering the benefits of tentmaking. These avant-garde workers support themselves, while working in some of the more remote corners of the earth.

Funds from tentmaking businesses are being used to set up businesses for national missionaries. Ferdie de Deguzman, a Filipino mission leader, told me, "The greatest hindrance to sending out Filipino workers is money. If the churches could support them, we could send out a thousand workers." A small, successful business can help overcome this financial problem. Businesses that are needed by a community may also provide a legitimate reason for a national worker to move into a town that is without a church. Initially, communities which receive national missionaries are at a loss as to why they are there. Having a profitable business is a natural and satisfactory reason for maintaining a residence. Providing benefits to the community through jobs or education endears the worker to the people, creating a platform for the message we bring.

Money for Mission Work

One obvious benefit of tentmaking is provision of money for the workers themselves. Tentmakers often earn more money than regular missionaries, though there are exceptions. Thus, we cost the church much less than a typical worker. Some tentmakers are fully self-supporting and some are partially supported. In either case, the church is saving money.

If businesses run by missionaries are successful, they can channel some funds into their ministry or into the support of other expatriate and national workers. In addition, having our source of income on the field reduces our need to return home at regular intervals to secure funds.

Vast Resources

Tentmakers have extended resources with which to experiment. We have financial resources and other business resources, as well. It is not uncommon, as we get to know suppliers or other local non-Christian businessmen, to invite their support for some needy project. Missionaries typically raise money solely from Christian sources. However, the tentmaker, without raising religious issues may raise funds from both Christian and non-Christian organizations and businesses. These monies may be used to support needy causes among the local people. One of our NGOs, working among the poor, is partially funded by wealthy non-Christians who want to do good for those less fortunate than themselves. In approaching them, we simply shared how our business helps bless the poor through this NGO, and we invited their help.

Vast Experience

In the same way that tentmakers have broader resources to draw from, we also have a greater pool of teachers, mentors, organizations, etc., to draw from. We are not limited to Christian sources for ideas, methods or accountability. Though we do avail ourselves of many Christian resources, we also utilize local and foreign leaders and mentors for ideas and counsel. Muslims who would never reveal cultural insights to church workers have no problem explaining to me how to use certain words and gestures to enhance my presentation, increasing my chances of making a business sale. These insights are also helpful in doing evangelism.

Modeling

"Whatever you do, work at it with all your heart, as working for the Lord, not for men."[11] People would rather see a sermon than hear a sermon; what we do far outweighs what we say. Missionaries who work are modeling something that's been lost in the West—the sanctity of work. With too many of our disciples we have passed on our sacred/secular division. We have exalted the "full-time worker," making Christian work an exalted position, rather than a Christ-centered way of life. Most of the Christian missionaries in the book of Acts worked secular jobs. These early Bible heroes lived, worked, and ministered among the people. They had no need for Bible schools; training was done, literally, while on the job. They sought to be in the world but not of it. Much of our example today tells nationals we are to be of the world, while not in it. It is important to model the balance found in serving both God and our fellow man effectively in the marketplace. Tentmakers can set a good example of hard work to both local laymen and Christian workers.

Tentmaking provides a positive working model for nationals. Regular missionaries from poor countries like India, Ethiopia, and Indonesia have told me that when someone converts, they expect to receive money for doing nothing. They observe the missionaries and note that they do not labor, nor do they appear to contribute anything of value to the society, yet they receive money. So upon conversion, some new believers expect the same. An NGO worker in Central Asia told me, "Having western missionaries come who are supported by their home churches leads converts to expect to receive support from western churches too. After all, isn't that how Christians live? Though encouraged to work, new believers have no model to follow, no example to emulate, no pressure to succeed in the real world; all they see and know is to get money from the West." Tentmakers who work alongside new believers show them how to work and live the Christian life.

In North Africa, one of the hot topics of the day is supporting MBBs to do ministry. In wealthy Singapore I was told of a Muslim woman who went around to various churches "converting" and then asking for and receiving financial help. People have been known to convert to get a job. For many poor people, a job is a job; if they can be paid for preaching or doing evangelism, it is the same or better than working a back-breaking construction job. In poorer areas, believers have approached me about working for me as an evangelist. The implication is that if I will pay them a salary, then they will witness for Christ. If we model an artificial gospel, we are likely to gain artificial converts. We need to clearly demonstrate that we are not overseas to make money; we do not witness for wages.

David Morris writes, "I [will] never forget a student from Arabia who told me that he wanted to become like me—so he would not have to work!!"[12] We need to model the Word of God and the work of God for

Christians and non-Christians alike. We need to teach new believers the honor of labor and of supporting themselves. People need practical examples of what it means to give rather than receive. Tentmaking provides a positive working model for nationals. It models a workable, livable faith. Tentmaking gives believers a balanced perspective of being in the world but not of the world. It shows how the church community should work and witness in the world.

Reproducible

Tentmaking is reproducible in the lives of new believers in nearly any environment. The first believers in any people group are likely to be persecuted, meaning they may lose their source of income. New believers who are discipled by tentmakers have a working model that can be reproduced in their own lives. Converts who do not have a working model, may either need to be supported by the missionary and his sources or extracted from the society so that they may survive. The former will hurt the new believers' reputation and their witness in the community; the latter prevents them from being a witness to the community.

Reduce Dependency

"He . . . must work, doing something useful with his own hands, that he may have something to share with those in need."[13] Tentmaking among converts may reduce dependency on the foreign missionary staff enhancing the national worker's credibility among his own people. Many non-Christians and some Christians believe the reason nationals become involved in Christian work is for the money they receive from the foreign mission organizations. National workers need to stand up and take responsibility for their own ministries, including their own finances. Tentmaking promotes, models, and provides opportunities for nationals to work and be responsible for their own financial support.

Involve the Laity

In our churches, we are told that the role of pastors and church workers is to equip the laity for ministry. Church members attend training classes on how to witness, how to minister cross-culturally, how to lead a Bible study, and so on. The laity is exhorted to "become involved in our needy world," but as one layman expressed it, "It feels as though we are there for the half-time pep rally, but we never get a chance to play in the game." Up until the 1970s, mission work was basically the exclusive domain of the clergy. The few laity that went overseas were primarily in support roles, helpers of those doing the real work. With the advent of OM, YWAM and tentmaking agencies like Global Opportunities and Frontiers, the laity began to realize they could have more than a supporting role. Tentmaking businesses and schools are being staffed and even run by men and women who take early retirement to use their skills on the field. Young entrepreneurs are seeking to test their creative skills in the uttermost parts of the earth. Truly, it is a new day. These workers are an answer to our prayers for laborers. Tentmaking as a model enables those who might feel they have little to offer to see the bigger picture, and where and how their skills may bring glory to God among the unreached.

Bless the Nation

Jesus said, "It is more blessed to give than to receive."[14] Successful businessmen who work with national businesses can be an economic blessing to the nation in which they work and minister. Tentmakers are able to use their knowledge and skills to enhance people's quality of life. By providing education and jobs, communities benefit. People's lifestyles are upgraded through the trading of new and better goods. In the eyes of the host country, the productive tentmaker contributes at least indirectly to building the nation. Even the most hostile governments welcome businesses and schools that contribute to the prosperity of the country.

A worker in Bangalore writes, "In a country like India, the building up of community through trade education is a big priority. Local governments appreciate examples of hard work to correct religious teachings which distract from work and improving productivity." The good will tentmakers create in the marketplace also fosters good will among the community and with the government. Such "win-win" situations create natural, non-offensive opportunities to witness for Jesus.

Biblical

Tentmaking is biblical. There are many biblical heroes who held jobs; Paul, Aquila, and Priscilla are only the most obvious.

SUMMARY

This list highlights many of the benefits tentmakers bring to the worldwide missionary efforts of the church. Of the problems mission leaders raise, language learning and the supposed practice of deceit are indeed issues of concern. Lack of accountability and focus, along with obtaining long-term visas, are issues of equal concern for regular missionaries. The other criticisms do not withstand any detailed and objective review.

Nonetheless, advantages and benefits are not the reason for choosing a missionary/tentmaking career. Each of us must seek the Lord's leading for where, what, and how He would have us glorify Him. His will worked in us must be done in His way. Tentmaking is certainly one viable way.

ACTION STEPS

- List ten misconceptions about tentmaking.
- List two weaknesses of the tentmaking strategy. What can you do to prevent making these mistakes?
- List ten benefits of becoming a tentmaker. Share five of these with a friend.
- Which of the twenty advantages of becoming a tentmaker appeal to you? Why?

Practice makes perfect, so be careful what you practice.

CHINESE PROVERB

Always be prepared to give an answer to everyone who asks you to give the reason for the hope that you have.

I PETER 3:15

chapter 4
PREPARING YOUR TENT

James, a Filipino, felt called to reach the XYZ people of the Middle East. Having an engineering background, he looked for a job in Sandyland that enabled him to live and work among the XYZ people. James' job required him to work long hours, so he had little time for language and cultural studies. Nearly everyone spoke English. As he had the opportunity, he made friends and shared his faith in English. Though he learned a smattering of Arabic, it was not a priority for him. After three years in the Middle East, James returned to Manila a defeated man. Though he had made several friends and shared the gospel with about a dozen XYZ people, he had no lasting relationships and found no one showing interest in the good news he longed to give away. While in Manila, he contemplated his next steps. He felt no release from God's leading to reach the XYZ, yet he was frustrated at the thought of returning for another term of fruitless service. While in Manila, he befriended Faruk, an XYZ man, who was studying at the University of the Philippines. In time, Faruk asked James about his Filipino culture and some of his personal habits. James was surprised to learn that elements of these were offensive to XYZ people. The next week, a friend of Faruk hosted a birthday party for him. James was surprised at the large number of Filipinos there. He realized that because of Faruk's ability to speak fluent English and be understood by Filipinos, Faruk had made more friends and had deeper relationships than he ever had in Sandyland. James determined to return to Sandyland, but this time as a student of the language and culture. With that in mind he enrolled in a university and did a M.A. on the history of the XYZ people. In studying the people and their language up close, James soon realized why he had not made any deep friendships. His habits and lifestyle were offensive to the very people he was trying to reach. His attempts at sharing the gospel in English, though quite understandable and clear from his vantage point, were totally meaningless to the non-western educated XYZ man. After two years of study, James returned to his former city. With his newly acquired skills, he quickly found a job with a local firm. The pay was less, but so were the hours. In addition, all of his co-workers were XYZ people. Within the next three years, James made several close friends and was meeting weekly with two men to study the Scriptures in the local language.

PREPARATION

Tentmaking missionary preparation covers many disciplines and requires much time and energy. Those who think tentmaking is an easy alternative to regular missionary work need to think again. Having been a regular missionary and a tentmaker, I have found that, if anything, tentmaking is more difficult and stressful than regular missionary service. Tentmaking requires more thorough preparation, not less. Tentmakers are fully business people and fully missionary, thus we need to be fully trained in both areas. It requires time, commitment, and discipline to become adequately equipped for service as a tentmaker. Too often we are in too big of a hurry to get overseas. Those who view tentmaking as a quick path to overseas service will be disappointed. There are no shortcuts.

Before departing to serve overseas, tentmakers are to be highly educated and thoroughly equipped. The research reveals that 86 percent of all tentmakers have a university education, with 41 percent holding a masters degree. Tentmakers who have borne fruit in evangelism and discipleship worked as Christian professionals for a church or para-church ministry for at least six months prior to moving abroad. In addition, these same tentmakers worked one year or more in a secular job. This is solid evidence that effective workers have invested in training themselves before entering the battlefield.

We are engaged in a mighty battle. In preparing, planning, and attacking, we must remember it is God who gives the victory (Proverbs 21:31). Yet, we fully understand that He has given us the responsibility to train and discipline ourselves for war (1 Corinthians 9:25; 1 Timothy 4:7). Every weapon within our reach must be used. Praying, preaching, giving—all must be brought into action. Health care, engineering, and computing must be used to advance His kingdom. Teachers, farmers, and students must shine their light against the forces of darkness. The kind of weapon we choose is not the key to success; the Israelites used hoes, axes, and sickles to attack and defeat the Philistines (1 Samuel 13:20). All of our talents, all of God's gifts, and all of our experiences and education must be sharpened to defeat the enemy. Nothing is unimportant. Every spiritual gift, acquired skill, and learned thought must be brought forward to the frontlines. No one can say, "I have nothing to offer." The easy enemy-positions have been captured; now the strong-holds are left. We are to attack the enemy in season and out of season, in the hills and on the plains. To fight in such a war, requires thorough preparation.

THE COST OF MAKING TENTS

Jesus teaches us to count the cost of following Him (Luke 14). Of the tentmakers I interviewed who had served as both a regular missionary and a tentmaker; all agreed that having an effective ministry as a missionary tentmaker is considerably more difficult than being effective as a regular missionary. If you are considering being a tentmaker, you must be obedient and count the cost, and having determined the price, you must be willing to pay it.

The Apostle Paul is an example of being thoroughly equipped for every good work (2 Timothy 3:17). As a teenager, Paul received the finest schooling in the Scriptures. As part of his rabbinical training he must have worked several years as a teacher of Latin, Greek, and Hebrew. Paul did the equivalent of his university studies under Gamaliel, one of the most famous instructors of his day. He was a young leader, the friend of many Pharisees and rabbinical leaders. His Roman citizenship allowed him access to Gentile nations. He was trained in the trade of tentmaking. Paul had formal training in both secular and religious knowledge and experience before he met Jesus. Jesus teaches us that we will be given responsibility based on our ability to handle it (Matthew 29:14–29). Paul was greatly used by God because he had the zeal AND the skills to be entrusted with much.

Sherri, a former worker in the Middle East, wrote, "I wasn't prepared for the kind of time commitment successful tentmaking required. It took a year to learn the language well enough to share my testimony and another two years before I had been around long enough for the nationals to trust and befriend me. Between job, language, and ministry, nothing seemed to be happening. In truth, I just lost hope and was lonely and worn out. Maybe someone else can take it, but it was too much for me." Joey adds, "Americans are in too big of a hurry for fruit. They forget that it takes nine months for a child to be born and at least two or three years for trees to produce fruit. Every farmer prepares the ground before planting, and a field fallow for years requires a lot of work. There are few short cuts. Plan on taking at least two years before even making any friends."

Like the Apostle Paul, tentmakers need to commit themselves to the finest training. We need to pray, think and plan long term. Reaching the unreached is not for sprinters; it is a marathon. It is like planting trees, not cabbages. It may take years before we see the fruits of our labors.

PREPARING YOUR TENT FOR STORMS
—DOS & DON'TS

There are five categories of tentmaking (T-1 to T-5). As with anything that offers variety, we need to choose the model which best fits the gifts and calling the Lord has given us. For example, when I bought our family car, I needed to consider the size of our family, gas mileage, cost of the car, the roads I drive on, and so on. In choosing to follow the Lord's leading overseas, there are a variety of factors to consider. Who do you wish to minister to? How much access to the local people do you expect your job to create for you? Where do you expect to locate? With which social class do you hope to identify? As with choosing a car, there is no one make and model that is the best for everyone. Each of us needs to consider what is best, according to the guidance He provides at this point in time. If you are seeking His will for your life, see Appendix D for a list of questions to consider in pursuing His direction for tentmaking service.

It is essential to learn to invite God into all our transactions, meetings, etc. Fred writes, "On the 20th of June, I traveled to Algeria to register our new company. I had to rent an office, start all the paperwork, etc. The second day I read a study from the World Bank, saying that registering a company in Algeria takes an average of 121 days and getting a phone-line 216 days. After seventeen days, I was back with my family. The company was registered and I had two phone lines." Tentmaking is a "God thing." Having prepared adequately, bid God to lead you in your dealings and expect Him to act. If we don't prepare, and we don't invite Him to act, surely He won't. Solomon teaches us that diligent planning, receiving lots of advice, *and* committing our actions to the Lord brings success (Proverbs 15:22; 16:3; 21:5). We are not to take foolish risks or entrust our money to strangers and then expect God to bless our efforts. Nearly every productive tentmaker has had one or more experiences of being cheated of at least US$100 in goods or cash. Mistakes and losses are part of doing business, as well as a part of God's maturing process. Keep pressing on in faith; learn to take some risks. Check yourself with others. Invite mentors into your life who will be active in holding you accountable. Ask these counselors to judge your ability to evaluate the market. Stay close to the Word. Keep to your regular routines spiritually, mentally, and physically. Learn to read regularly outside of your area of expertise.

In going overseas, it is important to know yourself. People who understand their own social style and personal tendencies are better equipped to adjust to cultural differences. By understanding ourselves, we are able to anticipate our responses to cultural differences. This assists us in managing stress and adapting to the peculiarities of the host culture. Invite people to share with you their impressions of your strengths and weaknesses. Have your leaders evaluate your spiritual gifts. Consider what helpful experiences in the church, ministry, and business are still lacking in your life. Input is important. I know a former American evangelist in India who led hundreds to the Lord. Due to a change in his circumstances, he switched to tentmaking. Being a good speaker he recruited numerous people to come work for him and raised over US$350,000 to get his business off the ground. However, he was bankrupt in four years and returned to the States. He is just one of several I know who were fruitful as regular missionaries but failed as tentmakers. What is the point? A dynamic Christian speaker/evangelist/missionary may be a terrible businessman. We cannot expect to be half-trained in tentmaking and then succeed at a full-time job. God is not mocked; we will reap whatever we sow (Galatians 6:7).

ROLE OF PRAYER

As the picnickers frolicked on the bank of the river rapids, a shout rang out, "A child fell in the river!" A crowd quickly gathered, and anxious eyes searched the rushing water for a glimpse of the child. Thinking quickly, the captain of the high school swim-team grabbed a nearby "tug of war" rope and tied it around his body. He tossed the other end to the crowd and dove into the rapids. The crowd watched nervously as the high school hero struggled to reach the child. When he reached the child, a cheer went up from the crowd. As he grasped the child and fought to stay afloat, he shouted over the roaring rapids, "Pull in the rope!" The onlookers glanced among each other and asked, "Who's holding the rope?" In the excitement of watching the rescue, no one had grabbed the rope. By then, the rope had slid into the rapids and was well out of reach. Helpless, the crowd watched as the figures in the water disappeared. William Carey, the founder of the modern missionary movement, told his church prior to departing for Calcutta, "You hold the rope and I will climb down into the pit."

Oswald Chambers reminds us, "that prayer is the greater work." The key to producing fruit through a tentmaker's life is prayer. That key is in the hands of the churches. Our sending churches have done but a small thing in giving of their tithes and offerings to support His work among us. Money is helpful, but money without prayer is powerless against the gates of hell. We can throw all the money we want at the gates of hell, but it is not going to make a dent. The solutions to all of our problems can be found through prayer. It is paramount that we recruit people to pray for the work. Over 95 percent of the workers surveyed said they had "recruited friends at home to pray for me daily or weekly." It is equally important that we keep these prayer partners updated on our needs and opportunities. Like air traffic controllers who receive regular updates from the pilots flying through their air space, prayer warriors need current information to keep the enemy at bay and His work in and through us moving forward. The gates of hell cannot prevail against prayer (Luke 18:3–8). The importance of finding people who will pray for us and of communicating to them our needs, opportunities, and requests, regularly, cannot be over stated. As one worker wrote, "God answers Knee-Mail!"

FINANCIAL SUPPORT

There are some churches who question the validity of supporting tent-makers. Though many of us earn money through our jobs, few (less than 10 percent) earn enough to adequately support our families and our ministries. The amount of church support will vary with the business income we earn and the cost of fulfilling our living and ministry needs. If the tentmaker is affiliated with a mission organization or team, the agency can monitor the tentmaker's income and inform the church what is needed on a year-to-year basis. Otherwise, the tentmaker should make arrangements with the church to keep them informed of financial needs.

Most Christians believe that tentmakers are fully supported through their jobs. However, the research verifies that only 6 percent of tentmakers are in this category, while 39 percent are supported by both churches and their job. The primary objective for tentmakers in moving overseas is to do evangelism and church planting. Our source of income is secondary to our primary purpose of serving God. Thus, there are many reasons why tentmakers should be at least partially supported by churches.

Language Study and Initial Set Up

During the first year or two overseas, the tentmaker needs to learn the language. Language learning is a full-time job, requiring full support for this period of learning. Furthermore, if the tentmaker is beginning a business, i.e. consulting firm, language school, etc., support will be needed for an additional eighteen to thirty-six months (beyond the initial language learning years) before that business becomes viable and profitable. During the initial two to five years, the tentmaker will not have any income, so the church's financial support is vital to both the success and survival of the worker. In many places, local banks will not make loans to the tentmaker, as the business, though intending to be profitable, is small and foreign operated. Thus, additional financial help may also be needed in the form of start-up capital.

Freedom to Minister

Salaries are one of the biggest expenses of any business. Tentmakers who receive financial support reduce the stress of having to earn money to keep the family fed. This enables us to reduce our business hours when there are ministry opportunities which conflict with the job. Having start-up support is often the deciding factor in achieving profitability. If we do not have additional income, it is unlikely the business would be able to "hire" our time and still allow us the flexibility to follow up relationships and duties outside of work, such as: doing evangelism with friends, discipling new believers, further language study, and general ministry duties. Each of these ministries may be very time consuming. To prepare what to share (witness or disciple) with friends often takes one or two hours a day for the first three to four years. Running errands is also time consuming. The services and infrastructure which make life so easy in the West are not in place in many countries. For example, to pay an electric bill often takes thirty to sixty minutes a month. Having some support gives us more freedom to minister.

Stress

Without adequate financial support, tentmakers with much less discretionary time have greatly increased stress. The stress of raising support before departure is just six to twenty months, but living abroad without enough income adds stress which lasts for years. The research shows that 80 percent of tentmakers receive 50 percent or more of their income from churches and supporters back home. Very few have succeeded without some support during their initial years overseas, and nearly all of these self-supported workers have poor or less developed language skills. Few people can do all the jobs and carry all the burdens of a tentmaker. Having adequate financial support to cover our basic living expenses greatly reduces our stress.

Bless National Workers

Once the worker's job is generating an adequate income, many tentmakers transfer their contributions from the church to support national workers who work alongside them in the ministry. Once the business is profitable and can afford to pay us a salary, we can use the extra monies to bless national workers. Our national workers are in some ways more effective in ministry than we are, but without the extra income we could not afford to hire them. Local believers who wish to minister have no place to raise money. Money from business revenues enables us to employ national workers who serve with us in the ministry, as well. Later net profits may, at the tentmaker's discretion, be diverted to support other mission work. A policy concerning the distribution of a worker's business income and net profits of the business should be made available to supporters.

Build the Business

In starting a business, the worker will need to raise a certain amount of start-up capital. Normally, churches will not give towards starting a business. Many churches would not consider that permissible. Gifts to non-profit charitable or educational businesses might be considered, but churches would rather support people than businesses. When the required start-up funds for a business are extensive, the team members may seek full support for their living costs and mission work and contribute their business income towards loans garnered for the start-up costs.

Salaries are costs of operating a business. By not paying salaries or paying lower salaries to the tentmaker, the business saves money, speeding progress toward becoming profitable. By accepting less or no pay from the business, workers are facilitating lower costs, thus shortening the time it takes to break even and become viable. Once the business is profitable, the worker can begin taking a full salary and reduce or redirect the support they receive from churches.

Expand the Ministry

As the business is profitable and expands, more monies may be released into ministry efforts. After the business is profitable, the church may reduce or stop contributing to the tentmaker's salary. However, often churches continue to support the tentmaker, encouraging them to invest the money in projects or pass it along to national workers who work alongside them. The church's additional funds may create new ministry opportunities. It is important that policies and plans of this sort be clearly communicated to those in authority and supporters at home prior to going overseas.

Faith Building

Support raising teaches us faith and dependence on God. It increases our prayer life. By sharing our calling with others and seeing people respond to share with us in His work, we gain confidence in God and His ability to work through us. These are meaningful lessons to be learned before going overseas, as the task we are embarking on requires a mature faith. In addition, the more we speak about the work, the more we review and ponder what we are going to do. This process helps us think through details and clarify God's leading in our lives.

Broader Support

Raising financial support gets us face to face with people, forcing us to share our vision and calling. In the process of speaking to people about our financial needs we are able to invite them to be involved in obeying the Great Commission with us. As a result, the Lord leads people to pray and get involved with us in a variety of ways beyond financial support.

Teach the Great Commission

As we share about our work, we also teach about God's vision for all peoples. Our message to potential supporters can help them grow in their grasp of His vision for the world. Thus, we are helping churches be obedient to God. Whether the emphasis is on prayer, witnessing, giving, or going, enabling others to be more obedient is good. The focus of support raising is on ministry, not money. Meeting with people and churches to present our future work creates opportunities to teach God's plan for all peoples. In ministering to churches, we seek to enhance both their vision of the Lord and invite them to be personally involved in His worldwide work. In doing deputation, our primary goal should be to help churches understand and obey God by serving Him among the unreached.

Character—Humility

Humility is not a point normally highlighted as a reason for raising support, but God has shown us that humility is something we need. 1 Peter 5:5–8 makes it clear that pride is the worst thing we can have in our lives. Doing things alone, i.e. "self-support," if we are truthful, is often a form of pride. Humility is an essential attitude for mature workers. Support raising provides us many embarrassing moments. This forces us to be humbled, strengthening our character in preparation for even more difficult and embarrassing situations which will surely arise overseas. One of the supposed advantages of being self-supporting is not having to go through the struggle and anticipated embarrassment of asking for money. But if it is God's will, why are we embarrassed? This is part of God's character development process so that we learn to depend on Him and not man.

Truly Missionary

Churches pray for those they pay. In my interviews with tentmakers, I met two T-2 tentmakers who were commissioned by their home church but not supported by them. When they returned home they found their churches had changed; one had grown significantly, and the other had a new pastor. Both of these tentmakers quickly learned two things: one, they knew very few people in the church; and two, no one was praying for them. People pay attention to their investments. If you believe prayer is crucial and if you want people to pray, get them to support you. If people are paying you, they will pray for you. Even workers who do not need financial support should receive at least a token amount of support from their church.

When I met with John's pastor in his church near London, he argued that as John would have a well-paying job in the land he was moving to, the church need not financially support him. I argued against this with the pastor until we reached an impasse. As a last resort I requested, "May I ask you just three more questions?" The pastor wearily agreed. I continued, "Has the church had any other businessman move into the 10/40 Window to work?" "Yes," said the pastor. "And how many cross-cultural workers does the church currently pray for regularly?" "Thirteen," he replied without hesitation. I then asked, "And how many cross-cultural workers does the church support?" There was a long pause, and then he smiled as his eyes were opened and he answered, "Thirteen." Today John is working abroad, and is supported ten pounds a month by the church. With the church's blessing, John shares this token support with a national evangelist who assists him. We may not need money, but we certainly need prayer. To ensure we are on the church "pray" roll, we must get on their "pay" roll.

Complete Our Objectives

Our primary objective in going overseas is to glorify God through evangelism and planting churches. Though we also have other objectives, they are secondary. If not for our primary objective, we would not go abroad. Some people question, "If your primary objective is evangelism and church planting, then why do you need a job? Why don't you just do evangelism and church planting?" The chief point for the churches to take hold of is that we cannot enter and live in the country as "missionaries." To live in the country and do the work of the ministry we must have some sort of tentmaking job and identity. That leaves us four options: operate a genuine business (probably at a loss), operate a business as a cover (not really have a business), work for another business, or operate a profitable business.

a. *Operate a business at a loss*. Clearly, this would be the easiest. However, if we operate a business at a loss, somehow the financial losses must be paid for. There are a few tentmaking businesses which continually operate at a loss. This costs the supporting churches thousands of dollars each year to cover the short-fall. This is not good stewardship, and if our work is a witness, this is also a bad witness.

b. *Operate a cover business*. A cover business is good for getting started in evangelism, but we have experienced in many creative access nations that once we have believers, it is then that the government will seriously investigate what we are doing, including our business. If our job or our business is not valid, we will be deported. So a cover business will facilitate the goal of doing evangelism, but not church planting. Also, must consider the ethics of telling the local government that we are performing a job when we are not.

c. *Work for another business*. As discussed earlier, tentmakers may work for other companies, local or international. Though the financial benefits are good, there are many other limiting factors to working for international firms. Local companies pay lower salaries. Often the salary is insufficient for the children's school, medical insurance, trips home, etc. Those who work for local companies often need additional support from churches to survive. More importantly, those who work for others often struggle with time management. They have little control over their visas (the ability to live long term in the country), where they live, and who their co-workers are. These are important issues if we are to fulfill our primary objective.

d. *Operate a for-profit business*. By definition, being a profitable business means we make money, but the fact is, making money is not our primary goal. It is a secondary objective to our evangelism and church planting goals, but it is an honest objective, for without it we cannot accomplish His primary goal. Making money is simply ancillary to our need for a viable long-term entry strategy to plant churches. Jesus tells us whatever we do, we are to do our best as if we are serving Him (Colossians 3:17). Moreover, a successful and quality business is a good witness to the local community, to the employees and nationals, and to our own friends.

Because making money is not the primary objective, we need the support of the church. That is also why we can return our profit to the church or re-invest it in other avenues of God's work, once the business is profitable.

Each of these four options needs to be considered prayerfully. God will guide some into each option. We need to listen to Him and obey His direction for our lives.

Admittedly, there are some tentmakers who have making money as a primary goal before doing evangelism. Unfortunately, many of these tent-makers give less effort to the ministry and more to the business. Working for the business is easier, more visibly productive, and even more uplifting to our egos. This diverts our time and energies from what was originally viewed as our primary objective for moving overseas.

Accountability

Workers are accountable to whoever pays their salary. If the church does not pay us, it might not feel it has the authority to speak into our lives about what we do. This is why it is good to receive at least a small amount of financial support and be commissioned by a church. Thus, before God, it is the church's stewardship duty to hold the worker accountable to God's calling. Too many churches still do not know how, or are afraid, to hold the staff and missionaries they support accountable for what they do with their time and the money provided. With money comes both authority and responsibility. Biblically, the church has the right to speak into a member's life. However, if I am overseas and the church is not financially supporting me, I can elect to do as I wish. I might even fall into sin and there would be no one following me up who could stop me from disobeying God. The reason some tentmakers fall into the trap of doing virtually all business and no ministry is a lack of accountability. As the churches are not paying us, they leave us alone to do as we think best.

The biblical model of a church is a body—one body. The parts are interdependent, not independent. If I am self-supporting, I can fool myself into thinking that I have no need for the church. Of course, being a godly tentmaking missionary, I would submit to the church, but what if the church and I have a disagreement? Then I can easily un-submit myself. Self-centered as this seems, this is in fact, what often happens on the mission field. As I am not interdependent with the body, I have no account-ability. However, if the church is paying me to serve in the uttermost parts of the earth, then I do have to fulfill the evangelism and church planting objectives I committed to, as well as work through any disagreements the church and I may have. If I do not, the church should stop paying me, likely calling me to return home. Being supported by the church keeps me accountable to doing the ministry and not only doing business.

The expectations and accountability of the church should be proportionate to the investment in the worker. Churches that support a worker $25 per month should ensure their worker is doing ministry but should not place expectations on the amount of time they expect the worker to be out sharing his faith. In addition, the church should not expect the worker to report more than once or twice a year. However, churches who support a worker 10 percent of his or her total income or more should have a say in how the worker spends that portion of his or her time each month. If the church is supporting a work of evangelism, they have the right to ask for reports about the worker's evangelism efforts. The church should also expect 10 percent of their worker's working hours to be invested in the activities they have agreed to pay him or her to do. That could be evangelism, running the business, or teaching in school. Jesus says that we are to render unto Caesar what is Caesar's. With employment comes authority and responsibility (Luke 19:12–27). If I employ you and you have accepted my terms for employment, I have a right to hold you accountable to the terms we agreed upon, whether I have walked in your shoes, or not.

Churches should also consider making weightier commitments to workers who are members of their congregations. If a church is truly one body, then 1 Timothy 5:8 has repercussions for churches that do not adequately support their own members. T-1, T-2, and T-3 tentmakers may not need as much support, but T-4 and T-5 workers need the complete financial backing of their church. If churches would concentrate on supporting their own workers, those workers could spend a greater portion of their home assignment at the church, serving the church, rather than traveling around the country to secure funds. Smaller churches that do not have adequate funds to support their workers should seek to form mission consortiums with like-minded churches in their area. In this way, a group of churches could support one another's workers, allowing them to gather their full support from one city or area, rather than having it spread out across the country.

THE IDEAL TENTMAKER

Tentmakers need discipleship and discipline. Romans 12:2 tells us, "Do not conform any longer to the pattern of this world, but be transformed by the renewing of your mind. Then you will be able to test and approve what God's will is . . ." It is important that we do not conform to the ways of the world. As in our relationship with Jesus, in missions, we need to involve both our hearts and our minds. If we overemphasize the heart, it rejects the mind. If we favor the mind, it rejects the heart. We are to love God with both; we are to use both to bring Him glory (Luke 10:27). We need to bring our hearts and minds together as we plan our mission strategy. It is not either/or, it is both/and. This balance is needed in the ideal tentmaker.

In my research, I surveyed and interviewed 450 workers serving in the 10/40 Window. I evaluated the effectiveness of each worker based on three factors: the number of people they led to Christ, the number of people they discipled in the Word, and the number of churches they planted. From the data acquired, there are ten characteristics that stand out that tentmakers should pursue in going abroad to serve the Lord. These are listed in order of priority. An ideal tentmaker would have acquired training and maturity in each of these areas. Note the first four areas reflect the character, temperament, and maturity of the tentmaker. They do not require any special training or degrees. Though competence is important, if we must choose between two workers, one with good character and another with good competence, choose character. It is easier to teach competence than character.

The top ten qualities for effective tentmakers are:
1. Spiritually mature
2. Socially adept
3. Emotionally stable
4. Persevering
5. Evangelistic zeal
6. Recruit others
7. Language fluency
8. Team player
9. Clear objectives
10. Accountable

Spiritually Mature

It seems logical that in a spiritual work, the workers must be spiritually mature. However, it is surprising how many undiscipled and immature workers are trying to knock down the gates of hell. Tentmaking missionaries must be spiritually mature. We cannot effectively preach the gospel by our own initiative and power. As servants of the Most High, we are but "jars of clay" who show the "all-surpassing power" moving through us in our work. It is "from God and not from us" (2 Corinthians 4:7). We are to join God in His work rather than invite God to join us in our work. Evangelism, discipleship, and church planting are supernatural works which must be empowered by the Spirit of God. Tentmakers must find access to the throne of grace in prayer, study, and the application of the precepts of His Word. We need to worship the Father in Spirit and truth, and be ever ready to give a defense of the faith to whomever may ask. An intimate relationship with the Father is not optional. Our faith must consistently be lived out, often in ungodly situations, so as to positively influence those around us for Jesus.

In business we are trained to emphasize our strengths and strengthen our strong points. However, Satan does not attack our strengths. He attacks our weaknesses. Tentmakers need to know and recognize their weaknesses so as to grasp the schemes of the Evil One as he tries to defeat and distract us. We need to have daily times with the Lord. Workers who consistently set aside special times to study God's Word, pray, and meditate are more effective than those who do not. The research quantified that workers who invest more than forty-five minutes a day in the Word and prayer are more fruitful in evangelism and discipleship.

In addition to spending time with the Lord, no spiritual discipline is more important to enhancing a worker's effectiveness than fasting. Workers who view fasting as an important spiritual discipline are very fruitful. I do not remember ever having a lesson in seminary or in my missiological training on fasting. Could fasting be more important than Bible study? More important than prayer? Yes, and yes, at least when it comes to effectiveness in evangelism, discipleship, and church planting. It may be assumed that those who fast use some or all of that time for prayer and meditation in the Word. Yet fasting and a good devotional life are disciplines which should be built into every worker's spiritual life.

According to the research, workers who have experienced a demonic confrontation are also more effective. It is expected that those who have encountered demons may be more effective. Sometimes the first step in a person's conversion is the casting out of demons. Again, I never received such training in advance, but I learned in the midst of the battle. If we are to send forth workers adequately equipped for every good work, then potential workers need to be trained in all aspects of spiritual life and ministry.

Socially Adept

Tentmaking missionaries need to be skilled in the art of making friends. Excluding support workers (those who come to assist missionaries), our ministry is with people. Good social skills are needed for building and maintaining godly relationships. Though many of those interviewed score as introverts on personality tests, those who are successful in sharing the gospel have developed the skills needed to both make friends and share the gospel. All workers need to be warm and friendly and open to new ideas. Workers who said that "most of my closest friends are nationals" also scored very high in evangelism and church planting. Hospitality is another key trait. Workers who regularly "have nationals in their home" or who "have taken a vacation with national friends" are more productive than those who have not. It is not surprising that those who answered, "it is hard for me to socialize with nationals" have a high probability of not being effective in evangelism and discipleship. Workers who spend their "free time with their family or alone" also have a higher likelihood of ineffectiveness. It appears that the more time we invest with locals, the more effective we will be in evangelism, discipleship, and church planting. Tentmakers who relate well to others enable their co-workers and friends to see their lives up close. Closeness to His light in us should attract them to what they see.

Moreover, workers who said, "I am adventuresome, an entrepreneur; I often take risks" also scored well. In preparing to serve abroad, train yourself to take small steps of faith (risk). Practice meeting strangers. Do not be afraid to make mistakes or embarrass yourself. When asked the most important skill for doing missionary work, one worker replied, "The ability to laugh at yourself."

Emotionally Stable

Tentmaking missionaries must be emotionally stable. Making tents is hard work. In ministering cross-culturally, we must learn to communicate in another language, learn new cultures, and share God's message in changing earthly contexts. Many a new arrival overseas exclaims, "I feel like a kindergartener!" And my reply is always, "You are!" Learning language and cultural skills forces us into many embarrassing situations. I have seen doctors and university professors brought to tears by their inability to adapt to a new language and culture. Character traits that the worker thought he had well under control, such as anger, bitterness, arrogance, distrust, disputing, malice, and negativeness suddenly surface and become severe problems. Interpersonal relationships with teammates and personally going through cultural stress and work anxiety amplify tension.

It is also essential to have a well-balanced self-esteem. By that I mean one's ego does not put down colleagues or demand center stage. Perhaps more dangerous still is a low self-esteem, since there is little on the field to boost one's self-esteem. People prone to mood-swings, especially those who shift frequently to depression, are likely to fail. Only workers who are emotionally stable should serve as tentmakers.

Persevering

Perseverance is easy to observe, hard to practice, and most difficult to learn. It is not surprising to learn that tentmaking missionaries who reside the longest on the field are the most effective. Workers need to consider serving long term. The increase in short-term workers is to be applauded, yet short termers rarely plant churches. He who gave up His life for us asks us to do the same for Him (Luke 9:23–25). Adoniram Judson, serving in Burma during the early 19th century, wrote his mission's headquarters in London, saying, "Please do not send us any more of those short-term wonders who come out here for seven years and then return only to live off of their experiences."[15] In Judson's day, "short term" meant seven years. Language learning, building friendships, and job performance all require discipline with a long-term commitment. Perseverance is essential in all areas of a tentmaker's life and work.

Evangelistic Zeal

Tentmaking missionaries who "are experienced in leading evange-listic Bible studies" before going overseas are highly effective workers. Potential missionaries need to be encouraged to gather non-believers to study the Bible. As one of the early steps in drawing people to Jesus is studying the Bible, people who learn this skill before going abroad are ahead in their training. Basic evangelism is taught in most churches and Bible schools, yet much of that training is more confrontational. Workers need to be able to share their faith openly and practically over an open Bible. Workers who "led ten or more people to Christ before going overseas" prove to be effective evangelists among the unreached. Workers who "prefer not to verbally share my faith, rather I let my life be a witness" and who "share my faith only when obvious situations arise" were not fruitful in their ministry overseas. However, those who did not win many to the Lord but "actively seek opportunities to ver-bally share my faith with everyone" scored well in effectiveness. For those who have church planting goals, the skill of being able to gather non-believers to study the Word is more important than witnessing or theological education.

Tentmakers who "befriended and witnessed to international students" before going overseas prove to be more effective. Befriending foreigners before going abroad has many benefits for both the non-believer and the worker. Learning from foreigners opens us to new ways of doing things. Interacting with strangers helps us better understand and even share in the struggles of one entering a new culture. Those seeking overseas service should be required to do some ministry with international students or foreigners in their community.

Recruit Others

Tentmaking missionaries are recruiters. Evangelistic work is similar to sales, so it is not surprising that those workers who "recruited others to serve overseas" are effective in evangelism, discipleship, and church planting. Workers who "recruited others to join the team I am on" or "recruited others to be tentmakers/bi-vocational missionaries" proved to be fruitful workers. A big part of recruiting/sales is simply informing others of the opportunities that exist. Tentmakers should be "inviters" who are regularly inviting others to join them in their life and work. Would-be tentmakers should learn the skills of inviting friends and strangers to meetings and Bible studies.

Language Fluency

Tentmaking missionaries need to learn the language of the people they are reaching. The research validates what missionaries have been saying for centuries, "Learn the language well!" Workers who answered, "I am fluent in the local language" scored very high in evangelism, discipleship, and church planting. Also, those who answered, "I am regularly involved with a national congregation or house church that uses the local language" scored well. Tentmakers have been correctly criticized for our poor language skills. Too many of us arrive on the field, jump into our jobs, and give language learning a part-time effort. We need to plan ahead, setting aside one to two years to study the language and culture full time or until we are able to share the gospel and perform our jobs in our adopted tongue. People prefer to speak in their native tongue. They are pleased and impressed when we invest the time and effort to learn their language well. Workers who minister in their own native language enhance their probability of being ineffective.

Team Player

Effective tentmaking missionaries are members of a team of workers who are bound together by a common vision or covenant. Teams interact differently; some operate closely like a volleyball team, while others barely know one another, as with a track and field team. Potential workers need to be guided to teams that fit their skills, gifting, and goals. Surprisingly, the most effective teams have eleven to fifteen workers, while teams with more than fifteen workers are the least effective. Thus, it would be wise to divide larger teams into smaller units. Also, teams having members from more than one home country tend to be more effective. Workers who are currently leading a team are very effective. One way to prepare is by playing team sports. Why not join a volleyball, basketball, or soccer team and experience the benefits of working together while contributing toward a common goal?

Clear Objectives

Tentmaking missionaries need to set goals and objectives. Workers who "have a clear strategy for planting a church" and clear pertinent goals are more successful in church planting than those who sought to plant churches without clear goals. Likewise, wise time management is needed so as to make the most of every opportunity (Ephesians 5:16). For example, the hours we spend in the office are more effective if the people we are working with are of the people group we are reaching. Workers who responded that "most of my co-workers are expatriates or foreigners" were generally ineffective. Those workers who worked mostly with the people they were serving were more effective.

Potential tentmakers should learn how to set realistic goals, such as time to be allocated to different activities, persons with whom to develop friendships, records to be kept or avoided, etc., and should learn how to be held accountable for those goals.

Accountable

Tentmaking missionaries who are accountable to others are more effective than those working as lone rangers. It is important for workers to learn to submit to authority and get input from older, more experienced workers. "Plans fail for lack of counsel, but with many advisers they succeed."[16] Knowing our hearts are deceitful, we need elders who will watch over our souls and guide us, keeping us to His standards for our lives. Effective workers invite people into their lives to give counsel and guidance in fulfilling His will. Those desiring to serve overseas should seek out elders who will mentor them through the preparation. Once overseas, other mentors should be invited into your life that have walked the path you are on. Many times two or three mentors are needed for various areas of our lives and preparation. For example, one person may coach us on our professional skills development, while another may guide us in developing our ministry skills. Fruitful workers welcome accountability and honest input.

In preparing for tentmaking, the above are the key qualities to consider and build into our lives. In addition, one worker from Indonesia adds good advice in writing, "Be sure new people understand the importance of being flexible and teachable; nothing happens as planned." Flexibility, teachability, and other character issues can be worked on under the guidance of a godly mentor.

SUMMARY

If it seems like a lot to do, it is! Yet John, a worker in Afghanistan, puts things in perspective when he says, "If you wait until you are totally ready, you'll never go." Understand that God will lead different people down different paths. Some effective workers have prepared for their service by developing only a few of these qualities. There are always exceptions, and we can never be 100 percent prepared. Nonetheless, the research shows these are the best ways for workers to prepare for a career of productive tentmaking missionary work. As you prepare, listen to His guidance for you and remember that when we meet Jesus face to face, He is not going to ask about our preparation, our job title, how many people we employed, or the number of people we led to Him. He will simply ask, "Did you obey?" (1 John 3:23–24)

ACTION STEPS

- What are some areas you still need to prepare in, before pursuing going overseas?
- Are you actively involved in your church?
- Do your church mission leaders know about your interest in missions?
- List seven reasons tentmakers should be supported by churches.
- What are four options for operating a business? Which best fits your calling?

- What are ten qualities found in the ideal tentmaker? How many of these qualities do you feel you have? What do you need to do to obtain those you lack?

- Is there an international student or co-worker who you could befriend this month?

- Who is holding you accountable in your walk with God? If no one, determine to find someone this month.

- Discuss your plans for overseas ministry with your church leaders and request they assist you in planning your future.

"A man always has two reasons for doing anything; a good reason and the real reason."

JOHN PIERPONT MORGAN

"You are not acting as you ought if you are moved by anything other than the glory of God."

CHARLES SPURGEON

The heart is deceitful above all things and beyond cure. Who can understand it?

JEREMIAH 17:9

chapter 5
MINDING OUR MOTIVES

Sue had a great love for God. She was an inspiring, sought after speaker. She spoke at churches around her county about her desire to reach the unreached and to complete Christ's great commission. She seemed like an ideal missionary candidate. Everyone spoke well of her zeal, fervor, and heart for the Lord. Sue invested years in preparing. She basked in letting people know of the sacrifices she was willing to make for Jesus' sake. However, after only five months on the field, Sue was headed home. Once the congratulations and crowds turned to language learning and loneliness, Sue could not endure. She soon discovered the shallowness of her walk with God and her dependence on the praise of men for the sake of her self-image.

CHECK YOUR MOTIVATION

Many people have noble goals but fail to take the steps to achieve them. Why? Because of the myths they believe. Tentmaking is not for dreamers. It is hard work. This book is written in part to debunk the myths. The first step in becoming a tentmaker is to consider God's leading in your life. In understanding His leading, it is essential you discern your true motives for wanting to be a missionary tentmaker. Why do you want to be a tentmaker? Fulfill the Great Commission? Money? Use your skills/education to serve God? Travel? Live a nice lifestyle? Help others? Take the gospel to a particular place or people? Different people are motivated for different reasons. Solomon reminds us, "There is a way that seems right to a man, but in the end it leads to death."[17] If you do not have the right motivation, you will not get far. It is important to be honest with yourself. Honestly ask yourself, "Why am I interested in being a tentmaker?"

Many people who have gone into tentmaking have failed to accomplish their original objectives. They went into tentmaking because they did not wish to raise support, they wanted a better lifestyle, or they wanted to help poor people. Their reasons for becoming a tentmaker were focused more on their own happiness than the will of God. They sought to fulfill their own goals for living a nice Christian life. But as good soldiers on active duty, our happiness should stem from pleasing our commanding officer, not ourselves (2 Timothy 2:4). We are not to choose the wide gate but the narrow one (Matthew 7:13–14). We are not to make our own happiness the basis for the choices we make or the things we do. Many, dare I say most of us, pursue friends, spouses, education, or jobs, with one thing in mind—ourselves. Incredibly, many people even go into missions to feel happy.

For believers and non-believers alike, it seems the primary motivation in life is to be happy. But honestly, I do not care if you are happy. Why? Because we live in a radically un-Christian society with a value system that is practically the opposite of the one Jesus Christ teaches. Jesus says, "If anyone would come after me, he must deny himself and take up his cross daily and follow me. For whoever wants to save his life will lose it, but whoever loses his life for me will save it. What good is it for a man to gain the whole world, and yet lose or forfeit his very self?"[18]

Tentmaking is not an excuse for keeping our worldly idols—including material wealth—and still being a missionary. Luke 9:25 is a good check on our motives for doing tentmaking. If we are seeking to gain the world, we need first to find Jesus. Each person's motivation needs to be nothing other than the glory of God. Jesus' purpose on earth was to bring glory to the Father (John 17:4), so our motivation should be the same. Everything we do is to glorify Him (Isaiah 43:7). Our decision to become a tentmaker or missionary should be characterized by a long term, significant commitment to learning. We need to seek thorough training and persevere until His will is accomplished, no matter what the personal cost.

SPIRITUAL ISSUES

"The choice is always between the crowd and the cross. When we choose the cross, then eventually there will be a breakthrough. If we suffer we shall also reign with Him (2 Timothy 2:12). If we are prepared to live as Jesus did, serve as He served, suffer as He suffered, then it is true that we will share with Him the joy of the harvest."[19]

Research reveals there has been a shift in the thinking of young Christian workers away from following God's calling towards fulfilling their own ambitions. A result of this is that young people are looking for ways to use their skills and talents in ways they enjoy, instead of seeking God's will for their lives and serving Him. Candidates want to use "their" skills for God but are not willing to be retrained to serve the Lord. This shows that there needs to be more teaching on commitment and sacrifice. This underlines that a significant factor in determining whether or not to be a tentmaker is one's relationship with Jesus. A tentmaker or missionary must be content with his position in Christ and be able to sustain that relationship through prayer and the Word without any props and promptings from the church.

The data shows that most tentmakers did not intend to be tentmakers, when they first went overseas but circumstances either forced or led them into it. However, the 21st century worker appears not to maintain the same high values of the past. Nowadays, there is an increasing number of T-5 tentmakers. More and more workers who are moving into tentmaking are doing so to gain an entry into a country, but they are not looking to do any real work. This research shows that the way we are identified and the way our identity correlates with what we do has a direct impact on our effectiveness as a witness. Working a real job *does* make a difference in how people relate to us and how believable our message is. T-5 tentmakers prove to be about as productive as T-2 tentmakers and significantly less fruitful in evangelism, discipleship, and church planting when compared to T-3 and T-4 tentmakers. There is a reason it is called the wide gate.

During the Gulf War, a Muslim background believer (MBB) commented to a co-worker who chose to remain in the country when anti-western sentiments were peaking, "I didn't know you were willing to die; I thought you'd just flee to America." One lesson we are learning: "The single greatest secret to effectiveness is the willingness of the workers to suffer, to endure, and to die. This means death to: popularity, pride, racial and cultural prejudice, material comforts, selfish ambition, a biblically unbalanced home life, etc." [20]

Before choosing to be a tentmaker, it is important to pray, study the Word, and seek God's face for His will for your life. If you sense He is leading you abroad, seek counsel from godly people who know you well and ask advice from experienced tentmakers. Then pray and meditate some more. I am confident that if you ask according to His will and put Him first in your life choices, He will show you His path for you (1 John 5:14).

WORK ISSUES

The Bible tells us we should work 85 percent of our days on this earth. In Exodus 20:9 we read, "Six days you shall labor and do all your work." Work, as with all things, is meant to be a spiritual endeavor. To find the right livelihood and determine God's best work for you, look in the job classifieds and also in the mirror. As you pray and read His Word, consider what God has gifted you to do. What burdens has He laid on your heart? What do you love to do for Him? A God-given desire may not seem to be a "calling," but it was enough for Apollos (Acts 18:27). What attracts you to a job: the people, the creativity or the problem solving? What experiences are you seeking in your work to mature in Christ? A strong desire or burden from God may be His way of calling you.

In seeking to discern God's will for our lives, let us examine Paul's life and motives for working as a tentmaker. Do these desires match you own?

1. Work gave credibility to Paul's message.
2. Work displayed Paul's integrity.
3. Work helped Paul identify with the people.
4. Work enabled Paul to model much of the message.
5. Work facilitated Paul in building a community that allowed him to reproduce his life.

Credibility

Making tents brought credibility to Paul's message. Paul did not wish to be a stumbling block to anyone coming to know his savior (Romans 14:13). Most of the unreached areas of the world are poor, and many have repressive governments. People in such countries do not understand why and how someone would leave a more developed land to reside in their neighborhood. After all, they are trying to emigrate to the West! The issue of true identity is one of the most critical factors to a tentmaker's success. Nationals we befriend want to know, "Who are you?" "What is your work?" People openly question why we would leave our extended family, freedom, opportunity, and home, for their poverty. The questions come non-stop. "How much do you make?" "How can you afford such a nice house when you get paid so little?" "What is your real reason for being here?" "This is a poor country with few opportunities; why would you want to live here instead of in your own country?" "There is more freedom in your country, why would you come here to work?" "Isn't it easier to earn a living in your country?" "What about your parents and relatives? Don't you miss them?" "Are you a spy, a drug dealer, a subversive, a missionary . . . ?" There are tentmakers who failed because they did not work through their answers to these questions in advance. Caught off guard, they are embarrassed or they lie. Some quit and go home because they cannot live with their conscience. Others are discovered by the local authorities to not be contributing anything of apparent value to society, and they are asked to leave.

If we are going to reside long term abroad, it is imperative that we be comfortable with our role and identity. People can often feel it when we are not answering fully and truthfully. This lack of openness creates a feeling of distrust. The best way to solve this problem of credibility is to make certain we really perform the work our visas say we do. When our work is clearly legitimate to everyone who is observing us, the pressure tends to ease. A relatively well-paying or prestigious position affirms a sense of authenticity, as does an affiliation with a government or with an international agency or company. A real liking for the job and enthusiasm in performing it also explains the tentmaker's rationale for being in the country. One solid motivating factor for doing tentmaking is to establish credibility in the eyes of the nationals we are trying to reach.

Integrity

Paul worked to demonstrate his integrity (1Corinthians 9:12). He did not want his salary, title, work, or anything to hinder the spread of the gospel. Paul wanted to make it clear to all that he was not preaching the gospel for his own benefit. When people see us working and know where our money comes from, we have little to hide. Living openly makes it easier to be bold in sharing about the love of our life. Paul could write, "We loved you so much that we were delighted to share with you not only the gospel of God but our lives as well, because you had become so dear to us."[21] It is hard to have intimate local friends when we cannot share our private lives with them. It is not easy for them to draw close to us when we live on a tourist or student visa, and they never know when we may pack up and leave.

Upon entering any country, we must answer the immigration question of "Purpose of Visit." The same challenge is amplified when over a cup of coffee we discuss the renewal of the lease of our home for another year, and the landlord asks in a confidential tone, "You can tell me, Jack and Jill, why are you and your lovely Canadian family really here?" If the answer isn't "To earn a living," it is the wrong answer, and there will be more questions.

When a tentmaker adopts an occupation simply as a cover, there is much pressure from those attempting to reconcile in our lives what they see as a contradiction. When a tentmaker's apparent position is logically untenable, suspicion is a natural reaction. There are external pressures as the local people try to figure us out, and there are internal pressures from an accusing conscience. No matter how dedicated we may be, when we as tentmakers cannot completely and openly share our faith and reasons for living among the people, it wears us down psychologically. Jon, a Filipino friend had worked "under cover" for six years with an NGO. Suddenly, he resigned to work for a local computer business. When I asked him why, he replied, "I got tired of living a lie." The wisest man who ever lived points out, "The man of integrity walks securely, but he who takes crooked paths will be found out."[22] Paul could not be accused of seeking personal or dishonest gain. In Thessalonica, his persecutors accused him of having false motives. Yet to the Thessalonians, he could declare the purity of his motives as his life and hard work were evident to all (1 Thessalonians 2:3–6, 9). It is imperative we have pure, godly motives for serving Jesus.

One worker among Muslims in Central Asia writes, "In the town where our widget factory exists, there is no church. . . . Widget has a reputation for honesty and integrity. In this town of strong Islamic fundamentalists, our foreign workers are called 'Mullahs' and are asked to pray at community feasts and functions. Our values of honesty, integrity and respect for the individual are being embraced by the approximately thirty local widget workers employed here. There has not been one instance of theft in our office or at the workshop in the year and a half that our widget company has been functioning. This in a society where theft at the work place is commonplace and is seen as one's right. Other NGOs in the area feel that everything is going well if theft in the work place is kept down to 20 percent. We are truly making an impact in the community that is laying the foundation for a better society."

Integrity is vital if there is to be an effective incarnational witness. Wobbly "platforms" make poor foundations for building a church. Integrity is a valid reason for becoming a tentmaker.

Identity

Working as a tentmaker helped Paul identify with the people (1 Corinthians 11:1). Identifying with the people through work creates natural opportunities to witness. We must understand that our local friends may not interpret the term missionary as we would. Identifying ourselves as a missionary might actually hinder our relationship and witness with them.

Even a national missionary, who is native to the host culture, might be considered a foreigner if he or she is not from the appropriate village, family, or people group. This is certainly true in Pakistan, Turkey, and India. Missionaries (national or expatriate) face identity and reputation difficulties when they are in places where they would not normally be expected to be. I used to live and work on the north side of the town where my sons attended the international school. However, most of our focus people lived on the south side. Whenever I would go over to the south side, people could not understand what I was doing there. When we moved both our home and our office to the south side, those questions quickly ceased.

Even when a missionary overcomes the barriers of physical access (i.e. gets a visa and lives physically close to the community), the larger and more difficult barrier of "image" and endearment must still be overcome. As a businessman in the community, our co-workers and employees introduce us to their network of friends, enabling us to rapidly become socially acceptable. Missionaries are often forced to construct a network of friends in unnatural places or with people who are considered marginal by their selected people group. An advantage of beginning my own business is that I may select the job and working location suitable to the image I desire to reflect to the people. This enables me to build networks among the people of my choosing.

To serve overseas as a regular missionary exposes oneself to many Christians. Regular missionaries who enter a country in relationship with a church are greeted at the airport by Christians, hosted by Christians, and quickly build relationships in the Christian community. In contrast, going to the same country as a tentmaker enables us to interact more with non-Christians and the relationships we make are more natural.

Some workers take pride in being full-time Christian workers and feel a need to be known as "full-time Christian workers." On more than one occasion, I have been rebuked for my lack of involvement in the local expatriate church, even told I was "a luke-warm pew-sitter," for going to church irregularly. However, it is not for us to defend or justify ourselves. We must each decide how we wish the people to perceive us. It is pivotal to understand the consequences of how people perceive us. Workers who do not invest in property or business and are not part of a team may be more open about their missionary identity and agenda, as they have much less at stake. Some Christian workers even act as if being kicked out of a country would be an honor. But the more we invest in the country, its people, property, and livelihood, and the more we acculturate, the wiser it is to live the life of a full-time Christian but without the "Christian worker" label. People believe what they see. If we work a job and receive a pay check, they will know; and if we do not, they will know that too.

The Scriptures tell us, " . . . let us not love with words or tongue but with actions and in truth."[23] As Christians in the marketplace, we naturally identify with those who are there. While striving to relate to their lives and struggles, we need not compromise our integrity. When we are tempted by the same temptations, and yet remain innocent, our co-workers and neighbors notice. Over time they will ask, "How do you do it?" We need not proselytize. Our actions will open doors for our words. When we tell them we can overcome evil, not because we are more disciplined than they are, but because of the power and grace of Jesus' indwelling Spirit, people listen. As one of them, we can show them the way out. Building an acceptable identity with people is a strong grounding for doing tentmaking.

Modeling

Paul had another reason for working. He wanted to be an example to the new believers. Many of the believers of Paul's day did not have a biblical concept of work. Paul knew it was not enough to speak to them about the importance of earning their own living. He needed to model it. Paul urged the believers in Corinth to imitate his way of life (1 Corinthians 4:15–17). In Thessalonica, he and his team not only preached the gospel but shared their very lives with the people. The team worked night and day demonstrating how work and ministry could be integrated (1 Thessalonians 2:8–12).

Working enabled Paul to model the message (2 Thessalonians 3:8). Working and identifying with the people serves as a good model for new believers. Modeling biblical principles in all areas of life is crucial to the discipleship of new believers. In true tentmaking and Christianity, we are involving God in our thoughts, words, and actions throughout the day—in whatever we are doing, wherever we are, and to whomever we are with. Many of us are good at walking with God when we are alone or involving Him when we are with other believers, but we must also include Him when we are with non-believers. This is needful for new believers to learn in cultures that have no Christian traditions. New believers naturally wish to emulate their leaders. If their leaders define "living by faith" as looking to God for support via overseas churches, it is only natural for their converts to do the same. I have witnessed fellowships from Indonesia to North Africa full of unemployed believers. In many cases, these MBBs are being supported by well-meaning churches in the West. In discipling new believers we naturally wish for them to emulate our faith and our lives.

However, I assume most of these western churches fail to grasp that many of these believers do not intend to get a job. Their goal is to live like the missionary who is discipling them, including being supported by western churches.

Working in a research lab in an Islamic country, a tentmaker found himself side by side with a number of Arab co-workers. On occasion, as a matter of routine, a piece of hose through which hot oil traveled would release from its connection, and the lab worker using the testing equipment would get a bath in hot oil. The response of the soaked worker, whether Arab or expatriate, was usually explosive. One afternoon the inevitable happened and the tentmaker became the center of attention as all eyes and ears focused on him to see his response. He calmly wiped the oil off with a towel, looked about the room at the staring faces and declared, "Praise the Lord." His testimony was worth one hundred sermons.

In an anthropomorphic way, God was at work in the act of creation. Thus, work is part of God's character. As creatures designed in God's image, we need to model for new believers that work is part of His plan and fulfills the purpose of our being. The Scriptures are a manual for life and they teach us, "If a man will not work, he shall not eat."[24] Missionaries who work real jobs model, rather than tell new believers how to live. Many poor people tend to think of work as a necessary evil or simply as a means of making money to survive. Some even believe the rich, including all westerners, never have to work at all. Believers need to be taught, and then they need to see that work is part of God's will for our lives. New believers need to work, even as we do, for working is part of the process God uses in conforming us to the image of Jesus (Romans 8:28–29). Proverbs 14:23 adds, "All hard work brings a profit." Believers need to learn to view work not only in terms of monetary gain, but also in terms of the spiritual benefit they may gain on the job, such as learning patience, self-control, wisdom, etc. I believe we all would agree that working a job builds character, which is a meaningful step in our maturing in Christ. We need to both teach and model that we are working for Jesus, not for men, and that it is the Lord Christ whom we serve (Colossians 3:23–24). Providing a good, reproducible model is a good motive for being a tentmaker.

Community

Work facilitated Paul's building a community in which his life was being reproduced in others (Colossians 3:16). Work adds value to the community. Tentmakers who create jobs, provide educational opportunities, or add revenue to the government and society will be welcomed. Providing work for new believers who have been ostracized by their families gives them status and keep them connected to the family that may wish to disown them, allowing them to bless those who are persecuting them (Romans 12:14).

"The priority of work is not profit but service to the community for the common good of all. As believers, our ability to be salt and light in the community, retraining and directing, is absolutely vital. Our modeling and influence will make all the difference in the community. In the past the emphasis was on evangelism by winning individuals. Today the emphasis is on evangelism by multiplying churches. This reflects the growing awareness of the importance of community and the place of the church in God's plan to redeem communities and cultures. Seen in this light, work becomes a vital part in holistic ministry to the whole community bringing a "redemption lift" to that culture."[25]

Having a real, acceptable job helps explain our presence to our neighbors. Working also gives context to our witness. As ambassadors of Jesus, we have been assigned a task that is "politically incorrect." Few government authorities welcome us and none recognize our ambassadorship. The importance of overcoming these hindrances is illustrated by an experience Robert shared with us.

"When I lived in Indonesia, the team I worked with targeted a village called the Stone of Mecca. In the beginning, we met with the village Muslim leaders asking, 'What can we do to help you?' They replied, 'We need better education for our children.' So we built a two room school house and started a kindergarten. In the mornings we taught the children and in the evenings we had English classes for adults. As the people came for classes, they asked about our being there. We shared the Lord with them and today there is a church of over ninety adult believers in that village. During these past two years due to the economic recession, many people were out of work, lacking even the basic commodities for living. Seeing this need, we began a grocery store to help provide food at cost. We gave away rice and tins of powdered milk to mothers who were nursing babies. But as the church grew, persecution came, and my family was ordered by the officials to leave the area. But the church of the Stone of the Mecca continues to grow under the local leadership of Joe, the man God gave us to train as the pastor. In the July 1999 issue of TIME Magazine, our village was one of several featured for the murders of Christians and the persecution that took place there. However, when I contacted Joe, I learned that not one of our people was hurt nor any of the church property damaged. The Muslims recognized our services to the community and respected that. They viewed us as being different from other Christians."

Living and working real jobs brings blessing to the community, gives credibility, provides an identity, and models biblical work to new and old believers and non-believers alike. Tentmaking done in the right way brings blessing to the community.

PERSONAL WORK ISSUES

To choose to serve as a tentmaker because of convenience or personal desire is a bad idea. The research shows that tentmakers who went overseas to work for a specific job are generally ineffective. Another curious revelation is that workers who "told others that they would be tentmakers" before going overseas are less effective. Workers who did not say anything about being a tentmaker are not necessarily more effective, but there is a mild indication that those who intended to be tentmakers before departing from their homeland are less effective. In addition, workers "who worked in a secular job at home similar to the type of work they are doing now overseas are less effective." This may seem illogical but not if you consider motives. Workers who go overseas because of their job tend to emphasize their job. Often they love their job, more than the people or ministry. As a result, they put their energy into building up their business, not their ministry. The research shows that the leading factor for doing tentmaking must be to glorify God by bringing others to salvation in Jesus. Any other desire may yield a successful business, but not a fruitful ministry.

MONEY ISSUES

Oswald Chambers said, "It never cost a disciple anything to follow Jesus; to talk about cost when you are in love with anyone is an insult." Paul did not go to the ends of the earth because there was a better market for selling tents. Paul is not remembered for making tents; he is remembered for being a missionary apostle.

Though at times Paul did make tents to supplement his income, there are other times he determined to earn his own livelihood for a very specific purpose. Paul made tents as a matter of principle. In 2 Corinthians 9, Paul makes a lengthy statement, giving all the reasons why he had every right to receive financial support from the church at Corinth, but he concludes that he and all of those with him chose not to do so. Apparently, the Corinthian church wanted to pay Paul and his team, but they refused. In 2 Corinthians 12:14–18, Paul reiterates his reasons for not accepting their financial help. There were two major reasons. First, as their spiritual father, Paul wanted to be a model, an example for his spiritual children. The Bible teaches it is the parents' duty to provide for the children and not the other way around (Psalm 17:14; 1 Timothy 5:8). And second, Paul said he did not wish to be financially obligated to anyone; he did not want people to think he was ministering for the money. He wanted to ensure that no one had the impression he might have dual motives for serving God. Nor did he want people to think they could "buy him out" so he would preach according to their desires. Paul sought to keep his life above reproach (1 Timothy 3:2). Paul saw a great need for modeling the new life in Christ. He wanted the Corinthians to know how to live and walk depending on the Lord and not on man. He showed by his example what it meant to be in the world but not of it.

Tentmakers can serve abroad for years at little expense to the church. The cost of living is steadily rising around the world. The average support for a North American couple serving in the 10/40 Window is now US$42,600 a year.[26] Most workers need one to two years to raise their support, some longer. Some applicants give up after several years of insufficient support-raising. Thousands of positions are available worldwide that pay round-trip travel for the family, good salaries with benefits and place the worker in a good context for ministry. Many of these jobs are good entry positions to scout out the land while looking for work more suitable to ministry or for studying opportunities for starting your own business, NGO, or school. Other religions are utilizing these opportunities, while we evangelicals debate the pros and cons of such strategies. And while we make up our minds, the price of sending missionaries sky rockets. We are making our message too expensive for export and too offensive for the less affluent nations. I was recently in a large Central Asian city where I met with T-3 tentmakers who were Latino, Korean, and American. Their monthly salaries were $980, $2,200 and $3,200, respectively. Why the difference? The reasons are obvious, but are they biblical or cultural?

Sue is my office manager; she is the best. She runs all of our businesses. When I first hired her, she was not a believer. She had been working for me about a month when she asked, "Mr. Lai, why do you drive a van and not a nicer car?" I told her, "Truthfully, I used to drive a nice car. But one day I realized that if Jesus had driven a vehicle, He would have had a bus or a van so He could take His friends with Him. I don't have a license to drive a bus, so I have a van because I want to be like Jesus." Sue quickly learned that money is not the major motivating factor in my life, and as of last year, it is no longer hers either.

We are told, "So whether you eat or drink or whatever you do, do it all for the glory of God (1 Corinthians 10:31). Martin Luther said, "A dairymaid can milk cows to the glory of God."[27] There are two kinds of tentmakers. One sees himself as a missionary first; the other sees himself as a businessman first. The research shows the amount of money we make (unless it is less than $700/month) has no bearing on our effectiveness. However, the research also reveals that those who pursue tentmaking for reasons other than spiritual reasons are ineffective. Our motives are critical to our fruitfulness. If our primary objective for becoming a tentmaker is to meet our own financial or ego needs, we will probably accomplish that. If our primary desire is to build a profitable business, it is likely we will accomplish that. And if our heart's desire is to plant churches among an unreached people group, that too, is likely to occur. God makes it clear; He says, "Call to me and I will answer you and tell you great and unsearchable things you do not know."[28] As Paul discovered, when our hearts are set on Him, God delights to grant us the desires of our hearts (Romans 10:1). What is your primary motive for wanting to serve as a tentmaker?

Support Raising

It was 1990, and as I was visiting Singapore, the local representative for Pioneers (a mission serving unreached areas) asked me to join him in interviewing a group of applicants. Wendy, one of the applicants, had a solid business background and an apparent heart for both the Lord and the lost. She said she was called to Turkey. After a round of questions and impressive answers, I asked Wendy, "Why do you want to be a tentmaker?" She answered, "I don't want to raise support; it is so embarrassing, and it seems so hard." My reply was soft but firm, "Embarrassing? Embarrassing is mispronouncing a word resulting in my asking a professional, pretty, local woman why no one would marry her. (That's not what I meant to say, I got my words mixed up.) Hard? You can trust God to use you to win Turks to the Lord, which has been done only a few times, but you find it hard to trust Him to provide your support, which, He has proven faithful to do thousands of times?"

Can we believe God to use us to reach Buddhists, Hindus, or Muslims, but not believe Him to supply our financial needs? If so, our motives are wrong because our understanding of God is wrong. Perhaps the issue is not our needs but our wants. God promises only to supply our needs. Jehovah Jireh is our provider, whether that be monies for college, a car, or serving in full-time Christian ministry. In twenty-three years of "Christian work," only twice have I circulated a request for money for myself. God says He will supply all my needs (Philippians 4:19), and He does. I believe our problem is that we often confuse our needs with our wants. Do I need a television or do I want a television? Do I need car, or do I want a car? Hudson Taylor put it this way, "God's work done in God's way will never lack God's supply." Money is a tool, like a rake, a hammer, or a bicycle; each enables us to do a certain task. I have heard regular missionaries criticize tentmakers for "being in it for the money." Yet I have noted in prayer meetings one of the most common requests of "Christian workers" is for money or things, such as a vehicle, land, a building, etc. I believe we have all received support letters which focus only on sending more money. We must look deep inside ourselves to discern our true motivation for serving among the unreached.

Some people are attracted to tentmaking because they do not have to ask for money. It is a matter of dignity, even of saving face. Tentmaking appeals to these people because they can have a better lifestyle than a regular missionary. On my wedding day, my Chinese, atheist father-in-law rebuked me for wanting to be a missionary. "What do you want me to be?" I asked. He exclaimed, "If you must do Christian work, then be a pastor, at least they make a good salary!" Even non-believers know missionaries do not make money! However, many tentmaking professionals are earning far less than their professional qualifications would normally demand. We are children of the King who owns the cattle on a thousand hills (Psalm 50:10). Thus, our vocational decisions should not be determined by economic considerations. Biblically and theologically, it is clear that economics should never rule over obeying the Lord.

Lifestyle

Many tentmakers have the potential to make a very good income, but the hours needed to make a lot of money and the money itself may be a distraction from our primary objective of reaching the unreached. Again, each of us must consider our own calling, needs, and situation. Jesus says, "Follow me." (Matthew 4:19) Paul says, "Follow my example as I follow Christ."[29] What is their example? Jesus clarifies, "Foxes have holes and birds of the air have nests, but the Son of Man has no place to lay his head."[30] Living the simple lifestyle means different things to different people. Personally, I have a nice home. I do not believe living a simple lifestyle means I must live at the poverty level. I do believe it means that every time I open my wallet, whether it be for my church, business, home, or family, I ask the Lord if I have His permission to make that expenditure.

Many followers of Jesus have difficulty discerning between their wants and needs. One of our team members drives a twenty year old car, but that car has a modern stereo system. One team member lives in a dilapidated shack, while another lives in a time-share condominium, replete with giant swimming pool, weight room, squash court, etc. It is not what we have that honors God but how we use it. It is not what we possess but how our possessions possess us. Unlike what our Muslim friends believe, we do not gain points in heaven for our lifestyle on earth. Each of us needs to seek His balance for our lives. The point is we do not bring glory to His name when we make our desires to be His will. Too often we do not seek His guidance for our everyday affairs. In pursuing God's will for our lives, we need to evaluate our motives for serving as tentmakers. Wealth, a nice lifestyle, or anything that may distract us from fully bringing glory to Jesus should be set aside when making our vocational choice.

WITNESSING ISSUES

In evaluating our motives for serving God overseas, we need to ask again, what is on our heart? Paul says, "Brothers, my heart's desire and prayer to God for the Israelites is that they may be saved."[31] In his writings Paul reveals several motivating factors for his ministry: his love for others and for God, his desire to encourage the believers, his obligation to God, his desire to finish the task of evangelizing the world, his absorption with the power of the gospel, and an inner compulsion.

Love

Paul is motivated to reach the unreached through loving others. There are over ninety times in his writings that Paul speaks of love, and fifteen of these times he specifically expresses his love to groups or individuals. He tells us to "Follow the way of love . . ." (1 Corinthians 14:1). Paul knew the way of love meant laying down his life for others (John 15:13). Paul longed to be obedient to God in loving others. If God has given you a love for a people group or country, go and share that love.

Encourage the Brethren

Paul gets excited when he encourages others. He tells the church in Rome that his desire for visiting is "that you and I may be mutually encouraged by each other's faith" (Romans 1:12). He exhorts us to "serve one another in love" (Galatians 5:13). Some workers do not serve on the frontlines but rather a few steps back in support roles. Their primary ministry is to serve the brethren. God does not lead everyone to witness face-to-face among the unreached. Some He directs to support and facilitate those on the frontlines. Jean joined our team with the goal of running our business. She works full time, often fifty or more hours a week. She carries the brunt of the work, enabling other team members to spend more time outside the office. Without her, we would undoubtedly be losing money. Her calling to help us facilitates and blesses us in many ways. If this is the desire Jesus has given you, take it before His throne and ask for His direction.

Obligation to God

Paul says, "I am obligated both to Greeks and non-Greeks, both to the wise and the foolish."[32] Paul is obligated to preach the gospel to everyone. Paul taught grace, and obligation. Grace is freedom. Obligation is duty. The two ideas seem to clash, but in the Holy Spirit, there is a balance. Jesus taught and modeled for us that 100 percent commitment yields 100 percent balance (Revelations 3:15–16). Any commitment less than that and we are out of balance. Jesus commands us, "Go and make disciples of all nations" (Matthew 28:19). In addition, Jesus says, "If you love me, you will obey what I command."[33] We are obligated to obey and to fulfill His purposes for the world. Obligation is a good motivator. We are obligated because God has given to us in such abundance. We are obligated because as His slaves, we are to obey His commands. An obligation to obey is a biblical motivation for reaching the unreached.

Finish the Task

Paul exclaims, "It has always been my ambition to preach the gospel where Christ was not known, so that I would not be building on someone else's foundation. Rather, as it is written: 'Those who were not told about him will see, and those who have not heard will understand.'"[34] Paul kept pressing outward, preaching God's love and grace in places no one had gone before. Jesus forewarned us that the end would come once the whole world has heard His good news (Matthew 24:14). Finishing His task is a viable motive for taking God's glory to the ends of the earth.

Power of the Gospel

Paul pens, "I am not ashamed of the gospel, because it is the power of God for the salvation of everyone who believes . . ." (Romans 1:16). The power of the gospel transformed Paul. He was changed from antagonist to apostle, persecutor to preacher. He knew the power of the gospel firsthand. The power of the gospel motivated him to bring others to Jesus. Many who are touched by God's power feel obligated to share that power. If God is speaking to you, take that obligation and release His power among those who have yet to hear.

Compulsion

Paul tells us, "For Christ's love compels us."[35] Paul was a tentmaker for the sake of Jesus Christ. He had no personal agenda. He sought no personal benefit. Paul chose not to receive money from the churches he planted for the sake of the gospel. He desired to never place a stumbling block in anyone's coming to faith (2 Corinthians 6:3). Paul's desire was that by all the available means people should be brought into a relationship with Jesus (1 Corinthians 9:22). For Paul, as it should be for us, the reward of sharing the gospel is enough. The title and position of "Ambassador of Christ" suffices; the pay and the lifestyle matter not. He was under compulsion. If you have a similar God-given compulsion, go.

ACCESS TO PEOPLE

Have you ever wondered why God chose to send His children around the planet as His primary strategy for communicating the gospel? Why make us His cross-cultural witnesses when He could use supra-cultural workers like talking animals, angels, visions, miracles, etc.? Perhaps the answer lies in the fact that each time His message moves from one culture to another, the method and strategy needs to be reinvented. The message is always the same, but new types of delivery systems need to be developed. As humans, we tend to focus on methods and strategies, sometimes at the expense of glorifying God. Perhaps this is God's idea of keeping us dependent on Himself. Maybe He requires this to guarantee that the message remains His message while our human methods remain expendable. So much of our training nowadays focuses on methodologies and strategies, rather than Jesus. We need to remember that the key to the salvation of our friends is His message revealed in our lives, not our methods. Contextualizing better, praying a bit more, getting our language down pat, and memorizing verses in the Qur'an are all helpful, but they are not to be the focus of our service. D.T. Niles, a missionary to India, once said, "Evangelism is just one beggar telling another beggar where to find bread." The transaction of sharing the good news requires communication, and communication requires both a messenger and a listener. I may be the messenger of a message, but if I have no one to share that message with, then I am really no messenger at all. Missions is all about relationships. Tentmaking is effective because it provides natural access to people with whom to build relationships.

On February 25th, my friend who works in the same building came to me and said, "I am in trouble; this year my office has a new contract. We are supposed to do $300,000 worth of sales each month and this month we have only done $120,000. What should I do?" I replied, "Pray." He looked at me funny, but I said, "Let me pray for you right now." So we prayed right there in the hallway. On February 28th, he came to me with a big smile on his face and said, "Can I buy you a cup of coffee?" I asked, "Why?" He exclaimed, "Guess what! An order just came in from Korea for $200,000. We are going to make our quota!" It was near the end of March when he came to me again. He was $100,000 short and asked me to pray for him again. We prayed and God supplied. This man is moving closer and closer to Jesus. Jesus' presence confers success. Jesus stood on the shore near Peter's boat, and His will, by a mysterious influence, drew the fish into the net. When Jesus is lifted up in our lives, businesses, and homes, His presence becomes the unction that maneuvers results so that He is glorified. By inviting Jesus into our business relationships, our co-workers cannot help but take notice. Utilizing tentmaking as a strategy to access the people you are called to is a good motivation for service.

Jesus said, "But I, when I am lifted up from the earth, will draw all men to myself."[36] As you seek His will for your future, you need to continually look to Jesus in faith. Your motivation for tentmaking should be to do your job as a fulfillment of His calling on your life. Your motivation is not to be self-serving or people-serving. Your motivation is to be God-serving, to bring glory to the name of Jesus.

SUMMARY

Paul was motivated to be a tentmaker for many reasons: credibility, integrity, the desire to identify with the people, to model the message, and to reproduce his life in community. Paul was motivated to do ministry because of his love for Jesus and others, his desire to encourage others, the obligation he felt toward Jesus and completing the task of world evangelization, the impact of the power of the gospel through his testimony, and the compulsion God had given him to tell others of what he had experienced.

ACTION STEPS

- Review how you first became interested in tentmaking.
- Reflect on your motivations for wanting to become a tentmaker.

Write them down.

- What are five good motivations for becoming a tentmaker? Which ones appeal to you?

After Jesus had called His disciples to Himself, He did an unusual thing. He took them with Him into the world. Not the nice world of spiritual retreats and controlled learning environments, but the world of prostitutes, corrupt government officials, the demonized, the terminally ill, and religious hypocrites.

UNKNOWN

"Come follow me," Jesus said.

MATTHEW 4:19

chapter 6

TESTING YOUR TENT—
Pre-field Preparation

Training—it means many things to many people, and there are many things we train, including our children, pets, and ourselves. Some view training as a negative term, preferring more acceptable terms for the 21st century, such as equipping, coaching, mentoring, or preparing. Yet Jesus calls us to be disciples, and discipleship is a life-long training process. Before embarking on training yourself for a tentmaking ministry, there are three qualifications you should meet.

One, that you are mature spiritually. You know how to feed yourself in the Word and prayer, and you are active in using God's gifts in your life both in a fellowship of some kind and as a light to your non-believing friends.

Two, that someone more mature has confirmed tentmaking is a good path for you. In the New Testament, each time God calls someone to a new ministry He confirms the calling through the church or other mature believers.

Three, that you do not need props to support your spiritual life (Christian tapes, books, sermons, even fellowship). These things are not bad, and in fact, we are commanded to be in fellowship (Hebrews 10:25). However, when you are living in the outermost corners of the earth, these may not be available.

How do you know if you need props? One way is to test yourself. Try training yourself by fasting from spiritual props for one month or more. On Sunday, instead of going to church, go to a park or quiet place and fast, pray, read, study, and meditate on the Word all day, listening to God. Read only the Bible. Listen only to God's Word on CD or tape, and do not listen to sermons or worship music. Tentmakers need to be able to manage their spiritual diet. When the props are removed, you need to know if your faith will still stand. If you are immature, or need props to hold up your faith, then you are not ready for tentmaking. Your priority should be to find someone who can train you further in the basics of the faith.

In training tentmakers, one of the issues to be dealt with is retraining the older generation of workers toward a new vision of missions. One worker writes, "When I consider what attitudes the new generation needs to have in order to work well in partnership with nationals and each other, I'm not sure the older generation has the best teachers. I'm thinking of my mission's context, but I can imagine the same applies in other organizations. We have a way of doing things that has almost become 'sanctified' because it is the way we were taught. Our leaders are saying we need to change the way we do things if we are to get done sooner. Yet when new folks come join us, the old paradigm is still the one they expect to function with. The new way of doing translation is often only given lip service." Putting aside old paradigms is a problem for most leaders and organizations. Yet, "teaching," by definition, requires an "old paradigm." In order for our teaching material to have any validity, it has to have been tried and proven helpful, and thus worthy of being taught to others. Nearly all of our past success stories are among the already-reached, using regular missionary methods. Yet, when compared with regular missionary service, there are some significant differences in tentmaking which tentmakers need to prepare for. Issues such as ethics in doing business, security, a dual identity, ministry in the work place, juggling different roles, and more separate us from regular missionaries. Missionaries have made tremendous advances among peoples who are animistic or atheistic, but it has been slow going into the strongholds of Buddhism, Islam, and Hinduism.

We are learning what programs and strategies do not work. We need to put some outmoded methodologies aside and look to the Lord for new ideas. We need to think through how to inform and instruct the churches, training institutions, and pre-field training programs, so that they have a clear understanding of what tentmaking is and the variety of ways tentmaking can be done. New workers need to seriously consider the source of the paradigm of their training and its effectiveness for the work they are being led to do.

We are adequately equipping people to serve among the reached, but what about the unreached? Those who are training tentmakers need to critically evaluate whether we are training new people into old methods that have failed. Are we encouraging new workers to learn from our failures and risk new ventures? Are we continuing old attitudes of paternalism and isolation, rather than showing how to release nationals to take over our duties while cooperating with like-minded others? Are we taking traditional missionary training schemes and giving them a tentmaking veneer? We need to be asking ourselves, "Just how old are our wineskins?"

PRE-FIELD EXPERIENCES

Time invested in preparing for overseas ministry can shape our entire career. The Bible exhorts us to be thoroughly equipped for every good work (2 Timothy 3:17). It is important to make good use of this time, refining strengths and strengthening weaknesses. A wise person will seek out a mentor who will hold him or her accountable to grow in these areas (Proverbs 19:20). Self awareness and good mentoring are needed for personal growth. There are four crucial areas each worker must consider and do some advance preparation in, prior to going overseas. These four areas are:

1. Church and spiritual life
2. Preparation and training
3. Work experience
4. Witnessing

Church and Spiritual life

The work and ministry God has for us to do is fundamentally a spiritual work. Future tentmakers need to be growing spiritually and be active in a local church prior to going overseas. The research reveals that the quality of a worker's devotional life has a direct bearing on his effectiveness in evangelism and church planting. Before going overseas, workers need to feed themselves and daily interact with the Master. Workers who do not have a daily devotional life before moving overseas are clearly less effective than those who do. Workers need to have shown the ability to spiritually feed themselves, reflecting discipline in various aspects of prayer and meditation.

A second important factor concerning effectiveness is that workers who "are personally discipled by someone more mature in the Lord before going overseas" prove to be more effective. Discipleship is being sadly neglected. Fewer and fewer candidates have had one-on-one discipleship early in their spiritual journey. They have not learned the value of accountability nor had someone refining their character with them. It is wise for mission leaders to ask potential applicants detailed questions about their spiritual growth and discipleship background. Applicants should be required to sit at the feet of mentors who will pour themselves into the applicants, discipling them and working with them in areas of weakness.

Workers also need to be actively involved in their local church. Having a ministry within the church allows both leaders and members to observe our giftedness. When people see our contribution to the church, they gain confidence that we can also contribute to God's work elsewhere. Too many young people church hop and give all their time to para-church ministries. Often students are attracted to the para-church ministries because they have the most gifted disciplers and quality discipleship programs. However, it is the church that will ultimately send, care, and support the worker once he or she goes overseas. If you sense the Lord is leading you overseas, it is essential to have a sending church. Find a church that ministers to you and in which you can also have a ministry. Share your plans and dreams with the church leaders. Invite the church to review your pre-field training and preparations. When you are ready to go overseas, request the church commission you as their tentmaker missionary.

Preparation and Training

As believers, we are to "Do your best to present yourself to God as one approved, a workman who does not need to be ashamed and who correctly handles the word of truth."[37] The majority of effective tentmakers have received training in either missions, Bible school, or seminary. A solid majority (78 percent) had training in missiology. A majority of the workers had both Bible and missiological training. Many workers prepared in traditional ways by attending Bible school or seminary (65 percent), missiological training courses (78 percent), short-term trips (80 percent), and language training (55 percent). Nearly 30 percent completed all four. Though missiological or cross-cultural training is imperative, the length and type of such training varies. In this area you need to know yourself, your fears, and your doubts. All workers, especially tentmakers going into business, should seriously consider investing the time to get some cross-cultural training before moving abroad. The research verifies that workers who do not have missiological or cross-cultural training are more likely to fail. Having training in how to learn a language also enhances effectiveness, especially when one has to learn an unwritten language.

How much training is needed? The best way to determine this is to visit the field to learn what is needed. Teachers and trainers at home naturally recommend that you do what they did, often encouraging you to follow them in their area of expertise. This is natural but often unhelpful. We are all different, and the ministries we are being directed to are different. Taking a short-term trip or doing an internship of three to eight months is often a good way to get a feel for what further training you will need. While overseas, you can question the workers to learn what pre-field training they received, and what was helpful and what was not. You can also learn what they would do differently. Ask someone on the field to coach you via e-mail as you take courses and prepare. Having someone to guide you in what to study, even what papers to write, gives greater focus and meaning to your studies. Get the training you need. When in doubt, it rarely hurts to get too much.

The most effective way workers can prepare to serve overseas is to invest one or more years ministering with international students. Ministering to international students needs to be given a stronger emphasis in the preparation of mission candidates. Workers who minister to international students before going overseas were shown to be much more effective than their peers. People pursuing overseas service should be exhorted to befriend at least three people from the country they intend to serve in. This would have three benefits. First, the candidates would experience relating to and ministering alongside foreigners. These relationships formed in a relaxed, natural, familiar setting would allow potential workers to make cultural mistakes in a place where it does not matter. They would also learn to be flexible, to listen, and to ask questions. Relating to international students or immigrants teaches us there is more than one proper way to do things.

A second benefit is the status gained in knowing the friend. Many international students are from the upper-class elite. Their friends and relatives back home could prove to be valuable allies in learning the language, finding a home, setting up a business, and even procuring a visa. If you move to the country before your friend returns home and take his greetings to his family, you will be welcomed with open arms.

While studying at Penn State, Frank sensed the Lord leading him to reach Muslims in a closed country. He made friends with fellow students from that country. During his final semester, he met Abdullah, a newly enrolled student. Twice Abdullah and Frank went out together with mutual friends. After graduating, Frank applied for a visa to the closed country and was denied. He went to London to apply at the embassy, but was refused there too. The Lord led him to try the embassy in Malta. He flew there and was rejected once more. However, while he was in the waiting room, he struck up a conversation with one of the embassy clerks. It turned out this clerk was Abdullah's uncle! When the uncle learned that Frank needed a visa but was rejected, he personally sought out the ambassador and pleaded Frank's case. As a result, Frank got a visa!

The third benefit is that these foreign friends would have an opportunity to hear the gospel and see it lived in you. Your friends should see differences between you and other Americans they meet. The differences should lead them to ask about your beliefs, allowing you to give them an opportunity to receive eternal life.

The research reveals one point which needs to be highlighted. This is a major concern, as it relates to a worker's marriage. The data strongly indicates that "workers whose marriage was not good (spiritually, emotionally, and sexually) before going overseas" have a very high probability of being ineffective. Again, having a good marriage does not mean the worker will succeed, but not having a good marriage before setting out greatly increases the worker's chances of being unproductive on the field. Experienced workers know that issues which were little problems at home become magnified once overseas. When interviewing applicants, their marriage needs to be thoroughly evaluated, and major unresolved issues need to be dealt with before sending them abroad. There is particular wisdom in not sending newly married couples into battle (Deuteronomy 20:7).

Two non-ministry factors are "reading books on missions and missionaries" and "exercising regularly." The survey does not explain why these factors are helpful. Personally, I find reading books on missions helpful. Reading about the experiences of others provides useful ideas for the times when we find ourselves in similar situations. In addition, the struggles of those who have gone before us and their dependence on Jesus serve as an encouragement to us. Nearly 84 percent of all workers read mission books or periodicals before going overseas. Such reading stimulates our vision, enhances our faith, and provides a library of information to draw on once overseas.

Exercising regularly is also helpful in increasing the probability of being effective. Experts tell us that exercising is good for our health; maybe it is good for our spirits too. Perhaps those who have the discipline to exercise regularly will carry that same discipline over into other areas of their lives.

Workers who experienced a demonic confrontation before going overseas are also more effective. Those who encounter demons and continue in the Lord undeterred are more prepared. It is not uncommon for animists, Buddhists, Hindus, and Muslims to manifest demons. Workers who are active in evangelism among the unreached will need to deal with spiritual warfare issues. These issues should be included in all missionary training.

The research shows that workers "who found it hard to initiate conversations about their faith" and workers "who share their faith only when obvious situations arise" are both highly ineffective. Also, workers "who prefer not to verbally share their faith, but rather let their life be a witness" also prove to be highly ineffective. Boldness and frankness in sharing one's faith need to be a part of any missionary training program.

Work Experience

The majority of tentmakers worked before they went overseas. Working a regular job provides experience and discipline that only the working world can teach. The type of work one does is not critical to our future ministry. Workers who had a secular job at home similar to the type of work they do overseas are actually less effective. This is not surprising because some workers, such as computer people, tend to be more focused on the demands of their work than on outreach. However, such people may be good facilitators, enabling others to do evangelism and church planting, while they keep a business or NGO running.

The research revealed that it does not matter whether you are self-employed, start your own business, are a leader at work, or work in a cross-cultural office; what matters is that you learn to work and that you do your work well. The data reinforces that those who put non-ministry goals above ministry objectives are likely to be ineffective in ministry.

Witnessing

As the plumb-line for effectiveness is evangelism, discipleship, and church planting, it is exigent that future tentmakers get practical experience doing evangelism before going overseas. The more experience and the greater the number of evangelistic tools mastered, the better. Workers who "regularly did personal or campus evangelism or house-to-house visitation" before going overseas proved to be very effective.

As the objective of missionary work is to win and gather new believers into Bible studies, it is not surprising that those workers who "led one or more evangelistic Bible studies with non-Christians" before going overseas were also highly effective.

Much of what field workers do is centered on building relationships. Workers who, prior to serving overseas, described their involvement with new believers they helped bring to Christ as a close friendship were also more effective. More of our evangelistic training needs to be centered on making friends and sharing the gospel through those friendships. Passing out tracts and "cold turkey" confrontational witnessing are particularly less effective in most Hindu and Muslim areas.

Without a doubt, all applicants should be experienced in face-to-face evangelism and discipleship before going overseas. Unless they will be working with a field leader who will mentor them in these areas or they are going as support workers, applicants lacking such experiences should delay going overseas until they have proven their ministry skills at home. Classes on evangelism will not suffice; hands on experience is needed. It is wise to try various evangelism strategies, such as passing out tracts and books, starting an evangelistic Bible study, learning and sharing illustrations such as the Bridge or Roman Road, open air preaching, friendship evangelism, community evangelism, etc.

Some missions discourage workers from having more than two children before going overseas. The research reveals another interesting tidbit. Workers who are married with children, particularly those with three children, are a bit more effective than those who have more or less. There is no doubt that more children incur more cost and seem to create distractions from ministry during the first few years overseas. However, the research proves the distractions may build additional relationships within the community, thus enhancing our witness. A family with four children may be expensive to keep on the field, but they are actually more effective in evangelism and discipleship than a couple without children.

BIBLE COLLEGE / SEMINARY

Traditionally, the standard way of preparing for the mission field is to attend Bible school or seminary. Tentmakers have been wrongly criticized for not being well trained. An interesting result of the research is that a Bible college or seminary education has no impact on the effectiveness of workers. It is neither a help nor a hindrance in enhancing the productivity of workers serving in the 10/40 Window. Actually, very few schools train students for ministry among Buddhist, Hindu, Muslim, or other unreached peoples. A few are offering intensive courses on ministering to unreached peoples, but they seldom have courses on church planting among the unreached. I know of none in the West with hands-on training. In contrast, Chris Marantika's school in Indonesia requires students to actually plant a church before receiving their degrees.

Bible schools are appropriately named "Bible" schools because they teach the Bible and train their students to work with Christians in churches as pastors, educators, etc. If God is leading you to become a pastor or serve the church either at home or overseas, seminary is a good place to prepare. Personally, during the four years I served a church in Asia, both my seminary credentials and the training I received proved quite beneficial. The missiological training I received in seminary has also proven to be very helpful. However, the reasons for sending missionary candidates to Bible school as preparation for overseas service among the unreached needs to be re-evaluated.

Why should missionary candidates go to Bible school or seminary?

"Missionaries must cross linguistic, cultural, and social boundaries to proclaim the gospel in new settings. They must translate and communicate the Bible in the languages of people in other cultures so that it speaks to them in the particularities of their lives. They must bridge between divine revelation and human contexts, and provide biblical answers to the confusing problems of everyday life. This process of cross-cultural communication means that missionaries, by the very nature of their task, must be theologians. Their central question is: 'What is God's Word to humans in this particular situation?'"[38]

There are three reasons why formal Bible education should be considered. First, if God is calling you to work with Christians, at home or abroad, a Bible education should be beneficial. The knowledge you gain and the tools and resources you are introduced to will be of value in your ministry. Bible institutions do a fine job of training people to work with Christians. Having a degree from a respectable school often opens doors to ministry in Christian circles. Second, if you have questions about your faith, want to go deeper into the Word, or desire to study the original languages, Bible schools and seminaries are most helpful. Many young people I have interviewed for the field had questions about their faith. Bible school is a good place to find the answers to your theological questions and put your doubts to rest. However, understand that a Bible school or seminary education is designed to deepen your understanding and use of God's Word, not to equip you to reach the unreached. And finally, if you wish to start new churches, you may wish to disciple your leaders in the areas of deeper Bible knowledge, church history, eschatology, ecclesiology, etc. As Heibert points out, all Christians who witness for Jesus are "theologians" in a basic form. However, if you are preparing to serve among the least reached peoples of the world, a formal Bible education need not be a requirement.

So why do most mission agencies still require their candidates to have at least one year of formal Bible education? A formal Bible education at respected institutions enables mission executives to be certain their candidates have a well-rounded understanding of the Scriptures. As discipleship in the churches and para-church ministries varies considerably and mission organizations do not have the facilities to disciple candidates themselves, sending all candidates to Bible schools or seminaries enables them to standardize their process.

The soundness of this paradigm should be open to questioning, if not change. Some agencies are talking of becoming more flexible with the Bible school requirement. I would appeal to agencies to begin to evaluate their candidacy processes and look more closely at including basic Bible training in field mentoring strategies. Field mentoring would enable mission leaders to evaluate the Bible knowledge of the candidates, while at the same time discipling them in missionary life and work. After a period of field mentoring, those candidates who show they do not have a good grasp of the Scriptures could still be required to study in a formal Bible college or seminary environment.

I have no doubt that formal Bible schools and seminaries do a good job of training pastors and Christian workers to work with Christians. However, even our "Schools of World Mission" have obvious weaknesses when it comes to training tentmakers for the 10/40 Window. We need to invest more effort in providing "practical," hands-on experiences. There was a reason Jesus took His disciples with Him and did not set up a school to train them. The answers to the questions that most Muslims ask can be learned in a few days of training. Arabic, not Greek, is what is needed on the field. Muslims do ask, "Is Jesus the Son of God?" But the answer is not complicated. Not once in seventeen years of Muslim evangelism have I been quizzed concerning my thoughts on infralapsarianism. Buddhists, Muslims, and Hindus want to know, "Who has the power to heal?" "How can I survive?" To many it is not a matter of truth; it is a matter of power. For tentmakers, these questions may be discussed in the classroom but best understood on the battle field.

I was recently asked by two high school students where they should go to college. The first told me that he wanted to be a pastor; the other felt he was being led to be a missionary to the unreached. I told the former to go to Bible college; I recommended the later attend a large state university. Today, fewer mission leaders to the unreached are recruited from traditional Bible colleges and seminaries. Why? I agree with what one worker wrote on his survey questionnaire, "When it comes to missions and evangelism, students from a Bible school have been to boot camp. Students from a secular university have been in battle."

SHORT-TERM EXPERIENCE

If you are considering long-term service, you should first plan to go on a short-term mission trip to the location of your leading. A short-term trip will enable you to test yourself, to see if you can adapt and live in that location. Many a candidate feels led to a certain people group or place, but upon arrival discovers, "This is not for me!"

Going on a short-term mission trip can be a faith-building and even life-changing experience. It can enrich the way you view both God and His world. A well designed trip will cause you to rely on God more and give you a better understanding of the need for laborers to serve the unreached. A good short-term experience should also test and clarify God's leading in your life.

Short-term missionaries come from all walks of life to do a variety of projects that may require a commitment from one week to two years. Those who choose to do a short-term assignment overseas may be of any age, from high school students to retirees. Over five hundred mission organizations offer short-term mission trips, most of which can be readily found on the internet. However, mission organizations offering trips to unreached areas are generally a bit more security conscious. If you wish to serve in the 10/40 Window with experienced tentmakers, you may need to contact those mission agencies directly. There are only a handful of on-site tentmaking short-term opportunities, but their quality varies, and due to security reasons, they cannot be listed here. Contact a tentmaking organization for more information.

The value and impact of short-term missions on the field is frequently debated. Some missionaries love having short termers and some avoid them like the plague. Yet no one questions the value and spiritual impact short-term trips have on the individuals who go. The research shows that 80 percent of those serving in the 10/40 Window went on a short-term missions trip prior to their moving overseas. Nearly 12 percent did their short-term trip to the location where they now serve. A solid 50 percent made at least a short visit to their area to scout out the land before moving there.

Churches also value short-term trips, as they build unity and zeal within the members who participate. Missionaries working with churches overseas generally favor having short-term workers for the help they supply. However, the majority of field workers interviewed would rather have someone else supervise the visitors. Apart from the value to the individuals and to the sending churches, the true value of short-term trips to the long-term efforts of our workers in the 10/40 Window is open to debate.

There are some agencies that specialize in short-term ministries; it is all they do. I read on one website that 50 percent of missionaries are involved in assisting short-term missionaries. That statistic may or may not be true, but very few of us see that as our main job. From a long-term worker's perspective, there is only one reason why we are willing to accept short termers: *laborers*. We need more long-term workers. We understand that young people nowadays are averse to making long-term commitments.

We also understand that "75–80 percent of all long-term workers went on a short-term mission trip prior to making a long-term commitment. Some estimates indicate that as many as 40 percent of those who go on short terms will return long term."[39] So missionaries welcome short termers with the hope they will come back.

Obviously, many will not come back, so a secondary reason why we welcome short termers is *advocates*. We are looking for people who will commit to pray for us often, financially support the ministry, recruit others to join us, and involve others in these ministries with us. We hope that when people return home, they will continue to be part of our ministry through their prayers, gifts, and encouragement.

The final reason we are willing to accept short termers is for the *help* they bring. Short termers have been helpful in caring for children while parents learn the language, teaching English language classes which create opportunities to share the gospel, and doing needed work in our businesses and NGOs.

Roughly one-third of the short termers I have worked with have neither returned, nor become advocates, nor were of any help. Thus, it is easy to understand how short-term programs may get a bad reputation.

Having worked closely with nearly two hundred short termers over the years (sent from churches, Bible schools, para-church ministries, mission organizations, and friends), I have begun to place short-termers into four categories: Burners, Servers, Learners, and Discerners.

Burners are usually people who come overseas for a holiday. They want to do something different and nice and possibly look good to their Christian friends back home. They take their camera with them everywhere. They use their vacation to burn up our time. They require a lot of attention and care, and they frequently remind us of the sacrifices they are making. Often they expect the missionary to serve them, as they see themselves doing us a favor. If you are reading this book, you are not a Burner. Burners would not read this book. People who wish to go on a short-term trip for a holiday should go with agencies which specialize in short-term ministries, as these ministries have the time and resources to provide the cross-cultural ministry experience Burners want.

Servers are people who come overseas to help. Each worker on the field has a specific job which needs to be done and the short-term Server offers to help do it. That may be anything from constructing a building, to minding the children, to fixing computers. Servers usually have a set project to accomplish, and when they return home they know whether or not they have accomplished it. Servers should seek to do short-term projects that the missionary actually needs to accomplish. Your objectives, expectations, and costs should be well clarified before going overseas.

Learners are those who come overseas wanting to learn about God, missions, the world, different cultures, and themselves. Everything is an adventure because they want to learn! Such workers are fun to work with but may or may not make a significant contribution to the work. Learners should expect to discover their ministry gifts and stretch their personal and spiritual horizons. If you are a Learner and open to what the Lord would want to do in and through you, most any type of short-term mission experience would benefit you. To get the most benefit from a short-term experience, Learners should set clear objectives and clarify expectations with those they will be ministering with before departing overseas.

Discerners are people who know God is leading them into long-term mission work and are seeking specific guidance for their lives. Discerners are the kind of short termers most long-term workers wish to have. Discerners need to be selective in where they serve. They should correspond with both the agency and the field workers with whom they will serve. It is imperative that Discerners have a real experience so as to test themselves. Whereas Burners, Servers, and Learners do not need to be overseas more than a few weeks, Discerners may wish to consider a longer short-term commitment. Ideally Discerners should seek out an internship which would both challenge and equip them for future service. Discerners should also look for an experience which will expose their gifts and skills to various work and ministry situations and opportunities.

The length of short-term trips varies. Some trips, usually two weeks or less, are exposure trips which give one a "look-see" of an area and what the missionaries there are doing. Server projects in particular can often be accomplished in two weeks. Longer trips or internships may range in length from four weeks to two years. The longer trips will involve you in the local ministry. The better programs offer missiological training as well. The length of your short-term trip should be matched to your objectives. If it is to scout the land for future ministry opportunities, one to four weeks should suffice. If you are struggling to determine God's direction, three to eight months might be better. I rarely recommend short-term trips longer than eight months, unless the worker is going to serve in a clearly needed support role or it is a well-designed internship. Three months is ample time to determine God's will as to your serving long term in a location, and less than eight months gets you home before culture shock can set in. Clearly, the contribution you make to the ministry will be hindered by your lack of language proficiency.

Another factor in determining the length of a short-term trip is culture shock. Culture shock normally is at its peak between the eighth and the eighteenth month. Short-term workers who return home during this period often leave with a bad taste of missions in their mouth and are less likely to return. Some, who come for twenty-four months, simply gut it out their final six to eight months, eager to go home and never to return. Thus, more than two years is better than one to two years, as it is more likely you will work through the effects of culture shock before returning home. Working through culture shock will in turn equip you for future bouts of this malady, allowing you to leave on a positive note, while teaching you vital lessons about God and yourself.

Expectations

One of the primary reasons that both short and long-term missionaries have unsuccessful overseas experiences is because their expectations are not met. It is essential that short termers have realistic expectations of what the conditions will be like and of what they will learn and accomplish. If you are going overseas to discern His will for you, there are eight questions you should get answered before committing to a short-term ministry. I recommend you get these answers from the field worker you will be working with and not from someone in their home office. You may review these questions in Appendix A. A short-term mission trip can be a key step in discerning God's will for your life. Whether you go as a Learner, Server, or Discerner, *go*!

CHURCH / PARA-CHURCH MINISTRY

Active church involvement is essential for all believers. The church is the bride of Christ and God works through it. It is the church who sends out laborers. Though many para-church ministries will also send out laborers, their financial support usually originates with the church. Para-church ministries, both at home and on the field, have strategic roles, but all workers should be actively involved in a local church before taking steps towards going overseas.

The research proves that workers who have no full-time Christian work experience before going overseas are likely to be ineffective. All workers, especially tentmakers, who are in a hurry to move overseas and set up a business or begin a ministry, should be advised to take six months or more to serve full-time in a church at home. The relationships developed in the spiritual and business realms, in addition to the valuable ministry experience, will aid the worker's effectiveness over the years. The fact that many workers (92 percent) are still in close touch with their sending churches shows the importance workers ascribe to their home church's involvement in their lives. Nearly 90 percent said "my church encouraged me as I sought God's will for my life," encouraging evidence that most of the workers' churches played a role in their going overseas. Exactly 69 percent replied that "I had an ongoing accountability relationship with a leader in my home church," showing that a majority of workers had a close relationship with a church leader. A large majority of workers were commissioned as missionaries or tentmakers by their home church. The church has a major role in sending tentmakers!

Prior to moving overseas, it is paramount that workers be involved in their church; sing in the choir, work with the youth, teach Sunday School, etc. As Lucy tells Linus, "Don't just sit there; do something!" The experiences gained will be helpful when beginning to gather a church at a later time. Try various ministries to see where you are gifted. Get involved with the missions committee. Be sure the committee members know you and your long-term goals. Ask for their input in selecting a mission agency and people group. Invest time getting to know your church leaders. Pick their brains, ask questions, and pray with them. Invite one or two to disciple you and hold you accountable in all areas of your life. Cultivate spiritual mentors who will encourage and counsel you when you are overseas. Seek out the prayer warriors of the church. Take time to pray with them and ask them to teach you how to pray. Invite them to pray for you too. Find church members who have similar professional backgrounds. If you already know your entry strategy, get to know men and women who are already working in the vocation you intend to pursue in obeying the Great Commission. If you are a teacher, get to know the teachers in your church or if you are a medical person, the medical people. These people may become primary advisors and be resource people for you in the future.

Be involved. Let people see your zeal and commitment. Workers active in ministering to others have little trouble raising prayer and financial support. People who see you ministering will be confident that you will continue to minister after you have left.

Finally, request that your church commission you as a tentmaker or missionary. Churches stand behind those they commission. A commissioning service is of great encouragement both to you and the church. It provides a point of reference for closure to what has been accomplished in your life and an affirmation for what is ahead. It is a recognition of your calling by the church as a body. This often leads to their committing to pray and financially support your overseas ministry.

MISSIOLOGICAL TRAINING

All workers should consider having missiological training before moving overseas. The research clearly shows that those without missiological or cross-cultural training are more likely to be ineffective. Having cross-cultural training does not guarantee success, but not having it increases a worker's chances of failure. When sharing the gospel, or working in a school or business setting, it is important to grasp how people think. Studying cultural learning techniques should help you grasp issues you need to master to communicate more effectively. All workers, especially tentmakers going into a business, should invest the time to get some cross-cultural training before moving abroad.

Missiological training varies greatly from short-term programs overseas, to seminaries, to institutes specializing in training for specific peoples or religions. Ted Yamamori lists some issues which should be a practical part of any missiological training program, tentmaking or otherwise. I call this "Ted's To Do" list. (With Ted's permission I have modified them a bit.) Before going overseas to a third world country, tentmakers should be able to do the following:

1. List and explain strategies for evangelizing and converting people groups where there are few or no churches.

2. Identify the techniques/entry strategies for living among people groups normally considered "closed" (CANs, RANs).

3. Explain and demonstrate techniques for communicating successfully with people from a different culture—paying special attention to dissimilar values, ethnocentricity, nonverbal communication (such as proxemics and gaze behaviors), and culturally value-laden conversion issues, such as polygamy or alcohol consumption.

4. Demonstrate a sound knowledge of the Third World—its strengths, as well as its weaknesses. Describe the more common Third World social systems and hierarchical structures. Explain the rationale for working "under" national workers.

5. Describe three or more church-planting strategies designed for countries where traditional churches are not tolerated. Explain and differentiate techniques for discipling, "friendship evangelization," "relationship evangelization," and building up self-replicating groups of believers. Outline and explain three or more church models.

6. Explain the basic ways for winning another person to Christ, especially when that person is a member of a cultural group different from your own. Be able to demonstrate these approaches in practice. Also, demonstrate actual use of these approaches with various ethnic groups under controlled, supervised circumstances where your approach can be critiqued and improved.

7. Explain and demonstrate techniques in actual practice for organizing, discipling, and perpetuating a group of believers in a secret setting. How would you participate in this group both as a leader or member?

8. Explain ways of teaching national believers to take up the missionary task, working independently of you, and without any outside support.

9. Develop and explain a personally satisfactory rationale for operating as a "covert" missionary.

10. Differentiate and explain two or more language learning strategies, including the tools used in those strategies to master the language of the people you will reach.

11. List and explain the basic tenets of the dominant religions and world ideologies (such as globalization) within your selected mission field. List ten strengths of each religion or ideology; list ten ways in which Christianity might better meet the local peoples' needs.

12. Show an ability to improvise and evaluate risk.

13. Experience community living, modeling the humility to put others first. Demonstrate the maturity to keep short accounts of sins/hurts/misunderstandings with co-workers. Show the wisdom to repent, reconcile, and make restitution when offenses of any kind are committed.[40]

When you can fully respond to all of "Ted's To Do" list, you have a solid missiological foundation.

Internships

One biblical step which takes advantage of experience without curbing creative innovation is the initiation of internships. More and more universities are partnering with businesses to provide hands-on internships for students. The students gain practical knowledge and work experience, helping them determine if this is the direction and work they really want to give their lives to.

The internships benefit the schools as they learn which aspects of their curriculum are more valuable to their graduates, and they enhance the school's capabilities and reputation. The businesses benefit as they can observe potential workers up close and with minimal cost evaluate the potential of hiring these workers. It is a win-win situation. Mission training schools would do well to instigate required internships in the context of overseas ministry preparation. Field tentmaking applications would put the classroom teachings to the test, allowing them to be appraised and perhaps modified.

In such a setting, the tentmaking field-mentor guiding the student must be experienced and competent. The field-mentor and school-mentor need to understand one another's training styles and objectives. Both need to be visionary, flexible, and gracious when integrating their programs in ways that encourage new ideas, as well as promote creative thinking and risk-taking that may enhance both of their ministries.

Some missiologists believe they have internships in place. However, a true internship is an ongoing team effort between both the field-mentor and the sending (school or church) mentor. It requires a close relationship to ensure the student's best interests are met and that what is taught in the school is well tested on the field. It involves interaction and sharing of ideas so the students are prepared to fully participate during their internship and not just watch as a tentmaker missionary does all the work. Corrective feedback from the field should influence what is taught in the school, and those parts of the school's curriculum which do not work on the field should be dropped. Most schools now have no "quality control" over the internships in which their students participate. In most cases it is actually the students who choose their internships, and the school only asks for a questionnaire to be filled out and submitted at the completion of the student's service. There is virtually no quality control and no accountability. In this aspect, secular universities do better than Bible schools and missionary training schools, as they work alongside businesses to ensure their students are receiving real benefit from their internships.

Internships are different than short-term experiences. Short termers usually serve in one of two capacities. Either they go overseas for less than two months, often to fulfill a special need or project, or they may be part of a longer, pre-designed program for training short-term workers. Operation Mobilization (OM) and Youth With A Mission (YWAM) are two of the more well-known and effective short-term missionary training programs. Like apprenticing of old, we should employ internships to adequately equip and motivate our young people.

Internship programs should not focus simply on seeing and experiencing new things in a religious ministry context. A good internship assists interns in walking through processes which enable them to see for themselves who they really are in Christ. We need to help the interns strip off layers so they can discern their own processes for making judgments and decisions and help them understand how their way of living is perceived by the people around them. The way the intern thinks, acts, and makes assumptions needs to be understood and reviewed. A good internship is more than experiences and facts, touching and tasting, feelings and photographs. It is the encountering of unexpected and revealing discoveries of oneself which the intern has never realized before. This self encounter should draw the interns deeper into the things of God and bond them to the people and the team they are living and working with. My experience is that only contextual changes generated through major life encounters help to change peoples' lives and especially their walk with Jesus. This is why training workers on the field is so much better than training in an artificial environment at home. Students who have revitalizing internships want to come back, not for the sake of the ministry or people group, but for the sake of their relationship with Jesus.

In considering internships, we need to understand the objectives of the parties involved. Schools wish to train and educate their students, equipping them for God's future service. Students wish to discern God's will for their lives, testing themselves to see if tentmaking or mission work is a good fit. Field workers are looking for help, but more importantly, desire to recruit long-term laborers. I would argue that internships should not be done with tentmakers or missionaries who are looking for temporary help, as this is of little benefit to the student. An internship should be a real and dynamic experience. Students should not just be taking care of the kids but should be involved in a viable ministry that truly engages their faith and skills. Naturally, there are language limitations, but learning the language should be a part of any internship. The experiences students have should be hands-on and real. An internship should not be designed to give the intern a good experience, but rather a *real* experience. If the tentmaker or missionary has to create things for the intern to do, that is not a good internship, as it does not expose the student to the real demands of tentmaking life and work. I believe internships should be for a minimum of ten weeks and a maximum of eight months. It normally takes a short termer one month to settle in and at least one week to prepare to leave. Ten weeks allows a minimum of one month of active ministry for students to experience cross-cultural life and work, test themselves in ministry, and experience God in a new way. Anything less than two months does not give the student enough opportunities to be tested and be stretched, which are essential for a real experience.

An English teacher in North Africa writes, "I feel in my case, preparation was overdone. I spent almost a year in courses, candidate courses, and a TEFL course. I read a lot of books that were required etc. I feel it would be more beneficial to encourage recruits to come to the field early and be willing to learn from the locals rather than knowing everything in advance. I think as workers we tend to not really listen to what the locals are telling us because often we 'know' that the facts are different (from all our books and courses). I think much more important than concern over not making mistakes is to be willing to enter a relationship with the people you want to work with, and that, you can only learn by doing."

Before going overseas, you do not fully understand what your ministry will be like or what the people and culture are like. Workers who attend Bible college or seminary prior to going overseas choose their assignments and courses based on second or third hand information. Doing an internship before getting formal training allows you to discover what you do and do not need to know when you return overseas. Investing time in the culture prior to attending seminary enables you to choose courses of study based on your personal experience. You can focus your assignments and research projects on topics which will be meaningful and helpful later.

WORK—BUSINESS TRAINING

Tentmakers need to have a viable skill, trade, or service they can use to gain employment in their adopted country. Whether those skills are learned in the classroom or marketplace does not seem to impact a worker's effectiveness. Over 89 percent of the tentmakers worked for one year or more before going overseas, with 11 percent of these workers having operated their own businesses. Both experiences showed neither a positive or negative impact on the workers fruitfulness in ministry. Effective workers have real jobs. However, many work twenty hours or less per week. Precisely 20 percent of all tentmakers said, "I have received an official commendation or award for my work performance." This same 20 percent were also highly effective in evangelism, proving that quality in the marketplace bears good fruit in the ministry. As Jesus put it, "every good tree bears good fruit" (Matthew 7:17).

Tentmakers who "choose to go into tentmaking because they enjoyed their job back home and wanted to use it to glorify God overseas" proved to be less effective. "Tentmakers who wanted to use their secular education and training for God" are similarly ineffective. The research reveals this to have become a theme among tentmakers. Workers who desire to use their chosen occupation or education and training to glorify God overseas are not effective. That makes perfect sense, for we are taught, "You shall have no other gods before me" (Exodus 20:3). Whenever we put anything ahead of God—job, family, hobbies, sports, skills, or personal comforts—we can expect to receive less than His best. Whenever we predetermine how to serve Him, we are not allowing Him to be in control.

SPECIALIZED TENTMAKER TRAINING

Workers each have their own unique skills, giftings, and callings. Where one tentmaker may be led to work with poor Hindus via a medical NGO, another is seeking to reach middle class Arabs via a small business. Thus, standardized tentmaker training schemes may not be the best method for preparing workers. Biblical principles must be taught and general missiological skills encouraged (as in "Ted's To Do" list), but training objectives should be determined by understanding each individual's qualities, background, and skills required for effective work in their area of service. Each trainee brings a varied background of life and ministry, education, and work experience. Training structures and relationships should be consistent with the long range goals of the tentmakers involved.

We need to question whether there is any biblical basis for the cookie-cutter approach nearly all institutions utilize in preparing students for Christian ministry. Too many formal training institutions have their own agenda and expect the trainee to fit their program. Such trainers normally view the quality of their curriculum and teaching as their final goal, whereas I believe the effectiveness of the trainee should be the ultimate objective. Relationships, not programs, were the focus of Jesus' discipleship and teaching. As His students, we should seek to emulate our teacher (Luke 6:40). Success should not be measured in grades received or on-site performance reviews. Rather, success of the program and its trainers will be judged years later in the fruit borne by those who were trained (Matthew 7:15–20).

Training should be done in the context of community. The ultimate objective of any evangelistic, discipleship, or church planting ministry is to build a Christian community. Good tentmaking moves beyond church planting to transforming the community. Workers who learn in community discover what community life requires and have the added experience of grasping the strengths and weaknesses to be found living and working as a team. Trainees must learn to forgive one another, repent, and reconcile when sins or mistakes are made. Training should include knowing how to teach, encourage, rebuke, correct, be accountable, and train others one-on-one and in small groups. Character qualities and values are most effectively communicated only when teaching includes modeling and reflection. Having community input will increase both the stresses and learning process.

Tentmaker training should teach the tentmaker entrepreneurial skills for initiating and leading a profitable business (NGO, school, import-export, etc.) and should equip him or her for fruitful ministry and continued spiritual growth. The strategies for training should be incorporated and built upon the learner's experience. All this will likely require different strategies for different learners. Knowledge learning should include discussion and debate. Skills learning should include instruction, demonstration, and guided practice. All theory should be verified as in accord with Scripture.

Workers who "set goals and are held accountable to goals" prove to be more effective, yet nearly half the workers surveyed felt there was not enough accountability in their life. Workers who "enjoy starting new projects and taking risks" are generally effective. Trainers need to ensure their programs teach goal setting and encourage risk taking. Leadership, team work, and community life should be taught, encouraged, and modeled.

Workers who "recruit other people to join them" also are more effective. Organizations need to encourage and train field workers to take an active role in the recruiting of new workers. Clearly some workers will be involved in recruiting much more than others. Nonetheless, every worker should assist in recruiting new workers and not just delegate recruiting to the home office personnel. Take note, however, that workers who declared "they enjoyed one-on-one contacts with people" were found to be slightly less effective. Friendship evangelism is all the rage, yet it does not seem to be so effective in the 10/40 Window. Again, trainers need to revisit the tools and skills they are giving new candidates. In addition to friendship evangelism, a variety of models including a bold confrontational evangelism should be taught.

RETIREES

Retirees are a greatly underutilized source of labor. They are experienced in the world, proficient at their profession, wise in relational skills, and mature in the Lord. Retirees can contribute in many beneficial ways. Many couples are even taking early retirement to serve the Lord. These self-supporting workers are a most welcome addition to our labor pool. Retirees have both work experience and spiritual maturity to share. Though retirees rarely learn the language and have a limited impact in the areas of evangelism and church planting, they can make significant contributions to either a business or NGO and team life.

Retirees should be encouraged to come as specialists and function in areas utilizing their specialty. Their advanced skills enable them to serve as on-site mentors for struggling entrepreneurs. I have known retirees who have mended holes in the accounting or marketing efforts of small businesses, served as handy men fixing whatever needs to be fixed, spiritually mapped a country, and operated guest houses for the team's visitors. Their spiritual maturity and openness to new ideas often results in their becoming a sounding board for struggling team members and team leaders alike. Retirees sometimes operate a hospitality home; relieving team members of hosting guests and taking them on tours. The children on the team love having grandparents around. Though many retirees can only serve for two years at a time, their experience, input, and service outweighs their limited time.

THE TENTMAKER'S BELONGINGS

When considering what to bring overseas, less is best. As I tell our workers, "If in doubt, leave it at home." Though we seek not worldly treasures, there are two items which cause workers special concern— their home and their car.

Tentmakers often own homes. It is an agonizing decision trying to determine what to do with the house. In most cases, there are only two options, rent or sell. Opinions and situations differ, but here are a few thoughts to consider. Renting the family home provides a base and a point of reference for the family while you are overseas. Some children need a physical home which serves as a security for them, a place they can always go back to. Even though you may not live in the home (as it is rented out) during short visits home, the children may visit the house and remember that it is "our house." In many cases, it is easier to rent your home than to sell it. Though friends may offer to help, experience has shown that renting through a realtor is more prudent. If the renter/manager is a friend and is transferred, or for some other reason is unable to manage the home for you, it may necessitate an emergency trip back. On the other hand, a realtor will handle repairs, collect the rent, and ensure that the premises are well kept. As professionals, they will also see the paper work is done right. And if the home becomes vacant, the realtor has both the contacts and the motivation of a commission for renting it out. The commission is usually manageable and worth it. Keeping your home provides a peace of mind, knowing you have a place to return to should you need it. One of our team members had to return home unexpectedly. He had to pay a fee to break his renter's contract, but the whole family was glad they had their home to walk into when they returned. With the stresses in their life at that time, I doubt they could have managed living with others while hunting for a different place to live.

Some workers choose to sell their home as a symbol of burning their bridges behind them. This is valid and not to be marginalized. It makes a clear statement to both friends and children that they are not coming back any time soon. Other workers sell, since they need the money from their home to start their new business or help pay for other debts. Again, these are valid reasons for selling the house. Prayerfully consider how God is leading your family. Evaluate your home's location, condition, and value in the light of God's leading.

An old car, like an old shoe, is comfortable and well worn but not worth much. If your car is paid for and you plan on returning home regularly, it might be worthwhile to keep it. If your car is new and worth something, or not paid for, it is probably better to sell it. When we return to the States for short visits, we have found that four out of five times, friends and even strangers in our churches are willing to loan us a car.

PLACEMENT

In finalizing the place of service, there are a few things new workers need to understand about the mission enterprise. Business management as a university degree began to come into its own in the 1950s. Since then, mission leaders have attempted to match new workers with positions that best fit their education, experience, and ministry calling. However, there is wisdom in matching both the skills and the personality of a new worker with a compatible supervisor and team. This is in contrast to the standard placement of workers that emphasizes their skills and training. Each worker's entire mix of spiritual gifts, training, work experiences, calling, and theological background needs to be considered when being placed in a new assignment. In addition, the background and giftings of the person who will supervise the worker should be considered. We need to review the practice of assigning people to jobs based upon available openings or the needs of the mission. Workers should be matched with leaders and co-workers who will bring out the best in them. We can pressure people to accept an assignment by appealing to their sense of team unity, commitment to the mission, field needs, etc. Yet giving an assignment based on any one of these reasons that is unsuited to the worker ultimately leads to a lack of motivation and productivity, and more importantly, likely leads to the failure of the worker.

Most mission leaders would say they strive to place workers in ministries which are a good fit for both the worker and those they are ministering to. To that end, home offices interview, test, and scrutinize workers before they are accepted into the mission. Yet once overseas, the truth is that if the leader knows of a need in location X and worker Joe is available, God's will must be for worker Joe to serve in X. This is where it is wise to build a relationship with your field supervisor in advance before moving overseas. In addition to familiarizing yourself with the leader, the team, and the work there, this relationship will provide better access to the decisions being made around you and the impact those decisions may have on you.

Jim Collins and a team of twenty researchers studied hundreds of businesses to learn the difference between good and great companies.

> "The executives who ignited the transformations from good to great did not first figure out where to drive the bus [their company or ministry] and then get people to take it there [make things happen]. No, they first got the right people on the bus (and the wrong people off the bus) and then figured out where to drive it. The good to great leaders understood . . . First, if you begin with 'who', rather than 'what,' you can more easily adapt to a changing world. If people join the bus primarily because of where it is going, what happens if you get ten miles down the road and you need to change direction? You've got a problem. But if people are on the bus because of who else is on the bus, then it's much easier to change direction . . . Second, if you have the right people on the bus, the problem of how to motivate and manage people largely goes away. The right people don't need to be tightly managed or fired up; they will be self-motivated by the inner drive to produce the best results and to be part of creating something great."[41]

Organizations that prioritize the placement of their workers according to only their calling, education, skills, and gifting are making a mistake. The Bible is about relationships. The younger generation is also all about relationships. If we understand that people are called to work with other people, then we need to apply that knowledge by matching workers with the right supervisors. Who people work with and work under is actually more important to their productivity and well-being than matching their gifting or skills. We may combine the right talents, gifts, and skills, and still not produce a winning team. Workers need to feel comfortable and safe with the supervisor they serve under. Increasingly, churches and para-church organizations have piled on more and more managerial or collateral layers in the process of reorganizing their organizations. Yet in creating new positions, mission leaders should be asking, "What is truly needed?" Too often the only question we are answering is, "What is wanted?" Jesus promises to meet our needs, not our wants. If we are prioritizing outside of His will, is it any wonder He is withholding His blessing? It is becoming more and more common to create positions for people who are returning home. Rather than encouraging and releasing these workers to pursue God's will in other areas, organizations are creating positions to keep their experience "in house." Moreover, young field workers then pattern their career after the older workers. The ultimate objective becomes climbing the ladder of the organization and not pioneering church planting. Would it not be wiser and a better investment of resources to study the issues to determine why people are leaving the field in the first place, and then solve those problems? We need to critically evaluate if the positions these moves create are a real asset or liability in the race to finish the task.

We need to also review the placement of our workers from the field supervisory standpoint. I have seen a variety of excellent workers return home because of leaders who did not know how to lead them. I confess that I am guilty of this very problem, contributing to the return of a few workers due to my own errors. I have failed in understanding the needs of other team members who come from different backgrounds or cultures. These mistakes have taught me to be more thorough in discussing peoples' expectations of me and the team. I have had to learn to be more selective and directive when inviting people onto our team. Each mistake is a lesson learned, but no mistake is an excuse for quitting. One young man went out to India for three years, full of ideas and zeal. When I saw him after his return, he said he was not going back. I asked him, "What happened to all your ideas and zeal?" He replied, "The mission sucked it out of me."

New workers need to be aware that mission organizations, not unlike churches and businesses, have their strengths and weaknesses, politics and pet programs. Placing an entrepreneur risk-taker under the supervision of a conservative plodder, or vice versa, can spell the end of the ministry for the worker. Unfortunately, we too often choose leadership based on age and location. True, several organizations are giving serious leadership to gifted young men, but there needs to be more discernment in the placement of field leaders who have leadership gifts.

More importantly, in this day of the internet and a world without boundaries, mission leaders are still being assigned according to geographic location. Supervisory positions, coaching, leadership, and accountability need to be based on relationships, not structures. Our structures need to be broken down and rebuilt to increase the effectiveness of our workers. It does not make sense for an experienced Bible educator to be supervising or mentoring a newly arrived tentmaking church-planter simply because the Bible educator lives in the same city and has been there for twenty years. For example, God provided our mission with a mature Asian couple. They were sent to an Arab speaking country, joining a team made up of North Americans. This couple was a "top draft choice." They are graduates of Moody Bible Institute. He is an ordained pastor who has both evangelistic and leadership gifts. Without much help, they had planted a new and thriving church before going overseas. They are highly respected in their church and their denomination. Yet upon arriving on the field, they encountered many problems. Their leader, though experienced, was not ordained. He did not have evangelistic gifts and he had never planted a church. He also had no understanding of Asian culture. After two years of frustration, this top draft choice couple was ready to quit. However, when they were placed under the direction of a leader based in Asia whose background and experience was more suitable, they began to thrive. Today their ministry in that Arab country is making good inroads.

Though the cost in both time and money to have supervisors travel nearly half way across the world to make field visits may seem inefficient, it is more cost effective than recruiting and training a new worker and having them quit after three years. Nowadays, monthly reports and frequent chats may take place over the internet to encourage workers and keep them moving forward. Annual or bi-annual field visits, in addition to interaction with other workers in the area, ensure their reports are accurate.

SUMMARY

Before going overseas, workers need to evaluate the preparation they need. Workers who have no full-time Christian work experience before going overseas increase the probability of being ineffective. An adequately equipped tentmaker should have some missiological training, at least half a year of full-time ministry experience, and one year of secular work experience before moving overseas.

ACTION STEPS

- Discuss the concept of training with several business leaders in your church and with your church's pastoral staff. Evaluate your need for experience working in a business, a church, or both.

- Do you feel a need to attend a Bible college or seminary? Why?

- Discuss with three people who know you well what further training they believe you need before going overseas. Review "Ted's To Do List" with them.

- What points on Ted's list do you still need to complete?

- Contact two tentmakers for a list of books they would recommend you read.

- Prayerfully consider going on a short-term mission trip or internship. Write to three tentmakers or organizations about serving with them. See what you can learn by working with them. Utilize the questions in Appendix A, once you have contacted them.

- Consider investing one year working in a business and an additional year working in a church.

"Success is the ability to go from failure to failure without losing your enthusiasm."

WINSTON CHURCHILL

"What I would like these young men to know before they embark for Nigeria is that it is God who is taking them to Nigeria, not they who are taking God."

REPLY OF A NIGERIAN PASTOR, WHEN ASKED WHAT NEW
MISSIONARIES NEED TO LEARN

Therefore, I urge you, brothers, in view of God's mercy, to offer your bodies as living sacrifices, holy and pleasing to God—this is your spiritual act of worship. Do not conform any longer to the pattern of this world, but be transformed by the renewing of your mind. Then you will be able to test and approve what God's will is—his good, pleasing and perfect will.

ROMANS 12:1–2

chapter 7
THE TENTMAKER'S TRANSFORMATION

We are created for God's glory (Isaiah 43:7). Therefore, missions, tentmaking, as well as all of life, are about God and His glory. It is easy for us to forget that God has chosen us and adopted us for His good pleasure (Ephesians 1:4–5). Though the Creator truly wishes to see all of His creation redeemed, many of us have been sent overseas so that He might take us deeper in our walk with Him. His work "in" us is more important than His work "through" us. The process of learning a new way of communicating and adapting to new ways of living and working are a part of His transforming process for us. Each new experience stretches us, moving us further from our personal comfort zones and closer to His loving arms.

Tentmakers are faced with an amazing complexity. Our call to evangelism and church planting pulls us in one direction, while our job pulls us in another. Our teams, wives, and kids tug on us from still more directions. How do we make it all work? God in the heavens is truly overseeing all the balls we try to juggle. He who leads us to use our work for His witness is not overwhelmed by the obstacles we face. He uses these stresses to test our worldly nature that He may perfect us into His image. But He does expect us to do our homework (1 Peter 1:13).

I have read the biographies of successful businessmen such as Lee Iacocca (General Motors), Bill Rosenberg (Dunkin' Donuts), and Jack Welch (General Electric). Their primary motivation for work seems to be either the challenge of building up the business or making money. As tentmakers, though we may enjoy the challenge and the money, neither is central to our motivation. Our sole desire is to release God's glory among those who do not know Jesus. Gary Taylor, a tentmaking consultant wrote to me, "In my sterile search for success, I have sometimes chosen to be effective rather than committed. I have chosen to be successful rather than merely being faithful. Sometimes my calendar is full, but my heart is empty. I have learned God doesn't ask me to be brilliant; He simply tells me to be a blessing and a witness. To be a blessing requires the empowering work of the Holy Spirit. And I am to witness His working both in and through me. My life must be lived so that it cannot be explained apart from Jesus. He wants to borrow our humanity to communicate His truths to the world."

A tentmaker's life and work is simply allowing Jesus to live His purposes in and through us. We must constantly remind ourselves that Jesus' priority is transforming us into His image. If He cannot transform us, He cannot transform others through us. There are many hard experiences God will allow us to go through overseas. These tough times are not meant to harm us, but to transform us into His likeness that we might yield fruit for Him in both ministry and business.

BECOMING ONE WITH THE PEOPLE

There is no such thing as the perfect tentmaking strategy. I have seen coffee shops, computer businesses, import-export firms, language schools, and NGOs both succeed and fail. The key is not the business or the location, but the people running it. You need to be thoroughly prepared to take on any assignment the Master gives you, whether that is a pulpit in Paris, an NGO in New Deli, or a computer business in Beijing. As you prepare, the following are areas of concern to keep in mind, study, and get counsel on. You should think through each of these areas as you develop strategies for your life and work among the people Jesus leads you to. These are also areas current workers should review to ensure we are continuously upgrading for the work He has given us:

1. The language in which you minister
2. The culture which will be the context of your ministry
3. Your personal bonding with your team and the local people

LANGUAGE

"You have to murder a language before you can use it properly."

A LANGUAGE TEACHER

Language is more than just a string of letters put together. Language is the channel by which people created in the image of God express their hearts and minds. Every culture and sub-culture does it differently. As we have already learned, nothing is more critical for enhancing our long-term viability and effectiveness in ministry than our fluency in the language. Language fluency and cultural sensitivity are keys to becoming an insider with our adopted people.

Language learning is not only important for sharing our faith, it is a big part of God's work in transforming us into His image. As long as we reside in our own country among our own people, even if we give away all we have, we are never totally dependent upon God until we have also lost our ability to communicate. Jesus said, "I tell you the truth, unless you change and become like little children, you will never enter the kingdom of heaven."[42] Learning a new language forces us into the role of becoming a child again. It is humiliating and at times, even depressing. Yet learning a language is part of God's transforming process for us in that it drives us to be dependent on Him for our very thoughts, keeping us in prayer and forcing us to be humble in ways which are unnatural to us. We need to view language learning both as an assignment from God for our transformation into His image, as well as a step toward sharing His glory with the people.

Nothing we do to prepare ourselves for His service overseas is as important as learning the language well. Many tentmakers have short changed themselves on language learning and as a result, they have handicapped both their business and their ministry. A worker in the Middle East writes, "I spent eighteen months in Arabic language school before starting my business activities. Having this behind me really helped to be more effective as a business manager and as a communicator of the message." Jake, also in the Middle East, adds, "The best advice I received was from a godly professor in the engineering department of my (secular) university; he said, 'Do not let professional preparation stand in your way.' His advice was to concentrate on being able to communicate in the language of the local people. I took two years out of my career to attend language school and that was the most important preparation I did. When it came time to find a job in my chosen country in my chosen field, the two most important skills that landed me the job were my language and the skills I learned at my previous technical position. They were not the sorts of things that I would necessarily have studied about or learned by taking some course."

Once you know where and with whom the Lord wishes you to serve, invest time in mastering the language. Depending on the difficulty of the language and your ability to master it, this could take up to two years of full-time language study. Enroll in a local university and study the language and culture. People are more gracious with a student, even older students. A student may make many mistakes that would be offensive if said or done by a teacher or business person. A student can also live more cheaply without raising suspicions. All of our expatriate employees have it written into their initial contract that they cannot begin work until they have completed at least one year of language study. As I want our employees to be able to do business in the local language (as well as share the gospel), this makes perfect sense to officials who question them on why they are studying and not working.

Well spoken language promotes rapport with the people and brings insight into the culture. As our language improves, so do our communication skills. One national friend put it this way, "English speaks to our heads, but our own language speaks to our hearts." And ultimately, the gospel must reach the people's hearts, so learning their heart language is not optional. Some people groups may speak more than one language. Those who speak the heart language of the people are more effective in evangelism. However, in some cases, business will be done in the trade language, requiring us to become proficient in both. This could require up to four years of study. Our Asian brothers in French-speaking Africa first learn English (to communicate with the English-speaking Christian world), then French (the national language), and then the dialect of the people group they are targeting. We each need to count the cost and ask ourselves if we are willing to pay it (Luke 14:28). Language learning is part of that cost.

Sometimes it is impossible to enter a country without taking a full-time job. In such cases, block out several periods during the week when you can study the language with a tutor. Many executives of multi-national corporations have tutors come to their office. Often night classes are available. Another option is to take one year and go to a nearby country where you can focus solely on language learning and then move into your adopted country and start working.

There is a strong relationship between the language level workers achieve and our use of the language in our work place. Workers who use the host language in the work place have an advantage in obtaining fluency. We need to encourage our staff and co-workers to speak to us in the local language, even if they can speak English.

There are many methods for learning a language. The most common strategies are formal schooling or personal study. If possible, I would recommend attending a formal course in the beginning, to learn the proper tones, spelling, grammar, and pronunciation of letters. Personally, I find the structure and accountability of a classroom helpful. But if you find the school's teaching inadequate or stifling, once you have an understanding of the basics, hire a tutor or language helpers. Tutors are usually local teachers who will give private lessons for a fee. As teachers, they should come prepared with lessons and assignments. You may find tutors by approaching a local university or school and asking if there is anyone who might wish to make some extra money tutoring you. Language helpers are untrained acquaintances with whom you meet just to talk. Finding a local who is diligent in correcting you in the fine points of the language and culture is not easy. Some, out of respect or a desire not to embarrass you, may hesitate to correct you. Tam is one of my closest friends. As a new leader in the church, I met with him and his wife for discipleship for nearly two years. One day I was talking with an associate in Chinese when he corrected me on a common word. Tam was standing there but said nothing. Later I asked Tam, "Why didn't you ever correct me on that word?" He replied, "We all know what you mean."

You should instruct your language helpers how to correct your speech and grammar. Moreover, you should prepare the lessons to go over with them. It is wise to have several language helpers so as to hear different accents and word usage. Some language helpers will need to be paid; some will volunteer. Though some will exchange your teaching them English for their teaching you the local language, I would do that only in separate meetings. One tentmaker's story explains, "I have had five language lessons now with Mrs. H. Due to fact that her determination to learn English far outweighs my determination to learn the dialect, I have now become her English language helper!"

In many languages there are different word usages by male and female speakers, so it is wise to choose tutors or helpers who are of the same gender. The more you immerse yourself in the culture, the easier it will be to learn the language. If you can, live with a local family for a time. Also, tune in to local TV and radio and read local magazines, newspapers and novels. The more you use the language, the more you learn. Do not be afraid of making mistakes, as they prompt correction and are often our best teachers.

Before beginning to study, set standards for yourself so that you do not take shortcuts later. Do you want to conduct business in the language? Teach a Bible study? Read the newspaper? Set goals and then stick with a full-time language program until you have achieved them. Most men love business because it provides a sense of value and satisfaction, i.e. we love ourselves. If your desire to learn the language is waning, check your heart, not your head. Could it be a love issue? If we really love those He has called us to, we might be more committed to learn the language and culture. Workers should make it their goal to be able to freely share their testimony and teach the Scriptures, as well as watch television and read newspapers in the local language.

There is a need for coaching/supervision to keep your motivation high and on target. Language learning is 90 percent motivation and hard work and 10 percent intelligence. Each team or worker should have an accountability person or language supervisor who monitors progress regularly. The language supervisor should hold the team member accountable for study time and progress in fluency. During the language learning year, you want to avoid spending too much time with other English speakers. Keeping a log of the hours spent in the community is one way of holding yourself accountable. Unless there is a separate room for seclusion or you do not have kids running around, the home is not an ideal place to study. There may be a public place, library, or restaurant where you can study; sometimes it is worth renting a small office. Going to an office each day also gives the neighbors the impression you are working.

A report from the Overseas Missionary Fellowship observes that westerners take an academic approach to language learning, while Asians absorb languages more naturally. There is a growing movement to de-school language learning. After all, language learning is a people activity, not a book activity. It is important to get out and expose ourselves to a variety of people from different social backgrounds. This has to do with the status we have in society. We need to communicate as our local counterparts communicate. If we are perceived as a business person, we need to speak like one—not like a western business person, but like a local. Socializing with people also exposes us to unspoken words. Interacting with people provides an avenue to practice speaking and listening, as well as opportunities to evaluate how people ask favors from one another. It is an opportunity to see how people give, receive, borrow, question, confront, etc.

Expect to become frustrated with your language progress; everyone does. We all hit plateaus where nothing new seems to stick. At times like these it is important to remember that language learning is a spiritual job, the job of building loving relationships. It requires the fruits of the Spirit: patience, faithfulness, and self-control. We must keep God involved in our language learning. Pray and read His Word in the language. The truth is we should never be content with where we are in our language ability. Language and cultural learning is an on-going process that ends only when we leave the field.

Many workers, though not yet fluent in the language are tempted to move quickly into a ministry role or position in a church or work place. Fight this temptation. It is important to first learn the language well. Be patient and you will reap what you sow. Language learning is hard work, and if you are learning two languages, it is twice as hard. Crucify your desire to "have a ministry." Instead, work prayerfully and strategically to make disciples and plant churches that reproduce. It is better to hold off on starting your business and ministry until you know the language well. Build for tomorrow, not today. It is a common mistake to make some quick progress in ministry only to be hindered further down the road due to inadequate language skills. If we do not disciple new believers in their heart language, they will not be able to reproduce their faith in their heart language. My wife was born and raised in China but became a believer while in university in the United States. She was evangelized and discipled in English and served in an American church using English. The first time we were back in China, after she had been a believer nearly five years, she was asked to pray at the end of a fellowship meeting. She stood up and froze. She could not do it. Though she had talked with people in Chinese, she did not know the Chinese Christian terminology. She did not know how to pray in her native language! We need to be patient and fully invest in language study. Perhaps the parable of the sower is about language learning (Matthew 13:3–8). The seed is the "word," and if our words are weak or lacking fluency, it will clearly affect the harvest. If we wish to reap a hundredfold crop for Jesus, we need to be fluent in the language.

Wives and mothers need special attention when it comes to language learning. An extra effort needs to be made to ensure that mothers have time to learn the language. Women are needed to reach the local women. Nannies may be hired or recruited for the first year or two to enable mothers to study the language full time. Some mothers even go to pre-school with their children in order to learn the language. They serve as volunteers. This helps the children become comfortable in interacting with the local children, while the mother is able to learn some language and make friends with the staff and other mothers.

Learning Two Languages

Where you need to learn both the trade language and heart language, research shows that the heart language is more important for evangelism and discipleship, and the trade language is more important for doing business. In reality, you should learn both, but the heart language is the primary objective and should be learned first. By learning the heart language first, the tentmaker is more likely to develop a dependence on the locals he desires to serve. This promotes relationships and interdependence. Also, learning the heart language may assist the worker in developing a student mentality, giving respect for the local culture and leading to a deeper sense of humility.

One advantage of learning the trade language first is that it may be easier and more helpful with government officials. However, language learning is hard work, and once a person has learned one language, he is sometimes burnt out. As a result, the tentmaker stays within the comfort zone that language provides, only learning the heart language marginally. Also, it is not unusual for a worker learning the trade language to adopt the biases of that language and its people against the people being reached. Learning the heart language first limits this biased input.

Whichever language you are learning, live in a neighborhood where that language dominates and plan to move when you begin studying the second language. When learning the second language, you will have to force yourself into situations where you must speak the new language. Friends who know you speak the other language, though they may know both languages, will find it hard to change over and speak the new language with you. This means you may need to find a whole new set of friends.

Becky writes, "After having lived in the Middle East for a number of years, I had become quite comfortable using Arabic in my job, daily affairs, and in hanging out with my friends. Then I went to have laser eye surgery. I happily went through all my preliminary checkups, the computer discussion, etcetera, talking with the young doctor in Arabic the whole time. Before entering the surgery, I also talked with everyone in Arabic. However, as they were putting me in scrubs and the surgeon was asking if I had any concerns, that's when my ability to use Arabic slipped away. Suddenly, the conversation became very personal and close to my heart and I found I could only communicate using my own language. This works similarly for most people. Sure, you can talk in a 'second' language about the weather and what happened yesterday. You may discuss your job or the business news. But when it comes to talking about matters of the heart—needs, hurts, feelings, trouble—that's when you want to, even have to, talk in your 'mother tongue.'"

Not using their heart language, not using it well enough, or using your own language more than theirs in your relationship might be the reason that a wall exists between your two hearts. Think about how difficult it is to pray spontaneously in a language other than your mother tongue. We need to make the sacrifice to cross over into their world of thinking and communicating so that we may present the claims of Christ in understandable terms.

I overheard Chiu of China, who serves in French-speaking Africa, say, "After learning English in Hong Kong, three years of Bible school in the States, and a year of French studies in France, I was all but burnt out on studying. Fortunately, my mentor kept on me to learn the local dialect. It took three years, but I am now the only foreigner who speaks the dialect well, and the good news is being spread. You cannot over emphasize the importance of learning the languages well."

Language and the Marketplace

How important is language in business? The history of exporting is littered with equally gauche linguistic and cultural blunders. When Chevrolet launched the "Nova" automobile model in Latin America, sales were terrible. Who wanted to buy a car whose name was "no va," which in Spanish means "no go?" And what could be more absurd than a washing powder that makes clothes dirtier, not cleaner? This was the message conveyed to Arab customers by one soap manufacturer's billboard when they forgot that Arabs read right to left.

Business people without language skills often do not realize how disadvantaged they are.

One western worker tells the story, "I was in Singapore and needed to buy some office furniture. The sales women were speaking in Cantonese, which I know. As they followed me around the store, they continued chatting in Cantonese about how much items really cost and how much they could squeeze out of this rich westerner for each item. I continued to speak in English. After I had decided which items I wanted, I waited for their price offers. I then began speaking in Cantonese. The women were so shocked and embarrassed, they wound up selling me everything I wanted at cost."

Another tentmaker in Asia writes, "I foolishly jumped right into starting our business, so circumstances did not permit us time to master the language." Learn from those who have gone before: learn the language first, and learn it well. When skillfully used, words make friends and open opportunities for sharing the gospel and building the business. Skilled sales people listen for the most effective words and word patterns and use them according to customers' responses. Listen closely to the words and phrases customers and prospects use when they talk about merchandise. The ideas these people express are their favorites. Therefore, these words have business and ministry value.

Though it is helpful to guess at the meaning of words in a social context, never guess in business or essential dealings. If you are unsure of your words, do not use them when doing serious business. When you come across words that sound like they would be effective in convincing the customer, check the dictionary to be certain of their meaning. Practice every new word before using it. Be sure that your pronunciation is correct. Steer clear of adapting one set of words and phrases for all descriptive efforts. The universal selling sentence has yet to be discovered. The customer who hears words such as "stylish," "gorgeous," and "glamorous" repeated over and over soon refuses to give them any value. If you are not fluent enough in the language, do not guess; use a translator to ensure clarity and honesty in all your business dealings.

Even the smallest of firms can make great achievements if they understand the language.

"With a staff of only eleven, Lincolnshire-based fresh produce distributor A&C Exports, Ltd. had been trying to break into the Italian market, but success eluded them until two years ago when they appointed linguist Karen Burdett to the account. Within a year she had sold 1,500 tons of potatoes to this nation of pasta lovers which today represents 20 per cent of their export business. 'Italian wasn't even one of her languages,' says joint director Lance Cornell. 'But she was determined to succeed, and after only four weeks of intensive study she picked up the phone. The effect was immediate. Although she told people she was still learning and might make mistakes, the fact that she was making the effort impressed them enormously.'"[43]

In a globalized world, culture plays a role that is as large as life. Learning a language takes time; learning a culture takes even longer. A wise tentmaker never ignores the cultural dimension of a society. For example, the Japanese avoid direct confrontation, preferring an exchange of information. Russians love combat; their very word for compromise is borrowed from another language. The Dutch favor consensus decisions, whereas Singaporeans leave decisions to the leader. Nigerians prefer the spoken word, Americans the written one. The Germans value efficiency and punctuality, the Spanish: relationships. Asian languages are high in context and tonal inflections. Latin American cultures are physically demonstrative. Even body language can be significant. Blowing your nose at a business meeting in Japan is the height of bad manners, as is crossing your legs so as to point the bottom of your foot at someone in an Arab setting. For effective communication, we need to understand these differences. Learning to wait, listen, and wait some more is important but hard for the task-orientated westerner. We need to apply Stephen Covey's words, "Seek first to understand, then to be understood."[44] Remember, the person may not be speaking in his first or even second language. When using English, speak slowly; use short words and learn to enunciate to ensure you are connecting, lest you talk past each other. Learning the language is more than words. We must study the etiquettes, ethics, and attitudes of the people as well. It is all part of entering into the world of the people and understanding how they process and express ideas.

Using a Translator

Though using a translator is not the best option for business or ministry, sometimes it is unavoidable. In those times, sensitivity is critical. You must express yourself simply and clearly, avoiding slang and jokes which only make sense to English speakers. Speak slowly. Speak using short and simple words. Subtle nuances, special terms, and catchy phrases are not going to translate. Use short sentences so that the translator can adjust to different grammatical structures. "Peter is kind and generous" will invariably be translated as, "Peter is good!" When translation is done on the spur of the moment, it is better to simplify. To ensure the people are hearing what you are saying, do the simplifying yourself.

There are many language tools to assist in language learning. Local bookstores may have dictionaries and children's books which are also helpful. Most mission agencies have materials to help with language acquisition.

CONTEXTUALIZATION

Contextualization without evangelism will not plant churches; bold evangelism without contextualization will plant "uncontextual" churches that might not last or reproduce.[45] Tentmakers must appreciate the uniqueness of other cultures and take pains to learn the ways of the people they are serving. Learning the local language is a part of this step, but in addition to language there are cultural innuendoes. Ignorance of these might show disrespect. Such areas include respecting the elderly and women, the appropriateness of handling or playing with children, proper greetings, what to wear, and so forth.

Contextualization is conveying the gospel message clearly into a new cultural context by becoming one with the people. Paul models this for us when he writes, "Though I am free and belong to no man, I make myself a slave to everyone, to win as many as possible. To the Jews I became like a Jew, to win the Jews. To those under the law I became like one under the law (though I myself am not under the law), so as to win those under the law. To those not having the law I became like one not having the law (though I am not free from God's law but am under Christ's law), so as to win those not having the law. To the weak I became weak, to win the weak. I have become all things to all men so that by all possible means I might save some."[46]

In a nutshell, contextualization is asking, "How far will I go in practicing 1 Corinthians 9?" Paul became a Greek to Greeks, a slave to slaves, weak to the weak, and all things to all people because he hoped to "save some." Paul's objective was not merely to instruct and to improve people; his heart's desire was for them to be saved. Anything short of this would have disappointed him. Paul desired for each person to be renewed in heart, forgiven, and sanctified. Our Christian labors should seek to attain no less. As one worker writes, "Whenever I have a question concerning culture, I always start with two questions: 'What does the Bible say?' and 'What did Jesus do?'"

The incarnation of Jesus is the supreme example of contextualization, and as His followers, we are to follow His example. Wherever we are, our lives in Christ should be contextualized by the very fact that our citizenship is not of this world. Thus, as one dear friend who manages an NGO in Africa puts it,

"Contextualization is about the incarnation and the cross. To me the Incarnation means that my lifestyle, and that of Muslim believers, should be deeply embedded in the local society and should look like the local lifestyle, with myself being tried and tested in every way as they are, yet without sin. And the cross means that I should be willing to give up many of the rights and freedoms that I have in the gospel (such as the right to a higher economic standard of living or the right to put my arm around my wife in the street or the right to eat in Ramadan), for the sake of the salvation of the local people. I should be willing to suffer as a servant among Muslims and to die for them. When I tell Muslims that God loved us enough to leave his glorious home to become one of us—taking our nature into his own identity—indeed to live as a humble oppressed servant among us, to give up his rights and to lay down his life for our salvation—when I tell Muslims these things, they must be able to SEE these realities in my own way of life (see Gal 3:1 and 6:17; cf. Acts 14:19–21; or see Acts 20:18, 24 or 1

Cor 1:18–19 and 2:1ff). If they cannot see the Incarnation and the Cross in my lifestyle, then my verbal proclamation is incomplete and incoherent. The missionary's life must visually *portray* what our words *describe*."

Tentmakers must understand that biblical absolutes will take on different forms from one culture to another. For example, the Bible says, "Do not steal" (Exodus 20:13). I think we would all agree that this is an absolute principle that applies in every culture. If a child leaves her toy on the street in front of her suburban house, can another child who happens by take it? Or is that stealing? An American would say, "Yes, it is stealing," but an Indian would say, "No." In ancient Israel, one could pick and eat fruit while passing through another man's orchard, but would that be legal today in southern France? Many Asians see the American practice of leaving the care of the elderly to a hospice or retirement home as a clear violation of the fifth commandment, "Honor your father and your mother." Clearly the application of moral principles as given in Scripture is influenced by a person's culture. As a result, tentmakers need to move beyond being bi-cultural to becoming tri-cultural. A tri-cultural person understands truth from three perspectives. We need to understand the truth as given in the Bible. But we also need to grasp how our own culture filters biblical truth, so we can discern what is of God and what is of our background. And finally, we need to know how the local culture cloaks truth, so we can reveal biblical truth in an understandable way to the people we are serving. In learning the culture, we learn to comprehend the values, meaning, and standards by which people are evaluating everything we do and say.

In general, people do not like change. People are much more hesitant to follow Jesus if they must cross racial, linguistic, or class barriers. Culture is very personal and is not to be taken lightly. Contextualization begins by showing an understanding of the differences between our own culture's values (which we should know well) and biblical values. When we can do this, we can more readily sort out what is of God and what is of man. By becoming aware of our own cultural frame of reference, we better understand why we react toward another culture in the way we do. In our witnessing and discipleship, we must continually be aware that the meanings of actions, values, or objects in our home culture may not have the same interpretation in our adopted culture. We must take time to listen and learn so that we understand how our message is being perceived and so that we do not deliver the wrong meaning. We should regularly question our friends, "What does this mean to you?" The applications of our teachings (the fruits) will show how well we are doing. And this re-emphasizes the need to become fluent in the language, for without good language skills, it is difficult to understand the culture and it is impossible to become tri-cultural.

For several years, my teammate and I would travel twice a month to a poor rural village without utilities. For one to three days, we would teach a small gathering of MBBs. On one visit, I was teaching about spiritual warfare. Two Muslims were sitting outside listening, which was not uncommon. We encouraged them to listen to our teachings. However, upon my return to the village two weeks later, I was arrested and charged with being a Communist. It took nearly an hour for me to discern what the charges where based on, but finally I understood that these two gentlemen had heard me teaching the fellowship about spiritual "warfare." Up until then, though the district leaders were hospitable, they could never understand why I kept coming to that remote village. On several occasions, I had openly told them I was teaching the new believers about religion, yet they could not believe I would make the effort to travel to that rustic, dirty little village just to teach religion. But now they understood—I was actually training a Communist rebel army to overthrow the government! Not only did these two men misunderstand, the MBBs did not grasp my teaching either. After we left, the authorities asked them, "Is Patrick training you to fight?" The MBB leader replied, "We don't know, but if he wants us to fight, we will!" It took a couple of hours of explaining the Bible to the authorities and showing them the passages I taught last time before they accepted I was not a Communist. Obviously, I did a poor job of listening and learning to ensure my teachings were being understood. But this is also why there is no need to fear mistakes. Mistakes are often our best teachers. As a result of this incident, the authorities did get a chance to hear the gospel.

Different cultures view God differently. Our worldview affects our view of God. Cultures are designed to protect us from problems. The way each culture prioritizes problems is different. Research must be done so that we understand: "What is the good news for this people?" Time should be invested in determining which methods of delivering the gospel are most acceptable. Another significant component of contextualization is researching felt needs. We must speak and live in ways that communicate understandable truth and love. It is important to read everything we can find on our people group and then validate what is learned by asking questions of our local friends. In validating a point of view, a value, or an objective meaning, it is good to get three or more opinions so we gain a well-rounded perspective.

Greg Livingstone adds,

"Evangelism which is not sensitive to human dignity, to culture and is unnecessarily provocative is not biblical evangelism. The New Testament is full of injunctions to be the salt of the earth, the light of the world, a Jew to the Jew (a Muslim to the Muslim? a Kuwaiti to the Kuwaiti?). There is always room for upgrading our evangelism to make it increasingly effective."[47]

Contextualized evangelism and discipleship are critical tools for the survival of believers in the midst of persecution. In many unreached areas, there are few second-generation believing families because nearly all the first generation believers have been extracted. The less we know about the people's culture and language, the more we may endanger new believers. It is ironic that we pray, study, and work for years, hoping to see a church started among the people. Finally, someone comes to Christ, but our lack of contextualizing jeopardizes their existence in the community. As a result, to avoid a believer's martyrdom, we must often extract him from the community, sending him to a far away city. Thus, we have made no progress in our original objective of planting a church.

There are many avenues by which we may enter the culture. Study the people's music, songs, history, sports, literature, poetry, arts, crafts, and religion. Some of the deepest cultural realities may be gleaned from the people's arts. Participate in their celebrations and festivals. Consider what redemptive analogies may be found in these observances for the sharing of the gospel. Learn their stories and proverbs, children's stories and cultural stories. Many of the world's societies are oral societies. Develop biblical stories for sharing the good news. Well told stories may have a longer lasting impact than any argument over abstract truths.

Having said these things, we need to understand that though we may strive to be contextualized in our business practices, home life, and personal lifestyle, there are limits to what the nationals will accept. When my family was deported from one country, it was partly because the officials deemed we were "living in the wrong area." In our quest to live among the people, we were living in an area that was not acceptable for a foreign businessman.

There are also limits to the process of contextualization. In most places Paul ministered, he was persecuted by both Jews and Gentiles. Wherever he preached the good news, that news was found to be divisive. It is important to understand that wherever the gospel goes, it will almost invariably divide families and cultures (Matthew 10:34–36).

BONDING

Bonding is another aspect of contextualization. The term "bonding" comes from the birthing of a child and its drawing near to its mother during the first few hours of life. Some hospitals help the newborn bond with the mother by giving the child immediately after birth to suckle and be held in the mother's arms. Doctors believe this initial closeness increases the bond between mother and child. Similarly, it is believed (though never documented to my knowledge) that workers who move straight into the culture without associating with other westerners adapt more quickly to the local people, culture, and language. Insights and deeper relationships will come naturally with those we bond to. Two types of bonding strategies are pertinent for tentmakers: team bonding and people bonding.

Team Bonding

Team bonding involves living close to your co-workers during your initial cultural adjustment time. The intention is to build harmonious relationships with your teammates in order to develop trust and a close team. After medical reasons, the second biggest cause of missionary attrition is poor relationships with co-workers. Team bonding is intended to reduce potential areas of team conflict. The disadvantage of team bonding is that you will initially learn the culture through the eyes of your fellow westerners whose opinions may be slanted or even wrong. This may bias your own opinions and cause between you and the people in your mind.

People Bonding

People bonding, or cultural bonding, involve living close to the local people you will be ministering with during your initial cultural adjustment time. Immediately upon arrival in your new country, you move in with locals and avoid non-locals, even your own team members. This period of cultural bonding usually lasts for one to six months. The intention is to build bonds with the local people, allowing them to be your cultural teachers and helpers. This should cause you to look to the people for guidance and direction when in need of ideas or help. The advantage of this type of bonding is that it draws you into the culture quickly and reduces fears of the people and their different ways. The disadvantage of this type of bonding is it may not draw you into the team, perhaps causing you to feel alienated from those with whom you are ministering.

So, which is better? "Team bonding" or "people bonding?" Over the years, I have seen how people who bond to a team tend to work as a team. These people stay on the field longer. However, they do tend to have a more difficult time adjusting to the ways of their focus people than those who move right into the culture. The one who bonds with the people will win the people's trust, get quickly into the language and perhaps see converts sooner. I have also observed that workers who "people bond" tend to team up with the locals involved in their ministry. But often, usually between three to six years, those who "people bond" have a major falling out with another team member, causing them to go home. So, who had the better ministry? Both will say they did! Workers have a tough choice when they know neither their team nor the local people well. If you already have a love for the people and have a strong commitment to them, then "team bond." In the same way, if you know the team well, then "people bond."

SUMMARY

Before departing for the ends of the earth, you should settle in your mind and heart that you are not doing God a favor by going to reach the unreached; rather, He is doing you a favor by leading you away from your comfort zone and causing you to be more dependent upon Him. Language and cultural learning are essential for all tentmakers. Communication is central to our task. Time must be set aside the first year for in-depth language and cultural study. Workers who do not set aside time to learn the language and culture within their first twelve months overseas rarely find time for concentrated study later. There is little point in going ten thousand miles across the world if we do not go the final ten inches. Effective communication is hard work.

ACTION STEPS

- Which is more important to God, His transforming process within you or His using you to reach the unreached? Substantiate your view with Scripture.
- Explain why language learning is the highest ministry priority for the tentmaker and why it must be done the first year overseas.
- Which language learning strategy will you use?
- Explain contextualization and its importance to evangelism, discipleship and church planting.
- Which lifestyle strategy will you choose to adopt? Justify your decision.
- Is there a segment of society you will focus on?
- Explain the pros and cons of team bonding and people bonding.
- Who will hold you accountable to your decisions?

"We are not in the job of persuading people; we are in the job of watching God open blind eyes."

GEORGE VERWER

Therefore go and make disciples of all nations, baptizing them in the name of the Father and of the Son and of the Holy Spirit, and teaching them to obey everything I have

MATTHEW 28:19–20

chapter 8
EVANGELISM AND
CHURCH PLANTING

A quick survey of evangelical mission agency websites confirms that each organization is committed to the bringing the lost to salvation in Christ and gathering those believers into churches. The words, the strategies, the focus for each organization vary, but our calling is the same, "Go, make disciples of all nations" (Matthew 28:19). Faith has various applications, but the focus is always on Jesus. Faith finds a way. The house was full, the door was blocked, but faith got in. If the door is shut, try a window. If the window is locked, go through the roof. Tentmaking is about trying the untried. Not everyone will feel comfortable with our strategies, but not everyone should. As his friends lowered the paralyzed man through the roof, it is easy to believe more than a few shouted discouraging words and attempted to stop them. Sharing the gospel involves risk. As Paul clearly states, "I am not ashamed of the gospel, because it is the power of God for the salvation of everyone who believes: first for the Jew, then for the Gentile."[48]

WITNESSING

We are commanded to "Preach the Word; be prepared in season and out of season."[49] As ambassadors of Christ, we should always be ready to give an account for what we believe, even why we are residing overseas. Much of our work is sowing seeds, but we are not to go overseas only expecting to sow seed. Jesus tells us, "You may ask me for anything in my name, and I will do it."[50] It is essential to understand that evangelism, discipleship, and church planting are spiritual ministries and as such, they require spiritual workers who use spiritual tools. Evangelism is not about methodologies; rather it is about God-given faith lived out in our relationships, available for all to see.

Jesus says, "By this all men will know that you are my disciples, if you love one another."[51] Our primary assignment is to love people into the kingdom. Jesus demonstrated his own great love for us in that while we were still sinners, He died for us (Romans 5:8). As Christ died for our salvation, we as His followers are to likewise die to ourselves for the salvation of the people He has sent us to. To share love, we must understand how the people interpret love. This reemphasizes the need to learn the language and culture. Our job is to cultivate a spiritually attractive life, and in understandable ways incarnate the message of God's love. God's job is to convict and convert.

The unreached are unreached for a reason—they have been resistant to the gospel. We need to understand that whenever non-believers perceive that becoming a Christian is a racial rather than a religious decision, there will be little response. In Buddhist, Hindu and Muslim lands, the greatest barriers to conversion are social and racial, not theological. It takes many encounters with Jesus, before they will trust Him. These encounters take many shapes and forms, but we will be an intimate part of each encounter, and love will be our primary tool of delivery.

Love must be an integral part of our daily life. We love people, not because of who they are, but even in spite of who they are. And in loving others we remember that "He first loved us," (1 John 4:19). Jim writes, "I had one Hindu co-worker who had a lot of anger and hated me. Everyone feared him. My approaches to him were likewise rebuffed. It seemed he went out of his way to be obnoxious, crude, rude, and socially unacceptable. I prayed that I could cultivate a genuine friendship with him and demonstrate unconditional love. This was not easy as he knew I was a Christian and made every effort to magnify his belligerence around me. But we eventually got along. Then he unexpectedly went into the hospital for life-threatening surgery. During his recovery my wife and I visited him briefly. After my colleague returned to work, he stopped by my office. I assumed he wanted to argue about our worldview differences, but what he came for shocked me. He came to tell me I was the only one, except his wife, to visit him in the hospital. We are now having sincere discussions about the Lord and His love."

It is important that we make genuine friends. Jesus did not view the disciples as "projects," or the people as "contacts" to be converted. We need to "get real" in our relationships with people. We must share our struggles with our friends along with our blessings. Our non-believing friends need to know that we are real people walking the road of life with them. Ask people for help. Too often we think we can build a relationship by doing a favor for people. However, when we help someone else, they feel indebted to us. People who owe us a favor or money will tend to avoid us or placate us. We need to learn to ask others for help. If we get indebted to them then they do not mind us being around. Kurt in the Middle East suggests, "I might ask them to explain a parable from their perspective. For example, saying, "Mahmoud I need your insight into the meaning of this story by Jesus. Jesus spoke as a Middle Easterner like you and I need you to help me with this." Bob in Asia adds, "Asking favors of friends has been real door opener. People want to help, but often don't know if they should."

My friend Joe writes, "How do Muslim background believers (MBBs) say they were first drawn to Christ? . . . How do we present Christ most frequently? Are these the same?" In a survey of South Asian MBBs, Dr. Dudley Woodbury, professor of Islamics at Fuller Seminary, discovered the following:

- A heartfelt attraction is what first draws most MBBs to the Lord.
- By contrast, most workers try to communicate the good news by describing abstract truths. While understanding that God's truth is a key part of discipleship, western workers may neglect the importance of a Muslim's need to *experience* the truth (who is Jesus) rather than to *know* the truth about Him."

In sharing our faith, we need to contextualize the message. We also need to understand how information disseminates throughout the society and then use these same channels for spreading the gospel. In most societies information spreads via established relationships. In such cases, it is imperative for workers to build relationships in a variety of networks. Most relational networks originate from either the marketplace or extended families. The best evangelists to any people group are members of that group of people. Marketplace relationships come naturally to tentmakers. Being accepted into family networks will take some effort. Asking questions about family practices at holidays and by inviting them to celebrate our own holidays may cause them to reciprocate our invitation. As a team, we encourage celebrating all kinds of holidays including May Day, Thanksgiving, birthdays, anniversaries, various countries independence day, any reason to have a party.

It is easy for days, even weeks to go by without discussing our Lord with anyone. It is important to discipline evangelism into our lives and relationships. I am not advocating rushing evangelism and sharing Christ in every conversation. Our team for example, encourages building relationships before sharing the gospel. The first few times we meet new friends, we rarely share more than "we are followers of Jesus." However, if we have played tennis with Farouk eight weeks in a row, and shared coffee with him a few times, but have not yet discussed anything spiritual with him, it is time to reevaluate our life and ministry. The gospel must flow through us, in whatever we do. We should have little to hide. Social psychologists note that we share the most important things in our lives in the first 30 minutes of talking to someone new—our job, family . . . our faith? With deference to the appropriate cultural context we need to learn to practice boldness. In addition, we should invite team members or other believers to hold us accountable in witnessing.

How we define ourselves is a key question. As tentmakers, though we may teach or operate a business, and are teachers or business persons, that should be just one part of "who" we are. Jesus must be incorporated into who we are and what we do and say. Consider: do peripheral things define us? Is our identity wrapped up in our family, our job, our titles, or our wealth? Or do we define ourselves through our relationship to Jesus? We need to enable His Spirit within us to define ourselves. Our lives should speak the gospel day in and day out. Our testimony is not only what happened in the past when we converted; our testimony is also what is happening in our lives today. When asked, "How's your day?" "Have you eaten yet?" or "How are you?" We can incorporate an indirect witness in our answers. For example, "The Creator has given us a great day, hasn't He?" "God is good, He has provided, yes I've eaten, and you?" "I thank the Lord; I am feeling well, and you?" These are simple, yet effective ways of differentiating ourselves from others, showing He is always in our thoughts.

People are watching our lives. Abdul worked for Alex for over two years. Abdul's job was to be a driver to Alex's family and run various errands for his office. Alex never talked to Abdul about his faith. One day Alex was sitting in the yard reading, while Abdul was cleaning the front yard. Abdul paused and asked, "Sir, could you tell me about your God?" "Why?" asked Alex. Abdul continued, "I have seen your life, you are different, and I believe it is because of your faith. Could you tell me about it?" That very day, Alex introduced Abdul to his friend

Jesus. We would not say it was best for Alex to wait to share his faith, but this time a message and receptivity did result from his actions.

Many tentmakers work along side expatriates and foreigners more than with nationals. We need to find jobs or design businesses that enhance our opportunities to work with nationals. We should hire people based on qualifications, but never be hesitant to hire a qualified non-believer. The work place is a great environment for others to observe the Christ in us. In the office I tell our employees that we work to invest and not just to earn. They know that we give some of our profits to charitable organizations. Annually I invite the management to suggest which non-religious organizations we should make donations to, and then I let them make the arrangements for delivering the check. Our business motto is; "To Bring Blessing to the Community." God is not the only one who loves a cheerful giver.

Proclamation versus Presence Evangelism

Ministry requires both our words and our actions. There are times when our actions alone must be our witness, but actions usually lay a foundation which provides impact and meaning for our words (verbal witnessing) which come later. Good business and good ministry incorporates both actions and words. In my experience, the actions always precede the words.

Before beginning His teaching ministry, Jesus Himself worked miracles. Normally when He entered a new town He performed a miracle, and after that began teaching. Proverbs teaches us to "Develop your business first, then build your house."[52] Ministry should flow through our work. Our national employees should know we are here not just to operate an NGO or business, but to glorify God. Pictures hung in the office, a Bible on the desk, praying about business decisions; all reflect our priorities. We have employees from several religious backgrounds working for us. All have seen the gospel through our actions and heard it through our words. One newly employed Muslim employee was clearly offended by our sharing the gospel at her first Christmas party. However, after working with us for a year, that following December she said to me, "Be sure I am invited to the Christmas party." People often listen better with their eyes than their ears.

As we live the life, we cannot neglect to speak truth into people's lives. In referring to a workshop he taught in the Middle East for workers in that region, a friend wrote me; "A number of people *really* didn't want to go out and do the 'practicum.' True, we went door-to-door, which may have had little relevance to their context, but it made me aware of how much we 'westerners' love *knowledge* and *information*, but have a hard time actually *doing* something. That sounds a bit hard and wasn't true across the board, but being 'doers and not hearers only' was a big part of the whole evangelism process."

Jesus tells us we are to be salt and light. We are told to proclaim the Word. Greg Livingstone adds, "You don't share the gospel, you share cookies. You are to *proclaim* the gospel!" Some tentmakers are hesitant to witness lest they lose their job. Jesus says, "Whoever would save his job will lose it!" (Luke 9:24 my paraphrase). We are not where we are to make money; we are overseas to be witnesses. We are not created to work and make money; we are created to be witnesses. A witness by definition must speak of what he has seen and heard. I noted that one of our team members who had excellent language and many friends was not sharing his faith. I asked him about it and he told me the problem, "I want to share, but each time an opportunity arises my mind questions, 'What if this guy turns me in? What if my sharing results in the closing of the business and everyone gets kicked out?'" I asked him, "Whose money built this business, Jesus', yours, or mine?" "Jesus'," he replied. "And whose reputation is at stake when you share? Jesus', yours, or mine?" "Jesus'" he again answered. I then stated the obvious, "So what have we got lose? It's not our money and it's not our reputations that are at stake. If Jesus wishes to shut down His business for His sake, then so be it. We are told to be witnesses for Him, the rest is His problem." We need to remember the primary reason we are overseas. We could do whatever job we do anywhere. If we are not going to speak the Word, then we might as well go home. The Bible is clear that "faith comes from *hearing* the message" (Romans 10:17).

One Asian worker in our area goes house to house asking people to do a survey. The first question he asks is, "What's your business?" The next question is, "If you die tonight where will you go?" Depending on how they answer, he then shares the gospel. He readily admits it is a trick to get into homes. He feels his job is to share, and God will open the hearts of those He is calling to Himself. But we need to ask, is this brother sharing good news or bad news? Not surprisingly, he has not seen anyone believe or even accept an invitation to study the Bible with him. Our witness need not be programd or forced. One strength of tentmaking is the natural contacts with people it provides us. Most witnessing opportunities just happen, they are not planned events. Nonetheless, I do appreciate that this brother is "a doer of the Word."

Better to make mistakes than do nothing. God can work through our mistakes, but He cannot work through our doing nothing. In fact, nothing is the only thing that is impossible for God! (Luke 1:37) When in doubt, share! It is better to say too much than too little, and usually it is better to say the wrong thing than nothing.

Evangelism Ideas

Many times our evangelism focuses on doing Bible studies. Have you ever evaluated how your friends interpret your invitation to study the Bible? Part of the problem could be in the invitation itself. We talk about "getting them into a Bible study" and "doing a Bible study." The very idea of a Bible study could in itself be too daunting for them. If you were back home and a Muslim invited the people of your church to study the Qur'an, how would they respond? There are a number of creative alternatives. For example, in the course of a friendship we can generate interest in, say, the life of Jesus or what He said about the kingdom of God, or His other teachings. We can discuss parables and relate them to local moral teachings. At some point, we can comment on this interest, and suggest that they might like to take a closer look at Jesus' actual words. And since the Bible is a big, unfamiliar book we can serve as their librarian. Offer to identify some passages which they might read on their own. If they respond to that idea, give them a passage or two for them to read. On the next encounter ask how it went. If they did read it, talk about what they discovered and then give them something else to read. If they didn't read it, this approach can still work. Just spontaneously open to the passage, read it together, discuss it, and then suggest another passage for them to do on their own. In this manner, you can create a one-on-one process that is so informal it can come across as a non-event. However, realize that their first handling of the Bible itself will probably still be a hurdle. Remember to handle the Bible with reverence, not setting it on the floor or using a marked-up Bible.

Get out and meet people. Where do people of your age and social background congregate? At clubs, the bus stop, recreational centers, coffee shops, the temple, or mosque? Then hang out in those places too. Prayer-walk neighborhoods and villages, stopping to greet anyone who greets you (Luke 10:5–9). Check the local paper for events, if the right people are there, stay and get to know some, if not, leave. Social services, English teaching, sharing your hobbies, education, etc. are tools to meet people naturally. Volunteer at hospitals, or with NGOs run by locals, or public events. Join clubs, play sports, engine repair, karaoke, do the things that your focus people enjoy doing. If they have special dances, or martial arts, or music, join in learning these things. One co-worker who enjoyed Shakespeare placed an ad in the paper for starting a Shakespeare club. Only one person replied. They agreed to meet the first Saturday of each month to read and discuss Shakespeare. After seven years of reading Shakespeare together the man accepted Christ. Yes, the path to Jesus can be found in HAMLET as well. "Using all possible means to save some," requires us to be creative and do things that will get us involved with people.

As you think through your evangelism strategies, remember that love is our primary outreach tool. We are to be "fishers of men" (Matthew 4:19). Professional fishermen do not just get in any boat, to go to any part of the ocean, at any time of day, with any net or tackle, to do just any thing. Fishermen have a strategy for catching fish. Without a strategy they would starve. One friend puts it this way, "It would serve us well to ask ourselves:

What kind of fish are we fishing for?

Where are we likely to find them?

What training is necessary?

What type of bait is best?

What time of day or night?

What kind of boats, nets, equipment, is needed?

What do we do if hours of fishing do not turn up the desired kind of fish?"

Community Witnessing

The team or community approach to witnessing is growing in impact. In the past, missions was done by highly motivated, godly individuals, reflective of the individualist western society of that time. Since the 1980s, there has been a greater emphasis on teams and teamwork. This is a step in the right direction. As we increasingly recognize the need to be a blessing to the entire community, we are discovering that the best way to reach a community is to be a community. Christ centered communities, living the life of Jesus in the marketplace, model a commitment and love that no other religion can match. As we live out the "one another" passages, others are attracted to our life and work. As emissaries of the kingdom when we model love and sacrifice within our community, it becomes natural for the local communities to be influenced by our model.

Normally evangelism is done one on one. One individual attempts to befriend another individual as an avenue to share the gospel. In the community approach many people are involved. For example, on our team we have Paul; he is great with computers. Saturday morning I meet Akbar at a coffeehouse and as we chat I discover that he is "into computers" too. Akbar agrees to have lunch with me on Tuesday, so I tell Paul to come too. He meets Akbar and they begin to hang out together. At a party Paul or I host, our wives meet Akbar's wife. Now the six of us are friends. As our relationship grows over the course of the year, Paul and I will have separate spiritual discussions with Akbar, or our wives with his wife. We keep one another informed of these discussions so we know what has been shared as a guide for future discussions. Paul and I together also review these discussions regularly with Akbar, so as to reinforce to him our biblical beliefs and commitment to one another. Often Akbar is embarrassed to ask me why I pray, or memorize verses, but knowing Paul is my close friend, Akbar will ask Paul about me. In the asking, Paul is then free to share both my testimony and his own. We have presented the gospel to several friends this way. All team members are encouraged to invite several team members into their relationships with national friends. We intentionally pair up friends who have the same interests, or have children of the same age. We are becoming known as a community.

A common hurdle to a person's becoming a believer is: Who will take care of them once they convert? Who will be their community? Our friends already know we have a community, which they have interacted with, so that is not a barrier. Rama, a Hindi friend pointed out, "White guys never see themselves as part of a group so they never connect with the rest of the world. People think of themselves in terms of their group, but whites only think in terms of themselves as individuals."

One North African worker writes, "As a team we have been trying to maximize our visits by doing something to touch our friends as often as possible. Our goal is to share with, pray for, or give something written on each visit. By something written we mean a note, article, verse or verses, or even a letter. This works, at least in the Arab World. Sometimes it is not appropriate to share or pray, but you can always leave a handwritten note. People love to see what the foreigner has written, they love to correct our mistakes, and they are often touched that we took the time to give them something in our own writing. For people like me with a twisted tongue in a foreign language, you can say what you really mean, and go to friends to help you write it correctly (more opportunities). It is good language practice. My experience has been that if you give a tract, portion of scripture, etc. that people shelve it more often than not. But something handwritten they are usually very anxious to read. It is also less threatening to authorities. It works well, too, for those who can take the time while on home assignment to send that archaic form of communication that has an envelope, stamp, address, handwriting, and a real signature!"

One weakness to a community approach is the team can become locked into a few friends. It is necessary that the leader ensure everyone is also making new friends while following up with old ones. A friend in China writes, "Our Singaporean co-worker has introduced CY and R (his new team members) to his friends. We ourselves have had friends over when CY and R have dropped by. We just assumed that they would be concentrating on building new relationships of their own. We had hoped that these new people who have just come to town would build up more of their own relationships, but to date, we have not had one person join the team who has figured out how to build new relationships. They merely follow along the relational lines we built the first year here."

It is common for new people to want to befriend the contacts the team already has, as it is easier than making new friends. Funny, how we choose the narrow and hard road to get overseas, but then choose the wide and easy path once we get here. It is the leader's job to ensure that old friends are being witnessed to and that new friends are continually being made. Every January, our team writes on a big board all the new people we have befriended the past year, and all the people we have shared the gospel with as well. We wish to keep checking that everyone is working together and making progress in sharing our faith.

Prayer and Witnessing

Prayer is a major outreach tool. Willy in China writes, "When we began praying for our 200 employees on a daily basis, 85 percent came to Christ." We should always be praying (1 Thessalonians 5:17), and we should be praying for our un-believing co-workers and friends. Whenever we hear of a family member who is sick, we will tell them we will pray for them and then remember to call them in 2–3 days time to find out if they are better. With good friends, I'll ask if I can pray for them right there on the spot, whether we are on the street or in the office. I want my friends to know I am a man of prayer.

Some people think prayer should be private—I fully agree (Matthew 6:5-7). But there are times we need to pray publicly. My objective in praying in public is not to draw attention to myself, but to God. Think about it, why did Jesus pray? And in public no less? Because He liked to talk to Himself? No, He was witnessing to the world how to pray. He was modeling for us what we should do. We in turn need to model prayer to our friends.

When I hired Sue to be our office manager I told her I ran my businesses by the book, God's book. And though she was not a believer I expected her to do the same. She only smiled. The third day on the job she presented me with a marketing plan asking, "What do you think of this?" I replied, "Let me pray about it and I'll get back to you." She looked startled but moved on. Later I told her the decision and shared with her how God guides me. In time, she got used to my involving Jesus in my office decisions to the point that occasionally she would hand me something and say, "After you've prayed about this, let me know what to do."

Another worker in Turkey writes, "I strive to set aside time each week to think of ways to try to better understand the cultural context in which I work and how to integrate God's truth in my professional endeavors. A vital part of this preparation is prayer. I pray for my students, my colleagues, and staff. I pray for an understanding of their worldview, God's will for their lives, and I pray my deeds and words will not be stumbling blocks. I also let my friends know that I am praying for them."

We are to pray for those we are in authority over. Let your staff and co-workers know you are praying for them. Periodically ask them what you can be praying for them. As God answers their prayers, watch as their minds and hearts open up to discussing His power and works. Of course, we are to pray as well for those in authority over us (1 Tim. 2:2).

Another worker in Central Asia who is using prayer to witness writes, "Recently a local luncheon was held and a MBB employee was asked to pray the closing prayer. He shocked everyone present by praying 'in Jesus name.' There were no foreigners present to impress by praying in this way. They asked him why he prayed like the foreigners. He responded wisely by saying that God knows no borders and that He accepts all who are pure in heart. This is helping the Muslims of this churchless town to see that it is indeed possible for a Muslim to become a follower of Jesus."

Men, Women, and Children

It is important that the wives are actively involved in witnessing. Admittedly in some societies it is easier for men to meet other men than women to meet women. Even so, once the men become friends; do whatever is culturally appropriate to get the wives to know one another. Ask Muhammed's wife to teach your wife the language or how to cook harira and tanjia or some other local dishes, or have her show your wife where to get a local dress made. When both the husband and the wife are involved in the relationship, as one spouse shows interest in the gospel, the other, due to the friendship, will be more trusting and open too.

Sharon writes, "Our strategy for uneducated women and kids is to teach the believing men how to be the head of household and for him to instruct his family. But in our context it has not worked. We have many men in the kingdom and very few women. Many of these men who have children also do not seem to be able to bring their own children to the Lord. We need strategies to reach women and children of male believers. And I believe that the Lord must lead us also to have appropriate strategies to reach women and children whose husbands and fathers are not ready." Though some women are called to be housewives, we require all of our wives, no matter what their calling, to learn the language and culture, for we must all be prepared to give a defense of the gospel.

Youth

In reaching out to the community, it is not unusual for young people, teenagers especially, to show an interest in the gospel. Personally we have found when young Muslims show an interest in the gospel, they are either severely punished or in a few cases, where they came to faith and would not recant, abandoned by their parents or killed. When it comes to proselytizing minors, the consequences are more serious. Should we then feel free to proselytize minors, especially when they seem more receptive? There are three reasons I discourage proselytizing minors.

First, God has commanded us to "Honor your father and your mother, as the LORD your God has commanded you, so that you may live long and that it may go well with you in the land the LORD your God is giving you."[53] Ephesians 6:1 reiterates and enforces this commandment as well. We should teach all people to obey God's Law, including children, meaning they should honor their father and their mother. It would be a contradiction to teach them to follow and obey God while at the same time encouraging them to dishonor their parents. I believe it also would result in bringing dishonor to the name of Jesus and to his followers.

Asmah was 16 years old when she first attended our house church. After a few months she approached me about receiving Christ. I told her to get her father's permission. She was reluctant, but after several months of prayer and building up her courage, she did. This led to a number of discussions with her father and in time, he and his wife along with Asmah were baptized. Not all stories turn out so well. Bakar was 17 and living at home when he also asked about being baptized. Again I told him to ask his father's permission. I never saw Bakar again, and later I was told that when he asked his father, he was hit repeatedly with a cane.

Second, when a teenager converts against his parent's wishes, this drives a wedge between the parent and child. The parent becomes angry at the child, at the one who witnessed to them, and also at the Lord Jesus. Whenever we break God's commands, there will be repercussions. We may—or may not—win the child, but we will certainly lose the family. God's goal is to win everyone, which means communities, families, as well as individuals. Too often we lose sight of the bigger picture. Evangelizing children against the wishes of parents and community leaders will close the door to reaching more than a few individuals.

Jack in Indonesia writes, "We had children coming to small groups and to the Sunday fellowship without their parents. As a team, we decided to honor the parents by allowing children to come only if they had their parents' permission. Usually, a local believer went to the parents and explained that their child had come to our fellowship and explained that the child couldn't come without their permission. Some parents wouldn't give permission but others were so impressed by our honoring them that they gave permission for the children to come. Many of these parents later saw the changes in their children, and some became believers as a result."

Third, as a father I would be incensed if someone tried to convert my children behind my back. I have both legal and moral responsibility for raising my children, and someone proselytizing my children would violate both. Jesus said, "So in everything, do to others what you would have them do to you, for this sums up the Law and the Prophets."[54] Thus, I cannot with a clear conscience, proselytize someone else's children without their permission. It would not be right, loving, or respectful.

Scripture teaches that love is the greatest gift we can give. Respect is a huge part of showing love. When we respect the parents' authority over their children, it demonstrates love.

CHURCH PLANTING

The ultimate objective of all mission work is to establish God's church where it does not already exist (Romans 15:20). The Nevius model of church planting describes a church as a body of believers who are self instructing, self propagating, self supporting, and self governing. The development of a strong movement of God in any people group involves three essential steps: evangelism, discipleship, and church planting. Evangelism and discipleship are not ends in themselves. The church is the bride of Christ. Evangelism should lead to a gathering of new believers who come together to form a fellowship, which becomes in time a church. Initially, new believers may be hesitant to meet with others lest someone report them to the authorities or their families. Yet as men and women believe, they should be discipled and gathered into fellowships for teaching and keeping the sacraments.

The first church the Lord allowed us to start was in a poor, rural village. As there was a significant Christian minority in the region, the believers, mostly Muslim background believers (MBBs), felt it would be okay to build their own church building. Though the team and I did not encourage this, as it was their church and their decision, they moved forward with the idea. The believers saved for nearly two years before they had enough to build a small building. One person donated land, and the day was set to start construction. The lumber was ordered; everyone was there to help. As the foundation poles were being put into place, two Muslim men from a nearby village walked by. These men were known for their radical faith and hatred of us. They innocently inquired what we were doing. The leaders responded, "We are building the first church in this county!" To which the men answered, "That's good; work hard." The church members were surprised at their answer and discussed among themselves why would they be so encouraging. Finally, one of the leaders ran after the men and asked them, "Why were you so encouraging towards our building a church?" The men replied, "Because when you are done, it will make a good bonfire." The elders knew this was no idle threat. Churches in other cities had been recently destroyed. They quickly gathered together to discuss what to do. Soon they decided against building a church and instead used the lumber to remodel one of the member's homes, which was in need of repair. His living room was enlarged so that it could be used as a meeting place.

In many places you will not be able to build a church building. Out of necessity, cell groups, house churches, or small groups will be the church model that must be developed. It is important to read and familiarize yourself with the different models of church planting. If possible, get involved in such a model. It may be wise not to commit to one strategy until after you have moved into your community and tested the soil to see what would be suitable for your environment. Having a well-rounded background of various church models which can operate out of a home will be helpful as the believers think through issues for gathering for fellowship and worship.

New believers need to be guided in maturing in Christ. This requires discipleship. Hudson Taylor said, "A man may be consecrated, dedicated and devoted but of little use if undisciplined." Discipleship is disciplining (or training) the new believers in the basics of the faith. Once the basics are mastered, discipleship continues into all other aspects of the faith. The goal of discipleship is to teach new believers to identify with Christ and be obedient to God's word, so that fruit may be harvested both in and through their lives for Jesus. As believers mature, leaders should be appointed in culturally acceptable ways. These leaders must be trained to shepherd the fellowship, evangelize unbelievers, disciple believers and plant other churches in nearby communities. In all church planting efforts, there should be a plan for raising up national leaders and as quickly as possible, giving the leadership of the fellowship into their hands.

In planting the church, you need to be clear not only about the people group you are reaching and the language you will be using, but about the segment of society you wish to focus on. For example, is there a social class or section of the city/country the Lord wishes for you to stress? Will you focus on the rich or the poor, the educated or uneducated? It is helpful to narrow the focus as much as the Lord allows, so as to know where and with whom to focus your time and energies. You will also wish to prayerfully consider the level of contextualization desired in the meetings, the worship, and even the design of the meeting place. There are six cross-cultural church planting spectrums to consider. The following "continuum" tool was devised to help clarify our church-planting, contextualization objectives.

The C1- C6 Continuum:

Six Types of Christ-centered Communities Presently Found in the Muslim World

"The following continuum helps describe and define, in terms of language, culture and religious identity, six general types of congregations (communities of believers) found in Muslim contexts. In some areas, all six types of Christ-centered communities can be found; in others, only one or two types exist. Even though each Muslim part of the world reflects its own unique blend of political, religious, historical, and cultural factors, the issues identified in the continuum at least offer a starting point to think critically about what it means to plant the church, even a church in a truly Islamic milieu.

C-1 Traditional church structure; using the local trade or national language. Often reflects western churches in practices and styles.

C-2 Traditional church structure; using the people's daily language. Very similar to C-1, only varies with the closeness of the heart language of the people.

C-3 Contextualized church structure; local language and local ethnic arts and culture reflected in the worship and ecclesiology of the church.

C-4 Contextualized congregation structure reflecting local language, local Muslim arts and culture, and the use of biblically acceptable/redeemable Islamic forms, vocabulary, and traditions.

C-5 Congregations of Muslims who follow Christ yet remain legally and culturally Muslim. By the local Islamic community, they are perceived as Muslims who are spiritually different yet still within the fold. Continuance of Islamic practices (e.g. going to the Mosque, fasting, daily prayers) depends upon each local situation and the leading of the Holy Spirit within the particular C-5 group. The distinguishing feature of C-5 is that these believers are true followers of Christ who have yet remained legally and culturally Muslim, and are part of a community of other such Muslim followers of Jesus.

C-6 Clusters of secret believers or individual believers within Islam. Such believers have little if any contact with other believers. With the extreme persecution converts experience in some places, this may be the only way one can survive. This could also be called an underground, secret church."[55]

A church planting list showing the "7 Phases of Church Planting" may be found in Appendix B. These church planting phases guide us to know where we are going in our church planting outreach. Each phase describes what we should be doing and our objectives, allowing us to measure our success. If church planting is the goal, there must be a plan for reproducing national leaders and leaving the church in their hands. To see this is done requires a process of both encouragement and oversight. Accountability of both church leaders and missionary workers, or a lack of it, may be the biggest reason we fail in our church planting objectives. Every worker would be wise to invite other leaders into their lives who will keep them on target (Proverbs 15:22).

A Church for Every People

I was attending a conference in Singapore when during a morning tea break, I joined a conversation between two local Chinese pastors. Both pastored English speaking churches, (English is a common language spoken by Singaporean Christians). Both pastors were enthusiastically sharing with me about the daughter churches their congregations had just begun. One daughter church was using the Mandarin language and another Hokkien, a Chinese dialect. In a question and answer period later that afternoon, one of the attendees asked the speaker if he thought the Malays (a Muslim minority group) should have their own church. Before the speaker could reply, one of the pastors I had tea with that morning shouted out, "They don't need a church of their own. They all speak English and can come to our churches!"

Frank Teo, a Singaporean who worked in Pakistan for eight years writes, "As in Pakistan with the Punjabi church, it is the same in Singapore with the Chinese church. If a Muslim joins a local church, not of their own people, they are rarely welcomed and never really encouraged to belong." Not once, but five times in Revelation we are told, "every nation, tribe, language and people" will be represented before His throne (Revelation 5:9; 7:9; 11:9; 13:7; 14:6). It is God's desire for each distinct group of people to gather to worship in the name of Jesus. Thus, I believe it is God's desire for every people group to have their own church. Our experience in North Africa mirrors that of Singapore. There are five people groups in our country, all Muslim, yet when we bring believers of two different groups together, they are polite but clearly uncomfortable. Teaching Hindu believers to join a church made of members of another caste, or of Muslim believers, is kin to teaching them to break the fifth commandment, "Honor your father and mother." Clearly, we are all one in Christ. Yet God's word is clear that there will be believers from every people group bending the knee to

Jesus. Church planting should be the objective of all tentmakers, and each people group needs to have its own church.

Reproducing Churches

Scripture teaches us to train "reliable men who will also be qualified to teach others" (2 Timothy 2:2). The principle of reproducibility should be applied to every facet of ministry.

Cultural expectations concerning "what is a church" should be tried, not formed. Believers need to be discipled in the principles but not the forms of "church." Believers need to discover in the Holy Spirit and within their own culture, ways they feel comfortable practicing their faith and ecclesiology. There is a danger of new believers uncritically embracing western thinking and models. We should go to great lengths to ensure that the emerging church meetings can be readily reproduced by those who attend. This means even with the first gatherings of believers, the potential national leaders should be involved in leading. Time and effort is to be taken to teach leadership principles and allow the believers to work out these principles within the parameters of their own culture. One co-worker writes, "We dealt with this in Egypt, where we had CBBs [Christian Background Believers] helping in the MBB fellowships. Of course, the church planters and the CBBs were always more proficient in leading the meetings, doing worship, teaching, etc., but that's not the point. We had to hold ourselves back and push the MBBs into (what it felt to them) uncomfortable positions of responsibility. Otherwise, there was never any incentive for them to take leadership—why should they? The CBBs and church planters have a vast background of knowledge and experience that they don't, so it always felt strange at the beginning, before they started to use the gifts that God had given them. This is where the individual discipleship is so crucial—to review with them what went well and what didn't go so well."

Likewise, we need to model preparation for teaching and leading using only the tools that are readily available to the local leaders. If they do not have access to commentaries, dictionaries, photocopy machines or a computer, then we should forgo those tools in our own preparation. It is completely normal for them to presume—and completely wrong for us to give them that impression—that teaching means they have to have a big library of books, know the original languages, etc. We need to teach them to prepare and teach with the tools they have at hand. We need to keep it simple. In many cultures, if it is not simple, it will not be reproducible.

Meeting Place

One decision that is easily taken for granted is where the gathering of believers should meet. If meetings are held in the homes of westerners, it is not unusual for believers to develop a syndrome that the meeting must revolve around the foreigner's presence. One fellowship in North Africa which began in the 1950s in the missionary's home, continues to meet there to this day. The first missionaries who began these meetings have retired long ago, but still there is a sense that the meeting should not happen without a western leader being present. When the missionaries leave for furlough or are away, the meetings stop till someone returns. To be a real church, the body needs to be self-supporting, self-governing, self-propagating, and self-instructing. After a time, the missionary should not be needed to prop up the church in any way, shape, or form.

It is not wise to meet at your place of business. One foreigner who owned and operated tours and a hotel in Vietnam led a number of his employees to Jesus. Every Sunday he held worship meetings in Vietnamese in one of his hotel's meeting rooms. Though he owned the hotel, employed over forty people and had nearly half a million U.S. dollars invested in the property, because of his church planting efforts, his employment visa was not renewed. Gatherings of believers of any size should never be held at your place of business lest you jeopardize the business. Though we model our faith in the office, I discourage team members from directly sharing the gospel in the office during office hours. If a co-worker or client shows an interest in hearing about our faith, we invite them to step outside for a drink at a nearby restaurant. There and then we share the gospel. In that way, should the person report us to the authorities, the individual alone will be blamed and not the business. Blaming the business could unnecessarily jeopardize the work of other team members, as well as the business itself.

Dealing with Persecution

Jesus teaches "in the world you will have trouble," "watch out for . . . wolves," and "persecution comes because of the word" (John 16:33; Matthew 10:16–17; Mark 4:17). Persecution is an inheritance of the believer; it is to be expected as Jesus promises it. It is not to be feared. Peter adds, "Dear friends, do not be surprised at the painful trial you are suffering, as though something strange were happening to you. But rejoice that you participate in the sufferings of Christ, so that you may be overjoyed when his glory is revealed."[56] Wang Ming-dao, who suffered much under the Communists, writes, "Some of God's promises are written in invisible ink, only in the flame of suffering do they become visible."[57]

How we deal with persecution is an important issue. Some workers extract their converts before they have to face persecution, sending them to the worker's home country for Bible school and a safe new life. But once extracted, it is nearly impossible for the believer to go home, as their family and friends will not accept them. As a result their family will never hear the truth about Jesus. Other workers choose to leave the new believers within their own community to endure whatever befalls them, trusting God to be their protector. I have heard stories of believers who were about to be killed and were miraculously spared, but I have also had friends who were not spared. Each of us must seek the Lord for His will. There may also be provisional ways of deferring or reducing danger, short of extraction.

In the long run, suffering somehow becomes a foundation block for church growth. Samuel Lamb, the pastor of the largest house-church in China was imprisoned for more than twenty years. He declared that "more persecution was followed by more growth . . . suffering is nothing to us. As long as we have the right attitude toward suffering God will strengthen us." [58] It is important to train new believers and even advise those who are interested in the gospel concerning the cost of following Jesus. Potential believers should be taught both the benefits and the potential costs of converting and of suffering. We need to help them count the cost (Luke 14:26–35). Tell them what happened to others who have converted. Make clear what they can expect from you should they face severe persecution—meaning a quick trip out of the country for a period of time, you will pray and fast for them, or something in between. There have been apparent converts who returned to their previous faith when the tentmaker did not protect and help them as they had expected. It is important to plan ahead.

Hiring Local Evangelists

Hiring local evangelists may be the most divisive issue on the missions horizon. Every one agrees that locals should be able to do a better job, but do they? The temptation money brings is too often beyond what many nationals can bear. Some western workers believe hiring national workers saves time and money, multiplying their labors exponentially. Others question the motives of nationals. Dr. Mary Chung, a Hong Kong mission leader says, "It is amazing how many students get called into full-time Christian service once their exam scores are released, and they realize they cannot go to university." Where churches exist, nearly every expatriate worker I have met has at one time or another been dealt with dishonestly by a local Christian worker, including pastors.

We need to think through how we pay national workers. Why? Obviously, national workers speak the language fluently, understand the culture, and can live on one-fourth the salary of western workers. However, is economics the most important factor? Hiring nationals places us over them as their masters. They tend to look to us, not to the Lord, for help. It creates a dependency syndrome. When others convert, they too expect to be paid to be Christians. I know of at least two ministries where every single believer is on the payroll of the tentmaker. I also know one tentmaker who, when an employee receives Jesus, he helps that employee find another job, so that there is little question of the employee's motive for converting. A further issue is that paying believers for Christian ministry is often perceived by non-believers as an extension of colonialism. Many times this results in the national worker being alienated from his people, defeating the purpose for hiring him. A worker in North Africa writes, "In some of the 'worst' cases, paying the nationals to minister has created a weak church with a high dependency on sponsors, and that becomes the status quo for any new churches that are planted. I've become very much against paying nationals for any kind of ministry, believing it weakens the church and creates many mixed motives." A short term worker whose church helped remodel a church in Indonesia told me, "Nearly half the church members I met were unemployed, yet many are not seeking jobs but proudly wish to live by faith and become 'full-time Christian workers.' When I asked, 'What does it mean to live by faith?' I was told, 'Pray to God for our needs and write the Singaporean and western churches for money.'"

Personally, I have had a few good and many bad experiences with hiring national evangelists. There are no easy answers. Paul said, "The worker deserves his wages" (1 Timothy 5:18), yet Paul did not solicit funds for himself or his team. How do we weigh that with national believers who say they do not have time for evangelism unless they are paid? John, a well-known church planter in Central Asia has this to say, "In our first three years here, we were part of a team whose fellowship grew from two MBBs in 1993 to 350 MBBs by 1997. Talk about exciting! But we took shortcuts . . . paying workers was one big mistake. Today there are only about 100–150 MBBs left. The shortcuts may give an exciting short-term appearance of results, but they didn't pay off." I know of two churches which collapsed, and many local Christian workers left the ministry when their foreign funding dried up. A few even left the faith.

People think about how they can survive before thinking about theology. As one Middle Eastern Muslim put it, "How can I move out of my present house until I have a new house to move into?" There are two ways to deal with the issue of hiring nationals. First, create real jobs for the local Christian workers. Teach them to work and disciple them in the biblical basis of work and how to witness through their work. Help the believers to set up businesses of their own. Having them work for you is an option, but that will not stop others from thinking they are still your servant and that their motive for converting is simply to make money. By giving new believers the training and tools to operate their own business or work for others, they can gain respect in the community, create jobs for others, and witness through their jobs. This also precipitates the issue of what their motivation is for following Jesus and you.

Second, test your people. When Joe first approached me about working for me I told him "No, I don't see you ministering to the people. But if you begin reaching out to the people, then I'll consider it." I let Joe starve for over year, but he did win four MBBs to the Lord and began discipling them. I then agreed to pay Joe for four years or until he had a sizeable group of believers, at which time we would work out a system to decrease his support.

Ned, working in Turkey, writes, "I would like to heartily affirm this element of accountability with funding. In spite of all the positive theory about how much more effective and cost efficient western funds would be if they went directly to nationals who are cultural insiders, my experience has been that most new believers in pioneer settings where the church is also fairly young do not have the spiritual maturity to properly handle funds without on-site, on-going, regular accountability. The results of this are often disabling to the recipient and can bring significant problems into the local church and ministry. Most local pastors, in my opinion, even if they have been pastors for a few years, are not at this point yet."

Churches that want to support nationals should channel funds through a mature and very trusted source who is on the ground and well connected to those who will ultimately receive the funds. Do not send money directly to the worker. It is wiser to use another structure or vehicle, preferably one in their country of origin. Such a person would not necessarily have to be a westerner, but this person should be well grounded in the faith, experienced at handling money, fluent in the language, a mature elder, or a seasoned missionary. In addition, this person should be accountable for how the money is used and provide regular updates to the donors. Never fund without an accountability framework. I would suggest a maximum funding of 50 percent, apportioned through periodic remittances. The concept is to leave the national with the major responsibility of raising further support.

The wrong use and attitude toward money is very important to Jesus. Jesus turned over the money changers' tables. He was angry because people were misusing His Father's house of prayer for personal benefit. Before hiring nationals, get to know them. Observe their lifestyle; listen to their dreams. Ask and probe the following questions of each person and of their close friends, including non-believers.

What are your motives for ministry?

Are you known for loving others?

Do you have a job? Have you proven you can keep a job?

Do you take responsibility for mistakes?

Do you have any "get rich quick" ideas?

Do you know how to balance a budget?

Do you know how to say "no?"

Do you sacrifice for others?

Are you generous? What ministries, other than your own, do you support?

Are you honest?

Do you know how to work?

Do you love sleep?

Do you save?

The deliberateness of hiring local believers for ministry largely depends on the local situation. Test the workers; ensure that they have the right motives. There are two simple tests to appraise a worker. One, give the potential worker $20 to purchase several items at different stores. Do you get the exact change? Are you given receipts for each item? Two, give the worker $20 for his personal use. After two days, ask him what he spent it on. Did he give any of it to others? These are simple tests which reveal a person's character. Consider closely with them the sacrifices they will need to make in the eyes of authorities, friends, and family. Be careful and prayerful.

DEVELOPING NATIONAL LEADERSHIP

Jim in Nepal writes, "After a church has been planted, it is important that the missionary encourage the rise of natural leaders within the young congregation and train them. As much as possible, the local group of believers must take responsibility for the church from the very beginning. It is essential that we train leaders who can wrestle with the theological issues that emerge within their cultural context. It is easier to train followers who merely believe what we say and imitate us. But such followers are spiritually immature, and when we leave, they are easily led astray by the first false doctrine that comes along."

It is much harder to train leaders, for we must teach them to think for themselves, to disagree with us, and to stand for their own convictions. We must learn to accept debates and honest disagreements on tough theological issues without cutting off a national brother or sister. We must learn the humility of admitting we are wrong, and we must be willing to see young leaders receiving more honor than ourselves. The goal of every missionary and tentmaker is to work themselves out of a job (2 Timothy 2:2). That requires us to reproduce leaders who can take over our ministry duties and in some cases, our businesses as well. There are many good books on leadership (Christian and non-Christian), which are helpful for training national leaders. Yet in training leaders of another culture, it is important to learn the cultural expectations of leadership. For example, Asians expect their leaders to be autocratic; Americans expect their leaders to be democratic. Asian leaders rarely admit a mistake; they would lie first. Whereas Americans value honesty, if their leaders make a mistake, Americans expect them to admit it.

New believers have little knowledge of the Scriptures and sometimes cannot read. They are dependent upon us for both an understanding of what the Scriptures mean and for guidance in dealing with the questions they face. It is our responsibility to teach the believers the Scriptures, how to study the Scriptures for themselves, and how to apply them to their lives. In explaining the Bible, we must allow the believers to work out the applications of the teachings within the cultural context of their community. As the believers mature, it is important to teach and model reliance on God for spiritual and physical needs. Many new believers prefer to be dependent on expatriates to make decisions and to provide for their needs. It takes forethought and effort to prevent that from happening.

Jesus sees the kingdom as in process. He, through us, is building His kingdom. If we do not build we are put aside. God delegated His building assignments to Adam and Eve, to the disciples, and so on. What is the greatest compliment Jesus gives? "You have great faith," He told to a Centurion who knew how to delegate. It is crucial to think in advance how to develop leaders. Encourage the believers "to teach us" how to be leaders within their cultural context. What is biblical we must undergird with biblical principles, and what is anti-biblical we must substantiate in Scripture.

We must cultivate leaders who can teach others. This includes showing them how to wrestle with theological issues and make applications within their cultural context. Early in the discipling process we should hand over responsibility for leading the fellowship to the nationals. If the church is to stand on its own, we must trust the believers to hear directly from the Lord. We must teach them to think for themselves and to defend their convictions from Scripture. We must trust the leaders and support their decisions. It is better to transfer leadership too early than hold on to authority too long. Try not to introduce foreign leadership structures; rather allow them to lead in culturally acceptable ways. Let the Bible, not our experiences, church background, or culture, determine how leadership is to be established. Do help them to learn how to plan and set priorities in culturally appropriate ways.

We must teach and model servant leadership. Teaching leadership is helpful, but modeling servant leadership is essential. We must openly share our strengths and weaknesses with those we are discipling. It is important to distinguish between positional leadership and leadership by influence. Jesus was a servant leader. Most leadership models are positional, whereas the idea in servant leadership is to influence other people. Servant leadership may be effective without an official position. Many cultures follow a positional leadership structure because it provides a title and money, along with influence and authority. However, it is wiser and biblical to set up a plurality of leaders or a leadership team (elders, deacons, whatever suits the culture). Defer appointing leaders until at least two people are ready to lead. If you appoint only one leader, it will be very hard to remove him or add another person as his equal to the leadership team at a later time. In many contexts it is natural for one strong leader to emerge, but in the long run that will hinder the expansion of the church. A brief study of the word "elder" reveals the New Testament emphasis for having a plurality of leaders. If one leader is prominent (first among equals), he should learn to function within the community as part of a leadership team.

Finally, leaders need help in dealing with fear. Ken Perkins writes in a study on persecuted believers, "When asked what individuals have learned from missionaries, the most common answer is 'to be afraid.'" We need to teach and show our future leaders to trust in Christ. We are to invite them to join us in praying for our needs. Give them a front row seat to our own personal struggles, so they may see how Jesus meets our every need and helps us overcome our struggles. We must teach and model trust, not fear.

SUMMARY

The ultimate objective of mission work is to plant churches where no churches exist. Before heading overseas, it is important to learn and practice various evangelism and church planting strategies.

ACTION STEPS

- How do you show love to friends and co-workers? Without using words, do they recognize the Christ in you?
- Familiarize yourself with ten evangelism methods or tools.
- Use five evangelism tools or strategies, such as passing out tracts and books, evangelistic Bible study, sharing illustrations, preaching, etc.
- Familiarize yourself with three church planting models, such as house churches, cell churches, community churches, etc.
- Which level of contextualization do you feel most comfortable with?
- How might prayer be used to share your faith?
- Will a community approach to witnessing be appropriate?
- How will accountability be done to ensure the team stays on task?
- If the believers are persecuted, how do you intend to respond?

- Appraise the advantages and disadvantages of hiring national evangelists.
- How will you train national workers to reach beyond their own people group?

"Which stone is more important: the one on the top or the one at the base? It is not what we build, buy or do that determines our worth, but our relationship to God.

Who, what, is the base of all our relationships?

The most powerful weapon on earth is the human soul on fire."

FERDINAND FOCH

By the grace God has given me, I laid a foundation as an expert builder, and someone else is building on it. But each one should be careful how he builds . . . If any man builds on this foundation using gold, silver, costly stones, wood, hay or straw, his work will be shown for what it is . . . It will be revealed with fire, and the fire will test the quality of each man's work.

I CORINTHIANS 3:10–13

chapter 9
FOUNDATIONS

I had the experience of sitting in my brother's living room in Florida while Hurricane Charley, one of the most destructive hurricanes in the history of America, passed over his home. When we were finally able to get outside, we were amazed to see huge trees, sometimes row upon row of them, toppled over. On further inspection, we noted that though these trees had grown to great heights, their root structures were growing just a few inches below the surface. If we are going to "finish the race," we need to put down deep roots, laying a solid foundation for our lives and work. There are four foundations which must be a part of the life and work of every tentmaker: a consistent spiritual life, a team with similar objectives, submission to godly leadership and accountability to godly experienced leaders.

SPIRITUAL LIFE

"No prayerless missionary can bring heathen idolaters who know not our God to their knees in true prayer until he becomes pre-eminently a man of prayer."

E.M. BOUNDS

There is no debate that of all our strategies, prayer is the most important. Most of our strategies are just that—our strategies; prayer is God's strategy. One of the major struggles we have as tentmakers is juggling all of our duties and tasks. Being God's strategy and not our own, prayer is an easy item to pass over in our rush to get through the day. There are two strategies I find helpful for bathing our life and work in prayer.

First, every tentmaker should raise up a team of prayer warriors who will pray for them on a daily basis. As tentmakers, we are fighting a spiritual battle. We need to utilize both spiritual weapons and recruit spiritual people to fight with us. In fighting the battle, the more soldiers we have fighting with us the better. Some people will physically come and join us, but others can join us through prayer. We cannot do a great deal to develop our support base once we are overseas. Therefore, we must take the time to have our support structures in place before we leave the shelter of our home environment. As actively as we recruit workers to join us on the field and others to financially support us, we need to recruit people who will battle along with us in prayer. When visiting churches, I often ask the pastor, "Who are the prayer warriors in your church?" I then ask to meet these men and women of God and invite them to lunch. I share with them our goals and invite them to pray for us.

For prayers to be effective, those who are praying should have accurate and up to date information. Thus, we need to regularly send prayer letters to communicate our needs. People often ask me the secret to what God has accomplished through our ministry. My reply, "We have over three hundred people praying for us." For over twenty years, we have sent out a monthly prayer letter. The impact those prayers have on the battle is beyond measure. Consider, I can pray for Mustafa's salvation for three minutes a day, or I can ask three hundred people to pray for Mustafa's salvation for ten seconds each day. Which will do greater damage to the gates of hell? One person throwing rocks at the gates for three minutes? Or three hundred people throwing rocks for ten seconds each, for a total of fifty minutes? (Luke 18:7). We need to recruit people to pray for His work, both in us and through us. We need to frequently correspond with those people so that their prayers have a strategic focus. The frequency of our communication encourages prayer. People who really pray want fresh information from the front lines. It is our duty to provide it. Secure e-mail facilitates our communication. Workers in open countries can also set up their own blogs where people may log on for regular updates.

It is essential that we pray at least daily for those under our authority. Hebrews 13 makes it clear that as leaders, we will "give an account" for our leadership. It is important that we lift up our team members and co-workers each day. Leaders especially need to know God's mind daily, for each person in the business and on the team. We must also remember our family and those we are reaching out to. This is prayer for guidance that must primarily be pursued by us in communion with the Trinity.

The second strategy for prayer is what Brother Lawrence calls "practicing the presence of God." Rather than fight against our busyness and the pressures we face, let us accept them and allow them to become opportunities to serve Him and to invite Him to work through us for His glory. We need to constantly remind ourselves that God is alive and that His Spirit is at work in us. We need to remember that each person, each incident that comes across our path, occurs for a reason. Nothing happens by accident. Everything is a part of His transforming work in us and others. We are here to do His business, His ministry, His way. Our duty is to be ready, willing, and available for Him to work through us.

Throughout the day, we should attempt to "practice His presence" in our thoughts and actions. This means to "pray without ceasing" (1 Thessalonians 5:17). We need to make business meetings times of worship in our hearts and answering e-mails a time of prayer. We need to walk through each moment of our lives with His Spirit in our hearts and in our heads. Whatever we do is to be done as unto the Lord (Colossians 3:23). We should strive to live each day, each moment, as if we are on our knees. For me, routines are helpful. I have trained myself to pray every time I switch on my computer, start my car, or open my office door. I have met several men who set their wrist watch to beep every hour to remind them to pray. Train yourself so that each time you begin a new task, you invite Jesus to do it through you. As we talk to other people, also be talking to God. This includes discussions at work, at home or with non-Christian friends.

Devotional Life

"Very early in the morning, while it was still dark, Jesus got up, left the house and went off to a solitary place, where he prayed."[59] Each day we must strive to be full of His presence, His strength, and directed by His guidance. We need to recognize our need and then strive to maintain a moment by moment dependence on our Lord, acknowledging that He alone delivers our daily bread. The research shows that workers who have longer devotional times are more effective. There was no measurement to assess the quality of those times, yet clearly more is better. As in spending time with our children, since we cannot plan for "quality times" with God, go for quantity.

How do we maintain a devotional life in the midst of juggling a team, wife, children, friends, the business, correspondence, etc.? The way is to "practice His presence." We need to realize His presence and love are available to us even when we are overcome with activities. It is no coincidence that Jesus' commission to go to all peoples includes His promise, "I am with you always" (Matthew 28:20). In whatever we are doing, He is there, so include Him.

Practicing His presence has many benefits. One of our businesses had been open for three years. Since the day it opened, it had been profitable, but when Sue, the office manager, brought in the end of the month report in June, she said, "We lost two of our best clients this month. They went belly-up due to the recession. I hate to tell you, but we will finish this month in the red." I replied, "Well, then there is only one thing to do." She countered, "You want me to do some advertising?" I laughed and said, "Yes, that too, but I need to pray." The next week I left for a four week trip. Upon my return, Sue greeted me with a smile. "I guess you were praying," she said. "We picked up four new clients last month."

Fasting

The research shows that the strongest spiritual factor related to effectiveness is that "workers who regularly practice fasting as an important spiritual discipline" are very effective. Many Christians have never learned how to incorporate fasting into their daily lives. I cannot recall my seminary offering a course on prayer or fasting. If you fast regularly, keep it up. If you do not fast, learn and ask others about how they fast. Join them in a period of fasting. As it was to the early church leaders (Acts 13:2; 14:23), it is vital as tentmakers to incorporate biblical fasting into our daily lives. TC in Southeast Asia adds, "When my Muslim friends find I am fasting, they are curious, and it opens doors to deeper discussions."

Power Encounter

It is common for people from poor backgrounds to equate technological power with spiritual power. As tentmakers, we can show people both technological power through our work and spiritual power through His Word. The research shows that 45 percent of all workers had encounters with demons on the field. It also shows that these 45 percent are highly effective in evangelism and church planting. This is logical as many Hindus, as well as a fair number of Muslims and Buddhists, include animist practices in their faith, practices which are demon-centered. However, in our western missiological training there is too little training on spiritual warfare. Dave Johnson, a worker in the Philippines, points out, "The name of the game is power. If we are going to win people to the Lord, they need to see the power of God."

When a people-group's world view is basically animistic (even for Muslims and Hindus), trusting in God without seeking to manipulate His spiritual forces seems unreal and incomprehensible. All people need to encounter God, be it through a truth encounter, love encounter, or power encounter. We need to utilize all means (1 Corinthians 9:22) to bring people into a saving relationship with Jesus.

A worker in Indonesia wrote this when I asked what he would recommend for pre-field training, "Preparation in spiritual depth and an understanding of spiritual warfare and of ministry in spiritual gifts to each other is *important*! Practice at home before getting on the boat!" A co-worker of his added, "People should have more awareness of spiritual battles, power encounters, and truth encounters."

TEAM

"Coming together is a beginning, keeping together is progress, working together is success."
HENRY FORD

A team is a community of "we," consisting of people who have a common vision and a common commitment. The details and doctrines may vary, but the love of the Lord is the glue that keeps a team striving to reach their objectives together. Good team work requires right attitudes and actions. In agreement with their common objectives, effective team members hold themselves mutually accountable for specific results. Good teams will project a synergy, enabling the team to perform in a way that is greater than the sum of its parts. As my high school basketball coach used to tell us, "There is no 'I' in team."

Good team members are not independent or dependent, but inter-dependent. Team members should freely share their knowledge and skills with one another, while searching for godly and efficient ways to achieve their goals. Team members should inspire one another, socialize together, make mistakes together, plan and debate together, and hold one another accountable to biblical standards in all areas of work, ministry, and life. A good team is like a family; there are no secrets, and there is nothing team members would not do for one another. A team can be a blessing, but it can also be a distraction. Focus may be the most important discipline for a church planting team to maintain. The team as a whole must have a clear sense of vision, purpose, and function. Each member of the team must grasp and agree with the team's objectives and understand the vital role he or she plays in achieving those objectives. Team members must communicate frequently with one another to ensure trust and understanding. The execution of duties should be shared in ways that everyone understands and appreciates each person's contribution to the team effort.

It is encouraging that 93 percent of all tentmakers serving in the 10/40 Window are on a team. Teams with members from more than one country are more effective than teams of one nationality. Over 70 percent of the workers surveyed serve on multi-national teams. Over half the teams (56 percent) have workers from more than one mission organization. The most effective teams, as with Jesus' team, had eleven to twelve members. Did Jesus know something we did not? Interestingly, teams with sixteen or more workers are less effective than teams with ten or less members. A team becomes more effective as it increases in number from three up to twelve members, after which the effectiveness of the team plateaus and then decreases at sixteen. Many team leaders like to limit the size of their team to five to seven adults. Once they have five team members, they stop recruiting. There are advantages to having a small team. One team leader writes, "now that my team is down to minuscule numbers, I've been able to spend more time with the friends we were called to serve." With larger teams, the expectations and burdens on the team leader increase exponentially. Then, even if the team leader is able to cope with the team dynamics, there is little time or energy left for their own involvement in evangelism or discipleship. Leaders of large teams need to learn to share leadership. Teams of more than sixteen members should consider hiving off part of the team to another area of the city or country, forming a new team. Most teams meet weekly or bi-weekly. Teams that meet less than twice a month are less effective.

Pat Cate, the former director of Christar, said, "There must be a balance between 'production' and 'production capability'—between building up the life of the team (training, member care, etc.) and the work of evangelism and discipleship. Too much emphasis on the team leads to introspection; the team appears to be thriving and well-adjusted, but they are living in their comfort zone." When no risks are being taken, little seed will be sown. On the other hand, too great an emphasis on results leads to high attrition. When attrition is high, the team's language and cultural acquisition remains immature and ineffective as new workers replace old ones. One factor that helps to prevent a team from becoming inwardly focused and losing sight of its goals is to be submitted to a coach/mentor who is not a member of the team. This coach should be mature in the Lord, experienced in the work, knowledgeable about the team and its goals, and bold enough to speak authoritatively into the lives of the leader and team members. Teams should have annual "check-ups" to ensure they are on target and accomplishing God's agenda.

Recruiting a Team

Most people are inspired to follow leaders who stand for something. It is paramount that leaders know their values and direction (the "vision thing") and ask people to commit themselves to helping make that vision a reality. In the beginning, many new team leaders wish to fill up their team with people just to have a team. This is a mistake. You should not start with the people who are available and try to fit them into your situation. If you do, much of your time will be spent in discipling and managing your own team members. We are not forming playground pick-up teams like immature, elementary school kids. Our teams should be made up of professionals who are mature in the Lord and experienced in their trade or business. Professional sports teams do not accept just anybody. All teams have standards, and those who do not meet those standards are cut. Likewise, team leaders need to know what type of skills, gifts, faith, and character they desire in team members. Before you recruit people, prayerfully determine God's assignment for the team and the right kind of individuals necessary to complete His assignment. Then ask God to put you in contact with those kinds of people. If the people are not a good fit, God will open other opportunities for them. Good leaders know they cannot and should not lead everyone.

The team leader's foremost responsibility is the training of his team members. An effective leader enables and empowers his people and does not do the work for them. The team leader is responsible to see that people and resources are used in godly and effective ways for both the work at hand and for future opportunities. Team leaders should strive to form close bonds with each team member, especially those being discipled to become leaders.

In evaluating prospective team members, there are two criteria to observe while interacting with an applicant and his friends and co-workers. These criteria are a calling and a teachable spirit. We want to ensure God is the one leading the person to work in our ministry, people group, or team. If someone is called by God to the work and the team, they are not to quit of their own volition. As God led them to start working with us, God must be the one who stops. If someone is teachable, they can learn the skills they need for working in the business or doing the ministry. More importantly, if someone is teachable, we can work through whatever problems may arise. Team leaders must be ready to respond in biblical ways to conflicts and disputes which arise from having a diversity of gifts and perspectives on the team. One leader in SE Asia writes, "What eats away at our spiritual life and team unity is not the cultural trivia we haggle over, but the covert presence of attitudes such as jealousy, selfishness, pride, loving the life of luxury, or loving the approval of man."

When evaluating potential workers, it is important to look closely at their character. In getting references from others, do not ask solely what the applicant has done; rather, attempt to get to know who they are. If a referee does not know the applicant well, that is not a good sign. If a person has good character, he will probably be a good team member. Always choose character over competence. A top accountant may keep good records, but if he cheats or has a sharp temper, he will destroy the team or business. People with good character can be trained to be competent; however, people with good job skills are not necessarily trainable in their character. Another important characteristic to evaluate is zeal. Choose a zealous worker over a balanced one. Jesus did not live a balanced life. He missed meals, worked long hours, and was often up late at night. In addition, He regularly got up early to pray. Balance is not a biblical term. God often praises the zealous believer, but He never holds up the balanced believer as an example to others. Zealous people make things happen.

I evaluate applicants for our team in two ways; first, I ask them what the greatest failure in their spiritual life was. If they do not have one, I know they have not matured enough for what we are doing. God uses suffering and failure to build His servants. Those who have not had major failures are due for one, and you do not want that first failure to happen under your supervision. Failure is God's tool for maturing us, so those who have yet to experience major failures are probably in the beginning of God's maturing process. Second, I have applicants work for a day or a few hours with one of the nationals we employ or have discipled. If the national says, "I can work with this guy," that is a good sign. But if the national says, "He talks down to me" or "I cannot work with him," no matter what the applicant's credentials or experience, I will not accept him into the team. Our ultimate objective is to reproduce our lives in nationals who will make up the church. If an applicant does not have a humble and a learner's attitude, it is another sign he is not ready for a tentmaking ministry.

It is necessary for leaders to clarify to potential workers what their roles/jobs will be and what is expected of them by both the team and the mission before going overseas. I cannot over emphasize the value of each applicant visiting the field prior to committing to a team, ministry or organization. Personal visits to the field are helpful in allowing the applicant to accurately assess their ability to live and work in the culture and minister with the workers there. A brief field visit also provides an opportunity for the team leader to assess the potential worker and determine if he or she would be a good fit. If it is impossible to visit the field, be sure to meet with the person who will be the team leader/supervisor to discuss with them your goals and expectations. The team leader/supervisor knows the real needs and situation on the field. The leader has the best information and insights into the actual life and ministry you will experience. As a field leader, once an applicant has agreed to our team's Memorandum of Understanding (MOU) and mission policies and visited us on the field, I personally visit their home church. Such visits provide an opportunity to observe what the potential worker's life has been like, obtaining a true assessment of their job, ministry and relationships. The relationships I make with the church leaders often prove to be helpful when the workers encounter problems on the field. Expectations about the life, work, and ministry of the worker need to be communicated clearly to the church, as well as to the worker.

Team leaders need to talk regularly with team members about all areas of their life and work, as well as remain updated on their expectations. Encourage co-workers to share both blessings and struggles. The leader needs to model this in his life. Ask team members their opinions. Take time to relax together away from the job and the ministry. When team conflicts develop, it is normally due to one of two reasons: one, a lack of clear goals at the outset or a misunderstanding of those objectives, or two, a failure to review those goals regularly.

Dick Scoggins mentors many leaders working in the 10/40 Window. He has a helpful list of things potential team members should demonstrate. Scoggins writes, "Each team member must be able to:

Serve others
Manage time
Practice generosity
Submit to authority
Feed self spiritually
Devote self to prayer
Encourage teammates
Esteem fellow workers

Manage household well
Be financially responsible
Adapt to new circumstances
Seek and accept team counsel
Practice biblical peacemaking
Communicate with supporters
Embrace team values and norms
Give thanks in all circumstances
Persist in spite of no visible results
Forgive and be reconciled to others
Function in accountability structures
Use skills/talents/gifts to benefit team
Obtain residency in harmony with team
Contribute to team celebrations and fun
Sustain godly interpersonal relationships
Participate in team activities and training
Cooperate in team problem solving
Cultivate biblical marriage/family relationships

As leaders, we need to think through the various aspects of life and work of the team. There are a number of areas to consider. Many leaders are using covenants or MOUs to spell out in writing the vision, strategies, principles and practices of the team. Teams that are all within one organization should still write up a covenant that adheres to the mission's principles, and practices but clearly spells out the team's own principles, practices, distinctives and objectives. Sample covenants or MOUs may be obtained from www.opennetworkers.org. Some basic issues a leader should think through and may wish to write up in a MOU are listed in Appendix C.

Selecting a Team

There are basically three types of teams serving on the mission field. For simplicity, I will call them a volleyball team, soccer team, and track and field (athletic) team.

Volleyball players must work together. Teams that operate like volleyball teams live and work in close community. Each player knows one another's role: spikers spike and setters set. One person cannot play alone. Workers interact with one another almost daily—working and witnessing, praying and playing together. A team member's identity will be linked to their relationships with other team members. Personal goals and decisions are subservient and submitted to the good of the team. In places where a people group lives in close community, this approach appeals to their needs.

Soccer teams (football for our non-American friends) differ from volleyball teams. When on the field, soccer players may play as a team or as individuals. One or two players may have a tendency to hog the ball. During the match, some team members are running hard while others are resting. Soccer teams will have regular team functions, but in many activities (work, local friendships, discipling), individual team members may inform other members of what they are doing but act independently.

The third type of team is like a track and field team. The team members are of the same organization and may meet regularly, but basically they live, work, and minister apart from one another. Team members may know what other team members are doing, but they are not actively involved in one another's lives or ministries. Team members may be doing different ministries; one might be evangelizing via teaching English, another might be helping the blind in an NGO, and another may be discipling MBBs or setting up a Bible school. Each team member is independent, having his own friends and ministry goals.

I would strongly advise you to visit the field and the people with whom you are considering serving before making a long-term commitment. If a short-term ministry or internship is offered, take advantage of the opportunity to determine whether the people, location, team and mission are a good fit. A personal visit is a great way to discern God's leading and see how your gifts, skills, and personality match the situation. Even as you would investigate different job opportunities at home, thoroughly question and explore what God is doing with the agencies and missionaries you contact. Solomon tells us, "The heart of the discerning acquires knowledge" (Proverbs 18:15). Do not hesitate to ask questions, listen, be discerning, and pray. When investigating a team, it is also wise to ask questions of the workers you may be joining to better determine what kind of team they are and what kind of work they are doing. Ask for the workers' e-mail addresses and write to them. See if co-workers respond similarly or differently. That is a good way of deducing how closely the team members are interacting with one another. Discuss with them how they deal with interpersonal problems. In Appendix D, you will find a list of suggested questions to ask missionaries and leaders.

This should help you dig deeper so as to better understand what is happening on the field and to compare various opportunities.

Selecting a team is another reason you need to know yourself. A team is not a church, but like a church, it needs a variety of gifts and skills. In approaching a team/mission, know what your gifts and skills are. It is good to have a written testimony, curriculum vitae (CV), or resume. Having this information available will assist leaders to better advise you on the places or people that would be the best match for your ministry. Many new workers claim they prefer to join a volleyball style team. However, when they encounter the level of accountability, openness, and depth of relationships a volleyball team requires, many cannot handle it. Before evaluating teams, ask people who know you well which of the three types of teams would best suit you and then search for such a team.

International Teams

The research reflects that international teams are more effective than mono-ethnic teams. International teams have the blessing of a variety of people, backgrounds and cultures, which can contribute to broadening the understanding and practices of the team. International teams normally lead members to more thoroughly evaluate their own cultural perspectives, causing workers to better understand their own cultural outlook. This gives the team members a greater appreciation of the benefits of cultural diversity. This understanding of differences within the team will carry over into relationships with nationals, resulting in a greater openness towards learning and applying new ideas. Having diverse nationalities creates opportunities within the community as well. Differing backgrounds and races enable us to show a different face of Jesus to our non-believing friends.

Being a member of an international team raises several issues which need to be carefully considered. The first issue, one that makes an international team special, is the language difference. People cannot communicate their innermost desires, considerations, and feelings as fast and as freely as they could if team meetings were in their native language. Though everyone has learned a common language, everything takes longer and is less refined in its expression. Misunderstandings are common. This lack of fluency in expressing oneself does have an impact on the cohesion of the team. Team leaders should not underestimate this issue. People who are unable to express themselves easily become disenchanted and frustrated. Some teams use the local language, or allow freedom of expression in any language. English may be the lingua franca of the 21st century, but for some Asians and Africans, English may be their third or fourth language, meaning they may know the local language better than English. In such cases, team meetings could be bi-lingual. Team members may be encouraged to pray and worship in whatever language they feel most comfortable.

With the different languages come cultural differences. A further barrier that is more easily addressed is that of social custom. The observance of social rules is significant for us to feel comfortable when interacting with others. If two people have different sets of social rules that make them feel comfortable, the result will be discomfort for both. For example, a German team member might challenge what an Asian worker said in order to clarify communication, but this challenge may be interpreted by the Asian as an insult. In such situations, do not be afraid to explain to others, "This is my culture." It helps the others to understand you and how best to communicate with you and with one another.

Understanding and respecting a variety of social customs within one team can build bridges, help communication, and encourage co-operation, which will serve as a witness to the surrounding community. Teams of diverse nationalities readily model cross-cultural love. To our non-believing friends, Christianity is no longer western but multicultural. It is not uncommon for friends to ask me, "Why are you a friend of this Filipino?" When we tell them that in Jesus there is no East or West, or how Jesus' love extends beyond culture, doors open to share deeper things.

Another issue is finances. Many workers—Australians, Dutch, Filipinos, Latinos and Africans—find it more difficult to raise money than Americans, British, Koreans and Singaporeans. Teams that operate viable businesses may employ these workers or consider how to subsidize them. In addition, compared to their Latino, African, and Asian co-workers, the western team members may seem to be living at a much higher level. Non-westerners need to understand that while they are sacrificing to be overseas; their standard of living is much the same as it was in their home country. However, for many westerners, though they appear to have more, their standard of living overseas is often much lower than what it would be at home. Within the team, some expenses, such as printing evangelistic materials or parties for non-believers, may be "team expenses." It is wise to discuss and resolve financial issues concerning standards of living, team expenses, personal needs, etc., before people move into a team setting.

On a multi-cultural team, it is important to be aware of how each culture reveres hierarchy. In some cultures, people listen to superiors very carefully before they express an opinion. Studies show that people from Russia, China, and Indonesia have a high regard for hierarchy. Other cultures, such as the Dutch, Australians, and Germans, revere equality. Those differences will manifest themselves in the ways individuals take initiative within the team.

Another fundamental cultural element involves the notion of high-context versus low-context communication. Low-context cultures, notably American, Northern European, and Australian, use language very precisely. Language is the principal means of communication. This is in contrast to high-context cultures like Japan, China, Latin America, and India. There, the major component of communication is in the context: people's surroundings, past and present events, and relationships. These cultures want to build a relationship first, and then they will trust. Thus, it is helpful for international teams to invest time in team bonding.

Each international team should create a leadership team of more than one nationality. The intertwining of cultural mindsets produces a new mélange which significantly changes the way the team needs to be managed. This leadership team should be capable of absorbing, reflecting, and working through the cultural aspects and challenges facing the team. A team of leaders is better equipped to understand the different cultural angles during the most critical phases of adjustment and can offer adequate steps to overcome hurdles. One person acting as the leader may be biased to his own cultural ways or may be regarded as being biased, without being aware of it. With varying languages and cultures, the chances of misunderstandings are greater. This is another reason why it is extremely important that your expectations, as well as those of the team leader, are clarified before going overseas. It is suggested that the discussion concerning expectations of a worker be done in the presence of the worker's pastor or a third party who knows both cultures well. This will surely reduce, though not eliminate, the chances for future misunderstandings.

One worker explains his situation, "Many TLs [team leaders] obviously don't recognise that cross-cultural team issues within the team are as important as the issues of the entire team embracing the new culture. Coming from the 'down under' part of the world means that we are often the minority in a cross-cultural team, and this usually means we are the ones who are expected to give up our culture. People have returned from the field because of the impossibility of making all the necessary concessions." The whole concept of teamwork will vary considerably from one culture to another. Asian cultures may view teamwork as a number of people working in a team under a directive team leader. Americans see teamwork more on a consensus basis. The Dutch are also consensus oriented, but prefer to talk about team issues as a group. Asians tend to support the leaders' ideas. If you ask for their input, they also expect you to act upon it. If the facts are inconsistent with their advice, you are expected to trust the relationship, rather than what appear to be the facts. Teams which have a plurality of leaders will solve many of these misunderstandings as they arise. Having had as many as nine nationalities on our team over the years, I feel the benefits of having an international team vastly outweigh the difficulties.

National Team Members

When inviting nationals to be a part of the team, it is important that they understand the team's values and strategies. Having a written MOU is helpful, but realize there will still be misunderstandings. Clarify how decisions will be made. It is helpful that nationals understand their recourse, should they have a disagreement with the leader.

Westerners are conceptualizers. It is our tendency to draw up concepts, which Arabs and Asians may need time to understand. Give the nationals time to act; allow them to be responsible for the duties they are assigned. Allow them to prove themselves. Do not be afraid to let them fail.

Supporting national Christians to work with you is a highly controversial subject. I have experienced both successes and failures. Failures came in two varieties. There were those who, over time, revealed their motives for joining the ministry were primarily to have a job and make money. If there was no salary, they quit doing ministry. The other failure was national team members rebelling because they did not agree with our contextualized approach or church planting strategy. The latter is actually more difficult, as you will wish to enable the worker for the task without compromising your team's principles and practices. It is good to regularly review objectives, methods, and strategies with the national workers.

In evaluating national workers for the team, study their past. Talk with those who know them well. Do they have a history of doing the type of ministry you are doing? If not, test them. Offer them a six month probationary period and evaluate how they do. Discern with them what exactly God is calling them to do. Will they still serve, even if they are not paid? Over time you can begin to reimburse them for their materials or transportation, gradually increasing the amount to include other items, such as food, lodging, medical bills, etc.

National workers who join the team will need an acceptable identity within the community. "Christian worker" or "evangelist" will probably be an unacceptable title or role. You may need to create a job where they will have an identity which can help with their support. This should not be a "cover" or fake job. Working a job is particularly useful in a pioneer setting. Even a part-time job models industriousness to new believers and helps them discipline their time. This job may be within your own place of employment or elsewhere, though elsewhere is preferable. Consider carefully the pros and cons of employing national workers for your own business or NGO, as it may imply to others that if they convert, you will also provide them with a job.

If the national workers do not wish to be employed, they should be required to raise their own support. Supporting and hiring nationals is discussed in Chapter 11. It is pivotal that the nationals clearly understand how they will be paid. National workers need to grasp that the team leader follows Jesus Christ, not people (1 Corinthians 11:1). Jehovah Jireh is Our Provider. Just as the leader trusts God to meet his personal needs, so the team members are to trust in God and not friends, churches, or the leader to meet their needs. In cases where team members (expatriates or nationals) receive different salaries, the reasons for those differences must be clarified to all. When supported, national team members should be paid by the team leader. Though the funds may come from a church or mission organization, most nationals see their paymaster as the authority figure to whom they are accountable. As one Indian working in a church in New Dehli so aptly stated, "I am paid by the churches in Singapore. Why do I need to listen to the pastor?"

When starting out, we need to come alongside our national co-workers with humility. They need to see us modeling the ministry they are to do before they can do it well themselves. Often our objective is to turn over the operations of a ministry to the national. In such cases, ensure ample time is invested: explain, model, and evaluate their performance before completely turning over leadership. In many cultures, it is common for people to assure you that they can do the job when they cannot. Watch and give guidance and encouragement before giving responsibility. When people are equipped and confident, they will perform better.

National workers who have backgrounds other than your focus people group will be familiar with the strategies they have used in their churches among their own peoples. Many will not be comfortable with contextualization or identifying with the locals you are reaching. Time is needed to train workers in contextualization and the reasons for the methods the team seeks to implement. It is not uncommon for new workers to complete the training requested of them only to do their own thing once they have been accepted onto the team. As locals with good language skills, they often believe they know better than the foreigner. In such cases, you need to clarify that this is not an issue of who is right or wrong, but of honesty and faithfulness in abiding by agreed upon team strategies and principles. This is a big reason why having a team MOU is helpful, as it clarifies the objectives and methodologies of the team.

In cases where the national does not agree or feel comfortable, he should be promptly, but graciously, encouraged to leave the team. It is wise to offer all potential national workers a six month probation, beginning from the time their language studies are finished. This allows time to discern their calling and their compatibility for working with the team.

When considering inviting both nationals and expatriates onto the team, remember that character is more important than competency and that experienced people are never as effective as passionate people. How do you determine a person's character in a brief interview? One method I use is during the interview process, I will ask, "If you were given $10,000 and told you must use it all within one day or return it, what would you do?" How they respond tells you reams about their character. For example, consider what they would buy. Question their reasons for buying those things. Also, did they offer to give any of the money away? Those who offer to give some of it to help others are probably generous and of good character. During the interview, I will ask about their community service and experiences with handling money: Have you ever been under-charged? What did you do with the money? etc.

Clarifying the team's philosophy of ministry cannot be overemphasized. Christian background believers (CBBs) from nearby people groups may have good language skills for winning the people being reached, but often they will have cultural prejudices as well. We need to discuss these prejudices, lifestyle differences, the use of Christian terminology, the colonial mentality, and salary differences. Who is the real enemy? Religion (Buddhism, Hinduism, Islam) or the people? What is the church? And, what will be done if persecution comes?

God's Team

God's team is a term that is used to describe all workers from various organizations who reside and work in the same city and have compatible ministry objectives. Some organizations/teams work closely with other organizations/teams, while some barely acknowledge one another's existence. As far as honoring God in relationships with God's team within the same city or people group, each of us should do as His Spirit leads. Often the Master gives us different businesses, security concerns, church planting strategies, or contextualization objectives, making it difficult to work alongside one another. In such cases, neither should compromise His leading, yet there should never be any animosity between ministries nor criticism of each other. We must recognize and honor one another's calling. One worker in Indonesia whose team has a contextualized (C-5) approach writes, "the best thing for us is to work in parallel, rather than together [with the other mission who is C-3]. . . . If the other workers run across anyone who only knows the local dialect (not the trade language), but is spiritually hungry, they send him our way; if we find someone who prefers to interact in the trade language, or in a more western setting, we'll put him in contact with them." Workers need freedom to follow God's leading for their ministry without the pressure of capitulating to the leading He has given others. More than one approach is needed for reaching a city or people group; sometimes cooperating closely enhances our approaches. However, there are situations where cooperation may jeopardize a ministry. In such cases, it is okay to admit God's leading is different and encourage and respect one another as you work separately.

LEADERSHIP

"A leader takes people where they want to go. A great leader takes people where they don't necessarily want to go, but ought to be."

ROSALYNN CARTER

Tentmakers need to be leaders and under leadership. Leaders are decision makers. My mentor often reminds me, "The most vital task of a leader is to ensure that his people are perpetually learning." We must guide and ensure our workers are continually upgrading in their business skills, character, competency, and community, and we must be doing the same. Sometimes we need to be like mother hens, watching our workers every move, and sometimes we need to give them a long leash. Leaders need to encourage both employees and team members to make decisions not requiring constant approval. As long as the team is accomplishing their objectives of profitability and evangelism, it is wise to maintain a wide window of indifference. Encourage workers to make mistakes. It is vital for team members to have the freedom to share their problems and opinions without fear. Colin Powell writes,

"Leadership is solving problems. The day soldiers stop bringing you their problems is the day you have stopped leading them. They have either lost confidence that you can help them or concluded you do not care. Either case is failure of leadership."[60]

Loyalty does not mean always agreeing with the leader; rather, it means stating an honest opinion for the good of the leader and the team. Leaders need to know if there are questions or problems. It is better to hear about them too early than too late. Discussion, debate, and even arguing can spur us to better things (Hebrews 10:25). But once a course of action has been decided, the debate ends, and each team member should be expected to own and act on the decision as if it were his or her own.

In listing the most desirable qualities in a team leader, the top three are humility, honesty, and a willingness to sacrifice for the team. It is also important that our employees and team members know we love them and will always be available in times of need. It is true that real leaders lead a lonely life. If you need to please people, leadership will ultimately be a burden to you. Leaders must make decisions, no matter how unpleasant. When you do, you win the gratitude of those who were bearing up under the difficult situation. We cannot allow the work or others to suffer for the sake of one person's feelings. Leaders cannot fear making people angry. Jesus made many people angry. Why? Simply because His standard was perfection, and nobody likes a perfectionist. I remind our team that Jesus is the leader of our team and the CEO of our businesses. If your standards are different than His, don't join our team or work in our businesses. Hurting people's feelings has saved many from hell. Encourage fun times. Regularly check to ensure all your workers enjoy their jobs and are aware of God's hand in the work they are doing.

Tentmakers need to be under leadership and accountable to someone who has the authority to rebuke and correct us, as well as train us in righteousness. In choosing a mentor, look for someone who creates opportunities for you to learn and stretch your faith. In selecting a team leader, does the leader have a vision for what God wants him to accomplish and clear goals for fulfilling that vision? Only insecure leaders need to chase the latest management fads. In selecting a leader, ask around to learn how he responds to criticism or how he reacts when you disagree with him. How does he make decisions? Alone or by consensus? Too quickly or too slowly? Do his team members feel loved? Do they feel the leader sacrifices for them? Does he create chances for employees to grow and stretch themselves? Is he also under authority?

In ministry, unlike most businesses, we often have a choice of who we work for. Take advantage of this, and get to know the field leaders before committing to work with them. Make certain they are God's best for you. And if your mission assigns you to a leader who is not helpful, request permission to seek an outside mentor for the areas you need help in.

Tentmaking Leaders

Tentmaking leaders need double vision, a vision for building their ministry and a vision for building their business or NGO. As tentmakers, we need to know ourselves. We need to know our leadership strengths and weaknesses, such as: business start up, business management, team leading, pastoral care, vision, etc. Some people are born leaders and will excel in many areas, but that is the exception, not the rule. In addition to the normal leadership qualities, there are three areas of leadership which are especially important to tentmaking leaders: zeal or passion, a servant heart, and an entrepreneurial spirit.

Passion, be it for God, the lost, or business, cannot be manufactured or learned at a weekend seminar. Passion is a God thing. Often the difference between winning and losing, making a sale, or getting the gospel out is an inner zealous drive to see the task done and done well. If you lack passion, you may be a great manager but never a great leader. Jack Welch writes, "If there's one characteristic all winners share, it's that they care more than anyone else. No detail is too small to sweat or too large to dream."[61] In Proverbs 23:17 and Romans 12:11, we are commanded to be zealous for God. But how do we manufacture zeal? There is no special program to attend or book to read (though some authors may insist otherwise). As our hearts are given over to God, so our passion must originate in Him. Thus, if you lack zeal, diligently seek the face of God and ask Him to build zeal into you. Find people who are passionate about the things that interest you; offer to work with them and learn from them. As with Elisha and Elijah (2 Kings 2:9f), entreat the Lord to pass their zeal into your heart. Zealous, passionate people are unstoppable. They do not quit until their passion is fulfilled.

Tentmaking leaders need to be servants. The business world honors wealth, fame, and power, while Jesus honors sacrifice, meekness, and humility. These diametrically opposed approaches to life are at the root of many Christian leaders' distrust of tentmakers. Tentmaking leaders must be quick to go the second mile: understanding how to lead with grace, while counting those we are leading as better than ourselves (Philippians 2:3). Leaders must appreciate the differences in our people's gifts and talents, knowing how to mix and direct the efforts of each worker to build up the business or ministry and to enhance productivity. Leaders also need to understand that their role is to help and support employees. Effective leadership provides active support to the critical goal of employee satisfaction and enrichment. This includes striving to develop an environment under which both employees and team members can grow and flourish. There will be times when ministry goals and business goals are in conflict. Tentmaking leaders must have clear objectives and the strength to implement those objectives, sometimes in the face of ridicule or monetary losses.

Rick Love, the international director of Frontiers, a tentmaking mission that plants churches among Muslims, instructs leaders in how to be biblical servant leaders,

> "A careful analysis of the leadership qualifications in 1 Timothy 3 and Titus 1 indicate that overseers are evaluated in four broad areas: leaders must manage their households well, teach sound doctrine, reflect self mastery and be team players. Numerous words in the qualifications listed in Scripture point to the priority of leaders being team players. Leaders must be hospitable (that is, focused on meeting the needs of others). They cannot be violent or quarrelsome (which destroys team life). Instead they must be gentle and peaceable (characteristics that build team life)."[62]

Jesus reflected vulnerability in His leadership. His disciples were not with Him during His temptations, but He must have shared that with them because it is recorded. Servant leaders do not need to be in control or always be right. We should not be afraid to share our weaknesses. A leader should be willing to lay down his or her life for those who follow.

Tentmaking leaders should be entrepreneurs, willing to take risks and try new ways of doing things. An entrepreneur sees the big picture and understands how everything fits together. Entrepreneurial leaders see things that others cannot. Our passion drives us to make our vision happen so that others can see what we see. Entrepreneurs generally do not need to attend leadership seminars to get ideas; they just know where they want to go and how to get there.

> "'One reason entrepreneurs—the ones most likely to make it, at least—behave like men and women possessed is that they have

experienced a flash of understanding known as *entrepreneurial insight*," says professor Ian C. MacMillan—a guru of entrepreneurship at the Wharton School who has counseled innumerable startup wannabes. They have seen, in their mind's eye, the better mousetrap, the great unmet need, the changing tide, the big opportunity. Because they see it so clearly, they feel they know exactly what must be done to prevail."[63]

In choosing to work under a leader, seek out someone who is passionate for what God has placed on your heart. Look for a servant, as well as an entrepreneur, who will speak truth into your life.

For New Leaders

It is noble to aspire to be a leader (1Timothy 3:1). But it is important never to take leadership lightly or to do it for personal reasons. Leaders are responsible before God for their decisions and the impact those decisions have on their people (Hebrews 13:17), and leaders will be judged by higher standards (James 3:1). If you sense God is asking you to lead, but you have not had much previous experience, tell your leader of your desire, asking what areas he feels you need to work on. If you are new to the work, give yourself at least two years to sit at his feet to watch and learn.

A good leader first learns how to follow. Take on a variety of tasks and roles to round out your background. Volunteer for assignments that are outside your comfort zone which will stretch your faith. Taking such steps will in time build up your confidence in God's ability to work through you. Increased confidence gives courage to extend yourself into new areas. It encourages you take greater risks and achieve far more than you might think you have the ability or faith to accomplish. A developing leader will often struggle with someone who is in authority over him. This struggle is critical to learning what authority is and the need to submit to authority. A good leader is first a good follower.

Rick Love writes, "One of the reasons leaders do not finish well over a lifetime of ministry is because they plateau. Routines turn into ruts. The wear and tear of ministry makes leaders shift to automatic pilot. This is a dangerous place to be. So we need to become intentional and proactive to break out of ruts and stay on a healthy growth curve."[64] How do we avoid the rust and ruts of life? A prime deterrent is planning ahead. It is amazing the number of leaders who have plans for the growth and discipleship of their team members but no plans for their own personal growth. We need to plan and make time for growth projects in our lives. Break down your life into the major areas in which you move and work. Then ask yourself two questions. "Am I eager for coaching and upgrading in these areas?" And, "What are some ways and who are the people who could stretch and challenge me in these areas?" Areas to consider are spiritual/discipleship, missiological/outreach, team/fellowship, family/marriage, business/tentmaking, character building and more. Once you have areas in mind, seek out mentors who are older and more experienced who can regularly speak into your life. Invite these people to spend time with you at your expense so that you can sit at their feet and learn.

God's work will not advance without leaders. Building a business, NGO, school, or church is not accomplished by chance. Success is by grace, the result of godly leadership and disciplined management. Leaders must set the example. The higher the level of leadership, the more spiritually mature we must be.

ACCOUNTABILITY

"Every man is as lazy as he dares to be."
EMERSON

Emerson had it right. People do not do what is expected; we do what is inspected. Phil Parshall, after forty years of serving among Muslims, said to me, "I have my doubts about tentmaking . . . most tentmakers I know start out doing business and ministry, but in the end it is all business and no ministry."

Everyone receives gratification from accomplishing tasks. Whether we are building a bridge or cleaning out the garage, we enjoy seeing the fruits of our labors. Productivity makes us feel good. It gives us value and a sense of worth. Those people groups which are still without a church in the 21st century are unreached for a reason—they are difficult to reach! Missionary work among these peoples has produced precious little fruit. Tentmakers, by definition, have two tasks to do. If one task is producing fruit and the other is not, it is easy to gravitate toward the more productive, fruitful task. Therefore, it is important that every tentmaker is under some structure or relationship which provides the needed accountability to keep us growing and active in fulfilling both of our callings.

Harold, a tentmaking facilitator with Operation Mobilization, shares his experience.

"The major concern of those working with workers in the Middle East is not recruiting them. We praise God for the upswing in prayer and interest in the Muslim world. No, our major concern is on-site effectiveness! On a recent visit to Morocco, where there are an estimated 80 envoys [tentmakers] with 10 different groups, one 'expert' said that he estimated that less than 10 percent of these were having an effective ministry in church-planting!"[65]

How do we do better in keeping our focus? In a word—accountability. Tentmakers need to find mentors who will hold them accountable to their ministry objectives. Many churches and workers believe that if a tentmaker joins a reputable mission organization, the organization will hold the tentmaker accountable to doing ministry. Unfortunately, often this is not the case. Many organizations, like many churches, have poor systems of accountability. Church leaders and regular missionaries lean toward the philosophy of "you don't ask me and I won't ask you." In addition, regular missionaries have no "box" for tentmakers. If the tentmaker pleads he is too busy starting the business to do language learning or too busy doing year-end accounts to log hours with the people, his mission supervisors back off as they know they do not understand the stresses and strains tentmakers face. As a result, we pretty much get to call our own shots. No wonder many believe tentmakers do not plant churches. Once you learn the teacher does not collect the homework, you stop doing the homework. No one likes homework, but a lack of accountability, like a lack of homework, only increases our potential for failure when the real test comes along.

I love the Charlie Brown cartoon where Charlie is shooting arrows into a fence and then going over and painting a bull's eye around each arrow. When Lucy sees what he is doing, she exclaims, "That's not the way to do it!" To which Charlie replies, "It's the only way I can hit the target." Phil Lundman, chairman of Petersen Automotive Industries, accurately points out, "Every organization needs support, accountability, and imposed consequences. But biblical discipline is lacking, if not invisible in most mission organizations."

Tentmakers must strive for more accountability. The research tells us that 67 percent of the workers are being held accountable quarterly or less. This is encouraging, but less than 50 percent of all workers set goals. If we have no measurable goals, how can we be held accountable? How can we be walking in faith if we are not trusting God for specific things? It is a Charlie Brown approach to ministry—whatever we do will be a bull's eye. In setting goals, there should be imposed consequences for not meeting the goals. There are two fundamental factors for improving our accountability structures: godly mentors and godly goal setting.

Mentors

Most tentmakers fail for one of three reasons: loss of focus, loss of balance, or they burn themselves out. All three of these problems are readily solved by having a mentor in our lives. A mentor must be able, experienced, and tell it to us straight.

Mentoring comes from the Greek word meaning "enduring." It is defined as a sustained relationship between a youth and an adult. Thus, a mentor is someone who is at least one step further down the path than you are. A mentor provides support, counsel, friendship, reinforcement and constructive example. Mentors are good listeners, people who care, and who freely share their successes and failures. Mentors are leaders who want to help bring out the strengths that are already there and strengthen your weaknesses. Mentors want God's best for you.

The wisest man who ever lived wrote, "Plans fail for lack of counsel, but with many advisers they succeed."[66] Mentoring is important because with each mentor we have, we multiply our thought input. There are opportunities that we may be blind to because we assume there is only one way of doing things. Mentors should be experienced in the areas we seek help in. Thus, at times we may have more than one mentor. Currently, I have a business mentor and a church planting mentor. Both men also hold me accountable in my character, spiritual walk, and family life. For ministry and business mentors, my wife and I always seek out mentoring couples where the wife is equally involved in the life of my wife.

Most people are too afraid of failure. Mentors need to give us room to fail. Yet if we stop and think, the majority of us would agree that our most important learning experiences often are the result of failure. One of the reasons mature people stop growing and learning is that they become less and less willing to risk failure. We forget that much of what we call experience or wisdom was learned from our failures. If you are going to grow as an entrepreneur and leader, a good mentor will help you learn to fail successfully, discerning with you God's mind for the trials and tests you face. The best church planting teams are impelled forward by a mentoring structure which is relationally centered, decentralized, non-controlling, and encourages flexibility, creativity, and entrepreneurialism. In addition, any mentoring structure needs to include and nurture real accountability so as to maintain high standards of leadership, which then is reproduced and passed on to the leader's teams and the churches they plant.

How do you find a mentor? Approach someone you respect who would be helpful to you in the areas you need strengthening in. Do not allow your perception that they are "too busy" to deter you from asking. Ask if he would consider being your mentor. Let him know why you selected him and what you hope to learn from him. Discuss your expectations and the amount of time you expect it will take. The problem will not be in finding someone interested in working with you. There are many people who want to mentor teachable zealots who are on the cutting edge of missions. The problem will be in finding people with the skills you need who can really sharpen you. Prayerfully determine in advance which skills you lack; talk openly and honestly about what you are looking for in a mentor and ask the potential mentor what he or she would be looking for in a trainee. It is wise to establish a trial period for the relationship, after which you will both evaluate the desirability of continuing.

Setting Goals

In Matthew 4:19, Jesus says, "Follow me." Where was He going? Did He have any idea? Obviously, He did. From Luke 10 we can see that He gave the disciples specific plans before He sent them out. In 2 Timothy 2:2, Paul says, "And the things you have heard me say in the presence of many witnesses entrust to reliable men who will also be qualified to teach others." So what did Timothy teach? Did he have a plan, or did he lead by feelings or guessing? I believe he had a detailed plan for each person he was accountable to before God (Hebrews 13:17). Proverbs 14:12 says, "A man's mind plans his way but the Lord directs his steps." Truly, God is sovereign over all things. Yet He is the one who has called us to be where we are. Therefore, He is the one who holds us accountable for our obedience in fulfilling the work He has sent us to do. Goals are not meant to be legalistic straitjackets but maps to help us know the way. There will be detours, so flexibility is a must. However, we need a goal, a specific purpose to work towards. Structure through goals helps to achieve this. Goals are aids to success in Christ's work.

All ministries exist to achieve results. However, some Christians are inclined to think of setting goals as worldly and lacking faith. But which requires more faith? To tell people the Lord is leading me to Timbuktu to witness for Christ, or the Lord is leading me to Timbuktu to plant two house churches among the Tuareg people within the next seven years?

The latter is a measurable goal. Whenever we ask people why they do what they do, they will talk about what they want to happen as a result of their ministry. Those hoped-for results are goals. We need to work together to quantify and qualify our hoped-for results. In His Spirit, we need to set a target at which we may aim our faith.

In taking my motorcycle driving test, I had to complete an obstacle course. One of the obstacles was to drive the length of a thirty foot plank that was eight inches wide. In practicing, I would invariably get all the way across the plank with my front wheel, only to have my back wheel come off the plank inches from success. I could never get it right until an instructor told me, "Focus on a spot six yards beyond the end of the plank and drive for that point." I did that, and the rear tire never went off the plank.

Goal setting needs to have SMARTS: Specific, Measurable, Active, Realistic, Time limited, and Stretch us. Goals need to be *specific*. If we are going to be accountable, we need to know where we are going. If you went to a church and told them, "I am planning to serve God overseas, but I do not know where I am going, or what I'll be doing, or how I'll being doing it," do you think the church would support you? Yet, once overseas, many tentmakers lose focus. Our big picture goals remain the big picture. We need to learn to plan specific steps which will put us on track to complete our big picture goals. Goals need to be *measurable*. You should know whether or not the goal has been accomplished. Goals also need to be *active*. A goal should show growth from one point in your life to another. It must be something bigger than myself that requires God's intervention. I am going to Timbuktu to start two house churches among the Tuareg people in the next seven years is both measurable and it is active. Goals need to be *realistic*. Goals should be attainable, not pie in the sky dreams. Start small, and work your way up. Jesus Himself established the principle that a person must be proven faithful in the little things before being entrusted with much (Luke 16:10). Make sure the goal you are working for is something you really want, not just something that sounds good. Goals need to be set within a defined period of *time*. It does little good to have measurable goals if we have an open-ended time frame. Finally, goals should require a *stretch* of faith. Jesus' statement, "you have not, because you ask not," has a parallel in much of life in the reality that "you attain little because you attempt little." Goals should push us out of our comfort zone. We should not be content with simply doing what we already can do, but as William Carey put it, "Expect great things from God; attempt great things for God."

A business which is ignored tends to hold itself accountable in that it will go bankrupt, but not so with a ministry. In all tentmaking ministries, there is the danger of becoming unbalanced, either giving too much time to the business and none to the ministry or all to ministry and none to the business. It is too easy to slide into the busyness of business where we can receive instant gratification while losing our ministry focus. Such imbalance results in a deferred glory being given to our Lord.

Jesus preached about the dangers of becoming preoccupied with work and the gratification it brings. He told the rich young ruler to sell all he owned and give the money to the poor. Early believers put a much greater stress on personal salvation than they did analyzing market trends and planning budgets. Does that mean these things are wrong? No, yet we need to remember to practice His presence with our God-given priorities. All of us, no exceptions, hit the wall from time to time. To overcome rejection, depression and discouragement, and for help with a hostile business environment or team member, a mentor can be a huge help. Proverbs tells us to "get wisdom" (Proverbs 4:7). Someone who regularly checks us on our goals provides wisdom, ensuring we stay on God's path.

SUMMARY

Prayer, fasting, and a good devotional life are pertinent to the success of the tentmaker. We need to have a consistent walk with God before moving overseas. Partnering with other co-workers who are of a like mind will enhance our effectiveness. International teams are more effective. Good leadership does not just happen. We should seek out leaders who will disciple and mentor us in the areas we need to grow. We need to plan ahead, thinking through what we expect life, ministry, team life, and leadership to be like overseas.

ACTION STEPS

- Recruit at least twenty-five people who will pray for you regularly. Commit yourself to sending them prayer requests each month.

- How would you evaluate your prayer life? What changes should you make?

- How would you evaluate your fasting? What do you need to learn about fasting?

- List the characteristics you believe should be in a good team member. Compare it to Scoggins' list. Are these areas in your own life?

- Ask two friends and your father (women, your mother) to evaluate your life against Scoggins' list.
- Is there a team you can join (sports, music, work, ministry) that can help you grow in your team skills?
- Ask three people at church and at work what leadership areas you need to grow in. Then seek out people who can help you mature in these areas.
- Who is currently holding you accountable in your daily quiet time? What you look at on TV or on the computer? Your family life? Your current ministry outreach?
- Write down the names of three people who might mentor you in work and/or ministry and talk to them about keeping you accountable.
- Write to several field team leaders for references and their teams' MOUs.
- Write out your goals for the next five years and the measurable steps that are necessary to accomplish those goals.
- If character is more important than passion, how would you rate your character? Your passion? What steps can you take to increase your passion for God? The lost?
- Consider the advantages and disadvantages of being part of an international team.

"Most churches are keepers of the aquarium, not fishers of men."

As iron sharpens iron, so one man sharpens another.

PROVERBS 27:17

chapter 10
FELLOWSHIP ON
AND OFF THE FIELD

SENDING CHURCH RELATIONSHIPS

Tentmakers are at the forefront of the greatest spiritual battle. Military troops in the frontlines of a military campaign need up to eight times their number in supporting roles. In the same way, tentmakers need a committed team to keep them adequately encouraged and supplied as they move God's kingdom forward. A solid sending church is needed for the tentmaker's well-being. The biggest roles of the sending church are prayer and encouragement. Nearly 100 percent of the workers surveyed reported that their "home church supports their ministry in prayer." Almost 60 percent of those workers receive letters or care packages from their friends or churches on a monthly basis. Packages with special foods, magazines, or other items from home are sure to uplift the worker.

Before heading overseas, tentmakers should invest at least a few months serving in a church. This period of service increases your understanding of how the church operates, solidifies relationships with the church leaders, and enables others to observe your ministry skills. In addition, you can begin to recruit prayer partners and mentors who can guide you in your overseas business and ministry.

Many churches need help understanding what tentmaking is all about. Some churches may not perceive a tentmaker to even be a missionary. As tentmakers are a sub-category of missions, like strategic coordinators, missionary doctors, etc., this should not be difficult. Yet the church does need to understand the various roles and distinctions between tentmaking and regular missionary work. One former worker shares his experience,

"When we left our church to carry out our vision, people remarked that we were no longer walking by faith now that we had registered a company! Whereas in fact we had just lost the complete life support system of our (mission) group! Even our home churches dropped our support since we did not fit in any of their mission categories."[67]

Some tentmakers negotiate a MOU or ministry agreement with their church. This is a set of guidelines drawn up with the home church, the mission agency (if one is involved), sometimes the employer or team, and the tentmaker. The agreement details expectations of the parties involved. It includes the areas of communication, job expectations, steps for resolving conflicts, prayer, financial support, pastoral care, and emergency procedures such as would be needed in case of a serious medical illness. Such agreements are helpful in solidifying the home church's commitment to the tentmaker and what is to be expected of the parties involved.

Communicating with the Church

Communication is basic to so many aspects of the church and its relationship with the tentmaker. Proverbs tells us, "Faithful messengers are as refreshing as snow in the heat of summer. They revive the spirit of their employer."[68] If people are going to pray diligently and intelligently they need to know what to pray for. If we expect churches to support us, they need to know how their money is being invested. Communication revives the spirit. In the 21st century, with e-mail, chat rooms, cheap phone rates, faxes, and express mail, there is no excuse for not communicating.

Tentmakers should be required to send their churches and supporters a bi-monthly or monthly prayer letter. Secure, monthly communication is doable. Personally, in twenty-one years overseas, we have never missed a month of sending a prayer letter. Audio visuals or other enhanced communication can be sent annually or as requested. Teams can make available a video or CD of the work at least every other year. With digital cameras and all the video equipment available to us, only security issues should limit our communication. Detailed goals and financial statements should be made available upon request. Such tools keep people current with His work in and through us, spurring the support team on in their prayers and ministries for us at home.

Though often there is much fanfare in the sending out of a worker, after a few months, with hardly any communication from home, it is easy to feel alone and forgotten. "Out of sight, out of mind" becomes more than just a cliché. How can you ensure that people on your home team stay involved? Here are four ideas:

1. Adopt an adult group

Visit small groups or adult Sunday School classes within the church and share God's vision for your work. Tell them you wish to adopt them as a support group. Give them some ideas of how they can pray and encourage you once you are gone. Commit yourself to sending monthly updates and prayer requests. Give them a list of treats, magazines, or other items they can send your family.

2. Start a prayer group

Before departing overseas, gather a group of people (monthly, bimonthly or quarterly) to pray for missions. Mentor this group concerning the people group you will be serving, your expected needs, and your ministry. Encourage them to meet and pray regularly for the people and your ministry needs. Recruit a champion who will gather the group as agreed and facilitate praying for your ministry after you have left. Groups become fun events for regular attendees, and their ministry of prayer will bless your ministry.

3. Encourage visits

Most agencies discourage having visitors the first one or two years to avoid distractions while bonding with the people and finishing your language studies. This is a wise practice. However, after a couple of years, encourage your family, church leaders, and friends to come to visit you.

4. Invite short-term workers

Nothing solidifies a church's commitment to you more than a personal visit. Request that some church members or an adult group visit and do a project with you for one to four weeks. If there is no construction work to be done, have them teach English or computers in the neighborhood. Some church members may have skills like accounting or computers that could be put to use in your office or NGO. The depth of ministry is not important; the people's visit will be enough for God to open hearts and touch lives.

THE NATIONAL CHURCH

Before we determine missiological strategies for fellowship, we should consider what the Bible says. The Bible is clear that we are to fellowship with one another (Hebrews 10:24–25, Galatians 6:10). Fellowship is as important to our spiritual life as exercise is for our bodies. We are to show love and practice the "one anothers," including living in unity with one another (Philippians 2:2, Ecclesiastes 4:9–10). Through the church, we are to be fed, encouraged, held accountable, etc. As believers, we are one body in Christ (1 Corinthians 12:12–31). As tentmakers, there are usually four options available to our family for fellowship and worship on the field: the new believers' fellowship (consisting of the believers we are ministering to), the national church (consisting of nationals from the nearby reached people group), the international church, and a private God's team worship service (made up of like-minded workers).

The first option is to attend the fellowship or church which the believers we are ministering to have started. Not many of us have this option because we are working among a people group that is churchless. Yet, in some cases there will be small groups of believers among our focus group whom our family can join for worship. There are pros and cons to this. If the children are fluent in the local language and customs, the family could serve as a model for new believing families. However, if the children do not know the local language well enough, having translation taking place during a service may be highly distracting. The believers, out of respect, will wish to defer to guests (any foreigner who acts like a foreigner) in meetings. This will hinder their ownership of the meetings. Also, the more foreigners involved, the more likely for western church methodologies and ecclesiology to be exposed to and adopted by the believers. Once a church of new believers has been planted, there are many other issues involved in having westerners attend that church which should be seriously evaluated. However, this is not a discussion on church planting. Therefore, the "national church," for our discussion, refers to the established churches among the peoples in our community who are already reached.

As tentmakers, there are a variety of "oikos" (groups of people) we relate to: our family, the team, co-workers in the office or project, neighbors, and the national (reached) church. But overseas, should that be the national church, the international church, or neither? Most tentmakers are confused or ambivalent about their relationship or ministry to the national church and the nearby expatriate international church. God has given us an assignment that does not include either one of these groups, yet we know we are to be in fellowship with our brothers and sisters wherever we are. Thus, it is pivotal to understand how our family and our ministries fit into the network of relationships that exists in the local society. This is also why it is essential that we know what the Master is calling us to do. The more clarity He provides, the easier it is to both make and eliminate choices.

Where do tentmakers go for their fellowship? Workers are split about whether it is preferable to worship with other foreigners or with nationals. A large majority meets regularly with other tentmakers for fellowship. The data uncovered that 54 percent of the workers "regularly attend an expatriate/foreigner English speaking church/fellowship," while 41 percent said, "I am regularly involved with a national congregation or house church that uses the local language." Nearly 90 percent of these workers were also in "active fellowship with other tentmakers or missionaries (God's team) in my area." This means many worship and/or fellowship with a different body of believers each week. The majority of workers are working among people groups that have few or no churches. However, most workers have churches in their city among nearby reached people groups. Though two-thirds of those churches pray for the unreached, less than one-fourth are trying to evangelize the unreached in their midst. Fear, prejudice, and lack of training are the three major factors referenced as hindering the local Christians from reaching out to the unreached in their midst. In the research, worship—where and how people worship—solicited the greatest number of hand written comments. Along with hiring nationals, where we fellowship seems to be a hot topic on the field. It is strategic for tentmakers to think through these issues before we are confronted with decisions which may impact the long term efforts of our ministry.

I ministered with a church in Hong Kong and assisted in a national church in a majority Muslim country which has a small but established Christian minority. From these experiences, I have learned there are many differences between working and ministering in an area where the church already exists but where there are few or no believers from the focus people group, in contrast to places where there is no church at all. Admittedly, every situation is different, so we need to be aware of the differences of our particular situation. It is also true that each team or tentmaker has different priorities. There are different factors which the tentmaker in a closed country needs to consider that a regular missionary in an open land never faces. Tentmakers need to anticipate and prepare for these potential problems.

If a tentmaker attends a national or international church and reveals his or her church planting agenda among a nearby people group, it is likely the church will in so many words ask, "What is in it for us?" Church leaders will want to know our goals and how we plan to achieve them. They will want to know what this proposed church will ultimately look like, how they should relate to it, and if it will bring the wrath of the government or religious leaders upon them. Be prepared to invest years helping them see, feel, and own the vision God has given you. Be prepared for some opposition as well.

I recommend you take some time to get to know the church leaders and discern what is on their hearts before revealing your ministry objectives. In meeting church leaders, pay close attention to their attitude towards the people you are directed to reach. Do they make jokes or show bitterness toward the people? Go slow in sharing your burden with national Christians. I know of several instances where well meaning local church leaders, citing Romans 13:1 and Titus 3:1, informed government officials of tentmakers who were witnessing to those outside the church's people group. As a result, the tentmaker was asked to leave the country.

Priorities and Church Involvement

Many Christian workers have a strong desire to have a role in the church. Just as we served in our church at home, it is natural to desire to serve in the church in our adopted land. However, timing is important. Until we are fluent in the language, most any kind of service should be delayed. If we need to learn two languages, it is common to learn the trade language and then become involved in a church using the trade language, but this may actually hinder our development in the heart language of the people we are called to reach. Language learning is hard work. After one year of language study, it is easy to feel we have accomplished nothing. After all, we have only learned to talk! There is not a whole lot to write home about. In our anxiety to "have a ministry," we can volunteer too quickly to serve in the church. It is wiser to wait and master the heart language so as to strategically enable the making of disciples and starting of churches that will reproduce using the heart language.

Many workers had leadership roles in their churches before going abroad. In truth, we miss the influence and structure a church leadership role gives us. It is all too easy to gratify our task orientated nature by taking on duties in the church before we are adequately prepared (1 Timothy 4:2)—adequacy meaning we have thoroughly completed our language and cultural studies. This is an example of how having clear objectives before going overseas and having someone hold us accountable to those objectives helps keep us on track. If we are committed to learning the language well, we need to complete that commitment. Thus, we need to be acutely aware of becoming overly involved in the local church, be it the national or the international church. It is tempting when there is little progress in the ministry to drift into working with the church, where tangible fruit is readily seen. Serving in the church temporarily strokes our egos, while quietly taking us away from His true calling on our lives.

In our city, there are both national and international churches. We allow team members to go to church on Sundays, but only from 6 AM to 12 PM. Children may attend at any time, and exceptions are made for parents to attend a church function if the children are involved in a class or event. Otherwise, team members are not allowed to attend church activities during the week without the team leader's permission. This limits getting distracted by the church. Yes, this has brought criticism from local and even expatriate believers who know only of our business agenda and not our ministry agenda. We have been told that we are just pew sitters, but so be it. The local churches usually have no outreach or concern for our people group. We do not wish for our local church attendance to be a distraction from our true ministry.

Working with the National Church in Open Countries

If you are led to work with a people group that already has an established church, then there are many advantages to associating with a local church. Local believers can be a great help in learning the culture and language. It is helpful to get to know the national church leaders. Even if we fellowship at the English church, anyone we lead to Christ needs to become a part of the national body of Christians. Get pastors' names, phone numbers, and visit them so that you have some local contacts. When you meet with them encourage them, and let them know you wish to be part of God's answer to reaching the unsaved in their community.

There is one major concern. In some situations we can become a target for resources beyond our means. No matter how we view ourselves, in most underdeveloped countries we are seen as rich foreigners. Whether we are poor college student or the wealthy vice-president of a bank, we are by local definition, "rich." When we argue with locals that we are not rich, inside they believe we are lying and have something to hide. We need to accept their definition of us. As such, we can become the target of a number of people who have legitimate needs. In poorer areas, expect a steady stream of church members asking for financial help. The problem will be that you will not be able to help them all. If you wish to share a portion of your income and time, the best idea is to work through a trusted national friend or pastor. Let him evaluate the requests and pass along any necessary contributions. In some cases, we are also viewed as a source of employment. Again, ask people to work through the pastor, as he is better qualified to determine both the need and the situation of those seeking help. Get used to being asked all kinds of favors. Andy from India clarifies, "Understand that church members will view you as rich. Be prepared to give, but know your limits. Do not feign being poor, as they will only think you are dishonest. We need to understand wealth in their terms, not ours. Develop a relationship with a trusted national employee or pastor who can help you evaluate when, how much, and whom to give to. Understand that Christians and Christian workers are just as likely to cheat you as non-Christians."

Working with the National Church in Closed Countries

Most tentmakers serve in CANs; countries which are closed to missionaries. Roughly 85 percent of the unreached peoples are in countries closed to regular missionary work. If a few churches or fellowships already exist among your people, you may wish to develop close ties with a local group or leader. But be sensitive to the leaders (local and expatriate) who began the work before you arrived (Romans 15:20). Seek their counsel before getting involved and be understanding of their church planting and contextualization strategies (Matthew 7:12). However, in most situations, there will not be such groups of believers with whom you can work alongside. Some CANs have churches among some of the people groups within the nation. Many missions insist if there is a local church in the nearby area, missionaries and tentmakers should work with the church. What should be the tentmakers' relationship with the national church? What are our options? In deciding to work with a church among a different people group that resides within the unreached group on which you are focusing, there are a couple of basic issues to question and study.

1. Are there prejudices against your focus people group within the church of the reached people group?

As with the early Jewish believers and Samaritans, prejudice may be a major hindrance to the spread of the gospel. God had to send persecution to get the Jewish believers to go to Samaria (Acts 8:1). It may take a similar divine intervention to get prejudiced Christians to reach out to the unreached peoples of their community. Normally, people will not admit their prejudices; they need to be observed. Do some research. Do the reached Christian peoples socialize with members of the unreached focus people? Do they take holidays together? Do the Christians eat where your people eat? Who do they make jokes about? Children are apt to reveal the prejudices of the adults around them. Ask children of the reached Christian people group what they think of the unreached people group. Ask people what they think of one another. In India, a Hindu background believer may have a heart for Muslims in his neighborhood, but if he tries to reach out to them, the Muslims still will not listen to him. The people's responses will tell you a lot. If the Christians have prejudices against others, clearly those prejudices need to be confronted, but consider closely why God brought you overseas in the first place. Are you sent to work with the church and to correct the prejudices of the Christians, or to plant a church among the unreached? Both are full time jobs, and one may work against the objectives of the other. It may take a generation or two to counter such deeply rooted prejudices. I have seen several workers come to Asia desirous of reaching the unreached, only to turn their efforts to correcting the unbiblical prejudices of the nearby Christians. This is fine if it is of the Lord. Meanwhile, the people group they were originally sent to reach continues to lack laborers.

A worker in Southeast Asia writes, "During our first four years here, I trained nearly one hundred Chinese Christians how to reach out to their Muslim co-workers. I gave seminars, small group teachings, and took trainees with me to share with Muslim friends. After our first term of service I reviewed what we had accomplished. I realized not one of the Chinese we trained was regularly trying to reach out to their Muslim friends. The prejudice against Muslims runs deep."

2. Will Christians be persecuted if they witness to other nearby people groups?

If you are working in a country whose government is hostile towards Christians and where converts are physically persecuted, great care must be taken not to jeopardize the national believers. There will be many within the church who fear the government and may report your ministry to officials to protect themselves. One worker writes of his experience, "My agency strongly advised me to work with the local church. Though it was of a different people than the one I was targeting, the thinking was that I could mobilize the church to help reach their unreached neighbors. Things went smoothly at first, but once a few Muslims converted, I began to receive visits from the police and immigration officials. After our third meeting, I was deported. As I was leaving the country, I asked one of the officials I had gotten to know, 'How'd you know so much about me?' He smiled and answered, 'Your own people (meaning the church) reported you to us. They did not wish us to blame them for your activities.'"

Greg Livingstone writes,

"Our tendency is to oppose pioneer church planting in Muslim countries because (from our perspective) poor judgment was exercised by someone in the past. Let us instead argue from Scripture. For example, it is perfectly understandable that some Christian leaders in Pakistan, Egypt or Indonesia (where there are many evangelical churches) would want to protect their congregations from harassment or violence from the Muslim community which might be provoked by evangelism among Muslims. It is understandable, but it is not a biblical justification for being disobedient to the Great Commission."[69]

3. How long has the church existed in the country and also in your immediate area?

If there is an evangelical church in the region or community, why is the people group still unreached? Most likely that church is among a minority people group who fears the unreached majority and the government which favors that majority. Thus, the church, for reasons of self preservation, prosperity, perseverance, or prejudice, has chosen not to be a light to the unreached people in their midst. If this situation has existed for only a decade or two, there is a chance the church may sincerely be willing to work with you to reach their unreached neighbors. Perhaps they only need encouragement, training, or a model to follow. However, if the church has existed among your people for three generations (fifty years) or more, I would have little hope of them significantly impacting the unreached group. Phil Parshall, a regular missionary to Muslims shared during a seminar, "I worked for thirteen years to get the Hindu background, Bengali church to reach out to Muslims, and nothing happened. The churches said they would reach out to Muslims, but they didn't. So we left the church and set out on our own. It was then that things began to happen."

Allow me to illustrate this using two Southeast Asian countries, the Philippines and Singapore. The DAWN movement and AD 2000 have had a tremendous impact on many Asian countries. I believe both the Philippines and Singapore have been models of their efforts. Both countries have diverse ethnic minorities. Both countries welcome missionary work and both have experienced explosive church growth the past thirty years. In the Philippines, there is now a church for nearly every people group; only eleven of the hundreds of people groups in the Philippines are today classified as unreached. These eleven people groups are all

Muslim and live in southern Mindanao. To the Filipino church's credit, two other Muslim people groups have churches, and there are at least five indigenous Filipino missions, plus several foreign missions trying to reach these Muslim people groups.

Singapore, by contrast, is 19 percent Muslim. However, there are just two faltering fellowships and still no church for the Muslims. What is the difference? History. It may seem to have taken a long time for the Filipino churches to reach out to the Muslims, but in reality the evangelical church in Muslim areas is quite young. And though many Christians fear the violent nature of the Muslims, the Filipino Christians do not have a strong history of prejudice against the Muslim community. Nearly all the Protestant churches in or near the Muslim areas are less than forty years old. The phenomenal growth of the evangelical Filipino church has been predominantly within the last forty years. However, in Singapore, though the percentage of Christians has increased significantly over the past forty years, the church has been well established in the Muslim areas for over 180 years. Christians in Singapore desire to keep their prosperity, and due to their prejudice against the Malay peoples, they have chosen not to reach out to them. Many would say though we are dealing with the fruits of the Spirit, I am comparing apples with oranges as Singapore is a first-world country and the Philippines is not. But that is my point, the Christians in Singapore have material and political gains to lose, which the Filipinos do not. Consider Pakistan, Egypt, India, and other countries where the church has existed side by side with Buddhists, Muslims, or Hindus for more than fifty years. Investigate why the established evangelical churches are not reaching out to the unreached people groups who live within their neighborhoods. Often the root issue is prejudice. Before working with a church to reach your unreached focus people, examine thoroughly how long and with what unwritten policies the church has existed among the people group.

4. In what ways could the church help your church planting ministry?

Consider the advantages and disadvantages of being involved in the church for outreach among your focus people group. Can the local church help you to learn the language and culture faster? In so doing, will they teach you their perspective or your people's perspective of the culture? If you help the church, will you be expected to take on duties which are not in line with your reasons for being there? For example, if the pastor takes a holiday, would you be asked to fill in for him? Should you have some people come to faith, will the church expect the new believers to attend the church? And if you begin another church, will you be expected to follow their ecclesiology, liturgy, etc.? When the new believers face persecution, how will the church respond? If local non-believers begin to attack the church, will the church report your ministry to the authorities?

Aris, a MBB in Indonesia, told me, "Every time we invite the Chinese to our meetings, they try to run the meeting. They do not understand that we do things differently." When I asked Abdul, a MBB in Pakistan about his role in the Anglican Church he worked at, he told me, "I am the church mascot. Whenever there is a big meeting and foreigners are involved, the pastor invites me and says a lot of nice words about me being their Muslim convert. But in my nineteen years as a believer, I have asked many times to be discipled or sent to Bible college, but nobody helps me grow." Hamidah, an Asian MBB said, "My husband (a MBB) has worked for the church as an employee for twelve years, but we are like a people without a country. Church families will have nothing to do with us, and we have no real friends in the church."

5. In what ways could the church help your tentmaking business?

Consider the advantages and disadvantages of being involved in the church for the sake of your tentmaking business. If you operate an NGO, perhaps Christians could become involved serving in administrative jobs or the distribution of goods. By modeling our love for the unreached, their work could serve as a springboard to break barriers of prejudice or fear, moving them into blessing and winning the unreached. In addition, there may be businessmen in the church who could guide you in registering your school or renting an office for your business. Take care though, as these may be opportunities you could utilize for getting to know non-believers too.

6. How do these dynamics or factors affect your ministry to the people God has brought you overseas to reach?

This is the principal question you need to ask. After all, it is God who is going to call us to account for our time and efforts. Each situation and each worker's calling is different. These are the issues to prayerfully consider as you seek His will for your involvement in the national church.

Pros for Relating to Christians on the Field

Before attending a local church, ensure that you are welcome. Do not attend an unregistered church, (which you did not start) lest you put the locals in danger. As a guest, if you are the lone foreigner attending the church, it could draw undesired attention to both the church and yourself. If there are Christians in the community who will welcome your people group into their church without insisting they change their culture to become Christians, you should consider ways to help those churches partner with you and become effective in reaching the unreached people. As one successful example, an expatriate team in Indonesia has merged its efforts with a local Chinese church and has started a C-4 service using the unreached people's heart language.

Believers can assist us as language helpers, and introduce us to places where the unreached people live and work. Moreover, the believers who have neighbors or co-workers among the focus people group can introduce us, speeding up our process of building friendships among the people.

Sometimes churches are hesitant to commit to a ministry they have never seen before. Modeling is key. Tariq is a MBB who pastors a church in the UK. I remember meeting him talking about converting Muslims; he asked, "Do you really think Muslims will convert?" I laughed and said, "Well, you did." He too, began laughing at his own incredulous remark. But he went on to explain that other than himself, he did not know of any Muslims who had converted. Where the church exists, we must demonstrate to the believers that it is possible for the unreached peoples to come to Jesus and gather together in worship. Then local believers will be able to envision the possibilities. This has been my experience in over a dozen countries where the local church at first seemed indifferent to witnessing to the unreached in their community. When a few people believed and were baptized outside of the church, local Christians then expressed interest and began getting involved.

Cons for Relating to Christians on the Field

In Pisidian Antioch, Paul began by preaching to the Jews. Yet, after one week of preaching, it was the Jews who stirred up the people (non-Jewish leaders) of Pisidian Antioch against Paul and his team (Acts 13:14–51). It is not uncommon, due to fear, prejudice, self preservation, political stability, and the hope to preserve prosperity, for local Christians to overlook the hidden peoples in their city. If the church has not reached out to the unreached people in their community for a century or more, what makes us think we can turn that around? When local Christians cannot imagine the unreached people in their midst being genuinely transformed by the Spirit, we need to defer judgment and quietly move into the community to do the work Jesus has assigned. As the local Christians see God at work through us, their hearts and attitudes may change.

One worker writes, "One of the highest leaders in the church in Egypt told me that the majority of churches will not accept Muslims and that it is not really fair to bring Muslims to the churches, since there will be no one for them to marry." Many churches in Muslim and Hindu areas avoid confrontation with the authorities by keeping to themselves. In some countries, pastors are cooperating with the government, so it would be dangerous for you to reveal yourself and your intentions to them. You need to be sure you know a Christian well before revealing your true intentions for living in the area.

Realize that there will be language barriers which lead to misunderstandings. Be prepared to apologize quickly, and fix your mistakes when you say something embarrassing to or about someone. Church members will ask you many questions about yourself, your reasons for moving to their city, your job, etc. Some workers feel uncomfortable answering so many intrusive questions. And should you not get involved in the church, expect to be branded as "lukewarm."

If you strive to mobilize the church to reach the unreached, do not set high expectations. I have met Indonesians, Malaysians, and Egyptians serving among Muslims in Central Asia who are reluctant to reach out to Muslims in the neighborhoods where they grew up. As one Chinese Malaysian serving in Turkey stated, "Yes, I work with Muslims here, but do not expect me to work with Muslims in Kuala Lumpur (her home). I could never do that."

THE INTERNATIONAL CHURCH

An international church may be available in countries that are not open to missionaries, as well as in countries that are. The number of international churches scattered around the world is surprising. Nearly everywhere that there is a sizeable expatriate community there will be an international church. I use the term "international church" for gatherings in which expatriates worship and have fellowship. I am aware that in many places these gatherings are referred to as fellowships, not churches, since they are often not fully operating churches.

Each international church is different from the rest. Some are members of established denominations, but most are not. Expect the international church to be different from your church at home. The common denominator that brings mostly English-speaking Christians together overseas is the English language. Thus, in the church, a wide variety of theological backgrounds, nationalities and worship preferences can be found in the church. Denominational mixes will include Methodists, Baptists, Anglicans, and Pentecostals.

The data confirms that workers who "attend an English speaking church or a church of their home language" are less effective in evangelism. However, there are additional things to consider when we seek His will on where to fellowship. One huge issue is the family. We need to weigh the cost of involving our children in a worship experience in their native language, versus taking them to a national fellowship where they are not conversant in the language. Of course, if your children are fluent in the local language, this is not an issue.

Advantages of Joining an International Church

There are solid advantages to attending an international church service. The international church provides a worship experience in a familiar tongue, and most tentmakers who are new in the country appreciate that. Worship with others is a necessary part of the Christian life (Psalm 150:1). The international church will usually provide Sunday School, Vacation Bible School, and youth activities. These help the children feel more at home in a strange country and provide positive biblical input.

As members come from a variety of countries, the international church also incarnates the characteristic of the Kingdom that we are no longer "East or West," "Jew or Greek," but one body in Christ. It is part of our witness to see ethnic barriers broken down. An international church can reflect this unity. One worker in a French-speaking African country writes, "Our experience here in North Africa is that we have two long-standing international churches—one English speaking and one French speaking. The English church is largely irrelevant to local life and has had little impact. The French speaking church, however, has seen a lot of fruit. What happens is that locals with questions about Christianity go there out of curiosity. Many have then met believers, been witnessed to, and come to faith. Seeing this, the MBB groups have now (with the international church's agreement) started to send people to attend the meetings to 'pick up' new people. When locals come to faith, they then try to integrate them into a local group! It might be termed officially sanctioned sheep stealing!"

Many of those who attend the international church are there on business. Tentmaking is marketplace theology in a missions setting. If the international church understands the work place and encourages people to be Christ's ambassadors there, it may also produce T-1 tentmakers who will join you in your ministry. It can be a place for training expatriates to minister to the nationals they interact with, as well. One worker writes, "If your group includes Americans, probably some have read a book on tentmaking or missions. . . . That is why, by having an insider relationship in the church, you can gently educate the larger group on ministering to the locals, the dangers of paying national evangelists, cultural extraction, prejudice, etc."

If a member of the team is involved with leadership in the church, you may be able to influence the church to take part in blessing the community or training members to reach the local people. In other places, the international church has responded to locals attending their meetings by setting up local house groups in their mother tongue. This may be done in conjunction with the team. Another worker, whose situation is different, provides additional insight, "I have seen two types of international churches in our city. The first type is those that do *not* provide a focus on the nationals but do include them in the life of the congregation. In these congregations, nationals come to faith and grow in their walk with Jesus, but I haven't seen them go out to plant other churches or even to evangelize much. The second type is those that DO provide a focus on the nationals, or at least have that as one of their goals. These churches seem to draw quite a number of nationals, and many (nationals) have been saved. Sometimes, they then plant an indigenous congregation with these nationals as leaders, but the form of the church seems to be far from contextualized. In some of the 'worst' cases, paying the nationals to minister has created a weak church with a high dependency on sponsors . . ."

Finally, one more worker shows us both the pros and cons of associating with an international church, "We have had both positive and negative experiences with the international fellowship. For our team, it proves to be a good source of wider fellowship. It also relieves the team of the intense pressure of having to be both team and church. Plus, several church friends pray for us, and some contribute money after returning to their home country, etc. The negatives have included being suspected by many due to our unknown focus, refusal to be on the church council, dressing different, etc. One lady led her driver to Christ and then sponsored him to Texas at the first threat of persecution. But several have introduced us to their language helpers, contacts, etc., and they have provided a wider net [of friends] on several occasions."

Disadvantages of Joining an International Church

In addition to being a hindrance to language development, attending the international church has other disadvantages. The most important factor to remember is that the more contextualized approach you have, the less you may want to be involved with an international church. When nationals believe in Jesus, they will emulate our practices. If we attend the international church, they will want to as well, and even if they do not, they will often desire to style their worship after what is done in the international church. If we attend that church, it is difficult to argue for a contextualized approach. Thus, the international church may actually become a cultural and social detriment to the development of indigenized local fellowships.

A worker in the Middle East adds, "I can see all sorts of drawbacks and difficulties for attending an international church when involved in an indigenous church planting work in the same locality, and I'm sure that you've thought of them all: financial temptations, lifestyle comparisons, travel opportunities, foreign language, etc."

Another drawback is the time involved fellowshipping with church members. By attending small groups once a week, a mid-week service, and helping with the youth program, it is all too easy to suddenly discover there is no time available to minister to the nationals. It is hard to bring our local friends into the expatriate fellowship as most nationals feel uncomfortable socializing in another language and building relationships outside of their established networks.

Jesus went out to the people. He met with them on their turf. Though He was a carpenter, He did not build a building, or establish Himself in one place. He did not expect the people to come to Him. He went out among the people to reach them in the places where they lived. Once they believed, then He called them to "follow me," so as to be discipled in the process of going to others. It is easy to build a "missionary compound" mentality around the relationships we make in the international church. This can become a hindrance to our outreach among the nationals. It is important to know the Lord's goals and calling. As one worker put it, "The reason we are involved in tentmaking is to reach people for Jesus Christ. If we find that the warm comfort provided by the church is interfering with our love and zeal for the lost, it's time to move out."

PASTORAL CARE

Many missions operate on the premise that missionaries, including tentmakers, need to be strong, independent, and resilient individuals who can care for themselves. That may be our billboard image, but in truth, we are all flawed and at one time or another need special care. Some workers arrive overseas with unresolved issues. Others arrive well prepared, only to stumble due to a lack of emotional support, guidance, accountability, or role models. The distance from family, friends, and spiritual mentors can drive some into depression. Others, due to unclarified expectations or pre-field screening errors, arrive on the field unprepared or unfit for the jobs they are assigned. While the worker's team or the larger God's team should be a primary point of support, some workers find it difficult to seek support from the people they must live and work with.

Personal and spiritual growth is not an automatic part of doing ministry. In fact, many workers manage to produce acceptable results in the face of spiritual barrenness. While giving generously of themselves, tentmakers can become spiritually empty and dry. Such personal and spiritual stagnation can lead to depression, dissatisfaction, disillusionment, and ultimately quitting. At the extreme end, it is often the precursor of succumbing to sin. In a vast majority of these cases, if workers would admit their struggles, they could be readily helped. However, the penchant to appear perfect causes many to wait until they are locked in the vice of sin, and then it is too late.

Tentmakers carry the weight of two careers. Our intentionality and work load open us up to greater levels of stress than what is normally experienced by missionaries and other Christians employed overseas. Gary Taylor, a tentmaking consultant, writes concerning two couples who had to return home prematurely due to emotional stress.

> "Our soldiers fighting the hottest part of the battle and getting wounded by direct, fierce, and frequent Satanic attack must have the care they need. I speak of pastoring, but a special kind of pastoring. The couples [who went home] were a regular part of a fellowship of expatriates in a country where even non-Christian expatriates huddled together in a church for cultural connectivity and uplifting. Fellowship and pulpit pastoring and professional counseling were available. But this was not the answer it might be back in Ohio. And they were well pastored in the community sense. But what does appear to be the answer, based on their own pleadings, is trained, informed, pastoral gifted tentmakers who are a specific supporting relationship with these tentmakers."[70]

Tentmakers have unique needs; as a result, we need unique care. Tentmakers should be linked to a missionary care provider to provide assistance and encouragement for the physical, emotional, and spiritual difficulties we encounter. Tentmakers should arrange regular on-site pastoral care visits through a mission organization or a qualified professional who lives in or visits the region regularly. This is one advantage of being linked to a mission agency. Missions have or are connected to a number of established networks of professionally qualified people who can be utilized to provide pastoral care. When serious problems arise, we need to be quick to admit we have a problem and ask for help. At such times, it is advisable to have a senior staff member on location who is able to provide ongoing pastoral care and oversight for day-to-day issues, as well as guide the worker through the problems they are dealing with. In the context of a business, it is better if that function is not confused with the company's senior management. If possible, there should be a different pastoral care contact for male and female workers.

Missionary care is a rapidly growing area of ministry, yet little is being done for the needs of tentmakers. Many mission organizations now have their own pastoral care departments, but there are also several excellent independent ministries for missionary care. Many missionary care providers, like Barnabas International, provide service at cost or even free of charge. Building a relationship with competent counselors in a pastoral care agency prior to the onset of tough times makes it easier to arrange for help when we hit rock bottom. Linking with a tentmaker or other missionary organization is a plus in any case, as pastoral care services are normally available.

Pastoral care is also helpful with debriefing and re-entry issues when tentmakers are preparing to go home. This applies particularly to long-term tentmakers. Debriefing in the local environment, as well as after returning to the home country, is helpful for resolving any outstanding issues between the worker, the employer, or the team. If this is not done well, issues may remain unresolved for years. There are examples of people who left their overseas employment situation angry and resentful. As a result, they found it difficult to reconnect with Christians at home or even to return to a normal work environment. Debriefing may also connect workers with resources which help them understand the changes that have taken place both within themselves and in their home community since moving abroad. Many mission agencies and some independent missionary care organizations have experience and resources available to assist with the re-entry process.

Conflicts

What do you do when team members have diverse visions for various aspects of the work? How do you deal with sin issues which arise? When a worker has a problem with his supervisor, how is it to be reconciled? In such instances, there is a need for biblical resolution with open and honest communication. In the case of a serious problem with a leader, it is advisable to bring in an outside counselor who is skilled at serving as an intermediary. A counselor who is respected by both parties should assist in bringing those at odds to a godly reconciliation. If a resolution is not possible, help should be obtained to find and agree to a godly separation of ways. A list of books and websites providing general information on missionary care may be found at www.opennetworkers.net.

We all have problems and failures. When you experience emotional fatigue, spiritual dryness, or depression, who can you to turn to for help? Before going overseas, contact a few missionary pastoral care providers. Select one, and invite him or her to visit you when in your region, and get to know them as a pro-active step for the future. Times will surely come when encouragement and counseling services are needed.

NETWORKING

Networks are both efficient and honoring to God. Networking enables workers to multiply their efforts by sharing the load of their labors. Most networks will have a point person who coordinates the activities within the network. This role is often performed by a NRM who is serving a particular country or people group. Some networks have formal membership with certain rules and requirements, while others are a loose connection of individuals. Some networks have an official relationship with the national government, acting as an ombudsman for workers serving in the country. A network should connect various ministries to share ideas and reduce duplication. This saves finances and reduces waste. It is not uncommon to find workers in two parts of a country working on similar translation projects or training programs without the knowledge of the other. Networks should bring together strategic leaders once or twice a year to review past progress, chart future objectives, and discuss the possibilities of sharing in projects for training, short termers, translation work, employment opportunities, contingency planning, etc., which are mutually beneficial to all workers.

Networks are also honoring to God. Jesus prayed for us to be one in Him (John 17:20–23). Unity, cooperation and coordination between believers should be as normal as the cooperation, and coordination between the parts of our individual bodies. The two major problems most networks encounter center around security issues and who pays the bills. These two points need to be agreed upon by all participants in the beginning. Differences in strategies and focus within a people group or country are usually understood and often complementary, but thoroughly discuss how security issues will be handled and how expenses will be paid.

Networks exist in most areas of the 10/40 Window. There are networks for T-2 and T-3 workers, pastoral care workers, NGOs, and micro-credit personnel. In addition, there are networks for many people groups and geographical regions.

SUMMARY

Before going overseas, be sure you have adequate spiritual and emotional support at home. Recruit people to pray for you. Request your church financially support and commission you. Once overseas, go slow in developing relationships with any national or international churches. The church you attend will affect your language and cultural adaptation and security, as well as generate other concerns. Look to build a relationship with one or two experienced pastoral care workers who can regularly visit you on the field to encourage and counsel you and who will be available to visit when tough times arrive.

ACTION STEPS

- What are some problems tentmakers working in a CAN will encounter that those working in an open country will not?
- What are six questions to consider before involving yourself with a local church? Answer them considering your calling, family, and ministry.
- List the advantages and disadvantages of relating to the national church, international church, or neither.
- List the reasons why it is beneficial to associate with a mission agency.
- If a conflict arises with your leader or a team member, what will you do?
- Familiarize yourself with the pastoral care workers within your organization, or peruse the internet for organizations which could assist you during tough times. Commit yourself to building a relationship with a pastoral care worker as a pro-active step for when tough times come.

"Jesus called his disciples to 'Follow me.' They did not know what was in store for them; they only knew they were to stay with Jesus. The twelve learned their work by keeping company with Jesus."

CHRISTY WILSON

In everything set them an example by doing what is good.

TITUS 2:7

chapter 11
THE TENTMAKER'S JOBS

"Tentmakers are very handsome," Ravi said to me. Not sure if he was paying me a compliment or if his English was poor, I inquired, "Why do you say that?" "Well, tentmakers must use one hand to manage their family, another hand to run the business, and yet a third hand to do their ministry. They must have some hands!" How true! The tentmaking father struggles with these three extremes in meeting the needs of the family, the ministry, and his job. Those who lead a team have additional responsibilities. Normally, there is just not enough time or hands to adequately do everything. So how do we get it all done? Unfortunately, there are no magic formulas or simple answers. As believers, we daily work out our salvation with fear and trembling (Philippians 2:12).

THE TENTMAKER'S TIME

Paul writes, "Make it your ambition to lead a quiet life, to mind your own business and to work with your hands, just as we told you" (1 Thessalonians 4:11). Quiet life, business, work, ministry? Who has time for quiet? It causes one to wonder if Paul really did work. No wonder he never had a family! Where do we find quiet in the midst of business and work? It is tough enough just adding on ministry!

The tentmaker's life requires discipline, planning, and determination. Prayer, meditation, and quiet do not come naturally to most tentmakers. Yet, notice how Paul connects the "quiet life" with effective business, work, and witness. It is clear our daily witness is rooted not in our business or work, but in the depths of our quiet devotional life in Christ. We need to have a proper perspective of work, ministry and family. We need to grasp that having a proper perspective does not entail putting aside anything that hints of being of the world (Luke 16:9). Rather, a proper perspective causes us to see our business and work as the channel for Him to connect us to the world. This connection enables His light and love to shine through us so that it may be seen by others. Like the stand upon which the lamp is placed (Matthew 5:15), our jobs enable His light in us to shine deeper into the dark areas of the world. However, the power of His light and the impact of His love, will be no stronger than what we have allowed Him to place within us.

It is out of a deep, inner life with God that our ordinary lives are lived out. His presence empowers us to behave and respond in godly ways to worldly influences, temptations, and problems. This inner response cannot be faked. Without a close, on-going relationship with Jesus, it is easy for our lives to become disjointed, losing their distinctiveness. We can become harassed and helpless like so many others. It is our inner response that ultimately wins respect and brings glory to God. We need to be aware of any tendency to pour out our lives for Christ without taking the time to refill our spiritual tanks.

Balancing Time with God, Work, Ministry, and Family

The tentmaker's lifestyle must reflect integrity, the character of his faith (incarnation) and the nuances of his environment (contextualization). Our work style must project commitment to professionalism. Time management books abound, but the bottom line is if we cannot manage our time well, tentmaking is going to be very stressful. At home and at work, we need to set priorities and stick to them. This is where it is necessary to have a supervisor or coach who will "shoot straight" with us and hold us accountable in all areas of our lives. With various balls to juggle—family, ministry, work, team—it is easy to drop one and let it lie. It is tempting to fall back on our natural (sinful) or national (cultural) ways of doing things. We need to frequently ask ourselves, "What would Jesus do?" Both our lifestyle and our business need to shine forth His light. It is pertinent to God's glory that we continually bring His presence into our work, home life, ministry, and other duties. Problems are experienced when aspiring tentmakers become so emotionally involved in the business they lose sight of the objectivity of their calling.

Jesus says to "use worldly wealth to make friends for yourself" (Luke 16:9). Our businesses are integral in living out our faith with friends and co-workers. In sharing the Word with my Muslim friends, I keep a record of what I have said so that over time I know what I have shared and how they have responded. When meeting with friends, I review these notes in my day timer or PDA. My desire is to share the gospel bit by bit with friends without dumping the whole Bible on them at one time. If we discuss heaven and hell one week, the next week I may steer the conversation toward forgiveness or prayer. Once my notes show that a friend over time has "heard the gospel," I will intentionally put it all together for him in one setting, not inviting him to receive Christ, western style, but inviting him to read and pray with me once a week.

Learning to pro-actively witness while we work enhances His glory as it shines through us. There are many ways we can have a silent but solid witness at work. When traveling (by car, taxi, train, bus, or subway), I will carry little Bible verse cards that I am memorizing. People are often curious about these cards and will ask what they are for. One time on a train in Asia, some college girls began laughing and talking about my large size, even talking about my feet, saying, "His feet are like boats. I wonder if he can walk on water." I pulled out my verses. As I did, one girl looked over my shoulder. Noting the verses were in her dialect, she exclaimed to the rest, "He speaks our language!" This gave me an opportunity to introduce myself and share the verses I was learning. I gave them each a verse to take home and consider for themselves.

Start each day at the office with several minutes of prayer and Bible reading. I have regular devotions at home, but I also do this at the office, in part to let my employees see my focus. When my managers bring new ideas to consider, I will often say to them, "Let me pray about it," reminding them that though I am the boss of the company, Jesus is the boss of my life.

Keep a small Bible in your briefcase and on your desk. Do not hesitate to refer to it for counsel. I was having lunch with a Muslim business executive, when he asked me to do something which seemed unethical. I asked him if I could talk to my boss first. Thinking I was going to pull out my cell phone and make a call, he readily agreed. I then opened my Bible and read a verse. He was flabbergasted that I would consult the Bible for a business decision. We wound up talking about spiritual things for over an hour.

Plan Ahead

Plan your work; work your plan. Solomon teaches us, "My child, don't lose sight of good planning and insight. Hang on to them, for they fill you with life and bring you honor and respect. They keep you safe on your way and keep your feet from stumbling."[71] Managing our time is not optional. Planning ahead helps reduce the tendency to make decisions based on what is pressing us, rather than on what is important. We must remain flexible but focused. We must continually distinguish between the urgent and the important and learn to say, "No." We must manage our non-work time well to ensure we stay in ship-shape, including worship, discipleship, lordship, stewardship, fellowship, and friendship. We need to train ourselves to regularly lay out our priorities for the major areas of our lives and faithfully review them in prayer. Think through a plan for the day, week, or month, and then follow it step-by-step. Each step, no matter how small or large, brings us closer to our objectives.

Measuring progress regularly helps keep us focused, lest we throw in the towel. Coaches or mentors serve as guides and cheerleaders, while the balls we juggle stay aloft. They also keep us real, telling us when we are out of balance, taking on too much, or neglecting major areas of our lives. Mentors also keep us mindful of our original goals. One business leader in the Arab world explains, "How do I manage to juggle so many balls? One, I have several personal coaches I can talk to. I regularly bounce ideas around with them, even little things. They tell me when I am overreacting or out of line. When I want to quit, they encourage me to go on. Two, I keep a flexible schedule. I am mindful that there are only twenty-four hours in a day and I do not need to work all of them. I make time for myself and my family. And three, I set goals. I have an inner reason for all I do, but I make sure I can quantify the results. Seeing things grow or change encourages me."

Combine Activities

Ministry and outreach need to become a lifestyle, not just events. Though there are times when the job, family, or outreach need our undivided attention, we must still plan activities that enable us to accomplish various tasks simultaneously. Scripture makes no distinction between the various hats we wear. As one tentmaker shares, "I came to the place where my work and my family did not prevent a significant ministry. I realized if did I everything unto God, all that I did, whatever I did, was a part of His doing ministry through me."

We must master the art of performing our jobs in valid, credible ways to show nationals how to be faithful in their jobs without allowing their jobs to become all-consuming. Daily, we need to review why we are going to work. As we teach our classes, program our computers, write marketing plans, and participate in meetings, we need to train ourselves to pause and reflect on why we are doing that particular task. And in our reflecting, we need to discuss with Jesus His reason for doing each task. Our primary motive for working is not to make money or impress others, but to bring glory to Jesus.

Some tentmakers struggle with how much time they should spend in the office. Understand that the vast majority of senior executives spend little time in the office. Much of their business is done at the golf course, the tennis court, the club, or in restaurants. It is perfectly natural to be out of the office, interacting with people. No visa stipulates the number of hours we must be in the office behind a desk. The boss might set hours, but not the government. So whether we are in the work place ten or fifty hours a week, we are not breaking any law. Yes, we are to fulfill the duties of the job we have undertaken, but if we can do the job in twenty hours a week, who will complain? If we work fifteen hours a week managing a national employee who works forty-five hours a week, we both benefit. This takes some of the burden off of our shoulders, and it makes government happy because we created another job. If you have doubts, ask the local officials. Would they rather have you employ people to do work or have you do it yourself? By hiring and training a national to do the business side of things, we are being honorable and fulfilling all that both God and the government require of us. Blessing the nations includes meeting people's needs. Creating jobs is among the best ways of doing that as it not only puts food on an employee's table, it builds his self-esteem. And of course, our employees or co-workers then hear the good news as well.

Nationals, especially officials, expect expatriates to live a life of ease. If we work for someone else, the company may require us to be in the office certain hours but few tentmakers have clock-punching jobs. Ethically, there is no conflict. Whether I put in twenty hours each week at the office or with my child, it is not the hours that determine whether I am an effective businessman or good father. I encourage our team members to take leisurely breakfasts and lunches. We truthfully tell our national employees who do have set working hours that we need time to brush up on language, meet with potential clients, and build relationships in the community. Our employees judge us by the quality of our work, not the hours we log. Just as I take off from work to coach my son's basketball team, I also give our national employees time off for special family functions. As an office, we have family outings, picnics, and parties. Our workers are encouraged to bring friends. At these functions, there will usually be prayer and sometimes a bible or moral story as well. If the business is profitable and provides secure jobs, the national workers will be content and we will have a stand upon which to shine God's light.

Those tentmakers with fixed working hours should seek input from other tentmakers on how to pro-actively pursue creative ways to quietly witness to co-workers. For example, Anna was limited by her company policies in sharing her faith. She decided to place a paper weight on her desk that said, "God Loves You." That very day, one co-worker asked her about it. Anna offered to have lunch with her and was able to share the gospel with her.

We can combine activities with our family and team members or friends we are reaching out to. Dick in North Africa writes, "My wife does not like parties or large social gatherings, but she understands the pressures on our time. We have learned to combine family, work, and social activities. At the office and at home, we celebrate holidays, using any excuse to bring people together." Jeff also adds, "We have been through six Ramadans, fasting in some way each year. Our first years, we wanted to identify with people, so we followed their schedule. It was part of learning and building bridges. Even if all our neighbors didn't hear us personally, word of mouth spreads fast around here. Because they thought only Muslims fasted, they were surprised that we would do something similar. We gained respect in their eyes. This year, we plan to make the month of Ramadan more ours, to redeem it. Reduce emphasis on food preparation and simplify everything. We want to emphasize the spiritual element for ourselves and anyone who comes to our home. . . . We aim to focus more on God." Holidays are great connecting points. Join in their celebrations, and invite them to yours. Birthdays and social holidays (like St. Patrick's Day and Valentine's Day) are great events for building relationships and sharing about the Lord.

When my sons were twelve and ten, I suggested we go off for a weekend together. When I proposed that their close friends and father join us, they readily agreed. The father had never thought about taking such time with his boys. He thought it a wonderful idea and wound up asking several other men and their sons to join us. Our little outing turned into eight car loads of men and their sons. As the leader, I set the schedule, ensuring we each got time alone with our boys. I also set the topics for discussion. I used various Proverbs as points of teaching and discussion. For several years afterward, some of those fathers continued to call me for advice on raising their sons. Being open with our lives and inviting others to join us does not necessarily hinder our "quality time" but can enhance our witnessing opportunities. It is not an issue of who I give my time to—the office, my family, or friends. Rather, it is an issue of planning events that bring benefit to all groups.

Delegate

Delegating is an indispensable skill for tentmakers. All tentmakers, especially leaders, need to master the art of delegating. People need to notice the difference in us. Our work is the most obvious and most public display of our lives. As we teach, model, and release others to act in our place, we learn to reproduce ourselves. Sharing responsibilities builds trust, confidence, and respect, not to mention saving us time. Most tentmakers do many daily functions that could be delegated to others. Where affordable, hire people to run errands, clean, and perform many of the boring, time-consuming tasks of life. The money spent is usually well worth it. Invest the time to provide quality training for all employees, whether a maid at home, a teacher, or a marketing manager. In time, this training investment will pay good dividends. As soon as you are confident the team member or employee knows how to perform the assigned job, let him do it, and walk away. Keep praying for the worker, and hold him accountable to your objectives, but give him the freedom to succeed or fail. God can work through others as easily as He can work through us. If failure really is our best teacher, then there is nothing wrong with watching others learn a lesson—unless it is extremely dangerous or costly. Ninety percent of the decisions we make are not "big" decisions. However, it is important to monitor and verify what is delegated. When the person reports back to you, take a personal interest and review the project/work, giving praise and suggestions as warranted.

In most businesses and communities, people seek power and control. But our heavenly CEO tells us that we are to not to be like that (Luke 22:26). We are to multiply our lives. Though we may feel we can do the job better ourselves, a good leader understands the value of investing time in people and reproducing our skills in others. Initially, it takes time away from other matters to train people. However, as more of the essential jobs are taken on by others, we gain back more time for a variety of business, ministry, and personal tasks.

If you own your own business, expect to work hard the first two to four years, but as soon as possible, you should hire qualified employees who can share the work load. Many T-3 tentmakers try to reduce their working hours to twenty hours a week or less. Rather than continually adding new business to fill your time, hire nationals who you can train to take on the brunt of the growing workload.

ENTREPRENEURSHIP

Research shows that successful tentmakers are creative and enjoy taking risks. The way forward in any business situation is to study the problem and then step out. This stepping out may be called risk or faith. As believers, we are to "live by faith, not by sight" (2 Corinthians 5:7). We invite the Lord to be involved in all that we do, say, and think. Therefore, whatever we risk is really a step of faith.

When starting a business, do not get scared by the bad news being spread concerning business failures. That is not to say there are no failures or losing companies. There will always be some. The key is discerning God's mind for you and then moving ahead in faith. Most discouragements come when we become distracted with the details. Persevere, learn to delegate, and be creative. I recall having a conversation with a colleague who lives in London. We were bemoaning the fact that some days it seems that progress is totally elusive. To accomplish a simple task may require the most extraordinary effort, and we end up doing the "Sunda Shuffle"—three steps forward and two steps back. He pointed out that because the major airlines have hubs which intersect at but a few locations, in getting to our meeting that day, he had to fly north to catch a plane to come south. His comment was simple but profound. In both business and ministry, especially in a cross-cultural setting, we sometimes have to take a circuitous route—one that may start us in the totally opposite direction—to arrive at our desired final destination. If you are facing temporary setbacks and frustration, keep an entrepreneurial flight plan in mind. Understand that you may have to travel an indirect route for a while until you can hook up with a direct flight which will take you toward God's ultimate objective for you.

CROSS-CULTURAL WORK ETHICS

When moving into a foreign country, it is assumed there will be some cultural adjustments. In the same way, the work place will require some study and adaptation. We need to be learners first and leaders second.

It takes time for local and expatriate co-workers to work together in harmony. Surely there are adjustments wherever one works, but when crossing into a new culture, we must plan to invest time and effort in understanding how the people work. We must be willing and ready to adapt ourselves to the marketplace culture. We are to learn how to pro-actively instill trust in our relationships with co-workers. We should ask questions about everything. For example, do locals operate well in teams, and if so, how? Do they make decisions independently, or do they require approval before taking action? Making uninformed assumptions about people's motivations must be avoided. It is helpful to have well defined roles and responsibilities. Many cultures use cryptic communication, placing a greater emphasis on non-verbal messages. Be prepared to repeat things, and be bold in asking questions. Do not hesitate to seek help. Asking help of others demonstrates teachableness and godly humility. Westerners often have difficulty reading between the lines, so it is good to ask clarifying questions, even when we think we understand. As one African Muslim said, "The American is very explicit; he wants a 'yes' or 'no.' If someone tries to speak figuratively, the American is confused." Avoid confusion, ask questions, and seek clarity.

If you are a manager, use caution and do not rush into decisions that involve employees. Always assume there is more to a story than meets the eye. This requires being selective in what you communicate or withhold at any given time. Realize that honesty may be perceived as a weakness. Wisdom is required in building trust and speaking truth.

Helping local staff to accept personal responsibility for their work and behavior is another issue requiring guidance. A tentmaker in Central Asia writes, "Our office equipment was not looked after and regularly disappeared: pencil sharpeners, chairs, a typewriter, etc. It was decided that each employee was to be allocated their own equipment. Equipment for general use was also assigned to one employee and kept within their eyesight. Workers had their names engraved on the equipment with the understanding that if it went missing, it would be replaced from their own salaries. Suddenly things stopped disappearing!"

Details can be hard for employees to grasp. All specifications have implicit physical and mental values that are understood by the company placing the order, but this does not necessarily mean these values are understood or recognized. This becomes a problem when your employees read "one yard" as "one meter," or "one inch" as "approximately 0.02 meters." If you give specifications in a business culture that does not understand details, you could face serious lawsuits if your product is sold in North America. That means everything has to be very carefully specified and verified.

Another detail is handling petty cash. Employees need to be taught that the money they are handling, though not their own, is their responsibility. It is not unusual in the Third World, both in business and even in the church, for people to go shopping for something and return with falsified receipts. Some suppliers even give employees a higher billed receipt in order to keep the difference between the receipt and what was actually paid. In turn, the employee continues to do business with that shop. As a manager, you need to learn the true price of things and keep control of receipts, checking that this sort of thing is not done. One help with this problem is giving bonuses based on accurate documentation sustained over a period of time. Periodic personal calls to suppliers are another way to check prices and receipts while building relationships. We need to have a godly attitude in dealing with such issues. We need to teach truth and honesty, while keeping in mind that the money lost is not nearly as important as the person's soul. Co-workers and employees need to understand our values in view of His light shining through us.

An even more fundamental idea is to give more ownership to employees by starting a profit sharing system. They will then be responsible to each other for the integrity of documentation.

It is important to realize that in different cultures, people work at a different pace. Walk the streets of Hong Kong or New York and be careful not to be run over. People always seem to be in a hurry. However, walk the streets of Rome or Jakarta and be careful not to run into someone else. The pace of life varies in different cities and cultures, and this impacts the way people work. A store in Asia may have eight employees behind counters that would have at most two employees in America. It may seem more efficient to dismiss the six unnecessary workers, but that will also diminish your quality control, accountability, and employee morale.

Dee, a tentmaker in the Middle East, writes of an experience she had, "During his first visit to our project, the vice-president of our international Christian NGO spent most of his time with two western leaders. During the briefing sessions, the VP was impatient when a local manager stressed the importance of some local practices that differed from head office policy. The VP also stuck to western food and drink, an indication of his lack of interest in the local culture. It is bad enough when leaders behave as if the world is a single cultural entity. But it is far worse when they highlight differences and fail to understand which differences are important." We need to learn to see people and cultures as Jesus did. We need to embrace the people and their cultural differences.

Most North Americans with secular business backgrounds have been well-coached in time management principles. Such principles are helpful overseas, but we must be flexible in order to manage the work. Goals and expectations should be lowered. Traveling around town will take longer. Many cities are infamous for their grid-lock. When things break, finding a reliable repairman can take weeks, instead of hours. Electricity, internet, and phone lines are not to be taken for granted. There will continually be other things that need to be done, such as the continuous supply of paperwork the host government requires. As a worker in Indonesia writes, "I have learned to strive to accomplish two tasks each day. Anything more is a bonus."

Attention to cultural matters is needed. Care needs to be taken not to assign a woman's job to a man, or vice versa. Nor can we give an apprentice's job to a skilled employee. In some cultures, seniority, not ability, dictates who gets promoted. There are feasible and profitable ways to work within each system. We need to learn the rules, make adjustments, ask for God's guidance, and give Him the glory in the process.

Various cultures also view time differently. In many countries, the clock has little significance. In Japan, you would not think to arrive five minutes late, but that would be early in most Arab countries. Workers will need to be taught the importance of beginning work punctually. When a client is told he will have a product or answer at a certain time and date, the promise must be fulfilled. Honesty, letting our "yes be yes and our no be no" (Matthew 5:37), is a biblical value. In many cultures, keeping relationships, not schedules, is what is valued. We should teach and practice biblical professionalism in the job. Though local cultural practices may go against God's Word and hinder the growth of the business, we must establish clear standards. People are watching us. In cultures that value relationships over schedules and friendships over quality products, reiterate your commitment to your customers and co-workers. "Whatever we do" is to be done unto Jesus (1 Corinthians 10:31). That includes maintaining godly relationships while offering quality services and products.

Remember that although we schedule and plan, many things are outside of our control. People are not a hindrance to our life and work but the very reason we are overseas. Allow extra time for everything.

One of the first things to be learned is how the culture handles interaction between members of the opposite sex. Do you shake hands, eat alone or together, and negotiate with members of the opposite sex? Some workers consider it their duty to teach the locals what Christian love is all about, especially as it relates to social interaction with members of the opposite sex. If they want to sit next to one another, shake hands, or even hold hands in public, they do, believing they are an example to the locals of the "Christian" way of showing love for one another. However, there is grave danger of giving offense to believers and unbelievers alike. It is not necessary for new believers to adopt western extra-biblical ways of expressing affection or doing business. In cultures where the sexes are segregated—and holding hands, kissing, and embracing in public are taboos—you are well advised to follow the locals' lead. Some cultures stratify their society according to rank, caste, class, age, or sex. In Japan, you use different pronouns, depending upon whether you are speaking to someone who is older or younger. Brahmins in India will have nothing to do with Untouchables. Though as Christians we wish to teach that God loves everyone equally, sending your Untouchable salesman to a Brahmin's business could cost you a sale, with nothing gained for Jesus either.

Different countries have distinct ways of doing business, as well as dealing with conflicts. Ask about the local social etiquettes soon after settling in. In many Asian countries it is common practice to use a middle man to get things done. Whether you wish to buy, sell, or inform a friend that he needs to use deodorant, a middle man is preferred. In many countries, there is an art to negotiating price. This relates to another huge cultural issue for Asians, that being "loss of face." Give an invitation to Chinese Christians after a service to come forward to "die for Christ," and you can expect many to step out and be willing to lay down their lives. Yet if you talk to them about "losing face" for Christ, the numbers will be greatly reduced. Nationals in both the office and the church who know you have an understanding of these cultural issues will respect you for this and be more likely to place their confidence in you.

Rarely does a Chinese, Indian, or an Arab believe your first price is your real price. This is not lying; this is negotiating local style. Giving your best price right up front is going to hurt your profit margins. In many cultures your relationship with the client is more important than even the price or quality of the goods or services. Plan to invest time, networking and building relationships throughout the marketplace. My good friend Nasser is a great networker, yet he rarely seems busy, and you will never find him behind a desk. When I asked his boss, "What does Nasser do?" He replied, "He brings people into my shop." And it is true; he does.

To reduce mistakes and pitfalls, it is helpful to meet with others having similar jobs, both expatriate and local, to glean what you can from the lessons they have learned. Ask questions about dealing with local authorities, holding employees accountable, how to hire and fire employees, how to relate to your managers, how to run effective staff meetings, how to resolve conflicts, best practices for training, leadership models, delegating jobs, etc. We need to learn to lead in ways that will motivate people to be productive. An Iranian said, "The first time . . . my (American) professor told me, 'I don't know the answer; I will have to look it up,' I was shocked. I asked myself, 'Why is he teaching me?' In my country a professor would give a wrong answer rather than admit ignorance." Western style leadership and ways of doing business, even daily conversation styles, may be unsuitable and easily misunderstood. By studying the environment and asking questions, you will enhance your prospects of success.

Job summarizes these tensions well when he says, "as long as I have life within me, the breath of God in my nostrils, my lips will not speak wickedness, and my tongue will utter no deceit. . . . I will not deny my integrity. I will maintain my righteousness and never let go of it; my conscience will not reproach me as long as I live."[72] We are all under stress; we make mistakes and become confused. Job's proclamation of his determination to maintain his integrity in the midst of stress is a model for us. We need to regularly remind ourselves that God is sovereign. He has placed us in our specific location and situation to demonstrate His love, grace, and character to the people around us.

Cross-Cultural Communication in the Work Place

A teacher told this story to a class of half western educated Africans and half tribal educated Africans:

A hungry hyena was going down a path when he comes to a fork in the road. As he approaches the fork, he smells food. He goes left for a while and then says to himself, "No, not this way," so he goes back and goes right. After a short way, he changes his mind and returns and goes left again. He goes back and forth, back and forth for almost a half hour, unable to make up his mind. Finally, he returns to the fork in the road and stands there, unable to decide which way to go. Hungry and anxious, the stress becomes too great and suddenly he explodes.

"Is this a true story?" asked the teacher. The westernized Africans laughed and replied, "No, of course not; a hyena cannot explode." Embarrassed, the tribal Africans hesitated to answer. Finally, one tribal African spoke up and said, "Yes, it is true, for it teaches that greed kills."

To the western educated mind, truth is based on facts. However, our ways are clearly not God's ways, and neither are they the ways of many other peoples. Peoples with different languages and cultures think, believe, and work differently. Some people, like these tribal Africans, think conceptually. In other words, their idea of the truth is based not on fact but on whether a concept is true. When sharing the gospel and doing business, we must understand how the people think and make decisions.

"Cross-cultural reality testing forces people to examine both their own and others' understandings of reality. Most people simply assume that the way they look at things is the way things really are, and judge other cultures' views of reality before understanding them. These judgments are based on ethnocentrism, which closes the door to further understanding and communication. Furthermore, ethnocentric judgments keep missionaries from examining their own beliefs and values to determine which of them are based on biblical foundations and which are on their cultural beliefs."[73]

To increase our cultural sensitivity within the marketplace, it is fundamental that we invest time in learning the language and learn to appreciate the differences in the culture. Use local décor or music in your office. Seek ways to relate and function within the host's cultural structures. Sponsor local sports teams or begin youth leagues. Give employees bonuses or time off for special services; this will enhance the company image within the community. Identify real needs in the community and develop action plans to meet those needs. We tithe from our businesses. Each year we allow the employees to designate part of that tithe to a non-religious charity of their choice. This blesses the community and encourages our employees. As one worker put it, "It is wonderful to work for a company that thinks beyond making money."

Remember, the bottom line to most businessmen is not Jesus, honesty, or love, but money. People (even Christians) can rationalize anything for the sake of receiving money. Thus, a tentmaker actually needs to be trained to cross three cultural barriers: the ethnic language barrier, the business and customs barrier, and the social and economic level barrier. Crossing these barriers requires good language and cultural skills, humility, and flexibility, enhanced by a deep devotional life and continual conversations with Jesus. Tentmakers should be characterized by qualities such as flexibility and a sense of humor, which allow us to adapt to life in a different culture. We should make a conscious effort to find beauty and value in unfamiliar situations. Consequently, tentmakers are not given to much complaining about our rights or lack of conveniences. A tentmaker's focus is not on the world and its comforts but on Jesus and His glory (Matthew 22:37–40).

In taking a job for another company, you will need to work under authority. No matter what company or NGO you work for, they will not only make demands on your time, they will often restrict what you consider to be your freedoms. Be sure you get a written agreement in advance on the number of hours you are expected to work, lest you find your time limited or unacceptable restrictions placed on your ministry. Check in advance their policy on witnessing. An engineer in a Middle Eastern country had been sharing Christ with other expatriates. His employer told him he would have to stop. There could be no more religious talk. He stopped for a while but soon realized he had come for a deeper purpose, and he continued his witness with greater discretion. During his five year stay, he was able to start a church. Remember, our job can complement our ministry objectives, or conflict with them. Much of that may be out of our control, so consider employment possibilities carefully before signing a contract.

Tentmakers should seek to network with other tentmakers or Christian businessmen in the area. With every job come new contacts. New employment opportunities are often secured through personal contacts. Take advantage of the relationships you build overseas. There are no guarantees on the length of your current employment. Should you decide to stay in the country, those relationships may be valuable in landing another job.

If you work in an open country, there will be missionaries in the community. Many regular missionaries may not understand tentmaking or be in agreement with your goals. In many cases, even when there are personality differences, the career missionary will have a better understanding of the people and the culture than the newly arrived tentmaker. Befriend the missionaries and learn from them. The missionaries' suggestions and reprimands are to be heeded. Remember, "Those who listen to instruction will prosper."[74]

NATIONAL EMPLOYEES

Leadership at Work

Tentmakers should be encouraged to befriend and witness to co-workers. However, those in positions of authority need to be wise and understanding in handling their staff. It is difficult to focus on servanthood when an overwhelming emphasis in the business world and the church is on leadership. But if we keep our focus on the Master and seek to do our jobs in accordance with His Word, we must remember that God has commanded us to be servants, not leaders (Matthew 20:25–28; 23:11). Of course, if we are leaders, we are responsible to make things happen. If we have supervisory duties at work, we need to provide a clear vision of our goals and objectives. It is wise to clarify from the beginning how decisions are to be made. Go the second mile to ensure each worker understands his or her specific role and job description. As a leader, it is imperative to invest time with employees. Regularly check with workers about their job satisfaction, training, and joys and struggles both at home and at work. Remember, we are managing people, not behavior.

There is a fine line between maintaining a professional supervisory working relationship with our employees and befriending them so as to share the Lord with them. To develop a relationship of mutual trust and respect, it is paramount that our life and work be consistent with the Bible. This is foundational to our witness. But how personally involved should we become with our employees and co-workers? One good guideline is the bigger the financial gap the greater the distance that should be kept. While there is no law that says we cannot become personally involved in national employees' lives, generally it is not a good idea with those we supervise. We do not wish to put ourselves in a situation where we compromise either the gospel or the business because of a friendship. Let other team members, national believers or short termers befriend and share the gospel with such co-workers.

Whatever happens, good or bad, spiritual or otherwise, we must maintain a professional relationship with employees who report directly to us. This professionalism requires a certain amount of distance. Becoming close to employees is encouraging and makes way for good growth and communication at work. However, in the long run, problems usually surface, forcing some hard decisions. If we become too personal, it is not uncommon for the employee to assume that we will overlook mistakes, lateness, and relatively minor offenses. However, often this leads to feelings of resentment from other employees who sense our favoritism. Should the employee make a serious mistake, there could be reluctance on our part to make an unpopular decision or exercise discipline or dismissal for fear of harming the friendship. This reluctance and delay could result in a lack of credibility to our leadership. Apart from employee performance, such friendships may bring a propensity to tell the employee information that is confidential or inappropriate. It is important we continually seek the Lord for integrity in our relationships with our employees and co-workers.

A good boss should be confident in the abilities of individuals, enthusiastic, caring, supportive, goal oriented, knowledgeable, a good communicator, patient, responsive, an excellent listener, and generous. Acculturation training is relevant as preparation for any cross-cultural job. Leaders are needed most in a crisis. As a manager, we may come under a lot of cultural pressure. This pressure may result in our being held hostage by various interest groups, such as employees, government officials, relatives, etc. Sufficient language and acculturation skills assist the leader in making difficult decisions.

As your language skills improve, invest time in learning about the local management and leadership styles. Evaluate the management methods used by locals for appropriateness in your business or organization. Learning the local ropes broadens opportunities for developing local lower and middle management, as well as leaders within the local church. Mastering contextualized leadership styles will assist in the raising up of new leaders who are both strong and dependable, who work with cultural integrity, and who are committed to the organization. Looking toward the future, such people become a valuable resource both inside and outside the business. For leadership development within the business or NGO, organizational benefits such as financial bonuses, promotions, recognition, and salary increases should be explored, particularly with local customs and culture in mind.

Workers' Rights

As a leader, Jesus never lied. He never attempted to take advantage of anyone. Jesus modeled selflessness and helpfulness. His relations with all people were loving and helpful. He saw people in light of eternity, not how they might benefit His purposes. His priority was people, not production. In running an NGO, school or business, we need to be spiritually driven, not materially driven.

A business is only as good as its people. People, not money or products, determine the speed of growth. Thus, it is both biblical and good business sense to invest in our employees' training and general well-being. "Human resources consultant, Kevin Sheridan, analyzed almost half a million employee surveys showing satisfaction with the boss's presence in the work place corresponded closely with perceiving that their employer cares. Spending time with your employees is one of the best ways to convince them you care."[75]

In many Third World countries, the rights of employees are often non-existent. Employees are regarded as disposable assets. Health insurance, retirement, safety issues, sick leave, maternity leave, child care or benefits, children's education, transportation costs, and opportunities for the physically disabled are a few of the many extras national companies overlook because they benefit the employee, but not the business. We can offer some of these benefits as blessings to our employees. Some tentmakers give paid time off for their employees to do charitable work in the community, and others give bonuses to employees who serve the poor or in other ways bless the community. Part of our witness is treating our employees with respect. This includes viewing their lives as a whole, not just the hours they put in at the work place.

Ongoing education, training, and professional development should be encouraged. In the West, we have more opportunities for growth and development. We have money for books, conferences, and travel. We should provide ways for employees, especially management or potential management candidates, to acquire new skills and upgrade existing ones. Set aside funds for employees to attend seminars. If no training programs are available locally, create your own in-house training. Invite churches back home to send out business people who can put on training seminars and provide the skills needed. Both the churches and your employees will be blessed. These seminars can be offered to the community as well, enabling you to bless the community, enlarge your network of friends, and endear the business and yourself to government officials who can assist and share credit with you in helping to make the seminar a success. Such ongoing development can be a form of mentoring. These benefits will enhance job satisfaction as both employees and management see they are growing in knowledge and acquiring new skills. Training will also help build loyalty, reducing attrition.

Confidentiality is a difficult concept for many nationalities to appreciate. Talking about issues and people at work is considered to be normal practice, even though the topic is outside the realm of those involved in the discussion. Gossip can be rampant and destructive. People like to do favors in order to put others in their debt; this ensures they will be privy to the latest news and information. Though it may be counter-cultural, it is important to teach employees what is and is not appropriate to talk about around the water cooler. There is also the issue of government agencies who will want employees to share inside information about the business. These agencies may use tactics such as financial rewards, physical threats, or housing benefits to coerce cooperation. When an employee is being pressured to provide information, it is best to work with them so that you may give the government undistorted information.

Hiring Nationals

Next to the gospel, the best news we have to offer people is jobs. People everywhere want to be financially independent. However, though most nationals admit to wanting our money, they dislike working under us, as it may feel like they are being colonized again. It is important to be wise, professional, and Christ-like in hiring national employees. Potential employees should be put through interviews and job testing which is relevant for the position they are seeking. Some cultures may have different hiring procedures. In Asia, many people are hired because of their relationship to a manager rather than their competence to do a job. It is not necessary to heed such cultural practices. The priority is to hire competent employees who will help the company prosper. It is good to start new people with a three to six month period of probation so that if the worker proves to be incompetent, he or she may be dismissed without any penalties to yourself or the company.

Hire employees based on merit, not their race, religion, or friendship. Hiring competent non-believers can be more than an asset to growing the business. An NGO worker in Central Asia writes, "We have found that it contributes to the work of church planting to include non-believing nationals as workers in our micro-credit programs. We do not prefer to use our micro-credit program simply as vehicles for C-4 or C-5 believers and MBBs to do outreach. This would mean that we had believers inside a 'believing' program directed only at those unbelievers outside it. Instead, we recruit Muslim persons who openly respond to a very tangible and practical call to help the poor (in this case, micro-credit). These efforts are very worthy and religious in the eyes of the local Muslim community. By design, we pepper our staff with contextualized believers, a few persons who have been trained to sensitively and naturally share the gospel with Muslims. Our hope is that, while working to help the poor in an emptying, self-denying sort of manner (Philippians 2:5f), we can share the gospel both with those we are assisting physically as well as with our co-workers."

Our team is focused on reaching out to a Muslim community. When hiring, if a non-Muslim applicant and a Muslim applicant are equally qualified, we will choose the Muslim. However, if the non-Muslim is more qualified, we will hire the non-Muslim. Our business needs to be operated by the best people we can find. David in Pakistan shares, "We responded to a referral by a colleague and hired a national believer who had supposedly completed three years of university level studies. However, soon after hiring him, we found that this believer had lied to the church about his qualifications and apparently was in a position to betray all the believers to the authorities!" Hiring friends has its risks. In poorer areas, it is often wise to train two people for one position because one person alone needs more accountability and encouragement, and he or she will not remember everything pertaining to the job.

A worker in North Africa writes, "If the only reason you would employ someone is that he is a believer that would be foolish. But on the other hand, if the only reason for not employing someone would be that he is a believer; this would also not make sense. We employed a believer for a work that was fitting to him, knowing that if people would say we only employed him for being a believer we could answer, 'Bring us someone else with all his abilities, experience, work ethic and trustworthiness and we will employ him.'" Solomon teaches, "An employer who hires a fool or a bystander is like an archer who shoots recklessly."

Hiring National Christians for the Business

If the national is working for the business, be sure he is truly earning his wages. Hire employees based on the contribution they make in the work place, not their religious views. Employees know when someone is on the dole. In hiring nationals, we need to be wary of hiring new believers. One NGO leader told me, "In Hardland, our NGO had to reverse its policy of hiring new believers to assist them with their livelihood. After growing to forty believing employees, we trained and then assisted thirty-six of the MBBs to find new, higher paying jobs. Immediately, these thirty-six stopped coming to church." Paul exhorts Timothy not to give new believers leadership too quickly (1 Timothy 3:6) and to test believers before giving them important responsibilities (1 Timothy 3:10). These are wise policies to apply when hiring local believers, no matter what your setting or situation.

Steffan in Bangladesh writes, "Beware of becoming the employer of someone you are trying to mentor or evangelize. It has the potential to create the wrong environment for effective discipleship. The mentoree must be economically free to choose not to grow in spiritual disciplines, not to evangelize, and not to be on fire for Christ, so that the growth that is really there can be seen, and further growth can be built on the foundation of Christ, not upon the mentoree's need for a job." It is good to assist new believers in finding a job, and it is wise to help them find a job working for someone else.

Hiring National Christians to Help in Ministry

There are times when we find it advantageous to hire nationals to do ministry but not work in our businesses. Hiring believers may enhance the team's ministry outreach. Nationals with good language skills and sensitivities to the culture can be effective evangelists and disciplers. However, we are careful that local believers do not become financially dependent upon Christian workers or too closely associated with us. Both could ruin their testimony. In the event of a crackdown by authorities, believers employed by foreign Christian workers often face death and imprisonment. Be careful not to mix business and ministry benefits. If a worker is paid to do ministry, he should not be involved in the business and vice versa. A worker in Central Asia told me that two of his workers moved to his city so they could be trained in ministry and employed in his business. However, when the local officials learned he had paid for them to attend an Inter-Varsity sponsored conference in a neighboring country, they were told to leave the city.

A related difficulty is the credibility of the native-born missionary (or pastor) in the eyes of the people. If the pastor or leader is being paid from outside the country, that leaves him vulnerable to the charge of doing it only for financial gain. This charge may taint their witness and is often strong enough to prevent a true hearing of the gospel. In addition, the possibility of support from outside raises the prospect of "rice Christians," people who say and do all the expected things, not for the love and service of God, but as a means of making money.

It is easy for us to place too great an emphasis on money. Too often our solution is to throw money and manpower at problems until they are solved or disappear. Luke, a worker in India, writes, "More money used does not result in more effective evangelism or church planting. In the short term, more activity is seen if evangelism is well funded, but on the Indian Subcontinent, it can be demonstrated that years later the fruit does not last. Who wants to plant a church that many years later is still not self-supporting and thinks that evangelism cannot take place because the West is no longer sending money to support evangelism? A quick glance at these missions financed from abroad naturally suggests that the religion which they represent is foreign. They are supported by foreign money, and they are often foreign in appearance. Eastern people almost universally look upon Christianity as a foreign religion, and they do not want a foreign religion. This is one of the biggest and most insidious of our difficulties. We are not preachers of a western religion, and anything which tends to create or support that misunderstanding is a thing to be avoided rather than encouraged."

Foreign financial support of national workers has repeatedly proven to be a stumbling block for the growth of the church. One local believer painted the picture this way, "Supporting us is like planting flowers in the desert. As long as the flower is watered, fertilized, and protected from the sun, it will flourish. But once these things are taken away, the flower will die." Many non-believers think that the only reason a person would convert is because they are being paid by a foreigner to preach Christianity. In supporting nationals, we need to examine whether we are building bridges or stumbling blocks.

An NGO worker in a Muslim country points out, "Western money when given to poor Asian churches causes a philosophical shift in their thinking. When Asians are paid by the West, the Asians feel they must imitate their employers so as to honor them. Thus the philosophical shift; they live, eat, minister, and worship as those who pay them live, eat, minister, and worship."

In my travels around the 10/40 Window, subjectively speaking, 70 percent of the nationals who are fully supported by foreign money to do a certain type of ministry are not doing what they are paid to do. But as there is little or no accountability from either the churches or the mission organizations, the funds continue to flow. Everyone feels sorry for our "poor" brothers and sisters, but is dumping cash on them the best way to help them? Several times when visiting America, I have been told of a wonderful project or national worker serving in the 10/40 Window that is being supported by churches or individuals in the West. However, when I visit those projects or workers, I find something very different than what the supporters told me.

When I visit America during the fall, like millions of other men, I enjoy watching Monday Night Football. The game is all the more enjoyable because of one commentator, John Madden. John was the head coach of the Oakland Raiders in 1977, when they won the Super Bowl. In discussing the game, John has insights and sees things on the field that I just do not see. I have watched hundreds of football games in my life, and John always has something insightful to share about what is happening on the field. Dick has been a missions pastor of his church in Texas for eleven years. We met at a conference in Africa where he had just invested one month visiting several workers, both nationals and Americans, which his church supports. After a few general questions, I asked Dick four specific questions about those ministries and workers. To each question he replied, "Good question. I wish I'd thought of that before. I don't know." As a professional missionary tentmaker, I understand the game. I see things that those who are less familiar with overseas ministry cannot see, not because they are dumb but because they are less experienced.

In attending a meeting of Christian leaders from many Eastern European countries, leader after leader from various denominations stood and said, "Please do not send us money; it only creates division. Do send us business people who can create jobs for us so that we can build ourselves up." At that same meeting, I had breakfast with an Indian leader of an organization that coordinates the efforts of thousands of Indian missionaries. His word to me, "I wish Americans understood how their methodologies and money corrupt the church (in India). If people really knew how their money was being spent, I doubt they'd give. If only you Americans knew how little we learn from your teachers (missionaries) who teach seminars with ideas and methodologies we can hardly apply or understand. We need to learn how to live our faith in the marketplace, how to work and witness. We need local models of doing business and missions." When I asked, "Why, then, do you welcome western teachers and seminars?" He smiled and replied, "We do it because with each seminar, jobs are created for those who work to put together the seminar. We do it because with each seminar there are opportunities to receive more charity. However, this charity divides us and puts our focus on getting easy money, rather than learning to depend on God." Jim, a western worker in Indonesia adds, "Our team has a rule that none of us will have any financial arrangement with a MBB unless the team as a whole agrees. The counsel of the team will help us see more clearly what God is doing in each situation."

We need to help new believers and churches experience God as their all-sufficient provider. We need to pray for God to give the churches the "grace of giving." As the church in Corinth gave out of their "extreme poverty" (2 Corinthians 8:2), we need to teach and model generosity to those we are discipling. The financial independence of a planted church, even in an impoverished community, does not have to be excessively difficult or burdensome to the community. To pay a pastor's salary only requires ten employed members to tithe. Any church having a sacrificial spirit should be able to support its own pastor.

Dismissing Workers

When there is an employee who is not performing or behaving as expected, deal with the issue immediately. First, ensure that their failures are not due to inadequate training. If there are problems outside the work place which are upsetting them, you may have an opportunity to minister to them. However, teach them that their work must go on. In such cases, a leave of absence may be appropriate. Seek out local business leaders for ideas on culturally appropriate ways of dismissing workers.

In cases of rebelliousness or incompetence, acknowledge the problem. The culture may dictate who should be informed of the problem, but discuss the issue with the offender immediately. Ignoring the problem or saying there "might" be a problem will only make you sound wishy-washy and encourage others to lower their standards. Begin to document the offender's failures so as to have an accurate record of the employee's actions. Give the employee specific guidelines for changing their actions and a time frame for completing the changes. Often, giving a warning and showing that a record of their actions is now being kept is enough to change the employee's behavior. However, if the employee continues to under perform or behave inappropriately, dismiss him. Sympathize with those who are affected. And be specific. Show empathy, and evaluate any potential repercussions. Speak the truth in love. Show Christ-like concern for the employee. Handled correctly, I have seen the Lord turn bad situations into good, both for the employee and the rest of the staff. Be sure to check the local laws so you know what rights the employee has.

MONEY & NATIONALS

Money is referred to hundreds of times throughout the Bible. Few topics receive more attention in the Scriptures. Jesus warns us "Not to store up treasures on earth . . . For where your treasure is, there your heart will be also."[76] Jesus turned over the money changers' tables and became angry because people were misusing His house to pursue profit. The correct use and attitude toward money is very important to Jesus.

An NGO worker in Asia writes, "Four times in the past seven years we had solid believers who were developing into leaders in the church and who were given responsibility for finances in our NGO. However, they did not handle money well, and two were tempted to pad their expenses. All had to be dismissed." People need training in how to manage money. We worked for nearly two years to teach Joe, the leader of our NGO, how to save his own salary in order to last the month. We taught him to keep records and receipts, documenting expenses when receipts were not available. Once he proved he could manage his own affairs (1 Timothy 3:5), we gave him responsibility over the NGO's funds. Today, we have indigenized the entire project. As an amusing side note, by his own admission, Joe often complains of people coming to him and asking for money, even as he once did me. He acknowledges it is easier to ask others for more money than to manage what he has budgeted. Nonetheless, he is learning to reproduce in others what he has learned about dependency and budgeting.

Loans to Nationals

Giving loans to nationals is another controversial topic. One way to look at it is to literally cast the bread upon the water (Ecclesiastes 11:1), meaning to loan freely without expecting any return. I have found in such cases, I am never fully repaid. It is also an option to hire the person to do odd jobs around the house or even the neighborhood.

I learned of one tentmaker's experience in Central Asia. "Our family has been asked for larger amounts. One of my friends asked for a couple of hundred dollars to get her husband's car fixed. They are from an affluent family, and I felt sure I would be repaid. I was, but I have always found that no one ever repays me for loans unless I request it. This was not comfortable at first, but I got in the habit. Another friend showed up before dawn one morning with an emergency medical problem. Her two year old had had a heat stroke during the night. The hospital could tell they were very poor and refused to help unless they paid first. This was one occasion when I gave her the money (about $100) without discussing repayment. In her case, it took several months before we were repaid. We have been asked for money to buy a sheep for a child's circumcision party, to fund new businesses, and for many other medical needs. We have found that the medical need loans are always repaid upon request, though it may take time. This is probably because they know there will be other medical emergencies someday. Business loans are rarely repaid, or at least, not fully, so we stopped making them."

My research has received mixed reviews on loans being repaid. Organizations and NGOs that specialize in micro-enterprise development have good repayment records, but individuals who loan money to friends or neighbors have mixed results. Though it speaks reams about our relationships, unfortunately it seems that non-believers are more likely to pay back the foreigner than a believer. A worker in India makes a good point, "We came overseas with a definite policy against loaning any money to our local friends. We wanted to make sure their motives were pure. However, when we saw what our friends did with each other, we noticed that they were constantly loaning money to each other when someone had a need, and the money was usually paid back. If we did not join in that cultural pattern, it would make us look like we were not a true friend. We have since loaned money to several friends to help them make it to the end of the month, and it has caused no problems. I would ask your friends what they do in terms of giving and sharing and ask God what to do in your specific location."

One of the best solutions to giving loans and paying nationals has been put forward by career missionary Brian Michell, the former director of the OMF in Borneo. He told me, "As a mission, we aim to support capital projects but not operational expenses. This means we would be happy to seek and channel funds for major projects such as church buildings, property, or special equipment and materials for ministries, but not to finance the salary and routine operating expenses of individual workers within the SIB [local church denomination]. Projects may be funded at one-third as a gift and two-thirds as a loan, which is to be paid back over an agreed upon period. We do channel funds for evangelists' salaries in areas where there is not yet an established church, but we do not allow this to continue once the church is established and has its own pastor. In doing this, we wish to remind church and evangelism ministry leaders to maintain a conscious transition and closure distinction between the stages of primary evangelism and the progression to pastoral nurture and church teaching and development."

Still another worker clarifies the importance of being an interdependent body. "Financial independence is not absolute; the New Testament churches were urged to help other congregations in times of famine, etc. Each congregation is independent, yet still part of a whole brotherhood— not to be isolated from mutual, even international encouragement and aid. Our goal is not absolute independence, for there are no international barriers in the body of Christ. Right after World War II, my home church in Seattle sent an American/Japanese missionary to Japan. There he was instrumental in starting over twenty churches. Those congregations are so grateful; every year they still send thousands of dollars back to the Seattle church for their local outreach. This is beautiful, international sense of family."

SUMMARY

Tentmakers need to balance many duties: wife and children, business, team, ministry, and more. It is important to plan ahead and when possible, combine activities. Training others to take on our duties and delegating as much as possible helps lighten our loads. We need to be aware that even as there are ministry-related social and cultural adjustments, there are also business-related social and cultural adjustments. Hiring nationals, both believers and unbelievers requires understanding and sensitivity. Motives need to be thoroughly explored. Nationals from poorer backgrounds cannot always handle a rapid increase in wealth. Jesus teaches that it is "more blessed to give than to receive" (Acts 20:35). Believers are to be generous. The decision to make loans is primarily an issue of generosity and obedience. Each situation requires prayer and wisdom.

ACTION STEPS

- What are two ways you could begin to quietly witness to those around you?
- What are some activities you do that could be combined?
- List three cross-cultural issues which could help or hurt communication in the office, depending on how they are handled.

- When hiring local workers, what questions would you ask them?
- What are some issues to consider when supporting national workers?
- What are the pros and cons of making loans to friends?

"The worst disease a missionary can get isn't malaria; it's dullaria, when you are no longer excited about the promises of God!"

GREG LIVINGSTONE

"I expect my players to have three kinds of loyalty: to God, to their families, and to the Green Bay Packers, in that order."

VINCE LOMBARDI

Be very careful, then, how you live—not as unwise but as wise, making the most of every opportunity, because the days are evil.

EPHESIANS 5:15–16

chapter 12
THE TENTMAKER'S PERSONAL LIFE

When I arrived in the village, I was surprised to see Fajar coming to greet me. A simple man, he was well known and liked by everyone. He had prayed to receive Christ the year before but had not shown much interest in growing. When he did attend the house church meetings, I wondered where he was spiritually. His first words to me caused me to both jump for joy and nearly faint from shock, "I have decided to be baptized; tell me how." "What happened?" I asked. All I could understand from his brief outburst was, "Islam is no good." Over the next day, the story unfolded. A week before, a Saudi Muslim evangelist came to the village. People were happy to hear this ambassador of Allah quote the Qur'an in proper Arabic and speak curses on the non-Muslims and praises on the followers the Islam. This evangelist was told that Fajar had occasionally come to our meetings and was showing an interest in the Bible. Much to Fajar's joy, the evangelist told him he wished to visit his home and talk with him. Being a poor man, Fajar's home has only three rooms, and two of them have dirt floors. The few times I had visited his home I had removed my shoes before entering, a local custom of respect. However, when the Saudi came to his home and saw the dirt floor, he chose to leave his shoes on. This incensed Fajar, but he said nothing. Later Fajar explained to me, "This evangelist was so rude, and he could barely speak our language. You are considerate and speak our language. If that is what his god is like, then I will follow Jesus."

LIFESTYLE

Expatriates from the West are often perceived as Christians due to our nationality, not our faith. As a result, tentmakers must distinguish themselves as real Christians through a Christ-like lifestyle. We need to go the extra mile in serving and modeling biblical behavior while being sensitive to the local customs and culture. How and where we live impacts who will befriend us. Our lifestyle needs to reflect our place in society. It does not make sense to the national for a business executive to be living in a slum. Teachers need to live at the level of a teacher, just as business owners must live at the level of a business owner. When I was arrested in the first Muslim country we lived in, one charge made against me by the interrogator was, "As a businessman, why are you living in the village and not where the westerners live?"

The research validates that the way we are perceived by the nationals does affect their acceptance of us. Anthropologists tell us that for every status, there is a role cluster, i.e., behavior and activities we need to demonstrate in the culture in order to validate the social status we purport to have. If we display behaviors inconsistent with our status, our neighbors will doubt who we say we are, thus affecting our testimony. If our actions and lifestyle do not match our title or job, nationals will not believe what we say but will give credence to what we do. On this basis, the nationals will assign us a different role which fits the lifestyle and behavior we show. For example, if I choose the status of a "business person," yet the community observes I live among the poor, work out of my home, and often engage people in spiritual conversations (behavior/roles of a Christian worker), the locals will probably doubt I am business person. Instead, they will see me as an evangelist, posing in a phony status. People will wonder about my true intentions for being there. Naturally, if we are marked as deceptive, our sharing about other things, including spiritual matters, will be tainted.

We must realize people are smart, and people talk. We fool only ourselves if we think people do not perceive our real intentions for living among them. We need to be who we say we are.

We must choose a contextualization strategy and a job which are congruent. If we are committed to a C-5 contextualized approach, our lifestyle issues are few; we must go native. But for the majority of workers, it is vital to think through how we live and where we live in light of who we say we are. In addition to living at the level of our identity, we need to live at the level of our supposed income. Workers (teachers especially) who live beyond their means must have a logical way of explaining any discrepancy. For example, it is nearly impossible to hide from national co-workers how much we are being paid. Paul, a teacher in our school, shares, "The toughest questions I have faced have come from my national co-workers. When they ask, 'How can you afford to place your children in the international school?' I struggle for an acceptable answer."

Locals generally expect expatriates to live at a fairly high standard. To work with a western firm and not live well will raise suspicions. As most westerners are perceived to be rich, it is acceptable to claim we are undergirded by family support from back home (assuming this is really so). Rarely do people ask the amount of that support. Some workers say they are living off their savings. Often those savings are last month's support check! Think through the questions people may ask about your standard of living. For example, when I lived in the village with my family, people would ask me why I did not have a nicer house. I would explain that in doing business, I needed to master the language. If I lived in a big house with a wall around it, I would not be talking to people (like that person) and I would be like the other foreigners who never learned the language. Over time, we pointed out that as our children's friends were in the area, we chose not to move. Though we lived a bit lower than we should have, we arranged our house nicely. Nonetheless, in time, living in the village still became a problem with the authorities.

On the other hand, the role and lifestyle of a person with the status of agricultural consultant, micro-credit developer, or health worker is similar to that of a holistic missionary. Their role has a defined place in society. Similarly, if you are in relief work or work for an NGO, it is more acceptable to receive support from home and maintain a nicer lifestyle—even to live in a wealthy area, while serving in the ghetto. Thus, strategies utilizing NGOs are more accessible to reaching the poor. University students are also expected to receive outside help, so living at a higher standard than the local student population is acceptable.

Understandably, it is common for us to have some stress in explaining our finances to friends. It is good to think through how to answer questions about our finances and lifestyle. It is also wise to do research, in advance, of ways to bring money into the country without it being traceable to a church or mission organization. Some countries do check the flow of money in and out of bank accounts. Nowadays, with ATM machines, it is easier to transfer monies, but not everywhere has an ATM.

Tentmakers need to come to terms with the fact that by the world's standards we are rich. Randy Alcorn writes,

"But who are these 'rich,' and how rich are they? The answer is that almost everyone who reads this will be rich, both by first-century standards and by global standards today. Statistically, if you have sufficient food, decent clothes, live in a house that keeps the weather out, and own a reasonably reliable means of transportation, you are among the top 15 percent of the world's wealthy. If you have any money saved, a hobby that requires some equipment or supplies (fishing, hunting, skiing, astronomy, coin collecting, painting), a variety of clothes in your closet, two cars (in any condition), and live in your own home, you are in the top 5 percent of the world's wealthy. Hence, when we speak of the rich we are not talking about 'them' but 'us.' Those we think of as rich today are really the super-rich, the mega-wealthy. But it is we, the rich, to whom Paul is speaking. The allowance of 'rich Christians' by 1 Timothy 6:17 immediately follows a sobering warning of what awaits those who desire to get rich (1 Timothy 6:11). If we are rich, and we are, we need not conclude we are necessarily living in sin. But we must carefully adhere to Paul's instructions of what our attitudes and actions are to be."[77]

My friend Mohamed speaks good English. He was talking with a short-term worker who was visiting. When he remarked how wealthy this young college student must be, the short term worker emphatically denied it. When Mohamed pointed out that he could afford to fly to Asia and take time off from school to travel, the short termer continued to plead his poverty. After a while, Mohamed needed to go. His parting comment to me in the local dialect was, "Your friend is not a very honest man, is he?"

We need to understand wealth and lifestyle in local terms. We should live and work in ways which make sense within the culture. As ambassadors of Christ, we are to proclaim His message in word and deed, but we must do so in humility and love (Ephesians 4:15).

We need to recognize good points in other religions and cultures. We should never be critical or take cheap shots at the beliefs or customs of others by comparing their worst with the best of Christianity. Learn to praise things of beauty and godliness and incorporate them into your own life. Jim writes, "We will join in the celebrations of Mohammed's birthday. No, we do not recognize Mohammed as a prophet, but we do acknowledge to our friends that he was a great leader, the founder of the Arab world, who rid Arabia of the practice of idol worship." Entering into the local ways of living is a huge part of acculturating. We must listen with respectful patience to the criticisms they have of Christian thought and practice. From their insights, we can gain new perspectives on how to live and witness in ways they can comprehend, as well as their perceptions of godliness. Many a worker has drawn closer to Jesus because of insights learned from critics of the Bible or Christian practices. Nonetheless, we still must boldly proclaim that Jesus alone is the Way, the Truth, and the Life.

Whenever workers go abroad, we take many suitcases with us. Often one or more of those bags contain our cultural baggage. For example, we have our own cultural ideas of what food is, how it should be cooked, and the ways it should be eaten. Everyone seems to understand the importance of relating to the locals in understandable ways, but that goes beyond just eating the local food. Few have grasped the benefits of driving local cars and wearing locally made clothes, even if they are designed in a western style. The tentmaker should live an incarnational life. It is only reasonable that we should be the ones to adjust to local ways of life. If changes are to be made, why should the tentmaker not make them? It is not a matter of doing in Rome as the Romans do; rather, it is a matter of obeying Jesus in loving your neighbor as yourself (Leviticus 19:18; Mark 12:33).

Housing is a key issue in relating to nationals. Homes should be set up in a fashion which is comfortable to the worker but not "foreign" to the local. It is important to have a place where you can relax, kick off your shoes, and be yourself. The data indicates that nationals are comfortable visiting homes which are totally contextualized, as well as homes that have a living area for national guests and a private, more western area for the family. However, nationals are uncomfortable visiting homes that are purely non-local in set up and décor. Before setting up your home or apartment, visit the homes of several locals who appear to have the same status as you. Consider how their living area is arranged and pattern your living area after theirs so that visitors will feel more welcome.

We are commanded to "practice hospitality" (Romans 12:13). It is unlikely we will see people believe unless we make friends with them. Exactly 92 percent of the workers see friendship as a key factor in their evangelism. Nationals need to feel comfortable when visiting our homes. However, while you may arrange the common living room to be hospitable to local guests, feel free to keep one or two rooms in the house for yourself.

The late Dr. Herbert Kane, my mentor while in seminary, often said, "A good missionary travels with only his toothbrush and his Bible."

Less is better when moving overseas. People notice the type of furniture, lighting and appliances we use. When we adopt the local ways, people also notice. Wearing their clothes, eating their foods, and adopting their décor, causes them to feel we are truly at home with them. Attention to detail is important. Utilize local appliances as much as possible. There is nothing wrong with having one or two appliances brought from home, but hold them with an open hand; be happy to share them with friends.

Our attitude toward our possessions is more important than what we actually own (Matthew 6:19–21). Wi Lee asked to borrow my stereo for a party he was having. He wound up keeping the stereo for nearly four months. I never once bothered him to return it, but when he did, he also asked for a Bible. When I asked why he wanted a Bible, he replied, "I wanted to test you and see how much this stereo means to you. If it were mine, it would be my life! But I see that you really believe Jesus is more important to you than things. I want to know why." Later Wi Lee believed. It is important to hold things with an open hand. People often took advantage of Jesus, as His disciples, we should expect to be treated the same (Luke 6:40).

Every country has customs that are followed within the home which should be kept in our homes as well. In many cultures, people remove their shoes before entering their homes. In Muslim lands, men and women often sit separately or in different rooms. Some workers feel that by mixing the sexes or wearing shoes, "they are teaching the locals a better way." Unfortunately, in most cases all they are doing is making the local feel uncomfortable, resulting in their never returning. Locals expect our homes and lifestyle to be different, so they will rarely criticize the way we live. When we highlight a difference, they will normally compliment us, but the real test of the compliment is not in what they say but what they do.

One Korean worker told me, "The first few years I served all my guests kim chee. Each one said it tasted delicious, but rarely did anyone ever accept a return invitation to my home. Over time, Rahid became a good friend, but he too rarely came to my home. Finally, I confronted him, 'Why don't you ever come to my home?' As he had said he liked my Korean foods, his answer surprised me, 'It's because you always serve me kim chee.'" Just as we learn to eat and enjoy the native food, so also we should serve it when we extend hospitality to others. If we cook their food well, everyone will be happy to eat at our home. If we regularly cook our own national food, some may enjoy it, but others will not and may stop visiting our homes.

In seminary, we were taught the ditty, "Where He leads me I will follow, what He feeds me I will swallow." Food is a major issue. Many argue that eating the local cuisine is not a big deal. But consider, if foreigners come to your country and reject your national dishes, how do you feel? As Americans, if we invite someone for Thanksgiving dinner and they say they hate turkey, potatoes, and pumpkin pie, are we likely to invite them again next year? To reject a person's food is to reject the person. Having grown up in a midwestern American city, I never ate spicy food. When we moved to Asia, I quickly realized the people love hot chili peppers on every dish. What did I do? Stop eating? No, I simply trained myself to eat spicy food by going out and eating the hottest food I could find for several weeks. It was hard; I hated it, and I felt sick. However, within a month, my taste buds adjusted and my body adapted. Nowadays I now truly enjoy spicy food.

We have the model of Paul, who adapted to the local cultures so that he "might by all possible means save some" (1 Corinthians 9:22). He adds, "Everyone who competes in the games goes into strict training. They do it to get a crown that will not last; but we do it to get a crown that will last forever."[78] We go into strict training to learn the language, witnessing techniques, operating a business or NGO, etc. We need to understand that part of this training is disciplining our taste buds and stomachs to eat as the people eat, sit as they sit, and dress as they dress. We are called to take up our cross daily (Luke 9:23). It is imperative to grasp that a part of this cross is giving up our freedoms so that we may demonstrate the love of Jesus (Galatians 5:13–14).

Self-discipline is needed to do His work. Paul adds, "I beat my body and make it my slave" (1 Corinthians 9:27). We claim we are willing to die for the people, but are we willing to eat goat's eyes, spicy curries, durian, and lamb kidneys for the peoples' sake? Muslims do not eat pork; good Hindus are vegetarians; some Buddhists abstain from beef; and the Chinese eat everything. We have found that by eating what the locals eat or do not eat causes them to feel more comfortable in our homes. If you do not wish to follow local dietary customs, when you have guests, be as sensitive as you can to their practices. Use paper plates and disposable silverware so they need not eat from contaminated dishes. We are to seek not our own good but the good of others (1 Corinthians 10:24). Before moving abroad, practice disciplining your body. Go without meat, sugar, electricity, or hot water for a week.

Some cultures/religions set up their homes in certain ways to reflect their piety. Muslims will hang Qur'an verses and a picture of

Mecca on the wall. Hindus and Buddhists will often have a small shrine or pictures of their gods on the walls. We also can put verses on our walls at home and at work and hang pictures which reflect our beliefs. Concerning clothing, the nationals have been there for a long time, and they usually know what is best. Though in some places the local dress may not be suitable for westerners, every worker should have some local clothes to wear when attending celebrations and special occasions. Because three different cultures work in our office, we have a day each month for each people group; all employees, no matter what their race or religion, are encouraged to wear the dress of that group. This has often resulted in employees wearing the dress of other peoples on other days as well.

There are many other things to consider in choosing how to live. One worker in Thailand found his blond hair and blue eyes to be a distraction, so he dyed his hair black and bought brown contacts. Have you ever thought about how men and women wear their hair? There is an Arab proverb which says, "A man without a mustache is not a man." With children, who does the disciplining? In private, that is your affair, but a mother disciplining a son in the Middle East could cause the bystander to lose respect for the mother. Will holding your spouse's hand cause others to lose respect for you and thus for your God? It is important to determine and understand the values of the adopted culture and their standards for holiness and power. Jesus says, "Whoever can be trusted with very little can also be trusted with much, and whoever is dishonest with very little will also be dishonest with much."[79] It is the little things that make a difference. Cross-cultural evangelism and church planting are enhanced by proper actions and attitudes.

Friendships between families of widely disparate means and standards of living are extremely unlikely. We may consider ourselves a friend of a local because we play tennis or chess once a week, but close friendship is reflected in the depth we are involved in one another's lives. Some questions to ask to determine the depth of our relationships are: Can we share mutual problems? Do we take holidays together? With whom do we naturally choose to relax? Do we share with them child rearing problems? Do we go shopping together for special gifts? Or discuss retirement plans? From whom do we seek financial advice? The test of true friendship is who we share the more meaningful areas of our life with. Economic lifestyles and not just cultural differences pose a huge barrier to social intimacy. As a result, though not out of any desire to discriminate, most missionaries associate with the poor only in the context of their evangelistic or social work. As tentmakers, our lives more closely reflect the people's lives.

Yes, this yields its temptations, but it also opens opportunities to build intimate relationships.

LIVING THE LIFE

God develops each of us over our lifetimes. He is more concerned about what is happening in us than through us. He knows where we should be headed and how to keep us pointed there. Each person's journey with God is unique. We are not unique by accident; it is part of His great design in keeping us dependent on Himself. But many of us have learned to walk by sight, not by faith. We have trained and studied so that we can "go it alone," even without God. Churches put forth formulas and methodologies which keep us busy doing the work of the church, while not giving much thought to the impact on our lives or relationship with Jesus. Formulas can be an insurance policy against thinking and relying on God. Methodologies are designed to reduce risk.

The average western Christian does not realize the extent to which he or she depends on others for the stimulation of their spiritual and intellectual life. There are church services, Bible classes, prayer meetings, cell groups, weekend retreats, choir practice, seminars, workshops, Christian radio and TV programs, Christian journals, missionary periodicals, devotional books, sermons and sacred music on tapes in our homes and cars, and an unlimited supply of Christian literature of all kinds for all ages. Workers serving in Timbuktu have few or none of these props. At most, they have a handful of books and a couple of cassettes. Tentmakers need to know how to nourish themselves and others spiritually.

Doug, working in the Middle East writes, "We get sidetracked into focusing on methods, approaches, theories, models, studies, manuals, etc., and lose sight of the fact that the one basic thing we desperately need is more of God—a passion for Him, seeking Him, knowing Him, being more full of Him, being changed more into the image of Jesus, walking more in the Spirit, etc. That is what we need to center on—not methodologies and theories, etc. We *need* revival! Without it, what will our lifetimes of service amount to?" God brings forth the fruit (1 Corinthians 3:7). Our duty is to fulfill His assignments, keeping our focus on Him.

"Looking to capitalize on Houdini's immense popularity and fame, a London bank challenged him to break out of their vault with its new, state-of-the-art locking system. They were certain that even the great Houdini would finally meet his match.

Houdini accepted, and on the appointed date, the press turned out in droves to see if the master could get out in the three and a half minutes allotted. But he had a trick up his sleeve! His contracts always specified that before he disappeared into the trunk or cell or behind a small curtain, he could kiss his wife. After all, many of his feats were seriously dangerous, so who could refuse the couple what might turn out to be their last goodbye? But what no one knew was that he was getting more than a kiss! As their lips met, his wife would secretly pass a small piece of wire from her mouth to his. Then, once he was alone or hidden behind the curtain, he'd use the wire to pick the locks. This time out, though, the wire didn't seem to be doing the trick. Here's what Houdini wrote about that experience . . . 'After one solid minute, I didn't hear any of the familiar clicking sounds. I thought, my gosh, this could ruin my career, I'm at the pinnacle of fame, and the press is all here. After two minutes, I was beginning to sweat profusely because I was not getting this lock picked. After three minutes of failure, with thirty seconds left, I reached into my pocket to get a handkerchief and dry my hands and forehead, and when I did, I leaned against the vault door and it creaked open.' And there you have it. The door was never locked!' But because Houdini BELIEVED it to be locked, it might as well have been. Only the 'accident' of leaning on the door changed that belief and saved his career. It's the same way with all of us. The things we believe to be unsurpassable barriers, obstacles, and problems are just like the bank vault door. The only lock is in our minds, and as long as we simply believe that we *can't*, well, we can't. But when we give the door a push we can be amazed to find that not only is the door not locked to us, there's really no door at all, just the illusion of one."[80]

All of us have inner barriers which prevent us from moving forward. Our minds say the language is unlearnable. Our taste buds say the food is uneatable. Yet God has given us His spirit of power, of love, and of self-discipline (2 Timothy 1:7). We need to discipline ourselves, no matter what the barrier seems to be, to step out in faith and give the door a shove. The biggest obstacles tentmakers face are often the ones we have created in our own minds. We are to set our minds on things above (Colossians 3:2), not the barriers.

Cultivating Your Spirit

Jesus says, "Follow me." The call to tentmaking missionary work is first and foremost, a call to be with Jesus. It is easy to allow the demands of ministry and work to pull us away so that we end up ministering and working for the business or ourselves, rather than with Him. Our secret times with God must have priority over our service for God. We need to remember the example of Martha and Mary. Jesus praises Mary for taking the time to listen to Him. The point is Jesus wants our attention more than our activity.

The Lord had His people "gather manna every morning" (Exodus 16:21). His manna is new every morning. We are never to live on the old manna. The old anointings will not suffice. It is paramount that we maintain our dependence on the Lord. It is too easy to think "we" accomplished the works of our hands. Our Master requires we recognize that He alone is our supplier and strength. All we have accomplished must daily be acknowledged as coming from Jesus. Without His grace, we cannot even pray for our daily bread. Separating the Lord from our jobs will result in a hunger and then an empty shell of a witness. We must keep our relationship with Jesus fresh every day. This involves the disciplines of prayer and Bible study or reading. Without intimacy with the Lord, life has little meaning or joy, and the bumps and bruises of life hurt a lot more. Our times with the Master should draw us further into the world, not insulate us from it. The natural fruit of being with God is a greater zeal to bring Him into our life and our world.

Tentmakers need to be people who open their hearts to God and listen when He opens His. Living in a cross-cultural context is no place to be leaning on our own understanding. When asked the source of his strength in persevering for forty-four years in his ministry among Muslims, Phil Parshall told me, "I have invested at least one hour of my morning to prayer and reading the Word." We need to evaluate our spiritual disciplines, our strengths, and weaknesses. Once overseas it is important to maintain our spiritual disciplines. The practices we had at home should be continued once overseas. It is wise to set goals in these areas and ask our mentor to hold us accountable for our spiritual growth, including: active steps we are taking to grow, devotional habits/spiritual disciplines (both personal and family), struggles with specific sins, Bible study, prayer times, Scripture memorization, promises claimed, journaling, etc.

Cultivating Your Mind

In loving the Lord with all our minds, we need to pro-actively determine areas in which we need to grow and develop mentally. We should take inventory of our lives. The mind, like the body, has a way of deteriorating. Take stock of ways we can grow in wisdom and expand our thinking. Having a reading plan is one good idea. Jake in Hong Kong says, "I have read a book a week for most of my life and have developed a simple way to read more effectively." Budi in Indonesia adds, "I place books into one of three categories; theology, methodology, and inspiration. I try to read one in each category all at the same time." Personally, I prayerfully choose a theme for each year and read and memorize along those lines. Church planting, training leaders, intimacy with God, and intimacy with my wife have been recent themes. It is important to get new input. Periodically read a book or magazine in a field outside your area of expertise. For example, if you are an English teacher, read a business book; you may pick up an idea for a teaching topic or a way to better manage your classes. If you are a contractor or designer, reading a book on animal habitats may be the catalyst for an innovative solution.

Listening to tapes and reading the newspaper are other helpful ideas. Keeping abreast of current events is useful when looking to strike up a conversation with the guy sitting across from you in the coffee shop. Some workers have taken courses at a local club or nearby university. Hobbies are helpful for giving your mind a rest, as well as developing friendships. John in Pakistan built a business around his hobby of fixing things. David in Indonesia, uses his guitar to make friends in his village. Music can be good for both the mind and the body. Remember, another David played the harp.

Cultivating Your Body

It is common knowledge that the greatest cause of missionary attrition is poor health. Yet, no generation in human history has had more ways to care for our bodies and reduce stress than we have. We can exercise, read, get a massage, play games, or watch TV or videos, but each of these is useless unless we use them. When we are tired, the production and quality of our work declines. We work slower, are less creative, and make more mistakes. All of us have to work overtime sometimes. Yet, prolonged hours at work stifle creativity, deplete our energy and rob us of our joy (Psalms 127:1–2). We should never take ourselves too seriously. We are not as necessary as we think. Whether it be work, play or ministry, it is all done for Jesus' sake (1 Corinthians 10:31). Our ability to relax and enjoy life is a testimony to those around us.

Balanced living requires caring for the temple of God, our bodies (1 Corinthians 3:16–17). Sufficient sleep, a balanced diet, exercise, and hobbies help regulate our bodies. Interestingly, another factor that enhances a worker's effectiveness is exercising regularly. If you exercised before moving abroad, it is important that you keep up a similar routine once you have moved. Regular leisurely breaks should be a part of every tentmaker's weekly schedule. Leisure allows us to play and be as Jesus tells us, "childlike." Jim writes, "As a tentmaker, I meet many Muslims on the job, but it is in situations of play and relaxing that my friends and I really share our feelings and our faiths. Rest and play is needful. Playing in the world gives us fresh points of contact with reality and a catalyst for new experiences, ideas, and people. As tentmakers, we need to learn to give ourselves permission to relax, play, enjoy life, and enjoy God for who He is."

In watching their health, workers should make sure they have regular medical check-ups and keep their inoculations current. Most cities have good doctors. Many doctors have been trained in the West and are more than adequate physicians; many will even speak English. However, the standards of cleanliness in hospitals may not be what we are used to. Most hospital rooms are shared with six to twelve others. In some countries, there are no meals served to patients in the hospital. The food is the responsibility of the family of the sick. That means there are often many people in and around the hospital. Unless you have a private room, you may have lots of company.

Be prepared with medicines. Though you cannot anticipate all the medicines you may need, take enough aspirin, favorite cold medicines and other vitamins or pharmaceutical items. If you wear glasses, take an extra pair and bring a photocopy of your prescription. Pharmacies vary from country to country, but many now carry the most common drugs. Prescriptions from other countries are usually honored. If you will be living in the boondocks, two recommended publications are: "Where There Is No Doctor" and "Where There Is No Dentist."

Vacations are another outlet for relaxing the mind and the body. Apparently, vacations can help keep people alive. "Yearly vacations cut the chances of dying young from coronary heart disease by one-third for middle-aged men already at risk for heart attacks. The more times men skipped their annual vacation over five years, the more likely they were to die in the next nine years, scientists reported at the American Psychosomatic Society meeting."[81] Everyone needs to get away periodically. Sam in Southeast Asia shares, "On our designated weekly day off, we do not always answer the phone, as it usually means a request. But we never pretend we aren't home; that would result in a greater offense if discovered." Personally, my wife and I get one week alone each year, no kids. It has done wonders for our marriage. Tentmakers should be encouraged to annually take one or two long weekend breaks in a nearby country for refreshment or special meetings to rest and receive encouragement. Exercise, rest, and vacations are needed to give the body and mind a chance to retool, refocus, and reenergize. Regular breaks enable the body and mind to move from dwelling on the necessary problems which flood our daily lives to thinking about ultimate matters.

Cultivating Your Social Life

Building up your social life may fit in with your ministry outreach, but friendships are not necessarily "contacts." Developing a social life with locals requires patience, good language skills, and boldness. It is good to strive to have both a close local friend and a friend of your own nationality. The local friend, in addition to being a friend, will be invaluable in gaining cultural and linguistic insights. A friend of your own nationality could be someone who would understand your dual identity and ministry struggles from your cultural perspective.

Attend functions you normally would not attend. If you are looking for innovative ideas for a store display, check out places that sell things outside of your line of work and that have a completely different customer demographic. How one store sells sports equipment may give you ideas about how you should sell your computer goods. Trying the unconventional is a proven way of getting your customers' attention and a great way for meeting new people. Get involved in clubs and local events. Dean in China says, "I go to events where I'll meet people from different industries or people who have interests different from mine. Unlike a networking event, I am not prospecting for new ideas or contacts, but of course sometimes I leave with some promising business cards." One team in the Middle East formed a band to play at weddings and parties so as to meet new people. Another team joins local soccer tournaments. Carl volunteered to coach the local rugby team. Mary volunteers to teach piano lessons to friends. Each of these are examples of ways of meeting people and making friends so as to share the gospel.

Cultivating Your Emotions

As Jesus' ambassadors to the nations, it is imperative that we keep our emotional balance centered. It is common knowledge that emotional ups and downs tend to get exaggerated overseas. It is helpful to know yourself. Be honest with yourself about your mental, physical, spiritual, and emotional needs. Set low goals to keep yourself from big disappointments. Know your role in society and at work. Learn the cultural perspective on how, and to whom, to yield to on decisions, and how and when to push for answers and action. Expect some failure. You will fall down; you will get hurt. Nonetheless, in prayer, keep picking yourself up and following the Lord. Ask the Lord to continually give you a positive attitude. Learn to rest in His Spirit in the midst of pressure. Even in situations where you think you know what to do, be patient, teachable, and humble with both national and expatriate friends and co-workers. It is likely your greatest stresses will come from team members and not the locals. If you have had emotional problems or areas of weakness before departing overseas, share this with someone and ask him or her to hold you accountable in these areas.

To be regarded as a missionary at home and a business person or other professional overseas can lead to emotional stress. This affects the whole family. Children can be very vulnerable to such stresses. My children found it hard to go to a MK (missionary kid) school but not be able to tell friends and teachers that their parents were missionaries. The local business children who attended the school were considered to be less spiritual than those of regular Christian workers. Jesse adds, "More than once, local Christians chastised me for not getting involved in the programs of the church. It is hard to quietly accept criticism from local Christians when the truth is I would not need to be here if the church were doing its job." Knowing our role, and being content with it, is a must for maintaining our emotional stability.

One of the greatest emotional destabilizers is culture shock. Culture shock is the transitioning process everyone experiences who lives in a foreign culture for two years or more. Upon entering a new culture, most people are enthusiastic for the initial two to six months. During this period, everything is new, exciting, and fun. However, sometime during the fourth to twelfth month, though sometimes later, a depression or negativism sets in. Depending on how it is dealt with, this gloom may last a few months or persist for years. During this period, workers tend to focus on the differences and the things that are "wrong" with the local people and customs. The degree that people experience culture shock may vary greatly. Housing, hygiene, the working environment, food, over-sleeping or not enough sleep, cleanliness, social activities or the lack thereof, and unrealistic expectations might each be symptoms of culture shock. Workers need to be aware of the process of adapting to a new culture, and they usually need some support and teaching to prevent burnout. Some workers never pull out of the negativism which culture shock brings.

Tentmakers need to know themselves. In learning our strengths and weaknesses, we need help in discerning our blind spots and determining our limits and the limits of those for whom we are responsible. Most of us tend to inch toward commitment like a snail crossing a sidewalk. We are so afraid of going over the edge that we create fears and cautions which hinder God's working through us. If we are truly pioneers, we need to realize some mistakes will be made, and they can result in penalties, both emotionally and physically, to ourselves, our family, and our team members' well-being. Though no one wants to fail, failure is a good teacher, and through our failures we learn what our limits are. Taking steps of faith is part of the risk of being in God's work.

SINGLE TENTMAKERS

Single women and men have unique opportunities and difficulties. Perceptions of singles vary from the attitude, "They must have lots of free time to do ministry, learn the language and spend time alone with God," to sympathy for "the poor, lonely single." Singles need to be recognized for who they are. Stereotypes only discourage and set false expectations. The fact is each person—single or not—is different. In some countries, like China, singles seem to excel in building relationships, while in some Muslim communities there is no such thing as an unattached adult. Singles, female or male, are an anomaly. In business, singleness is not much of an issue. Single men, in particular, seem to be at no disadvantage in the marketplace. Some employers might even prefer to hire singles, believing a single has more time and energy to devote to the job.

There is a cost to singleness. Before going overseas, singles should be thoroughly questioned on their willingness to accept their role as a single and the possibility of life-long singleness. It is wise to include in a MOU (Memo of Understanding) clear guidelines of what is acceptable or unacceptable for singles on the team. This is especially important in cultures that have distinct roles and social rules of conduct for men and women. Working in foreign cultures exacerbates the need for comfort, which in turn creates vulnerability to sexual advances, internet pornography, and ill-advised arrangements.

Provide options for housing. It is not wise to force singles into pairing up with other single team members. Understand that the singles are strangers and sometimes from different cultures. It shows insensitivity to expect singles to live together as a harmonious family. For older singles, adjusting to team life and sharing their time and ideas may be a greater adjustment than adjusting to the new culture. Allow the singles to build their own relationships and determine their own living situation. Singles on the team may choose to live together, but they may also be adopted by a local family, live with another local single, or live alone. We need to appreciate that singles face unique difficulties. As a single person, though they have the work of one, they also must do everything for themselves. There is no one to share the household chores, cooking, shopping, etc. As a single male, it may be culturally difficult to hire house help.

Singles need mentors and advocates who meet with them at least weekly. Many teams fail to realize their single women appreciate having a "champion" to speak up for their ideas in team meetings. Singles can often feel left out, like a fifth wheel. They are easily overlooked while other team families take their children to the park. Singles sometimes have problems with anger, loneliness, self-pity, and self-centeredness. Mentors need to learn of their struggles and be available to help and listen. I recommend that each single worker be "adopted" by at least one couple on the team. This couple's home should provide a home away from home where the single feels free to visit at any time as a place of refuge, for use of a computer, or to find a listening ear. Many organizations place a lot of emphasis on knowing where their people feel called to serve. Perhaps it would be better to first consider the team on which a single might serve, to ensure the team understands the special needs of singles and have a mentor prepared to work alongside them.

Singles must understand that life on the field requires some give and take. Families may not expect you to baby-sit for them, but sharing one's home and family does require time and energy. Be quick to help with chores, and be sensitive to the families' needs for time alone. Be real with your co-workers. Couples do not expect singles to be perfect. Like the rest of us, it is expected you will forget and make mistakes. As one single worker in Central Asia writes, "We do need to be real about where we are and be able to communicate it. Sometimes we grieve the loss of a marriage relationship. Sometimes we rejoice in the blessings of being unmarried. Emotions fluctuate for each of us." There is a cost to serving Jesus, single or married. We each need to learn Paul's secret of being content in any and every situation (Philippians 4:12).

SUMMARY

Our lifestyle is a huge part of how we and our message are perceived by the locals. We need to live at a level that is consistent with our job. Adapting to a new culture is an issue of mind over matter. Self discipline is needed in learning to eat, drink, dress, and live as the locals. Prayerfully determine where to live and how to furnish your home. The little things do make a big difference. "Know thyself" has a special meaning for the tentmaker. Ways in which we cultivate our spiritual, mental, physical, and emotional life at home should, if possible, be continued on the field. Before moving overseas, it is critical for tentmakers to learn to cultivate their spirits, minds, emotions, and bodies without the props the church has to offer. Single workers need special care. They need guidance in determining their role within the community. They should have an advocate within the team who will help them with the questions and struggles of daily life.

ACTION STEPS

- In what ways will the location of the home impact your family and ministry?
- Discuss with your spouse how you intend to arrange your house and practice hospitality.
- How will you discipline your mind to submit to your will and spirit? What steps can you take now to train your body to do that which may be unusual or difficult?
- In what ways do you currently cultivate your spirit, mind, emotions, body, and social life? How can you continue these practices overseas?
- What are some issues which are unique to singles?

- If married, how can you reach out to the singles on your team?
- If single, what are some "family" issues you need to be sensitive about with families?

"If the kids are not happy, Mother is not happy, and if Mother is not happy, nobody is happy."

BILL COSBY

Spoil your spouse, not your children.

UNKNOWN

Many women do noble things, but you surpass them all!

KING LEMUEL

chapter 13
WOMEN AND TENTMAKING

(As a man, I do not feel I can do justice to the subject of women. Titus 2 talks about older women mentoring younger women, so I have invited my wife to contribute to this chapter.)

WOMEN TENTMAKERS

Despite the many biblical examples of women involved in evangelism and even tentmaking, like Priscilla, Euodia, Syntyche, and Lydia, missions has been mostly a male domain. Women are among one of the largest unevangelized identifiable segments of societies throughout the world. There is not a community to be found that does not include women. Around the 10/40 Window, women are using creative access strategies to reach other women through drama and music, language clubs, crafts, small businesses, children's day care, exercise groups, story-telling, cooking and baking, flower arranging and more. Though women in the West may feel stereotyped and that there is a glass ceiling in business and other areas of life, in the Third World this is truly the case. Women tentmakers can expect to fight to be heard and to work twice as hard for success as in the West.

Women, both single and married, need to be encouragers of one another. Back home there are many support groups within the church and the Christian community for women, but not so overseas. As my wife points out, "Women know how to talk and pray, but we don't know how to sharpen one another." Women need encouragement and training in developing services and businesses for outreach.

Sacrifice and suffering will take on a new definition for women tentmakers. They need to have listening ears and guidance for dealing with issues they never encountered before. Older women need to be encouraged to take up the mantle of mentoring younger women (Titus 2:4–5), walking them through the "how tos" of ministering to others. Greater efforts need to be made to adequately equip women of all ages and stages of life for living and working among the unreached.

THE TENTMAKER'S WIFE

There is a well-known saying, "Behind every good man is a good woman." This is certainly true of tentmakers. King Lemuel asks, "A wife of noble character who can find?" No greater challenge exists for the tentmaker than to balance the demands on his time. Spouse, children, team, discipling ministry, evangelism, work, communication with friends, churches, and family back home—the list goes on, and it seems endless. Guidance and accountability are hard to come-by overseas. This multiplies the stress on tentmakers' marriages. Though there are a few men who follow their wives' tentmaking job overseas, nearly 100 percent of the married females among those surveyed were overseas due to the husband's position. Tentmakers need a spouse who is equally committed to the husband's calling. The wife of the tentmaker may have a different role outside of the business or even ministry, but she needs to be on her husband's team and not on his back as he tries to juggle the many responsibilities.

Husbands need to establish clear boundaries to maintain a balanced life. We must daily ask Jesus to empower us in His Spirit. Paul models and teaches that we are to be filled with Christ's Spirit in whatever we do (Ephesians 5:18). His Spirit empowers us to live godly lives in the body of Christ (5:19–21), in marriage (5:22–33), as parents of children (6:1–4), and at work (6:5–9). The Lord is our enabler in whatever we do. In pursuing the Lord's service overseas, we need to ensure we have understood our priorities and have thought through a plan for keeping our time and energies centered in Him. Whether they are actively involved in the NGO, business, or ministry, our wives are to be an integral part of our whole life.

Marriages of cross-cultural workers are especially vulnerable. Satan knows if he can destroy our marriage, he can destroy our ministry. The second most common cause of missionary attrition is relationship problems. In my opinion, most of these relationship problems are rooted in matters between the husband and wife. Though rarely stated as the cause for going home, marriage problems have contributed to many more casualties than are attributed to them. Few workers wish to announce to the world their marital problems. Unresolved marital issues often cause other problems to be exacerbated. In the end, the other issues become the reason the couple goes home. However, the root issue is often marital stress. My research validates that those workers "whose marriage was not good (spiritually, emotionally, and sexually) before going overseas" have a good probability of being ineffective. Having a good marriage does not guarantee success, but not having a good marriage before setting out greatly increases the worker's likelihood of being unproductive. Experienced workers know that the issues which were little problems at home come under the magnifying glass overseas. In interviewing applicants, their marriages need to be thoroughly evaluated, and major unresolved issues need to be dealt with before sending them overseas. Cross-cultural living, with help from the Evil One, causes old sin issues to resurface. Many times workers have said to me, "I don't know why I am struggling with this again. It's been years since I have had this problem."

The Calling of the Wife

The research reveals that having a clear call or leading from God to serve overseas is the number one motive for workers to go to the 10/40 Window. Believing God has led us in this work helps us persevere through the tough times. Though some couples have endured on the field solely on the husband's calling, in most cases such couples either go home within four years or have serious ongoing marital problems. It is not uncommon in America, Europe, and Asia to find a husband who is called to a particular ministry with a wife who is barely involved because she does not share that same calling. The ministry the husband is involved in is his career. A similar scenario can work well overseas in places where the wife has all the conveniences, fellowship, and emotional support modern societies have to offer. It is quite another thing when she has none of these benefits.

Serving cross-culturally involves every family member, so it requires the whole family's commitment. Many organizations wisely discourage moving overseas with teenagers, unless the teen has clearly counted the cost and agreed to pay the price. A discontented wife or teenager is likely to shorten the career of any tentmaker (Proverbs 19:13). Jesus tells us that the husband and wife are one flesh (Matthew 19:5). Couples should learn to function together, not just live together. There will be times when the job or ministry will take precedence over the family, as well as times when the family will take precedence over the job or ministry. As He has guided us, He knows our limitations.

In many jobs in the West, it is not unusual for the husband to be sent on a business trip for a week or two. In the same way, there may be times when the tentmaker couple will be separated for business or ministry purposes. Jesus tells us there will be such times of separation (Mark 10:29–30). And just as He calls us, He will care for us. Such separations should be prayer-fully thought through. Children should be involved in discussing moves and periods of separation so that they are not surprised or hurt by Mommy or Daddy's sudden departure. If one spouse is not clearly led to serve abroad, separations, even for a few hours when there are problems at home, can become overwhelming struggles. The concerned spouse will have difficulty trusting God for the family's safety, health, education, future, etc. Fear will likely reign, pulling the other spouse out of the ministry and work he or she feels sent to do. Yet if the couple's love for each other is deep and strong, surpassed only by their love for the Lord, there will be few, if any problems that cannot be solved.

If a husband feels led to serve overseas, but the wife is unwilling, it may not be a lack of calling; it may be that her phone is off the hook. The husband should invest time understanding his wife and the concerns she has and work through her fears and worries with her. Then as one, you can help one another put your trust in the Lord. It is important for the wife to be willing to embrace God's will, wherever He may lead. Both husbands and wives need to receive strength independently from the Lord. One worker speaks to these issues, "You will do a great service to ensure that the wife is not just 'coming along with you' but that she is going to be, in at least the private sense, a co-owner of your calling in business and ministry and of all the stress and blessings which will accompany it."

Who Am I?

Possibly the greatest priority for God in calling us to the mission field is the transformation He wishes to work in our lives. When we first move overseas, we take along a lot of cultural and spiritual baggage. Expect the Lord to do a major house cleaning in your life. Be ready for it. It is painful, but it is good for you. He loves you enough to want to transform you into His image, but expect it to be a struggle (1 Peter 4:12–13).

In many cultures, married women are referred to as "so & so's wife," instead of by name. In the homeland, a woman may have her own identity, but this is not true within many third world cultures. Widows and unmarried women are often attached to a family or household who provides a "covering" for them. At home, there are many social activities which women may readily participate in. In some cultures, respectable women are never seen in public places or allowed out of the home. Servants or the men do the shopping. In such situations, language learning may seem impossible. Loneliness may become a huge issue for women.

Many tentmaker wives struggle with their role and even their identity.

She was called and commissioned as a tentmaker, the same as her husband, so shouldn't she be involved in the business and outreach? But if so, who will raise the kids? Where does her responsibility to her husband and the children end and her responsibility to the Lord begin? Or should it be the other way around? Yet aren't these all one and the same thing? So why do they seem to pull her in a hundred directions? Even as she struggles with all these questions, concerns about "Who am I?" are not at the forefront of most women's thinking. Mothers have more immediate and pressing problems which require their energy, like learning to communicate with the vendors at the market while trying to keep her two children out of the cow dung at their feet. Seemingly trivial matters compound daily, depleting her energy and joy. Training the children, meeting their emotional needs as they adjust to a different culture, learning the language, running the house, and seeking to love the Lord with all her heart and share that with the woman next door leave her exhausted at the end of the day. And then the husband returns home expecting her to meet his needs! She has no time left to think about her own well being.

The role of the wife is often ignored and left to play out as the performance unfolds. We must learn to recognize and deal with the wife's basic need of having some significance. Failure to do so leads to health problems, marital stress, depression, and a tragic misuse of a gifted servant of God. In a meeting with Tina and her husband, Dave, she suddenly exclaimed, "Why is all the attention given to Dave? I am a human being too. God called me to be here just as he did Dave. Why does it seem I am always crying—'Pick me! Pick me!'" Having many roles, yet with no clear direction, often accentuates feelings of guilt that arise in a woman's heart. As a woman and a wife, a mother and a missionary, she senses she has fallen short of her dreams.

Tentmaking wives not only need to script their roles for themselves, they need to rewrite who they are in relationship to their husbands. Some women, especially those who used to have a full-time job at home, derived status and comfort from being "recognized" as a contributor to society. As wives of tentmakers, many women struggle to find an identity within the parameters of their husband's status. Sometimes, though a couple cannot carry a visible badge of "missionary" or "Christian worker," they must live at a missionary standard of living. Thus, they can neither openly relate to other missionaries, nor relate to wealthier expatriates. This hinders the wife's need of making deep friendships with other women to whom she can bare her soul.

Each spouse needs to have a sense of significance and fulfillment.

This will come more naturally for the husband who is out in the community. Thus, the husband needs to invest time in building up his wife's identity and confidence. It is common for wives to become jealous of their husbands' ministry and freedoms, and this, if not resolved, will become a seed for marital stress. Help is needed for the wife to sort through options and priorities for child care, education, and ministry, both in the community and alongside her husband at work. My wife reminds me that in twenty years of tentmaking ministry, the accountability and mentoring of older women in her life have kept her focused and moving forward. She recognizes that she would be lost in the shuffle among the many responsibilities we have as a couple without their input. Personally, my mentors have helped me to understand what it means to live with my wife in an understanding way (I Peter 3:7). Wives need regular reassuring and encouragement from their husbands. They need help coming to terms with reality and recognizing their priorities in different phases of their lives. They also need to be reminded that whatever they do, they do it as a service to God.

Joyce Bowers speaks of four "wifestyles" to give cross-cultural wives some guidelines and defined meaning to their roles. The four roles are homemaker, background supporter, teamworker, and parallel worker. "Homemaker: she is primarily a full-time wife and mother. Her main focus is on the home and the support and nurture of her family. She is an enabler to her husband in his work. Background supporter: she actively supports her husband and his work. She is moderately involved in outside activities, many of which relate to her husband's assignment. Her main focus may be on ministry that can be carried out with the home. . . . Teamplayer: her main focus is on a team ministry with her husband and both work full time. She feels free to choose a variety of activities, some of which relate directly to her husband's work. . . . Parallel worker: she sees her missionary role as distinct from her husband's role." In Bowers' opinion and my observations, not many tentmaker wives fall in the category of parallel workers. There are also many combinations and variations, especially at different stages of our family situations. Each role is valid; we need to know ourselves and thank God for the role He has given us.

My wife adds, "Women seek roles which we feel will give us an identity from which we can draw comfort. But it is only in a deep love relationship with Jesus Christ that a woman will truly find what she seeks. No husband, no job, not even raising well-adjusted and successful children can satisfy for long. We women need to find our identity in Jesus Christ. When women lose their first love, we allow our own abilities to determine our identity. Every person as a disciple of Jesus has gifts to be offered back to Him for the building of the kingdom. We must find our identity as disciples of Jesus and then let our roles flow from that identity." Husbands, we need to be diligent in leading our wives deeper into the heart of God (Ephesians 5:25–27).

As children grow or other factors in the home or ministry change, the roles and priorities of the wife should be reevaluated. When the children enter school, the wife may find she has more time or energy to pursue other activities. She should be encouraged to try new venues of service, utilizing talents which may have been used sparingly while focusing her attention on the godly development of the children.

A greater issue here is not actually what the wife does, but how she perceives herself and how the husband perceives her. Though their roles may vary greatly, both spouses need to agree on the wife's role. It is important to be united on how the wife should respect and deal with local cultural values, with special concern given to those practices which are deemed unbiblical. Husbands need to be supportive of their wives, helping them define their role and publicly recognizing and honoring it. A wife who is well adjusted, happy and content in the Lord is a pillar on which a happy home is built. I know of many men who might have quit during very difficult times, if it were not for the emotional and spiritual strength of their wives.

It has already been stated that culture shock affects everyone who moves overseas. Good communication is a good preventative. The husband's culture shock is often cushioned by his busyness and his well defined role at work, in the community, and at home. The wife, on the other hand, struggles with the well-being of her family. Though the wife is busy with the house and the children, her many duties can seem insignificant to the ministry of her husband and the calling they came overseas to fulfill. Discouragement and frustration set off culture shock. Communication between husband and wife enables the couple to enter into one another's lives and find meaning to the struggles they are facing. Affirmation and adequate support from the husband in the confusing roles the wife has to juggle help smooth the effects of culture shock.

Some husbands are so focused on their work that they neglect their families. Others unwittingly make unreasonable demands of the wife, even to a point where she becomes physically or emotionally ill. Husbands must understand that while we enjoy the excitement of traveling, growing the business, teaching, ministering, etc., the wife remains at home continuously burdened with household responsibilities and the care of the children. In addition, often the wife has no fellowship with anyone of her intellectual caliber. A good wife is worth more than rubies (Proverbs 31:10). But like any gem that needs polishing and care, husbands need to beware of their wives' issues and work with them to overcome their fears and struggles.

Wives need to understand that the tentmaking husband struggles with two extremes in meeting the needs of his family. On the one hand, he wishes to meet all the needs of his wife and children, while on the other hand, he wishes to fulfill all the demands of the ministry and business to bring glory to Jesus' name. In a practical sense, there is just not enough time to adequately do it all. Thus, it is important for both the husband and wife to be equally committed or called. In addition, male supervisors need to be more sensitive to women's issues. Supervisors should include their own wives in coaching couples. During pre-field orientation, specific attention should be given to discussing various "wifestyle" options for married women. The wife's life and work should be made a part of the workers' annual reports, along with goals for the year and a summary of ministry activities. Such reports would provide insight for discussion with supervisors, as well as documenting the work they accomplished.

Wives and Ministry

Whatever roles tentmaker wives choose to have, the list of ministry opportunities for women equals or even exceeds those of men. Our ministry to those around us is an outflow of God's love through us. As women are more active in the work force in our home culture and are gaining more recognition and affirmation, there is a temptation for them to consider their ministry roles as missionaries as primary and their ministry roles as a wife and a mother as secondary. I want to affirm women in their ministry role of being a wife and a mother. Titus 2:3 talks about older women teaching the younger women to love their husbands. My wife clarifies, "The first and most significant role of a wife is being a wife. That is not just a play on words. Many women feel their children are first priority, but we need to study what the Bible teaches." A family begins with the husband—wife relationship.

My wife continues, "in Proverbs 31, the context of the passage includes the woman's role and work in relationship to her husband. The first role given to women is to be a helper to the man (Genesis 2:18). As wives, we need to consider the role of a helper seriously in relation to the man God has given us. A good helper knows her role and her husband's needs.

Another passage that helps me to live out my role as a helper is Proverbs 31:11–12, 23. As a helper, I want my husband to trust in me to meet his needs and bring him good. And as a result, he will be respected in the city gate." A helper is not to be treated as subservient. As couples grow in understanding and trust, husbands should enable their wives to exercise their gifts and talents in both the business and the ministry.

I thank God each day for the woman helper God has given me in my wife. Before you think that I have a submissive and quiet wife, she wants to add, "Being a helper is not a natural role for me—at least it wouldn't be what I'd script for myself. I like to lead, and I am opinionated. I will be the first to admit that I also have a sharp temper. But as I grow in the Lord, and with Patrick's patience as the head of our household, we grow in understanding of one another as husband and wife. As we work together, we also recognize one another's strengths and weaknesses. He affirms my role as a helper for him, and I learn to submit to his leadership." We are still perfecting our roles as husband and wife. After twenty-five years of marriage, we still have our struggles. Yet we recognize that struggle is part of God's growing process. Open and honest communication is essential to our growth. Loving mentors who hold us accountable when we have conflict have been the key for us in fulfilling the calling He has given us as a couple.

For mothers, another significant ministry is that of shepherding their children. Children are a heritage and a reward from God (Psalm 127:3). Verses stating the importance of how to bring up our children abound both in the Old and New Testaments. We need to remember the responsibilities God has given us as parents. The folding of diapers, tying of shoes, and chauffeuring kids between school and sports activities can seem insignificant in a results driven world. We need to remember the little things we do for and with our children are significant in God's eyes, and He is the one we ultimately seek to please. When we focus our eyes on the eternal, those little mundane tasks take on greater meaning.

Godly parenting reflects the glory of God in a society where there is no light. One woman wrote, "I was at the park with my children two days ago. Asha was there with her children. She has observed that my children do not throw tantrums like hers do. She was wondering how I manage to do that. I was able to share with her how my husband and I follow God's instructions in our parenting." We are His living testimony; as we live our lives, our friends see how our children grow and how they live out the principles we teach them.

God spreads His glory through the lives of children (Psalm 8:2). It is no surprise the research indicates children are an asset, not a hindrance to ministry. Children make terrific ambassadors for Jesus. Many mothers have built eternal relationships with women through friends they initially met through their children. At the park and in the market, people often fawn over our kids. Helping out at their school activities or local youth functions are great ways to meet other mothers.

Another significant role for a wife is that of minister. In some cultures, it is harder for women to meet others, but children and knowing the language are helpful bridge-builders. Thus, it is important for wives to learn the language and to learn it well. Time should be set aside for the wife to learn the language. If she has young children, this may be difficult. A plan should be designed for her to have tutors, special classes, books, and other tools, which will facilitate her language acquisition. Though her duties may be many and the process slow, some goals should be set to keep the mother moving forward in her language studies. Our team has been able to encourage European high school graduates to spend their "gap" year living with us for three to nine months to provide child care and do homeschooling while the mothers study the language. Local nannies can also be employed to care for the kids. Learning the language not only allows the tentmaker's wife to be able to communicate the love of Christ, it helps her feel more at home in the culture. In whatever ways she desires to contribute to the ministry, our wives' well being and love for the country is crucial for enabling us to be productive in whatever we do.

Mothers often find local mothers within their neighborhood who have similar interests or whose children have the same interests. These neighbors are normally curious about the foreigner in their midst. Ask them to teach you how they keep house, cook, wash, sew, grow flowers, etc. Share responsibilities for watching the kids. Learn and use new vocabulary as you acquire these skills. Invite them to learn how to bake or make homemade ice cream. There are as many things to learn as there are jobs to be done in a house, and each provides an opportunity to shine your light for the Lord.

Sue in Central Asia writes, "Recently, my language helper wanted to learn how to cook pasta. We agreed to have an hour of language learning and then cooking. I had bought the meat, so when she asked if she could bring anything, I said no. I then realized that she wanted to give me something in return. So I arranged to meet her for breakfast and then we went to the market together. As I was buying some vegetables, I noticed she wanted to pay but I was too quick. Thankfully, the Holy Spirit prompted me, so I told her if she could run over to the other stall and get me some noodles, I would appreciate it very much. She did so and seemed more relaxed." The best way to get to know others is not by serving or helping them. Actually, it is by allowing them to serve, help, teach, or otherwise invest in us. When we serve them, they are likely to feel indebted to us, but if they serve us, they are likely to feel we are indebted to them. People tend to feel more comfortable with those who are in their debt, versus those who they are in debt to. Who are you more comfortable being around, the person who you owe a favor, or the person who owes you a favor? Asking favors of friends is an excellent way to build relationships.

Many local women are lonely; most are more afraid of meeting a foreigner than you are of them. Do not be afraid to take the first step or say the wrong word. Nationals everywhere are gracious to the guests in their midst. Linda, in the Arab world adds, "Since I arrived, different women have expressed their disappointments, struggles and pain to me. These precious windows of opportunity into their lives have sometimes shocked me. I realize that sometimes we are 'safer' people to talk to as we are outsiders in their eyes."

The home often furnishes opportunities for a personal testimony of the Lord's gracious work in our lives. The inner workings of the home, if outsiders are invited in, may be a better witness of our faith than anything we could verbally share. Real discipleship and a godly household go together. Donna in Indonesia adds, "My friend who is engaged to be married is going into it with much fear, largely due to marriage breakups in her own family and what Islam teaches. I asked her if she knew of any marriages which she thought were ideal. Two out of the three she shared were Christian marriages. She obviously knows more Muslim couples than Christian couples but look at which marriages stood out to her!"

My wife adds, "Women are relational beings. We easily build relationships with local women. As believers who strive to live out biblical principles, our relationships provide terrific opportunities for sharing how we live our lives according to biblical truth. We should not be afraid to share those principles with our local friends. Biblical principles are instructions for living on earth. These principles apply to all peoples. Just because a woman is a Hindu or a Muslim does not mean she cannot learn and apply biblical principles. In reality, we begin the discipleship process with our friends before they believe. Much of that discipleship is a result of our modeling. We can also be intentional and verbally introduce biblical principles to our friends. Such sharing paves the way for presenting the full gospel. Without Jesus' Spirit, we know our friends will have more struggles applying the truth they learn. However, if they see the wisdom of the principles we share, but lack the ability to apply them, this is an open door to tell them of the role and power of the Holy Spirit in our lives. Later, when they believe, they will already have a good foundation to build on." Through relationships, women have many opportunities to involve themselves in ministry. We should not confuse ministry with tasks. Ministry comes out of our relationship with Jesus. It includes sharing our love for God and depending on Him to speak through our actions and words. Some women are able to find the time and resources to plan and prepare stories, studies, and other materials to reach out to women. Some want to but have little time and energy for such tasks. We should not compare or covet a more significant role in ministry. As God accepts us in our roles and ministry, we need to accept ourselves and one another's roles and ministries.

Potential Problems

Women are generally more relational than men. The biggest problem faced by most women is finding compatible fellowship. Back home there is a smorgasbord of options for fellowship, but overseas you must take what you can find, and sometimes there is nothing available. If for no other reason than this, wives need to be part of a team for fellowship. Wives should be encouraged to get together for tea, to watch a movie, and to have fun, besides doing Bible study and praying together. Annual retreats for women are also an encouragement. Women who are experienced at ministering to women should be brought in on occasion to share with the wives, while the men stay home with the children. Such activities refresh our wives, "recharging their batteries" for the daily challenges they face. Make provision for your wife to join with other women, even if it requires traveling outside the country.

The women in our team agree that by God's design, they were put together as a team. But they also agree that if they were in the same church in their home country, they would probably not be close friends. Their differences in personalities and backgrounds would make it unlikely they would choose one another as friends. Because of the limited choices for camaraderie here and the belief that they are called together by God's design, they have worked at growing to love one another as sisters in Christ. They will admit it has not been easy. There have been problems and misunderstandings. But as one wife on our team said, "We don't just study the 'one another' verses, we live them." And another wife added, "It gives us an opportunity to understand the meaning of love as stated in 1 Corinthians 13."

Not all women find evangelism and church planting to be their passion. In many countries wives cannot work. Some wives, especially after their children have entered school and again when they leave for college, do not know what to do with their time. With each new phase of life, discuss creative ideas and explore opportunities with your spouse. In several countries, tentmaker wives have begun their own businesses out of their homes, employing local women to make handicrafts, operate a catering business, and operate a hair salon. Such businesses give them opportunities to employ local women who they can befriend and witness to as they work. Other tentmaker wives have started interest groups or do volunteer work.

Security

Wives and children need to be aware of security issues. The wife and children must understand your dual identity. Rehearse answering questions likely to be asked with each family member. After four years as traditional missionaries working in a church and a one year furlough, we returned to a Muslim country as tentmakers. However, I neglected to inform my children of our change of jobs. All they knew was we were going back overseas to reach out to Muslims. The second day of kindergarten, the teacher asked all the children, as a kind of ice breaker, "What does your daddy do?" You can imagine her surprise when my son said with pride, "My daddy is a missionary!" You can imagine my surprise when the teacher confronted me with that! That evening we had a thorough discussion with the children explaining Daddy's new job.

Be prepared for the possible event of one spouse being arrested or having a sudden, serious illness. Both spouses should know the passwords for computer programs and how to use e-mail and the telephone to contact your supervisor, home church, and country's embassy. Both spouses should also know where your personal papers are kept, including passports, will, insurance policies, and bank accounts. Copies of all documents, including passports should be kept in a readily available file. It is a good idea for the wife to have her own debit/credit card so she can get money in an emergency. The children should know where to go, and how to contact people who will help them should Dad and Mom have an accident or be arrested. Each family should have its own security guidelines and emergency plan which are updated annually.

Security issues are a source of stress for many tentmakers and their families. It is important to talk about these stresses with your wife and kids. Do not assume that they do not have fears. The children's fears need to be acknowledged. They should be taught how to handle various security concerns. It needs to be handled with discretion according to their ages and maturity. When our children were young, we taught them that when they were asked about my job, they should just say, "My dad works for Widget company." If they were asked more questions, they were to reply, "I don't know. Ask my mom." It is not uncommon for the wife to know her husband is a banker but not know what he really does as a banker. Wives should not feel they have to answer in detail about what their husbands do.

MAKING A TENT A HOME

One of the most important decisions you may make upon arrival is where to live. Most tentmakers build relationships through their work place and their neighborhood. Some missionaries, realizing their best relationships are with their neighbors, intentionally move periodically so as to share the gospel more. The house you choose will affect the way the local people view you and will play a significant role in the general well being of the family. It is vital for wives and children to feel at home. It is nearly always worth the extra time and effort to make family members feel comfortable with their living space.

Where to Live

A newly arrived worker might ask, "Are we living in the right area?" Without having visited, I would normally reply, "Probably not." Nearly every new worker moves into the wrong area at first, but that is okay. In fact, it may be wise to live in the wrong area at first. Until you pass through culture shock, you worry about cleanliness, electricity, water, food, schools, etc. It is better to become comfortable in the culture and then in stages move to places which are better suited for ministry. That usually requires moving more than one time.

Cultural bonding suggests you start out as low, as poor, and as simple as you can. However, if the wife and kids burn out within six months, is that worth it? Before arriving overseas, discuss with the family the kind of home you would like to live in. I would strongly suggest the family agree to the goal of living at the lowest level your profession allows within the people you are reaching. If you start out higher, or in an area where your people group does not live, don't sweat it. Most workers need a "starter house." In the beginning, most workers make their biggest and greatest number of cultural mistakes. Thus, there is benefit to living away from the area in which you expect to be most effective, so that the majority of your mistakes are in a different area, and you will not offend people you later hope to reach out to. Yes, sometimes mistakes may also endear you to your neighbors, but only sometimes. Sometimes we so embarrass ourselves that we want to "move away." In any case, it is wise to commit to staying in your first home one to two years, and then reevaluate.

In selecting a location for your home, there are many practical questions you should ask. How many bedrooms do you need? What size a house has your family been used to in the past? Which neighborhood is suitable for the family? Is the price within your budget? Is the water and electricity supply regular? Is there a telephone line? Do the utilities and phone work? (Take it from one who did not check and learned that though there was a phone and a line, it never worked.) Is it important to be close to good schools and a playground for the kids? Is it open to breezes and sunlight? Is public transportation accessible? Is it quiet? Do the wife and kids feel they would be safe there? Is shopping, banking, and medical care nearby? Is there a safe place to park your vehicle overnight? Before moving in and paying the deposit, be sure any changes you request or improvements are completed by the landlord. Rents are usually negotiable, and often you can get a ceiling fan or an air-conditioner added at no extra charge. Most landlords prefer foreign renters, as foreigners have a reputation for maintaining property well. If most factors are equal and you have to decide between living near a good school for the children or near Dad's place of work, choose the school. It is much easier for Dad to commute than for the kids.

As important as the logistical and convenience questions are, you also need to consider ministry related questions. Where do the people you are called to live? Do you wish to surround yourselves with neighbors who will be easy to befriend and relate to, or would you rather have a home away from the crowds that can be a place of refuge? To which socio-economic group are you going to minister? What size and kind of house can you rent without appearing to be a "rich westerner?" Is the layout of the home conducive to ministry? Does it allow for private family areas not easily accessible to guests? This may be important for security reasons, as well as privacy. If the house is furnished, is the furniture appropriate for receiving the kind of guests you desire? For example, a Chinese landlord in Indonesia may furnish his home in a way that is unbecoming to the Muslims you desire to have visit. If your NGO or ministry will primarily serve the villages, should you live in the city or a village? In the village, you will certainly be living in a fish bowl, but you will probably have deeper friendships and learn the language better too.

Some cities restrict where foreigners may live. You may need to go through official channels to sanction your accommodation arrangements. Be prepared to pay two or even three months rent as a deposit. Some areas require the entire year's rent up front. If possible, so that you are not tricked or cheated, use a recommended realtor (if they exist) or a friend to help house hunt and negotiate the rental contract. However, though the local friend may know the language, he might not have ever rented or bought a home before. It is wise to ask for help from someone who has previous experience in renting or buying property.

Thoroughly discuss these questions with your spouse before committing to your new location. In the end, husbands, remember a home is the wife's office. When in doubt, let the wife have the final say on where you live.

Some workers prefer to rent a home, while others prefer to buy. You may have a choice about housing, but you may not. In some cases, an employer will provide housing. If the company provides housing, your choices may be simple—take it or leave it. If the company gives you a choice, consider closely all the options. Multinational companies usually maintain houses in the section of the city where the expatriates live. If your goal is to reach out to your neighbors, this may prove too restrictive.

In most foreign cities, there are few middle class houses and even fewer for rent. Overseas rental homes tend to fall into one of two categories: "very large and very nice" and "barely adequate." While few workers can afford large homes in their home country, they likely can overseas. Prayerfully determine God's criteria for you; then ask and He will provide (Matthew 7:7). As rents are usually affordable, with the landlord's permission, feel free to invest in the property and make changes so as to make the home more livable.

Most expatriates rent homes, but with globalization and perhaps inflation in some countries, there are advantages to buying. Before buying, you need to ask yourself several questions. Can I afford to buy? And is the market good? Is the government stable? (If not, it might confiscate your property.) Is the government an ally of your home government? Are there restrictions on foreign ownership? How long do you intend to reside in that place? Homes do not resell as easily in most countries as they do in the West. Many countries do not have home owners' insurance, so if there is damage, due to hate crimes, you could be liable. It is wise to rent your "starter home" for a year or more before determining whether you should buy.

One worker in China, reflecting mixed considerations, writes, "We have bought our property because we plan to be here long term, possibly ten years. By buying, the money is in our pockets and not someone else's.

I think after saying this that people should evaluate the place and the political, economical, and crime situation in their country. I feel buying property is much better than renting for those living at a location long term." Another worker in South East Asia adds, "Being new on the field, our buying a house was very good for us psychologically and emotionally, as we had moved around quite a bit the previous year. Buying a house gave us a sense of belonging and stability we very much needed. It has also tied us down to one place (good and bad). I think my wife has more of an emotional need for a place of our own than I do, although I found it very helpful, especially in terms of not worrying about what everybody was thinking about me. Once we bought a house, I viewed it as my neighborhood and was not so worried what others thought. We also bought in a better neighborhood with the thought of having a refuge rather than ministering to our neighbors."

In setting up your first home, there is no need to go native, unless you are committed to a C-5 contextualization strategy. With your "starter house," give yourself time to acclimate and settle in. Though it is good to have an area to receive guests, you should also keep an area for yourselves. Children will need the freedom to decorate their space as they like. Though there may be limits due to the culture, having some space of your own is helpful, even for the experienced worker. Naturally, your house will not be like your house in your homeland, but it can provide some reminders of your home culture.

It is important for the wife to have the freedom to make the house a home. In the first few years, as we knew we would be moving often, we made the mistake of not taking the time to make the house a home. This was unsettling for my wife and children. Even if you know your house is but temporary living quarters, hang some pictures, buy a few plants, and get some throw rugs. The point is to enable your wife to make the place a home. It does wonders for her sanity, and in times of stress, it is good to have a place that looks and feels like home.

Household Help

In many countries, it is normal for both upper and middle class families to have household servants. The idea of having help with cooking, dishes, cleaning, and errands may sound great at first, but before deciding, think carefully about the pros and cons.

Ask yourself, why do I even need house help? Do my neighbors have similar help? Do I need part-time or full-time help? If you are in business, it should be socially acceptable to have help, but it might not be if you are a student or working in an NGO. In some countries, all expatriate workers are expected to have house help. In our early years, we did not have help. One day a close MBB friend and I were sitting in the living room while my wife vacuumed around us. He rebuked me, "Why don't you hire one of our women to clean your house? Do you know your neighbors see you as selfish? If you don't provide jobs for our people, how can you expect us to respect you?"

A knowledgeable national helper is wonderful. They know where and how to shop. Running errands can be complicated and time consuming. A helper can save you time, energy, and stress. Helpers know the local prices and may save you money as they can bargain better. In addition, the helper can cook local foods in a way that will please your local guests. Though western supermarkets may be available, the money a helper saves shopping in the local market during the course of a month may cover her entire salary. A helper can be a great blessing for learning the language and culture too. A helper will know where to buy things and where and how to pay bills. Some countries still require bills to be paid in cash, meaning waiting in long lines each month to pay the bills.

In the beginning, few helpers are reliable or even helpful. Mothers who have never managed house help before will have to invest time in training them. A common mistake women make is treating the helper as a friend, not an employee. Helpers need to be trained, managed, and held accountable, just like other employees. Each day's work needs to be planned in advance. If the chore or food being prepared is new to the house help, the wife should do it with the worker to ensure she does it the way you like. You may wish to join her for running errands too, both for the experience and to familiarize yourself with the time and cost of running each errand. Do not assume the house help will follow a weekly schedule. If Monday is the day to wash the car, the helper may not do so if the car is not dirty. Time must be invested each day to review what you expect the helper to do. The helper will be happier and so will you.

There are two problems which may arise from having household help. One is theft, and the other is security. Make clear to the help that if she steals anything, she will be dismissed. One way to help her with temptation is to promise her an annual bonus based on her honesty. And if her local knowledge or contacts save you money, split the difference with her. Security-wise, house help will know about everything inside your home and who your visitors are. It is common for authorities to request that the helper make reports to them about activities within your home. Do not discourage this, as she really has no choice. But be aware it may be happening. One idea is to hire a helper who has poor English; the less they know the better. Be sure they are illiterate. Another idea is to hire a worker from outside the group you are focusing on, but this is not as helpful for language learning.

The Simpler Life

Twenty years ago there was much talk about living a simple lifestyle. Today's younger generation has little clue what that is. As tentmakers, you must be prepared to do without many of the items you are used to. You may bring a few indispensable household appliances with you, but do not expect them to last long. The heat, dust, transformer, lack of grounding, and irregular power surges are likely to ruin them soon after arrival. Every major city in the 10/40 Window has electricity, though sometimes not as reliable as in the West. In many cases, the voltage is different, requiring the use of transformers for the appliances you bring. Check in advance about electricity voltage in the city you are going to. The outlets overseas are also different. In smaller cities or remote areas, laptop computers are better as they can operate with a battery, and plugs are designed for various voltages. Except for laptops, it is wise to bring few or no electric items.

Limit the amount of clothing you bring as well. Buying clothes locally and wearing the brands which are known to locals will help your acculturation process. One Chinese American working in China could never figure out how locals at all levels knew he was an American even before he said anything. When it was pointed out to him that the brands of his clothes betrayed his identity, he went and bought a local wardrobe. He was soon able to pass for a local. I know of Latinos working in Central Asia who had similar experiences.

Shopping will be your first hurdle. It can be exhausting simply trying to decide where to shop, what to buy, and how much to pay. Different cultures have different cultural rules for buying and selling. People in many countries expect you to bargain. Invite a local friend to go with you to the food market, furniture stores, and other shops to explain how the local system of buying and selling works. Make a list of what items cost to use for future reference. When I lived in China, I regularly took a taxi from my apartment to the commuter train station. Each day I had a different driver. They usually quoted me the same price, $2.40. Sometimes a driver would ask for more, but I would say, "No, I'll pay the normal rate, $2.40." The driver would always nod, and I would feel good about knowing the local price. After several months, I happened to take a taxi with my neighbor, a local Chinese. At the train station, my friend paid $1.80. As I speak Chinese well, I asked the driver, "How come, he pays $1.80? Isn't the normal rate $2.40?" He smiled and replied, "That's the price we charge foreigners." Every driver knew the system! Whatever you buy, expect to pay more. As one local friend explained, "You are not being cheated; it's called a 'white skin tax' which you are charged for being a foreigner and living here."

Every trip to the market is an adventure, so make it fun. What is a few cents here and there? Learn to laugh at yourself; being over charged a few coins here and there is not worth losing your peace of mind.

Family Time

Many tentmakers state that one of their greatest difficulties in living overseas is privacy and getting time alone with the family. Learning culturally sensitive ways to protect some family privacy can be a great challenge. When you want time alone, do you lock the doors, pull the shades, and hide in your house, pretending no one is home? When a visitor knocks, do you drop your plans for them? What do you do if visitors will not take a hint and leave when it is time for your kids to go to bed?

Carving out time with the family (western style) may be impossible overseas, especially if you cling to western values of "family time." In America, many preachers have a lot to say about "family time." However, some of their ideas, though portrayed as being based on the Bible, are not necessarily biblical; they are expressions of American culture. One of the biggest blessings of working in another country is the chance to step outside your own culture and discover there is more than one way to do things. Such new revelations also cause us to search for what practices in our adopted culture—and correspondingly in our own culture—are really biblical. For example, where in the Bible does it say that godly families will put their children to bed early each night? And where does it say that children take priority over guests? Or that loving husbands wash dishes?

Perhaps you have grasped by now that living overseas as a tentmaker requires a new way of thinking and living. The family IS our ministry, even as a guest IS our ministry. In Eastern and in biblical culture, when we welcome a guest into our home, the guest comes under our care, as if he is one of our family members (Leviticus 19:33–34). Jesus models this in both feeding and healing those under His care. Yet, when informed His family was present, Jesus questioned, "Who is my mother, and who are my brothers?" Pointing to his disciples, he said, "Here are my mother and my brothers" (Matthew 12:46–50). We hear very little preaching on that passage. Having a cross-cultural marriage has forced me to evaluate things from another perspective. It is not unusual for Asian children to go to bed after 10 PM. Do they grow up damaged, unbalanced or in poor health as a result? No more than western children. So why is an 8 or 9 PM bed-time such an issue for westerners? When the children came to Jesus in Matthew 19, they were with their families out in the wilderness. What kind of parents were these? Or was it the kids' summer vacation and there was a KOA campground nearby? Jesus' teaching was not on parenting or family lifestyle, but on God-honoring principles. These principles are influenced by many things, including culture. When we move overseas He will lead us to adopt many of the ways of our adopted culture. This may include aspects of how we raise our children and how we spend time with them. Most children do not miss being raised in their parents' homeland; only we, the parents do. It is helpful to study what Jesus says about raising children using only the Bible and not our cultural interpretations and applications.

While visiting one family who we were recruiting to our team, the elders of their church brought it to my attention that the couple regularly allowed their three year old to stay up until 10 PM. The wife was Asian. She did not see this as a problem. However, it was causing the church leaders to think poorly of them as parents. Citing some examples which my wife and I saw as cultural differences, one church leader argued with me that because they were undisciplined parents, they would be poor missionaries. I pointed out to the parents that there was a cultural misunderstanding in their parenting style with the church leaders. Being sensitive and not wanting cultural misunderstandings to be a barrier to their calling, they adjusted their parenting habits, including putting their child to bed early. Amazingly, in my next visit five months later, the church leaders perceived them to be good parents and good candidates for the mission field as well.

We need to think through how our culture affects our views of family and parenting. Jack in India clarifies, "When guests arrive, we drop our plans. In our culture, usually the man is the one who entertains. My wife simply makes tea and serves cookies and then leaves to do whatever she needs to do, including tending the children, homeschooling, even putting them to bed. When the women visit, they join in doing whatever the wife is doing, whether that be laundry, dishes, or caring for the kids. Yes, it interrupts homeschooling, but is it better for our kids to learn to serve, honor, and witness to our guests, or memorize their multiplication tables? Clearly, the latter can be done anytime."Dealing with the constant flow of guests can be a struggle if we look at life through western glasses. Jim, a worker among Muslims writes, "Often people arrive when we are having family devotions. When that happens, we welcome the guests and invite them to join the family. The children know they are to sit still and wait till the guests are made comfortable. My wife brings the guests food and drink, and then after making the appropriate greetings, I continue along, sharing the message with the children. Yes, it is an interruption. But we get many opportunities to witness by living our family life out in the open and not keeping it private. On the rare occasion that a guest chooses not to join us, my wife serves the guest a simple drink, and then she continues the lesson while I sit with the guest. But it provides me with an opportunity to share with the guest what we were doing."

Westerners try to protect their families and their time. Rather than seek to protect ourselves, perhaps we should "abandon" ourselves. Children are only bothered by what bothers the parents. Another worker adds, "Living cross-culturally is a transformational opportunity. Some things are shed, others are modified, and yet others remain almost exactly the same. It is hard to know ahead of time what among our western values may end up being shed or changed. Welcoming changes, anticipating challenges, and being willing to be remolded are valuable attitudes. You and your family will find your non-negotiables challenged and your personal boundaries stretched."

We always need to remember to ask ourselves, "What did Jesus do?" Privacy is an American value. It is something we have acquired within our sinful culture. Jesus sought times alone to meet with the Father and to train His disciples, just as you might with your family. However, when in the culture, He lived according to the accepted standards of the people, except where they broke biblical teachings. He ate local food, dressed like a teacher, submitted to His parents and was a generous guest to His hosts.

There is nothing wrong with living according to our own cultural practices. Yet, having sacrificed and prepared for years to be His witnesses, we need to prayerfully consider whether or not Jesus would have us make a few minor concessions in our personal preferences. If private family time is a high value, take it to the cross, as you have done with so many other things. The best evangelists are those who have a steady stream of people in their home. There was a two year period where our guest room was empty only sixteen days. I think that helped our boys' discipleship, not hurt it. Family time is good and is important. Some workers need more than others. When our house was full, after the boys came home from the local school, I had to carve out time away from the house to be alone with them. But as with Jesus and His disciples, it may be necessary to get out of the house or the city to have such times. Learn your spouse's, your children's and your own limits. Realize it is acceptable to take one to three days away with the family a few times a year. Knowing yourself and your family is a key in determining what is helpful.

John, in Central Asia, sums this up well when he writes, "My exhortation is to discover the beauty and logic of your host culture/people to the greatest extent possible, whether or not you end up adopting their values over your own, or modifying yours in some way. When you meet them on those terms of appreciation and respect, the differences can become enriching rather than frustrating."

SUMMARY

Women tentmakers are needed to reach the unreached women of the 10/40 Window. Yet, women can expect great hardship, as well as great blessings, as they pursue His will overseas. It is essential for women to know who they are in Christ. Women need to grow in their sharpening and mentoring skills. A good marriage is an essential foundation for a good ministry. Husbands and wives need to develop good communication skills before departing for the field. Parenting issues should be regularly discussed and discipline of the children consistently enforced. Ways to contextualize family times should be considered. Women also need to think through how they wish to set up and operate their home overseas. Husbands need to be sensitive to the wife's social, security, and family needs.

ACTION STEPS

- Mentoring is essential for growth. Who is, or can be, invited to be a mentor in your life, ministry and marriage? If you are an older woman, who can you mentor?

- What ministry do you have or desire to have overseas? How can you better prepare or equip yourself for this ministry?

- Wives, what marriage and child raising issues do you need to discuss with your husbands? Do it this week.

- Which "wifestyle" do you see yourself fulfilling? How does your husband or leader view your role? Discuss your role in the home and in ministry with him.

- What image do you wish for your home and family to project to the community? How will you accomplish this?

- Discuss ways your spouse and you can make special moments for one another and the family.

To live away from my family is the severest form of martyrdom.

CELTIC PROVERB

A man who is a success at home and a failure at everything else. . . is indeed a successful man.

WRITTEN ON THE WALL OF A LIBRARY
AT AN ARCHEOLOGICAL DIG IN ATHENS

Fathers, do not exasperate your children; instead, bring them up in the training and instruction of the Lord.

EPHESIANS 6:4

chapter 14
THE TENTMAKER AND HIS CHILDREN

David Howard, who invested forty years in mission work, told me, "By far my deepest regrets are in my relationship to my family. If I could live my career over, I would always put my family first, something I too often failed to do." Well-defined lines between home and work do not exist unless we work to define them. It is common to take on too many tasks which keep us away from the wife and kids for long hours. The ones we love the most are often the very ones we take for granted. The wisest man who ever lived told us, "Train a child in the way he should go, and when he is old he will not turn from it."[82] We need to invest time in our children. Children are likely to become what we put into them and live up to what we believe of them.

The most difficult decisions faced by tentmakers are not business or ministry related; they have to do with our children. To what culture do they belong? Where should they be educated? Where will they ultimately find a place in life? Is it fair they have to make sacrifices based on my decisions? Sacrificing our children is one way our heavenly Father teaches us about the cost of discipleship and what it meant for Him to give up His only Son for us. For my wife and me to sacrifice our education, our heritage, and our lives is comparatively easy. As Oswald Chambers said, "It never cost a disciple anything to follow Jesus; to talk about cost when you are in love with anyone is an insult."

Two reminders are helpful for parents. First, realize that all parents struggle with these issues. Though it is true we did not grow up in our adopted culture, nor have we experienced raising children there, we do know God, and He is the same wherever we are. If God has called us, He has also called our children. Our adopted culture will become "home" to our kids if we encourage them to make it their home. Our homeland's culture is not better, safer, or godlier than our adopted country. The safest and best place we can be is in the center of God's will, wherever that leads us. We need to have God's perspective on raising children. Second, as slaves of Jesus, even as it is not "our" education or "our" lives, so the children are not "ours." Since the children belong to Jesus, we can trust Him to provide and care for them. Settling the issue of who your children belong to may be the most important decision you make before going overseas. It will impact many decisions you make on their behalf.

Two-thirds of the workers rate their children as "happy" or "doing well," but that means one-third are struggling. Training requires planning. If we are to train our children, we need to think through our parenting strategies. I am amazed at the number of Christian workers who have no discipleship plan for their children. They have plans for their co-workers, team members and converts, but none for their children! Fathers, we need to prayerfully consider what it means "to bring up our children in the training and instruction of the Lord" (Ephesians 6:4).

I am blessed to have a cross-cultural marriage. Most people, especially westerners, believe the way they were raised is the best. As westerners, we never really evaluate how much of our upbringing is biblical and how much is cultural. Having a bi-cultural marriage has forced my wife and me to look to the Scriptures concerning child-rearing issues. We have been surprised at what we found. An American education, playing baseball, learning the piano, having well-trained school teachers, and eating Big Macs are cultural rights, not biblical rights. No one grasps this better than the Korean missionaries whose children attend international schools and as a result often speak better English than Korean. It is common for Korean MKs to grow up with little understanding of Korean culture and history. They become more comfortable in the West than in the East. Their upbringing makes them unfit for Korean universities. This causes many Korean MKs to attend a university in the West, and ultimately settle there. Would you go into missions if you knew your children would have to change their nationality? Our citizenship should be in heaven (Philippians 3:20). How we raise our children may be the ultimate test of where our citizenship truly lies.

Informing the Children of the Move

For tentmakers, because we serve in restricted access nations, the way we communicate our identity to our children is important. Some families choose not to disclose their missionary identity to their children. The children are informed of Dad's new job but not his dual identity. It does not mean the parents avoid talking about world missions or reaching the unreached. Rather, they are discreet and wise in how they communicate with the children. They place the emphasis on their lives, not their words. Some go to the extent of not including their children in visiting churches or involving them in any of the mission presentations they give. This shields the children from handling security issues and the undue stress that comes with it. Some families feel that everything they do needs to include the whole family. We need to exercise wisdom in what to tell our children and how much to include them in our decision-making processes.

Because we switched from being regular missionaries to tentmakers when the children already knew our missionary identity, we had to help our children understand our new role. We also prepared them to answer difficult questions by replying, "Ask my mother" or "I don't know." It is important that parents prayerfully consider how to communicate with the children concerning their move and job change. Plan ahead. Decisions made today will impact decisions of the future.

Preparing for the Move

As you make plans to move, your children will know that something is happening. Involve them in the adventure of moving abroad. The older the child, the more information and preparation they will need. Teenagers will have many questions and fears. Several pastoral care ministries offer help for those moving abroad with teenagers. Check the internet for ideas.

Normally, it takes one to three years from the time you decide to go overseas till the moment you get on the plane. These years should be used to prepare the children for this next stage of the family's life. Invite the children to share in the process of cross-cultural preparation. Take them to a few ethnic areas of your city. Point out the differences. Eat some of the food. Help them learn the joy of trying new things and that differences are good. If people from the country you are moving to live nearby, take the kids to their neighborhood to get both a look and a taste of where they are going. Share with them about the culture, foods, clothes, schools, and kids. Find books or films about the land you are going to and study them with your children. Make things positive so they do not develop fears or misapprehensions of the people or culture.

Children are quick to pick up biases from parents. Explain to them what life will be like. Talk to them about the new friends they will make and the new language they can learn. They need to be assured that they will have fun and friends in their new home. In moving overseas, it is important to bring along the children's favorite toys. Leave the appliances, but bring the kids' toys. Take books, hobbies, and crafts as well. If old enough, give your child a camera, and let her use it to document the move. After you arrive, the child can record new sights and experiences. If possible, ship some toys in advance, so when the children arrive they find their things. Familiar toys will ease their transition. With older children, you might wish to select a city, a sports team, a music group, etc., to relate them to their homeland identity. Allow the children to have some paraphernalia from this adopted group in their new room as a reminder of their roots. The problem of rootlessness is often overcome by the closeness most missionary families experience.

Routines are indeed important to children, but they do not have to be regimented or complex. Some routines can be kept when raising support, and these will provide some familiarity and stability when you arrive at your new city. Create something unique for your family to do at meal times, bed times, brushing teeth times, or even when starting the car. Memorize a unique prayer of thanks for bed times, hold hands at a meal, or sing a song when starting the car; these can be comforting, portable, repeatable routines that make the kids feel more securely loved.

In the same way that a church is both a building and a body of people, teach your children there is another meaning for "home." Train them that home is not just a place, but also a position that is in Christ and in the family. Study Philippians 3:20 to teach them of their dual citizenship. Assure them that home is where Dad and Mom are and not in the old or new city or in your physical residence.

Inform them of the new language you all will be learning. Discuss how the learning may take place. Joke with the kids about the advantages their brains have over yours in acquiring language. Do not hide the fact that it will be hard, and at times you will want to quit. Make a pact with one another to become fluent in the language. Doing this ahead of time will serve as a reminder and reference point when tough times do arrive. If the kids learn the language, they will be happier living overseas. If they do not learn the language, their social and educational options may be limited to the expatriate community.

In planning your children's future, think "big picture." Things may change, but good parents plan ahead, keeping their options open. Make educational decisions looking ahead ten years from now, not just year by year. As with yourselves, do not rush the children into the culture; go at their pace. Remember, the child nearly always reflects the parents' attitude toward the culture. If the kids are struggling, it may be the parents' problem, not theirs. With older children, set targets for where they ultimately want to be in language learning, making friends, and eating local foods. Keep encouraging them to move toward their goals. Do not set a date deadline, as things change and dates put unnecessary pressure on them. Set clear objectives, so you can help them measure and see they are making progress. At each step that impacts them, involve the children in your decision-making process, but do not leave final decisions to them. With positive reinforcement, most children adapt faster than they think they can.

Training Your Child

Proverbs 22:6 is often quoted. We are to train up our children, but how do we teach them the rules if we do not understand the game? As parents, we need to be aware of what our children are doing, and we need to involve them in our lives. Children learn by instruction and modeling, not by osmosis. Pray with them about your concerns so they learn to ask you to pray with them about their concerns. Have them accompany you when visiting local friends. Take them to work and explain how you integrate your faith with your work. Teach them the Scriptures, memorize passages together as a family, and ensure they understand God's heart for all peoples. Keep open the lines of communication. Consider where you will get involved and where you will not. For example, what do you do if your children are continually being bullied at the park? Or the best schools require all students to study Islam? Or you live in a culture which is not kind to children? Is it important that your kids become acculturated? Do they need help making friends? Remember, getting involved does not always mean we have to protect them, nor is it our duty to resolve problems for them. Each problem they encounter is an opportunity to teach and apply biblical principles.

Children are very flexible. Rarely do they worry about the same issues we do. Children under the age of ten draw their self-esteem from their parents. They mimic their parents' words, actions, joys, and fears. Model for your kids what they should do. When my son was offered a plate of chicken's feet, he froze. Immediately, his mother reached over and took a foot off the plate and ate it, smiling the whole time. Watching intently, he followed her lead and happily began eating too. To this day, he loves chicken's feet.

The older the child, the longer the adaptation may take. Be upbeat with the kids. Some parents make comments like, "The food isn't too spicy, is it?" Though well intended, such questions are only going to encourage negative answers. Be patient and be positive. Remember, our western values may teach "cleanliness is next to godliness," but that is not in the Bible. As children make friends, their friends will naturally help them acculturate. When I visited Jim's home, I noted that his children refused to eat the spicy curries which are added to most local foods. The parents were embarrassed at their children's eating habits. Jim and his wife struggled over what to do, as it meant bringing peanut butter sandwiches when visiting friends or having a battle with the kids over the food. When I visited a few months later, the children were happily eating the local dishes. What happened? Simply put—peer pressure. When the children began attending the local school, they observed all their friends eating the spicy food, so they copied their friends. Within a year, they even preferred the local cuisine. The important thing is to provide opportunities and encourage your children to play with local children. Do not limit their trying and doing things other kids do.

When my son was four years old, he would play with friends outside near our apartment building. One day, I noticed he was sharing a can of Coke with a friend. Usually I would speak to him in the local language around his friends so that he would not feel different. But fearing they stole it from a nearby vendor, I quizzed him in English, "Where'd you get the money to buy that?" When he replied that his friend went garbage picking and found the open, half drunk can in the dumpster, my mind went ballistic. But rather than make a scene, I calmly replied in the local dialect as any concerned parent would, "Okay, don't spill any on yourself." Later that night we talked about the situation. Instead of rebuking him, I asked him if he knew the rules about garbage picking. I then set boundaries for what he could and could not pick up off the streets, teaching him to give what he found to others who are less fortunate.

Kathy is British and one of the sweetest nine year olds you could ever meet. She is number one in her class in several subjects in the local school and is a well-adjusted child, one that would make any missionary parent proud. However, one day she came home shaken and complaining about feeling sick, not wanting to go to school. With some questioning, her parents discovered she was being bullied at school. Her big, six-foot tall father went to school, found the bully and whispered calmly in his ear, "Son, I am holding you responsible for the happiness of Kathy at school. If I hear about you again from my daughter, you'll regret it!" The problems at school stopped immediately, and Kathy's joy returned.

In his lecture, "What I'd Wish I'd Known When I Started Out," Phil Parshall gave two pertinent points for families: First, be careful with girls. If you have a daughter, do not entrust her into the care of another male, but always use female babysitters and caretakers. Even trusted servants may stumble. Second, teach your children the culture and provide opportunities for the children to learn the local language. Getting the language early, even by sending them to the local schools, is more important than their learning math and science. It is a win-win situation to send your young children to the local schools. The children learn the language and culture and make many local friends, while the mothers meet the children's mothers. Jenny, a mother serving in Central Asia adds, "If our children do make local friends, we have a responsibility (and opportunity) to get to know that family and to encourage the friendship. We need to trust that the values we give our children at home will help them when they come in contact with contrasting values in the street, local schools, or home, *and* we need to emphasize to our children the areas where our adopted local culture lies much closer to biblical ideals than our home culture."

In the culture we are working in, it is common for parents to belittle their children. We often ask parents about this habit. Most never realized they did it until we pointed it out. Often, as we discussed this practice with our friends, they admitted they did not like the way their parents criticized them when they were children. This has led to several opportunities to teach young couples about raising children.

Our own children may be affected by harmful cultural values. Remember, it is the parents' attitude which is key. Instead of criticizing the ungodly practices of the locals and its effect on your children, take the opportunity to teach the children forgiveness, their position in Christ, and compassion for those who do not yet know God's love.

Kids do not need to have expensive toys or the latest gadgets to have fun. Games can be made up of all kinds of things. One worker writes, "Life is what you make it. The hotel in which we stayed left quite a bit to be desired. It was hot, dirty, and run-down—literally filled with bugs of all kinds. That night, as I tried to settle in my one year old, my four year old, and my wife, I felt a tinge of guilt for not having a better getaway situation. We had been working in the Ukraine for months and sorely needed some downtime. So I set about to try to eliminate as many of the bugs as possible over the next hour or two. My four-year-old (Christopher) began to really 'get into it.' He joined me with his own rolled-up magazine as we set about on a military 'search-and-destroy' mission to eradicate those bugs from every corner, nook, and cranny! About an hour later, close to midnight, as we stood perched side by side on top of one of the beds, just daring another predator to show his face on one of our blood-stained, battle-scarred walls, Christopher turned to me with those smiling, puppy-dog eyes and said something that Penny and I have never been able to forget. 'Dad, this is a great game . . . killing bugs. Let's always remember this night.' I couldn't believe it! The very activity that I had thought of as a royal hassle had become, for him, a game! All he needed was a rolled-up magazine and a room saturated with prey. We had a ball."

One problem young missionary children deal with relates to their image of God. MKs often view God as a rival for their parents' love. Children are unable to grasp the nature of missionary work. They do not understand the struggles their parents have in thinking through how to raise and educate them. The only thing the children feel is they are competing with God for their parents' time and attention. As a result, some missionary kids become bitter with God and reject their parents' faith. Parents need to invest time in their children to ensure they know they are loved by both God and their parents. Children are never too young to be taught discipleship and the meaning of sacrifice. Help the children grasp how God calls the entire family into His service, and clarify the role each family member plays in fulfilling His calling.

Teach your children how to get around in case of an emergency. Take them to different places in the city and see if they can find their way home. Review what they should do should they become lost. Even a five year old will surprise you with their ability to navigate if you teach them. As you would at home, ensure they know their phone number, how to contact the police, and who to call if there is a problem. Explain health issues, especially how to eat and drink local foods and what to avoid, but do so in a positive way. Encourage them to try new things. Living overseas will not emotionally damage your children. In fact, living overseas should be the richest experience you will ever give them.

Discipline

When my son was six years old, we visited my close friend Wi Lee. During dinner, my son disobeyed my directive and as a result broke a flower pot. I quickly reviewed with him what he did. After he acknowledged his transgression, I gave him a hard spank and then sentenced him to five minutes alone in the living room. When he returned, he promptly climbed up on my lap, to which Lee's wife exclaimed, "He still likes you!"

Various cultures discipline children differently. It is important to maintain discipline, without offending the people's cultural values. If I had been more culturally astute, I might not have spanked my son then and there. Lee was my close friend and western educated, but I had forgotten about his wife. Family styles of discipline need to take into consideration the principles and customs of the nationals. A balance of raising and disciplining children that mixes local and home styles should be sought. We need to ensure our children are taught properly, which includes respecting local customs. In some cultures, children—by western standards—are not disciplined at all. Climbing on furniture, operating appliances—anything is allowed. In your own home, it is okay to set limits and politely mention these limits to your guests. As you are a foreigner, they may not understand your practices, but they will respect that it is your home. However, in a few cases, families have not returned for another visit, perhaps fearing they might make some mistake which would offend. My wife reminds me, "Remember our belongings are really His belongings." Give friends grace as Jesus has given us.

It is wise to watch for two warning signs in our children: a critical spirit and feelings of superiority. Listen to what your children say. Their conversation can take on tones of bitterness toward the host country. When living abroad, the children mostly observe the nationals, but they listen to what the expatriate adults are saying. Children who are exposed to critical attitudes will likely become bitter themselves. These children may move away from playing with the local children and abstain from local foods and customs.

Beware of feelings of superiority. Children can readily be convinced that their ways are best. If they hear adults boast of their home culture, its technologies and standard of living, the transition to the assumption that they are always right and have the best idea is an easy one. Children quickly find comfort in the thought that they are better than the locals. It is not unusual to see a bratty western child bossing his local maid around. These feelings of superiority and bitterness are common in children when they first go overseas. It is important to deal with such attitudes gently but firmly. Anna in Southeast Asia writes, "We wish to teach our children to view people as people. We do not want the children thinking of locals as 'one of them,' in the same way as some adults never become genuine friends with our neighbors as they view them as part of a 'target' group. We need to teach our children to appreciate that all people are different, and God likes those differences. We want our children to learn from and respect the differences."

Westerners need to understand that many cultures consider our children to be wild and ill mannered. Our American children often cannot sit quietly for five minutes, let alone endure an entire church service. Our children interrupt to ask for things and demand their own way. Western kids also have different interests than local children. They enjoy playing computer games, reading books, and playing with their vast assortment of games and toys. Our children have little motivation to get to know local children who have different ways of entertaining themselves. We need to train up our children to be ambassadors of Christ. Guide the children in learning to play with the local children in the ways they play, without all the western paraphernalia. We need to teach our children how to enter into their friends' world.

One father whose son became fluent in Arabic commented, "The most important thing is to show acceptance of the culture (integrate, socialize, admire, respect, etc.). It is also very important to show a willingness to try learning and speaking the language oneself." We all think we do this well, but it is possible that we have subtle attitudes of looking down on the religion, the culture, or the local children's behavior, which we communicate to our children. We may need to share with our children our own struggles with language learning. One boy told his mother he felt stupid when he was on the street and did not understand what was being said. She shared with him that often in people's homes she felt stupid too, as she did not understand everything being said. He was encouraged that it is okay to feel that way. He was able to handle the difficulties better, knowing his mother understood.

Education

Decisions concerning our children's education may be the most difficult and among the most critical. Teachers and friends have a huge impact on a child's identity. After leading your child to faith in Jesus, your choice of school may be the next greatest decision you make concerning your child's life. In my research, no topic elicited more responses and opinions than children's education.

Children under the age of eleven seem to adjust more readily to a new school and friends and are quicker to pick up the language. It is generally accepted that the older a child is, the more difficulties he or she will have in adjusting to the language and culture. It is normal when children begin nursery school or kindergarten in the home country for there to be one to five days of tears and weaning from the parents. Overseas, this weaning process is prolonged, unless the child already knows the language. Bee, in Central Asia, puts it in perspective in writing to her co-worker, "If your daughter can go to a local school, language-wise it will put her far ahead, but yes, it will be very, very hard for her the first two to three months. It rips a parent's guts out to see their kids struggle, but once the kids get the language and have some local friends, life is very, very nice."

The younger the child, the shorter the weaning process. My rule of thumb is for every year of age, expect one week of struggling. The tears and tantrums may last up to twelve weeks, but if the parents stick to the program they choose, the child will adapt and, in time, succeed. As language is a powerful divider, many tentmakers choose schooling options that keep their children in a mostly English environment. We choose this option because of the low quality of local education, because local schools are saturated with local religious teachings, or because we disagree with the discipline techniques or lack of discipline in the local schools. These are legitimate concerns; however, there are also ways to overcome them.

In their book, "The Third Culture Kid Experience," Dave Pollock and Ruth Van Reken suggest that in evaluating options for our children's education, we should consider the total approach applied within the education system. This includes styles of discipline, teaching, grading, and motivating students. They rightly point out that schools teach culture, language, and values, as well as academics. They remind us that one purpose of being educated is to create options for higher learning in the home country. Another idea is to involve each child in a fun activity (sports, dancing lessons, martial arts, horseback riding, choir, craft classes, etc.) that the child really enjoys, and is available only in the local language. This will create a motive for learning in a less stressful environment.

While some workers who live in remote areas may have fewer options, most tentmakers have nine options for their children's schooling: local public schools, local private schools, local Christian or mission schools, international schools, international or mission boarding schools, homeschooling, correspondence courses, sending the children back home to live with relatives or friends, or quitting the field and taking the children home to attend school. In considering these options, husbands and wives need to agree on God's priorities for educating their children. Parents need to keep in mind the child's spiritual, emotional, and social development, as well as their academic training. Every child develops differently, yet many workers agree there are two phases in a child's development to ponder when selecting schooling options. The first phase is children age eleven or under. The second phase is teenagers. Our schooling selections should be based on each child's personality and maturity; it is not recommended to have one plan for the whole family.

1. Local Schools—Public and Private

Children should begin in the local schools as soon as possible. Many countries have half-day nursery schools for three to four year olds, which is an excellent place to acculturate a child. Once in the local system, you can determine how long to keep them there, but starting children in the local school system after the age of twelve is very difficult.

There are many advantages to placing younger children in a local school. Attending the local school is the best way for your children to become acculturated. Children who begin young usually learn the language and culture better and faster than their parents. The kids make local friends, learn to eat the food, and live as the locals live. The local life becomes the normal life. The children will rapidly become "belongers," feeling a part of the culture and community. They become bridges to the neighborhood, introducing you to the parents of their friends. Whereas adults are discouraged from witnessing to minors, your children can model and in some cases witness to their friends and their parents about their own relationship with Jesus. Many questions will come up to be discussed at home, which can lead to precious conversations. Also, the children's holiday schedule will coincide with the office and national schedule.

One mother comments, "In our urban setting, I have seen this to be one of the most decisive factors as to whether or not a child will become fluent in Arabic. There is almost no gray area. The children who attend the Arabic schools become fluent, and those who receive an English education speak negligible Arabic." Another mom adds, "We have found the local school excellent for the enculturation of our children (and ourselves!), and they all speak fluently, feel at ease in our country, and know how to behave in a culturally acceptable way. I recommend this particularly for those who arrive on the field with pre-schoolers." One mother confessed, "When we put our younger boys in Arabic school for a year, both of the older ones said they wished we had done that with them at that age!"

There are also disadvantages to attending the local public or private schools. Ideally, children should begin attending local schools before they are ten years old. Like new kids everywhere, they may be teased and bullied on the playground. Children who are very sensitive may not react well to the shaming and teasing that goes on. Many third world schools teach by rote memory, discouraging creative thinking. Thus, a lot of time is spent reciting and memorizing. The children may learn bad language, attitudes, and behavior. The kids may also be required to study the local religion. A few MKs fall behind in their English skills. Children with learning disabilities or other handicaps probably will not receive the special attention they require. For older children, the local school is a hard option. They are in the process of forming their own ideas and values, when suddenly they are thrown into a world where everything is different and new. Not only is the language different, but the whole educational system is strange to them.

One mother points out, "Many of these problems may also happen in our home countries (not wanting to go to school, teasing, hearing bad language, bullies, etc.). I really think that sometimes we are too afraid of our host culture and people. They don't have more influence on our children than we allow them." And another mother writes, "As far as memorizing and learning by rote are concerned, I would like to emphasize the positive side of it, at least for the first four years (elementary). With our two eldest, we tried to get them out of memorizing passages/poems that were too long. Not so with number three, who entered the local system from the beginning. He enjoys it. Apart from that, we have been learning more about oral cultures and communication, particularly storying the Bible. This method teaches a skill which is invaluable in the societies where we live. We should be learning these skills ourselves and certainly not depriving our children if they have the opportunity at an early age." It is important to monitor each child's progress daily to be assured he or she is learning and developing as you believe God intends.

If your child is being inappropriately disciplined or shamed, it is important that the parent takes the time to talk to the teacher. Teachers generally respect foreigners. Make it clear to the teacher that hitting, shouting, and threatening do not get better results with your child. Explain how you and if appropriate, God use different types of motivation. Let the teacher know what motivation techniques work for your child. Tell them to inform you of any difficulties or problems before taking action. Let them know you wish to work with them for the benefit of both your child and the entire class.

The difference between public and private schools for younger children is negligible. Private schools usually cost more, but the quality of education should be better. Private schools often use the national language or even English, rather than the local dialect. If the school uses English, the advantages and disadvantages will be similar to those of an international school. If your child attends a private school he or she may need to travel further to school. This may hinder their relationships with the neighborhood children. If the school is near home, it may solve some of these concerns.

More and more mothers are supplementing their child's local education with homeschooling materials. Many schools have only morning or afternoon sessions. Either before or after school, the parents or tutors may teach English, History, Bible, or give additional assignments in subjects in which the local school may be weak. This is an attempt to combine the best of both worlds. The children acquire the language and culture and make local friends, while getting the elements of a more well-rounded education.

When and why do you stop sending your kids to a local school? Most tentmakers agree that you should stop when the pressure of the local school, plus the extra homeschooling is too much for you and your kids. One mother clarifies, "Each kid is different, but you can push your kid harder and farther than you think. But any of the factors listed in the negative side of local schools might be reasons for parents to take their children out after a few years." Obviously, the longer the children remain in school, the stronger they will be in the language and culture, and the deeper their relationships will be with local friends. Jack in the Middle East offers, "We do not need to be afraid of our children learning about the local religion or picking up foul language or habits. As a father, it is my duty to train up my child to be salt and light in such situations. The sooner they learn this the better."

Cynthia Storrs of SHARE Educational Services says, "I do not generally recommend trying to put a child older than ten or eleven in a second language learning environment." She suggests, for school-age children coming to the field for the first time, that we consider dropping them back a grade. Having an extra year of maturity increases the child's self-confidence. In repeating the grade, the child is already familiar with the course material (math, science, etc.) and can concentrate on learning the language. For teenagers, Cynthia adds, "I would not recommend trying the school on an academic level, but rather send the child for a year, sort of as an 'exchange student.' The goal would be to learn conversation/make friends only, and continue her 'real' education on the side, with correspondence courses." Another idea would be to send the teenager to school part time for physical education, art, music, and sports activities, and continue "real" courses through homeschooling. This allows the teen to meet some friends and learn some language. However, the teenager would need tutoring in the language before starting such a schedule.

Families who move overseas with children between elementary grades two and eight should consider holding the child back a grade level. I would also recommend intensive tutoring the first year by a native speaker who also speaks the child's language. The initial objective of the tutoring would be to learn survival language. It can be very humiliating if a child cannot ask, "Where is the bathroom?" or similar helpful phrases. Later, the tutor should explain concepts the child has difficulty with at school, and review homework and questions. The desire is for the child to understand the language and learn the lessons, not to be academically perfect.

2. Day Schools—Mission and International

The number of mission schools around the 10/40 Window is steadily decreasing while the number of international schools is increasing. Mission schools and international schools generally have better qualified staff, and the education is based on either an American, British, or international curriculum. Westerners can also identify with their methods and values. The quality of education does vary and should be investigated before committing to the school. These schools often specialize in training the students for going on to university in their respective countries of focus. They do provide a quality education, freeing the parents from the need to do supplemental homeschooling. Mission schools are normally run by denominations or a consortium of mission agencies.

The school you choose should be accredited and rated by an international governing body. The ratings are helpful in comparing the school's academic standards to others in the region. The cost of these schools is often excessive. If you are employed by an international firm, be sure your contract covers the cost of your children's schooling.

3. Boarding Schools—Mission and International

The quality of mission and international boarding schools varies greatly. Some provide excellent care for youngsters, and others allow them to do as they please. Boarding schools help the students learn self-reliance. Often the children develop life-long friendships. If you are moving often, a boarding school will provide continuity for the kids. Most boarding schools have two extended holidays a year, enabling the students to return home for six to eight weeks. The major negative is the children are away from the parents, and there is little control over their spiritual development. Many adolescents feel cast aside and unloved when sent away to school. Some students also find the rules stifling. Research has found that the single most important factor in whether one does well in a boarding school situation is whether he or she is an extrovert or an introvert. Extroverted youngsters do much better in adapting to boarding school. Nonetheless, some introverted children have done well in boarding schools. Each child should be evaluated according to his/her maturity and personality. Boarding schools in the home country are an option to be considered too.

4. Homeschooling and Correspondence Courses

Homeschooling is growing in popularity in North America. Homeschooling gives the parents control over what the children learn and with whom they associate. Parents can choose textbooks and teach subjects as they please. Homeschooling provides flexibility for the family, enabling you to take vacations or return home at the most suitable times, rather than being locked into school schedules. It also allows you to do more in less time, as no child needs to sit quietly while the teacher helps other students. More constant monitoring ensures the children learn their lessons well. Homeschoolers overseas must realize that in many places, opportunities for extracurricular activities will be minimal. If their social needs cannot be met, teenagers will feel a sense of separation which may lead to depression. Without schoolmates or local friends, it will be harder to learn the language, so it may be necessary to employ a tutor. Three workers who arrived on the field with children older than first grade wrote that they homeschooled their children for two to three years, until they felt comfortable in the new surroundings and had gained some capability in the language; then they entered the kids in the local school. Another mother writes, "Realize though your children go to a local school, some homeschooling will need to be done."

Online internet schools are a new but growing form of homeschooling. These correspondence courses have similar advantages and disadvantages to homeschooling. However, especially for older children, the involvement and demand required of parents is reduced. There are many good correspondence courses available over the internet.

5. Send the Children Home

A final option is to send the kids back to the home country for their education. This is more popular among Asians who fear their children will fail to keep up their studies in their native language. Children may stay with relatives or trusted friends who will instill the proper values in the children while they receive a good education. The major drawback to this is the limited amount of time the parents will have with the children, as school holidays will be too short for extended visits.

Language Learning for the Children

Older children usually require a defined goal or extra something to motivate them to learn a strange language. It is important to discuss with the children reasons for their learning the local language. Get them to brainstorm with you about the advantages of learning the language. Share ideas, ranging from being able to talk with other kids, shopping at the market or mall, watching TV programs, or other advantages that will come as adults. We must be careful to search our hearts and surrender our personal dreams for our kids to the Lord. We need to avoid the temptation to manipulate our children into choosing our goals. Jim, an American born in Indonesia who has been serving there as an adult for nearly twenty years says, "Kids learn language purely by the motivation of wishing to be like my friends. We do our best to stay away from expats, and as a family, we try our best to love our Muslim friends. Also, we stay away from saying things like 'In America, _____ is better.' Rather, we say, 'We choose to _____ because we choose to follow Jesus.'" Offer rewards (candy, stickers, privileges, special family activities, or give points) for going to a store and buying something alone, learning new words from a TV show, etc. Memorize prayers or songs together in the local dialect.

From the outset, be positive with your child and create occasions and reasons for him or her to want to learn the language. Even if you decide your children need not be fluent in the language, it is wise for them to learn enough to deal with situations they may encounter: buying things at the store, explaining to someone where their home is if they get lost, politely greeting visitors and offering them refreshments, telling a bus or taxi driver where to go and when to stop, finding out how much the cost of something is, being able to ask for and understand directions to a place, and reading local street signs.

There are many ways and occasions to help your children learn the local language.

1. Local School

Placing the children in a local school immerses them in the language. As discussed earlier this is the most common method young children use in acquiring the language.

2. House Helper or Babysitter Who Speaks the Local Language

Hiring a house helper who speaks only the local language is an excellent option for pre-schoolers. Employ a female local house helper or babysitter. She can play and watch the children while the parents are busy with other things. Encourage her to play games and communicate with the children in her language. In the beginning, you may need to do some translating, until the children begin to catch on. Provide materials with lots of activities and games and pictures. Play board games, Uno, and other games in the local language. Purchase children's games, tapes, videos, wall charts, and picture/vocabulary flashcards in the local language. Be creative. You could also invite some neighborhood children to come and play with your children. The neighborhood children will teach them local games (tag, hide-and-seek, marbles, etc.) or sports and the words needed to play them.

3. Teach the Children as You Learn

As you learn your language lessons and review your materials, have your child join you. You may do this with class materials or tapes. One mother shares, "When my daughter was born, I spoke enough language to use it with her whenever there were people around, showing from the beginning that that is what we do as a family. This prepared the child well for going to play-school later on, where she picked up a better accent." Another mother adds, "I didn't worry about my poor pronunciation; it was important to me that the kids enjoyed learning the language, so I made it as fun as I could. One thing kids like is to compete with mother, so we memorized verses together. The kids loved it when they would remember some word or phrase I had forgotten. This was also an excellent motivation for me and one of the best ways to memorize!"

4. Play with Local Children

For children of school age, playing with the local children is also fostered by attending a local school. For the children's sake, your own language learning, and the sake of the gospel, carve out time to befriend the parents of the friends of your children. Encourage your children to play outside with other kids. There may not be sawdust playgrounds and cushioned slides, but if the local kids are safe playing in the park or on the street, our kids should be safe too. One mother in Central Asia comments on her son who learned the local language well, "He played in the streets with the local boys. They had their wars; they had their good times. Some of the boys became friends, while others were jealous and did all that they could to make life miserable for him. Then, as he grew older, he went and hung out in places that local boys hung out. We realized that for him to have friends, he had to be one of the boys."

Another mother in Asia points out, "One thing that helped our kids make friends with local children was for me to play with them all together. Because (local) children's interests and games are so different, at first our kids had a hard time understanding. As I played with them, I could teach the neighbor kids our games and model how to handle problems with the kids. One idea we used was the card game Uno. I would teach them all together; then when they were all having a good time, I could leave and they'd carry on. Once, I invited neighbor girls about the same age as my daughter into the house, and I taught all of them how to cross-stitch. (I provided all the yarn and fabric.) As I talked with the girls, I translated key words for my daughter, and she was soon picking up most of the conversation. We were given a box of old roller skates, so we let our son invite neighbor boys in to play with them. We helped at first in translation and organization, and soon our son could organize things himself. Not much language is needed to have fun."

5. Hire a Tutor

Another alternative is to hire a tutor who will come to your home and teach the children. If you hire a local teacher, she should be able to develop materials without much input. Locals with no teaching experience may need constant input and direction. However, a teacher may not be flexible and may want to teach by rote memory. If the tutor speaks English, make sure she spends more time speaking the local language than English. Be prepared to guide and encourage the tutor, especially in the areas of doing enough repetition of drills (she may stop the first time the child gets it right), focusing on a limited vocabulary, and maintaining discipline.

Check the nearby language schools as there may be local language courses available for children. Some workers have organized vacation school language programs for their children. They hired and trained local women to teach the children, dividing them into different levels according to age and ability. The children were more motivated to learn being in a class with their friends. And since it was vacation time, they were able to focus on the language without the distractions of other schoolwork.

6. Electronic Helps

Children learn language by hearing and observing. Utilize computer programs, television, and videos. Usually you can buy children's programs which are dubbed into the local language. Allow your children time to watch cartoons and educational programs, such as Sesame

Street. If possible, videotape these shows and have them watch the videos over and over. Repetition is important for gaining comprehension. You may want to have them write down words they hear and understand, and praise them for using each new word. Children love any electronic thing. Investigate to see what resources are available in your local language.

In addition to learning the national language, another issue that may need consideration is dialect. In many locations, the dialect spoken on the street is different from the national language and what is spoken on TV. This can be confusing and make language learning more difficult. The language or dialect you want the children to learn will depend on your family's objectives. If you want them to just be able to play with local children, the local dialect will suffice. If you want them to be able to read and write and understand television, you may want to teach them the national or standard form of the language.

Third Culture Kids

It is important for missionary parents to understand that their children will have struggles with their cultural identity. Third Culture Kids (TCKs) are geographically and socially removed from their parents' culture. As a result, the children are not products of their parents' culture, but they are products of two cultures. Most tentmakers see themselves and their children as citizens of their native country. After all, that is where they feel "home" really is, and that is what their passport confirms as their nationality. The parents tell stories of the home country, cheer for their teams in the Olympics, read papers from home on the internet, discuss the politics at home, and on return visits, go to great lengths to introduce the children to the history and heritage of their "home" land. Parents assume that in times of crisis or when they retire, they will return home and their children will attend college, marry, and settle there.

However, though we may believe our children are Americans or Canadians like us, in reality they are not. But neither are they Asian or Arab. Their first culture, the culture in which they truly feel at home, is a mix of cultures. TCKs are the products of their parents' culture and the local culture they were raised in; however, not feeling at home in either one, they generate a new, third culture. TCKs are drawn to others who have had similar third culture experiences. When parents fail to grasp this, it results in unfulfilled expectations and often leads to the children having an identity crisis. Workers must understand and accept the reality that our children will never be fully citizens of our home culture.

Recognizing that our children belong to a special third culture can help us understand and deal with the difficulties they face. Knowing this, we should be wary lest we push upon our children our dreams of "going home" to study, live, or vacation, conjuring up wrong impressions of what their life will be like "back home." Rather, we should prepare them for entry into a culture that may be more strange than familiar. It is advisable for children going "home" for college to attend a re-entry program to assist them in their move and adaptation.

Growing up overseas provides TCKs with certain advantages as adults. TCKs are exposed to the adult world quite early. While still children, they may master social graces which enable them to relate naturally with adults. TCKs are good learners. They may not jump into new situations immediately, but when they have observed the rules and the limits, they know how to adapt and make the best of new situations. TCKs are open to new ideas as they have experienced that there is more than one way to do things. They tend to be creative and have a sense of self-reliance. Most TCKs are highly motivated and well educated. Studies validate that missionary kids are usually high achievers. When compared to their peers who graduated from western high schools, a greater percentage goes on to become leaders in their field of work. TCKs are not deprived, but they are different. They may have missed out on the sports, music, and toys of their peers in the parents' homeland, but as a rule, wherever they settle, they are mature, intelligent, positive contributors to society.

Counting the Cost of Children

John's parents arrived in his new country when he was ten years old. A month before, his father, who had prayed and sought for two years for work to move into this new land, was offered a prestigious, well-paying job. His father had studied the language and the culture in university and was fairly fluent in the local dialect. However, his mother and the three children knew nary a word of this difficult language. With little warning and only five weeks to pack and say their goodbyes, the family moved into a simple, three bedroom house in a large city. They had no team, no friends, and no contacts outside of Dad's office. John's parents opted to bond with the culture. Two days after moving into their new house, John and his young brother and sister were placed in local schools. John and his siblings struggled with the ridicule "foreign" kids often face when moving into a new school system. His mother tried desperately to learn the language and to drive on the "wrong" side of the road. The shopping market seemed to stretch for blocks. How would she ever find anything?

Every night, John complained to his parents about the "unfairness" of it all. What's so great about America? Why did they have to move to Seattle, anyway? He missed his friends and horses in Dushanbe. Today, twenty-three years later, John is a successful businessman and a leader in his church. He is married with three children of his own.

Why is it that the vast majority of Tajiks, Egyptians, Chinese, and others who immigrate to America can throw themselves into the American culture without language or cultural training and make it? Why do many missionaries struggle? Perhaps the issue is bridges. When people emigrate to the United States, they believe they are moving to someplace better, so they burn all their bridges. Jesus speaks of this when He says, "No one who puts his hand to the plow and looks back is fit for service in the kingdom of God."[83] Most missionaries return to their home culture often and nearly all intend for their children to remain "American" or "British." We talk about fully contextualizing, "going C-5," but in truth, we have our limits.

Tentmakers and regular missionaries need to recount the cost in terms of their children's lives. Deny ourselves? Yes, but deny our kids? Die for the people? Yes, but die to our home culture? Sacrifice my personal dreams? Yes, but sacrifice my dreams for my children? And what about their own dreams? Could this be what the Master was talking about when He spoke of "dying to self?" (Luke 9:23–25) Perhaps that is why He said, "If anyone comes to me and does not hate his father and mother, his wife and children, his brothers and sisters—yes, even his own life—he cannot be my disciple."[84]

For even the most Christ-centered worker, the limit comes when our children are involved. Paul clearly understood that couples would have more struggles than singles (1 Corinthians 7:32–33). How can we require our children to make sacrifices based on our decisions? However, immigrants to America do not have this problem. Why? Simply because they believe the move they have made is an upgrade, a step-up for both themselves and their family, and to that end they toil and sweat to succeed. Thus, they can burn their bridges and fully acculturate their family. They need not worry about education or language, for there is no turning back. Adapt or die. Thus, the root issue is, is becoming a missionary our decision or God's? Do we really believe God knows what is best for us *and* our children? Do we really believe serving Him overseas is a step-up in all areas, or only the spiritual area? Tentmakers need to thoroughly count the cost for their wife and family.

SUMMARY

Our children are part of God's team to reach the unreached. The choices we make concerning our children's education need to be made prayerfully and with wise input from experienced workers who know us and the area we are serving in. Discipleship and discipline of the children also need to be thoroughly discussed. As the Lord has called the entire family to be overseas, we should trust Him to provide for the needs of each member.

ACTION STEPS

- Discuss with your spouse a plan for preparing the children for your move overseas or up-coming home ministry assignment.

- Do you have a discipleship plan for your children? Commit to making one with your spouse this month.

- Think through specific steps your children can apply to increase their knowledge of the language.

- Develop a plan for integrating your children into the language and culture of the people.

- Evaluate the different schooling options. For each child, weigh the strengths and weakness of each option.

- What are some negative attitudes you may be subconsciously passing on to your children?

- Discuss with your spouse specific things you can do and say to promote a positive attitude among your children toward the people you are ministering to.

- Have you counted the cost of becoming a tentmaker in terms of the lives of your children? Take some time to do the math.

"It was the best of times, it was the worst of times."

CHARLES DICKENS

Foxes have holes and birds of the air have nests, but the Son of Man has no place to lay his head.

JESUS

chapter 15
THE TENTMAKER
AND HIS HOME BASE

A popular children's song says, "Make new friends, but keep the old. One is silver and the other gold." Friends really are treasures—as treasured as gold and silver. The need for friends does not diminish with distance. Friendship provides intimacy, fun, new experiences, and reinforcement of self-worth, whether a person is married or single, with or without children, young or old. We need people who value us for who we are, not for an outside motive. A solid home base of friends and family that upholds us with prayer and finances is essential for every worker.

Often, especially in the early years, a tentmaker's support base is in his home country. It is common for tentmakers to feel alone, shunned by the locals. There are often difficulties in drawing close to other workers. As friends and family move on with their lives, we are no longer tracking with their changes. Phone calls provide a connection, but not the closeness we desire. Friends and family become more distant, more foreign. Soon we begin to feel rootless, like a person without a country. "Where is home?" This question has many answers, but none of them feel correct. The best way to maintain closeness with our family, friends and churches is to make personal visits back "home." For most, that means return trips every two to four years. These trips are often draining and sometimes disappointing. It is important that expectations for return visits are kept low and you do not try to accomplish too much in a short visit.

Keeping in Touch

Keeping in touch with family members is crucial to most tentmakers' sense of well-being. Writing cards, making phone calls, sending small gifts, and even sending flowers are simple ways of reminding dear ones of your love. Keeping your children connected with their grandparents is much easier with e-mail, but there are still old fashioned, meaningful ways to communicate. My mother went down to the local library and brought home reams of children's books. She put a picture of our children on the table next to a tape recorder, and then read aloud to them seventy short stories. Every night, after prayers, we would turn out the light, turn on the cassette player, and grandma would read the kids a story. There are many creative ways to involve grandparents and family members at home in the lives of our children.

Linda in North Africa writes, "I am reminded of a dear friend who visited us when my mum had come to stay with us when our son was born. She commented on the specialness of the brief times we get to spend with family. Our times are much more precious and intense than if we lived in the same city. My mum realized that there were many special things she had done with me which she hadn't done with my sisters who live very near her, like helping with thank-you notes, writing in the baby books, being with me twenty-four hours a day for a week. Sometimes, we have had belated or early birthday parties when we're with family, so that the cousins can be present." Many families keep pictures of family members handy and use them as reminders during family prayer times. One child chats online with his grandfather every Monday night.

VISITS HOME

All workers are allotted time for a home ministry assignment (HMA) or furlough. Tentmakers who are not related to a mission organization may use their vacations to return to their home country. Some overseas companies fly their employees and their family home once a year. In the past, missionaries served on the field four years and then returned home for one year. But with travel and communication improving, it is becoming common for workers to return home more frequently but for shorter periods of time. The reasons for HMA vary: to visit friends and family, report to churches, or have a vacation. It is wise to plan your HMA in advance to ensure you accomplish your objectives.

Many workers loathe HMA because of the travel required and the demands put on them to visit many churches, friends, and relatives. The attitude of the parents towards HMA makes the biggest difference. If you look at furlough with excitement and anticipation, your children will as well. If you are filled with dread and reluctance, they will be too. Do not try to hide the difficult parts of HMA. Instead, talk to the children about the hard parts, and do things to prepare them for it. It is amazing how helpful children can be when they know how much it is needed.

When we were regular missionaries, my family did not enjoy the one year HMA. The many transitions were exhausting. It began when we had to give up our home overseas and store our stuff. Part of that process included finding and training someone to take over our ministry while we were gone. When we arrived in the States, we had to find a new place to live and borrow or buy furniture and appliances. We had to invest time to pay bills and manage the upkeep of the house. When it was time to go, we had to return all the stuff we borrowed. In addition, there were so many new people in our home church, including a new pastor, that we felt like guests. Once we returned overseas, we had to find a new place to live and unpack all our belongings. Taking eight to ten weeks HMA every two years keeps us in closer contact with our church and enables us to continue our work and ministry on the field. We do not need to give up our home overseas or rent a place in the States. In the States, we are traveling much of the time, so we stay in other peoples' homes. Being gone for short periods does not require another worker to fill in for us either. Since opening our businesses six years ago, it has become impractical to be away for longer than six weeks at a time.

HMA Objectives

How we view our home ministry assignment (HMA) is central to what we accomplish. Is the time back home part of the job—meaning we are there to report and serve the churches? Or is this to be a time of vacation and rest and catching up with family and friends? Determine which it will be in advance. Nearly any worker will tell you the worst furloughs are when you try to combine both. If you wish to take a vacation when on HMA, block out special time to be away from churches and friends who expect you to report on your work or minister to them. Vacation is vacation. If that is your objective, have fun.

Before departing for the homeland, put together some pictures of the people you are going to visit and show those pictures to your kids. Talk about these people at the dinner table and pray for them. This will help the children remember what friends, relatives, and the pastor look like. Buy a number of small gifts to share with those you visit. Coins or paper currency that is of low value, postcards, inexpensive trinkets that represent the country, and your own photos help cement your visit in people's minds. Prepare a scrapbook with highlights of your life and work that can be perused easily in a few minutes and can be passed around at meetings. It can serve as a conversation starter. Include pictures or items that will answer frequently asked questions. MyPublisher.com allows users to make coffee-table books from their digital photos. Put together a ten to fifteen minute Powerpoint or video presentation to share with small groups. Those working in unrestricted areas may also give away prayer cards or photo magnets with your names and addresses. It is always encouraging to visit a home and see our family photo on a prayer map or refrigerator door. Prepare several messages: a sermon, a ten minute message, some stories, as well as some things to share with teenagers or children.

The biggest questions we face on every HMA relate to our children. "What do we do with the kids?" "How do we keep them happy?" Everyone wants to see the kids, but churches that really care about their workers do not mind whether or not the children come for a visit. The church, after all, is supporting the husband or the couple to do the ministry, not the children. It is good to clarify with supporting churches their expectations for the wife and children in fulfilling the ministry. Most churches leave the choice up to the couple. A few churches will expect the wife to be involved in the work, but none expect that from the children.

If the church is supporting me, they are supporting me to do the ministry we have agreed upon. As with any job, the salary we are paid meets our family's needs. Businessmen do not take their wife and kids on business trips and on the rare occasion they do take the family, they do not sit in on the father's business meetings. We found that though all churches say they prefer to see my wife and children, if they did not visit with me, it did not affect the churches' support of us. When churches ask about my family coming with me to visit, I just explain the stress it puts on the children, plus the financial burden of them traveling with me. I then request that they excuse my wife and children from visiting. Churches are very accommodating and understanding. They want to reduce our stress and struggles, not be a part of them. Before our children left for college, my wife would make one to three church visits with me during our HMA. Each trip was one to three weeks in length. During this time, in addition to visiting the church, we would visit other friends and prayer partners in the region.

So what did we do with our children? We gave our kids three choices: they could stay with friends at our home church, they could stay with their grandparents in Texas (who complained they never saw their grandkids), or go with us to visit churches. In eighteen years, the third choice was rarely selected. Most children hate being put on display. They want and need stability. Even when churches involve the children in special fun events, our children feel they are on display. Admittedly they are different, just passing through, not really belonging. Often, our children spent one to three weeks with the grandparents and one to three weeks with friends. While my wife and I traveled, ate tons of food, shook hundreds of hands, showed the same slides and answered the same questions over and over, the kids had a blast. On three occasions, thanks to helpful friends and some advance planning, the kids were able to play on local Little League baseball teams. Several times I have returned from overseas alone for three weeks of deputation, leaving my wife and sons to carry on life as usual on the field. To this day, our kids appreciate the choices we gave them. Occasionally, it was logistically necessary for the children to tag along with us. This was the exception, not the rule. Wiser workers view their home assignment as part of their job, and they keep their families out of it.

Plan your itinerary well in advance of your returning. I recommend planning at least six months in advance. Prioritize who you need to visit. For us, it was family, prayer and financial supporters, long-time friends, and sponsoring churches. Though you want to see others, often it just is not practical. Be satisfied with short visits. Realize it is impossible to "make up for lost time" with all but a few of your closest friends and supporters. With the rest, you will have to make do with a quick visit, meal, or phone call. Make a list of those you need to call before returning home, and ensure time is set aside for calling. Discipline yourself to call one person a day, and limit calls to fifteen minutes so that you do not ignore those you are visiting.

Time, energy, and monies are limited. We find that people are willing to adjust their schedules to ours if they have ample warning. Many workers are driven by guilt concerning HMA. They feel they need to visit everyone who supports them and show them the children too. Guilt is not a good basis for making decisions. Supporters give to God's work, not you or your work. If your ministry is all about you, you should visit everyone, as you will be the one who encourages and blesses those who give. But if you consistently communicate that it is God's ministry, people will understand they are giving as to the Lord and not you. Trust God to bless them. He will do a better job, anyway. Having a plan that the family agrees to well in advance of your return greatly reduces stress for everyone. There is no need to stay with or call on everyone who supports you; people understand.

I would also suggest that you work out of hubs, regional bases from where you can visit a number of people and churches. Pick a place that is convenient, roomy, and fun. It may be a church, a relative's home or even a hotel. Stay one to three weeks in that place. Have your family stay there, and then drive for short visits and meals with friends and supporters in nearby places, returning to the hub at night. It only takes a few hours to renew a connection. Though your schedule may be packed (after all, you are working), there is no need to stress out the wife and children.

We inform all our supporters that we are committed to visiting them every five years. We have supporting churches in Connecticut and California, our home church is in the midwest, my parents live in Texas, and my brother lives in the southeast and my sister in the northwest. We would put a lot of miles on a car if we covered that scope on every visit, not to mention adding more gray hairs to my head. As with any job, we prioritize. We plan one trip to visit those in the east, and on the next trip we visit those out west. We always visit the grandparents and usually (not always) our home church. Part of our advance planning is making a list of people, both friends and churches that we cannot visit but will telephone. Though everyone would like for us to visit, they fully understand why it is not possible.

It is time to rethink our HMAs. One mother writes, "Our second furlough was only two months. That was disastrous. We packed in an extremely busy schedule, and my husband felt it was very important that I be at all meetings, so that meant the kids had to go too. My daughter was extremely stressed out. My family, especially my sister, felt like I had no time for them. Forget about resting. By the time we returned to the field, we were exhausted—much more than when we had left. For a year, I would cry every time I talked about that furlough."

If possible it is best to visit churches during the spring or fall when most church members are around. Visiting at Christmas is great for family but terrible for visiting churches. Summers are also good for visiting friends and family, and you can pack fewer clothes, but many churches are empty during the months of July and August. If we wish to raise funds and encourage prayer, we need to be there when the people are available. Keep in mind that the objective for visiting churches and supporters is to report and to bless them. HMA is work, not vacation. When people see you are there to serve and bless them, they are more likely to get excited about your ministry.

Our HMA is part of our ministry and as such, needs prayer support. Request your prayer partners to pray for your HMA; for the churches you will visit, the family, and for safety as you travel. Do not allow your prayer supporters to rest while you are home (Isaiah 62:6–7). Keep them informed of prayer needs. Ultimately, we are relying on God to sustain us through this marathon trip—to keep our fenders straight, our tanks full, and our luggage on the same flight. Schedules are tight, sleep is wanting, and stress levels can be maxed out. We need prayer for these things.

Another way to make the most of your visits is by having group meetings. I will regularly meet one to three businessmen for breakfast and another two or three for lunch at a coffee shop that is convenient for them. We will ask one family we know well to invite others over in the evening for coffee and dessert. In this way, we can socialize with three to five families at once. In some cities, we will have "desserts" five nights in a row. Some friends will host a dinner, or in the summer, a barbeque. It is common for people to bemoan the little time we have with them. When they do, I remind them that our life and ministry overseas is God's priority. I also remind friends it is our desire to get back as quickly as possible to God's assignment for our lives. After all, they are not supporting us to travel around the States and enjoy ourselves. When I spell things out like this, everyone readily understands and agrees. No one feels cheated and no one has ever said, "Well, I guess I won't pray for you anymore." In fact, a few people have commented on our zeal for His work, resulting in their recruiting others to pray for us.

For those times when you must take the kids, request to stay with families who have children of the same age. Having friends and things they can play with makes the trip go faster. Bring a few videos or DVDs for the kids to watch on your laptop or a borrowed TV during meetings. Most folks do not begrudge a child watching a video while the adults visit. Plan for some down-time. With the children along, do not make the schedule so tight that you forget what is important; be sure you have time for the kids. Reserve time for getting away to an amusement park, zoo, sporting event, or concert. See nearby sights with just your family. Staying with church members and friends builds relationships, but every now and then you need a break. Invest in a hotel room. A hotel with an indoor pool or something fun for the family is a great option and a real de-stressor. Yes, it costs money, but it is cheaper and more biblical than losing your temper or exasperating the kids (Ephesians 6:4).

Sometimes an expenditure of ministry funds is necessary for our family's survival. It is a time when you can relax, have fun, and focus on one another and not others. I am as frugal as anyone. In fact, my wife and kids would tell you I am "cheap." But I have learned that it is unwise and unbiblical to be cheap with my kids (1 Timothy 5:8). It took two near nervous breakdowns by my wife, for me to learn this (Ephesians 5:25–28). (That shows that I'm not just cheap, I'm stupid too.) Jesus is Our Provider. He will provide the funds and guide us in their use, and that does not always mean penny pinching.

Speaking of hotels, one worker writes, "One of the best decisions we made was to get a hotel room by the airport before our early morning international flights. We could have gotten up at 5 AM and made it to the airport on time. But that meant increasing stress at a time when stress levels were already off the scale. We have learned to say our goodbyes the afternoon before, check the bags into the airport luggage hold, and then go to the airport hotel to watch TV, swim, and have a leisurely dinner. Then in the morning, all we do is grab our carry-ons, get the courtesy airport bus, and in ten minutes we are at the airport. That extra two hours of sleep and not having to worry about traffic and airport lines made our flights much more enjoyable, causing us to return overseas a bit more refreshed."

One lesser objective of HMA is to replenish our supplies. Leaving Mom and the kids at a friend's while Dad travels gives her time to shop. You can also save time by purchasing things over the internet and having them waiting at your last stop before returning to the field. There is no way to completely de-stress a furlough, but you can take most of the stress off your wife and children. Build in times for breaks and depressurizing.

Travel Tips

If you must travel with the children, here are some travel tips. First, remember that four small suitcases are easier to fit into a trunk than two big ones. Soft suitcases are easier to squeeze in corners than hard ones; however, you may need one hard case for breakable items you may wish to bring back with you. Make the car family-friendly. Have a book box, coloring books, music, and story tapes—anything that can be done in the car. Portable CD or cassette players with kid-friendly headphones work well to give everyone some quiet time. Kids can watch movies on your laptop too. We kept a ball, bat, and gloves, a Frisbee and a few other outside toys in the car. For every hour of "quiet" driving, the kids earned ten minutes of play time. Sometimes they would collect minutes for a longer break to play baseball, explore a river bank or visit a fast food restaurant's play land. It was completely their decision where to stop and what to play. For the sake of the kids, forget about gas mileage efficiency—the bigger the car, the better. For one trip we were loaned a mini-van, it was fantastic. On another HMA we borrowed a four-man tent and between every city we visited, we took one to three days to camp. So though our weekends were intense, we had Tuesdays to Thursdays to camp and have family time.

Be picky about to where you stay. If you need three bedrooms, let it be known; otherwise, you add to the stress on the family. Watch your health. Meeting people and staying in different places exposes your family to all kinds of germs. You need to compensate by getting enough rest and passing up that chocolate dessert.

If you have routines when you are overseas (family devotions, prayer times, exercise, bed-time reading, etc.), maintain them when you are together in your home country. Build in times to have devotions; memorize a chapter and pray in the car. One worker told me his family would utilize local exercise gyms three times a week. Often, things go better with Mom in the back seat. Keep track of all miles and expenses. Paying for everything with one debit or credit card simplifies record keeping. Picnics en route may be fun and buying food from grocery stores is less expensive, but if it adds stress to Mom—go to McDonald's.

New Life

When you return to your home country, recognize you are not the same person who embarked to win the world two or four years ago. Many workers are unaware of the profound changes that take place within themselves as a result of living overseas. Often we expect to re-assimilate with a minimum of adjustment. We may think of ourselves as Americans or British who happen to be living abroad, but in truth and grace, God has been transforming us.

Many workers are surprised and even hurt to discover that relationships with our relatives and close friends back home are strained and distant. We expect people to be excited or at least interested to hear about our many experiences. However, it does not take long for conversations to shift to topics of local interest. Peoples' lives have moved on, and you will soon realize we no longer have the same place in them. Churches and even good friends do not know what to do with us once we have shown our pictures, given our report, eaten the potluck, received prayer and said thanks for their prayers and support. In their uneasiness, they ask, "When you are going back to the field?"

As bi-cultural people, we no longer "fit" back home. We have seen and experienced too much. Most people fear we will move them out of their comfort zones, while others treat us as heroes, but like the lion in the zoo, kept at a safe distance. This loss of identity is both social and cultural. When we return, we can no longer identify uncritically with our home culture, government, or even our home church. Consequently, if we point out different perspectives or criticize ideas, they are taken aback and view us as disloyal.

If an expectation for HMA is to be blessed, you are likely to be disappointed. As ambassadors of Jesus, we are always on duty. Because of the changes in ourselves and in others, be aware of peoples' needs and fears. Seek to be a blessing and not to be blessed. Do not wait for people to ask you about your ministry before engaging them in discussions about their life. Once your time for sharing is up, unless people ask, do not try to tell them more. You may have a lot more to share, but be humble and be quiet. Take the limelight off yourself and put it on others. Ask questions about the church, their work, their family, and their struggles. Stop and pray for people; share a verse with them. As with all of life, HMA is not about us; it is about God and sharing His love with others. Never are we told to put ourselves first, so why do it on HMA?

Children

Most MKs I have interviewed and befriended do not have fond memories of their parents' furloughs. There are many reasons for this, but the two themes that kept being repeated are, "I hated the instability" and "I hated having to perform for everyone." Before embarking on your HMA, explain to your kids the reasons why you are taking this trip. Let them know this is work, not vacation. Sometimes, people ask me, "How is your vacation?" At such times, I am quick to correct them that HMA is not a rest or vacation; in fact, it is more stressful than life overseas. Let the children know why you need to visit these churches and people and that they are an integral part of your life and work overseas. Prepare the children for the differences in the way people live and the way you will be living. This can include manners, different types of food and clothing, and how to behave when in other people's homes. Practice the kinds of questions they will be asked, and help them think through their answers.

As with anything, our attitude as parents makes a big difference. One father writes, "Get your kids on your team. I took the kids on a six-week support-development trip to forty-three cities. I learned real quickly that my children were not neutral agents (like luggage) but were either loose cannons making the ministry harder or active helps to my ministry. So, we decided to get them on our team! We had team huddles each day about what our goals were for the day and what part each member of the family could play in reaching those goals, and we'd pray together. At the end of each day, we'd huddle up again and praise God for the things we experienced together as a family. We also tried to make it fun with timed contests to see if we could beat our previous records in how fast we could unpack the car and set up in a hotel room."

Unless your children truly enjoy performing in front of others, do not include them in mission presentations. Forcing your children to share only creates unnecessary stress, when the trip has already elevated stress levels to the max. Some families are gifted in creativity and can involve each family member. If that is your family, work out a routine, skit, song, or reading, so that each child knows what is expected of him or her. But if your children are fearful, even hesitant, give them the option of not attending meetings. A worker in Thailand writes, "Make family a priority. If our children were with us, we did not require them to do anything in our presentations. Only if they wanted to participate in some way did they do so. We felt they were not there to be 'on stage.' We were there to share with our mission partners, not show off our children or our parenting skills. Our son was there because he is a part of our family, but not 'the missionary'." Remember your children are visiting a land which is foreign to them.

RE-ENTRY

Everything that goes up must come down. That is a basic law of physics. The law of the tentmaker is similar: everyone who goes out must come back home. A few workers retire overseas, but not many do. Having lived abroad for many years, we have become bi-cultural. The longer we have lived overseas, the more difficult re-entry to our first culture may be. As God intended, our time overseas has changed us, mostly for the good, though we may carry some bitterness with us as well.

Marjorie Foyle writes,

"Missionaries returning home often feel confused, unusually fatigued and uncertain on behavior and dress. They feel insecure, lost and lonely. Re-entry stress is a reversed culture shock, enhanced by bereavement reactions. People avoid close relationships with nationals and stop being respected for their work. It is important to avoid starting immediately with deputation work. On arrival three things need to be discussed: holiday plans, debriefing and medical examinations. Housing is also an important issue. Some families have suffered living with in-laws, which makes the parents stressed and the children behave badly. Single missionaries want to have plenty of contact with their family, which is not the same as living at home."[85]

If a worker has returned prematurely due to an emergency or an illness, there will be housing, schooling, and job needs. The reason why they returned home must be addressed. Guilt at having to return may be a serious problem. These workers need to be listened to, affirmed, and encouraged. They need to be assured that feelings of sorrow and loss, even loneliness, are normal and part of the re-entry process. Workers will need lots of prayer, guidance, and practical help to find their footing. This is one place a good member-care-worker can have valuable input. It often takes six to eighteen months before a worker feels a semblance of comfort in being away from what was expected to be their life's work.

SUMMARY

Home Ministry Assignment is work. Ministry and vacation should be kept separate. HMA can be one of the most stressful times in a missionary's ministry. HMA needs to be planned in advance, and every family member should be informed of those plans that affect them. Upon returning home, recognize that both your friends and you have changed. People's lives will have moved on without you, and in most cases, relationships will not be the same. When returning home for long periods of time, plan to be debriefed by member-care workers. Give yourself time to adjust.

ACTION STEPS

- What are some creative ways you can help your children stay in touch with grandparents and friends?

- In planning visits to your homeland, what ways can you de-stress these trips for the wife? For the children? If you have been taking the family with you to visit churches, discuss other options with your spouse.
- List five things you can do to make traveling in the car easier.
- List seven things you can discuss/do with the children to make their HMA more enjoyable.

In the beginner's mind there are many possibilities, but in the expert's mind there are a few.

CHINESE PROVERB

"I have discovered that any time there is a new breath of the Holy Spirit in His church there is always a tension that is created between those who experience and embrace His new breath and the existing structure and leadership of the church. Tentmakers are certainly experiencing this tension. We threaten mission leaders and confuse church leaders without intending to."

A TENTMAKER

"The way we see the problem 'is' the problem."

STEPHEN R. COVEY

If any of you lacks wisdom, he should ask God.

JAMES 1:5

chapter 16
TENTMAKING TENSIONS

As I walked into the Armory at the Urbana Missions Convention, it was hard to miss the large traffic light near the center of the cavernous hall. The blinking red light at the top flashed "GO!" "GO!" "GO!" As I approached, I realized the light was part of a booth set up by Frontiers, a tentmaking organization. I asked a worker at the booth, "Shouldn't the word 'GO' be on the green?" He smiled and replied, "No, you see, as workers among Muslims, we see things a bit differently."

In leaving my job as a regular missionary and moving into my tent-making job, many "red lights" suddenly appeared in front of me. Most of these red lights were put there by well-meaning missionary leaders who did not understand tentmaking, its options and possibilities. If you want to succeed as a tentmaker, you are going to need thick skin and a concrete confidence that God is the one leading you. If you feel Jesus is leading you to be a tentmaker, I would say, "Go for it—Green Light!"

I often remind people that as a regular missionary, a "full-time" Christian worker, I served "full time" among Christians. But as I walked to my office at the church each day, I saw the world passing by on its way to a damned eternity. I realized that if I was going to reach the world, I needed to follow Jesus' example and be in the world but not of it. I did not need an office in the church; I needed to be out on the street. I needed to leave the comforts of Christendom and enter the world without becoming part of it. For me, that meant giving up my role as a missionary so I could get into ministry.

So many people think they need "just the right conditions" to take the next step. They believe treading water is the "safe" thing to do. Yes, tread-ing water is safe, but it does not move you forward or get you anywhere. As tentmakers seeking to start a new business or embark on a new job, we need to understand there is no such a thing as "the right conditions."

Besides, our concern should not be the conditions but the timing—God's timing. Conventional wisdom may be shouting at us that everything is wrong! But if we have a concrete confidence He is leading us, we need to step out in faith. Countless tentmakers who started their own businesses or switched jobs in mid career have told me one of their secrets to success was their ignorance. They were too ignorant to know what they were doing was not the "conventionally wise" thing to do.

The stresses of tentmaking missionary work can be enormous but not unbearable. His rod and staff are our comfort (Psalm 23:4). Friends and family will not understand what we are doing. Church leaders think we want more money. Regular missionaries question our motives. Some co-workers will want to quit at the first financial losses or government inquisition. Money, kids, marketing, visas, permits, team members, cash flow, spouse, accounts—need I go on? As tentmakers, we need to be sure our foundation is built upon the rock, for the wind and the waves are sure to test us.

VIABILITY

Isa is a Christian leader who works in a Muslim country as the director of an NGO. He started this foundation, raised thousands of dollars, and then went to the government and said, "Our foundation would like to help feed the poor of your country." Though few foreigners resided in the country, Isa's help was graciously accepted and permission was granted. By 1991, when the Gulf War broke out, Isa's foundation was feeding eleven thousand people every day. They employed nearly one hundred people in an area where unemployment is close to 50 percent and the majority of people live below the poverty line. Despite his help, because he spoke out for his faith, Isa had many enemies. When the war came and the government sided with Sadam Hussein against his country, men broke into Isa's home looking for evidence to prove he was a missionary. Isa is a social worker, not a missionary. Nevertheless, some radicals thought he acted like a missionary, and they wished to prove it and deport Isa from the country. They raided his simple two-room house and found some Christian literature which they said proved he was a missionary. A mob gathered and threatened to arrest him, but first he needed to be turned over to the police. The police were told, "We have proof; Isa is a missionary." "Wonderful," they replied, "we will come and arrest him and throw him out of the country as soon as we have permission from the chief of police." The chief of police was informed, "We have proof; Isa is a missionary." "Wonderful," said the chief of police, "we will come and arrest him and throw him out of the country as soon as we have permission from the governor." The governor was called and told, "We have proof; Isa is a missionary." "Wonderful," said the governor, "we will come and arrest him and throw him out of the country as soon as we have permission from the Secretary of the Interior who oversees Isa's foundation's work." The governor told the secretary, "We have proof; Isa is a missionary. We are ready to arrest him and throw him out of the country." The Secretary said, "Wonderful, now be sure you take responsibility to feed the 11,000 people tomorrow. And be sure you find jobs for Isa's one hundred employees so as to ensure they do not riot or blame me for their problems!" So the governor called the police chief, who told the police, and in the end nobody arrested Isa. To this day, Isa and his foundation are still there and as a result of his faithful witness, there are now several small groups of believers meeting in the country.

Viability is a tension for tentmakers. Some tentmakers do not wish to work at their jobs but use their business or NGO identity as a cover to do ministry. There is nothing wrong with this, but understand that T-5 tentmakers who have a paper-thin entry strategy often fear being discovered. This fear hinders our boldness in witnessing. Gary Taylor, a tentmaking consultant points out, "Many tentmakers want to work ten hours a week or less. It's what we can get away with, rather than a sincere desire to work and witness." My research validates that workers who are secure in their identity are more effective. A tentmaker's viability is important. A tentmaker's job is often referred to as his "platform" for entry into a country to do ministry. By definition, a platform is designed to lift up a person so that he may be noticed and his message heard. Jesus teaches the advantages of having a rock-solid platform (Matthew 7:23–27). Our friends and neighbors are quick to discover the platform we are standing on. If that platform is made of sand, they will know and more importantly, we will know that they know. When we have a viable business, NGO, or other platform, we have a sure foundation which gives us the confidence to speak out our message.

A viable platform that is established in an unreached city serves as a holistic testimony to the community. As we are the first picture people have of the gospel, holistic models go beyond "preaching the gospel." We are to love others with our actions, as well as our words (1 John 3:18). Viable businesses and NGOs enable unbelievers to touch, taste, and see the good news, as well as hear it. A business platform can demonstrate the biblical ethics of honesty and hard work and bless the community. People are always watching us, which is good, for clearly our actions speak louder than our words. A solid platform will stand the test of the wind and the waves. Our work place creates opportunities to respond to the common practices of favoritism, bribery, lying, and cheating from another perspective. As we interact with everyday business situations, we model biblical principles in the midst of corrupt and complex cultural situations.

An employee of a large or even small multinational company living on a shoestring is a complete anomaly overseas and is very suspicious. We must plan to live at a level compatible with our income. As we are not getting rich, profitability alone is not a sufficient objective to explain our presence in the country. We need to share with our local friends our business and personal objectives in ways that explain why competent people will work for lower compensation. Personally, I often share my relationship with Jesus in such discussions, explaining how He led me to move overseas and bless people through education and creating jobs. It is important to think through how you wish to present yourself to friends in ways they (not just you) will feel comfortable with and understand.

Viability enhances longevity. Working for a successful business or NGO greatly facilitates multiple renewals of our visas. This eliminates one of the worker's greatest worries—how to remain in the country. A viable job also reduces our stress over defining our role in the community. With a weak or fake platform, we must be careful of what we say to prying friends and officials. With a concrete platform, we can not only tell people what we do and our role in the business, we can also invite them to our office and strive to do some business with or for them.

Over an eight year span, I have given three "business as missions" seminars at the annual meeting of a tentmaking organization. As one of many seminars being offered, the first two years mine only attracted two workers. However, this past year the room was overflowing with over thirty workers. When I asked about the increase in interest, several workers replied as one, "We have discovered that we can get into our countries via T-5 faker platforms, but now that we are getting converts, the officials are investigating us more closely. Team members who do not have viable jobs are threatened with being deported."

TIME

Managing our time is often a tentmaking tension. Owning a business is a good way to help get control and ease this tension, but it requires a long-term commitment. For the first two to four years of operating any business, you should expect to work hard and many hours. Jeb started a computer programming business and struggled for years to make it profitable. The first few years, he worked many eighteen hour days. He had little time for language learning or making friends in the community. Finally, he got a break and was able to hire some national Muslim co-workers. The new employees reduced his working hours and enabled him to build deeper relationships. It took Jeb nearly seven years to reach this point, but now he is operating a profitable business with over thirty employees. Though no one has converted, many have heard the good news. Jeb's viable business has freed him to get involved in a number of community activities.

Workers can take the wrong job too, and end up not having time for ministry. Sonny worked for four years, putting in sixty to seventy hours a week as the director of a local community college. Though he was able to hire four locals to work directly for him, he admitted he had neither the time nor the language skills to share the gospel with anyone. He finally quit to study the language and start his own small business so as to gain control of his time.

It is paramount that you understand your role in your new job, the amount of hours you are expected to put into your work each week, whom you will be working with, and whether you are you permitted to talk about religious issues with co-workers. If your job gives you access to the people you are reaching, it is easier to combine ministry objectives and work objectives. However, it makes it tougher if you do not have permission to witness while at work. And then, once you have shared the gospel with your six co-workers and they have all rejected the Lord, will you still have time to build and follow up new relationships outside of the office?

The research reveals that how we are perceived in the community is much more important than what our visa states as our purpose for residing in the country. The amount of hours invested on the job is not as crucial as some might think. In the New Testament, several disciples are called fishermen, yet they did not fish every day. Paul was a tentmaker, yet he made tents only sporadically. A person may have many identities: a teacher, businessman, father and ornithologist. But because he is not doing one of these every day or week does not mean he is not what he says. Many successful businessmen do but one or two deals a year. They may work hard for one or two months, but as their commission is US$60,000, they need not work as hard for the next few months. In many cultures, contract workers will take a job until they earn enough money for their needs, a motorcycle, wedding, or house, and then quit. At times, when people ask me why I have not been at the office much lately, I honestly reply, "Business is doing well, so I don't need to put in so many hours this month." If they ask about getting richer, it gives me an opportunity to share Matthew 6:24 and the priorities of a follower of Jesus.

The best model for work is sharing your duties. Some teams who have started businesses bring in three people to do the work of two. In this way, though everyone works in the business, no one has to work full time. Other teams apply what we call the 50/50 rule, where their work load is shared equally with another team member or national. James in the Middle East writes, "Currently we have the 50/50 working well, but that definitely was not the case when I first arrived. You may find it necessary to work 100 percent for the first few years. The 50/50 balance is fantastic if you give your new team members at least a year initially for full-time language learning."

SECURITY

A friend e-mailed me, "I wanted to send you an e-mail about a guy who contacted me. John Abay said he was a pastor wanting to work with Muslims. He said he was interested in knowing others who worked among Muslims, and to help him, I mentioned some mission organizations and some people I knew who were working in this field, including you. I recently got an e-mail from a man who said he was one of two converts under Abay's ministry and said that John had been arrested and that the other convert was dead. He wanted my help. I contacted Compass Direct, a news organization that reports on the persecution of Christians, as well as a human rights group. These organizations checked these things out, and their sources said that this info from the convert appeared to be bogus. So this Abay seems questionable. He did contact a missionary couple I mentioned to him, and they thought he was fraudulent. Has he contacted you? . . . I'm very sorry if it's caused any problems/risks for you. That was certainly not my intention."

Jake, a friend who was working in the Middle East, was just expelled from his country. It seems a local co-worker typed his name into Google and discovered from a church's website that Jake was there to do missionary work. Another worker planning to work in a nearby city distributed prayer letters while he was visiting a church in Oklahoma. He was just a few weeks from departing for Asia. In the letter, he gave his name, address, the mission, the country, the company he was being employed by and information about the local people. That letter fell into the hands of a local Muslim and wound up being printed in our local paper with an accompanying article about the deceitful practices Christians use to convert Muslims. Obviously, the worker never made it into the country.

Security is a huge issue for tentmakers. When I have my life savings invested in my business, I do not wish to be kicked out of the country due to someone else's mistake. I have been told by two countries that I am not welcome to return. One gave my family just forty-eight hours to pack up and be gone. In the first instance, our Muslim neighbors reported us for converting and gathering believers. Though it was a very stressful time, I have no regrets. However, in the second country, we were reported not by Muslims, but by local Christians who have connections with the government. In that same country, a government informant had given our MBB fellowship money and allowed us to use his home for meetings. Meanwhile, he was recording everything on a hidden camera! When confronted, this Christian brother showed no remorse and quoted Romans 13:1. He truly saw foreigners who came into his country to witness to Muslims as troublemakers who were placing the minority local churches in danger of reprisals from the government. I have been told similar stories by MBBs in Pakistan and Malaysia.

The local church need not always be avoided. One brother in China found the officials to be very helpful. He writes, "The mayor and the head of a university are both Christians who have been helpful with bringing in more people." The point is to be very careful when working with local Christians. Do not assume they understand and agree with your calling and intentions. Observe how much time they actually spend with your focus people group. Listen to how they pray to glean what is on their heart. Invest time explaining the risks and your security concerns. Do not place security burdens on locals who cannot shoulder such responsibility.

There was an article published in the twentieth issue of "Nida'ul Islam," an evangelistic magazine trying to convert Christians to Islam. The article written by Br. Amir Abdullah states some of the names and ministries of Christian workers serving in the Muslim world. Naturally, their view is different and some of the facts are misunderstood or clearly not true; but the message is clear—we are being watched. Western news organizations are also showing an interest in tentmaking. "Mother Jones," a British magazine, published an article in its May/June 2002 issue, portraying the tentmaking work of Frontiers in a poor light. Their article was reprinted in scores of Muslim periodicals around the world. Time Magazine headlined tentmaking in its June 30, 2003 issue.

So how can we be effective in evangelism and church planting, keep the recruits necessary for expansion coming in, maintain the synergism needed to build a business, and keep our activities hidden from the wrong eyes? Jesus says, "we are to be shrewd as snakes and as innocent as doves"

(Matthew 10:16). Having a viable job is one key. Learning to not answer questions or defray responses as Jesus often did is another key. I am continually surprised at how many tentmakers seem to have a need to talk about their work to complete strangers. The term "tentmaking" is known in the Muslim world. We must learn to be "economical with the truth." Jesus did not answer every question he was asked. We need not tell every official our life story. Yet, if the full picture of our activities is revealed, we should have spoken and acted in ways that no one could accuse us of having deceived them. We should never, ever, have to lie or feel a need to lie (Colossians 3:9). Brother Andrew, the founder of Open Doors, reminds us, "These people getting caught [smuggling things for money] are depending on their own cleverness. Their motives are probably another disadvantage. Hatred and greed are heavy loads. Your motive, on the other hand is love. And instead of priding yourselves on your cunning, you recognize how weak you are . . . so weak that you must depend totally upon the Spirit of God."

Many tentmakers are overseas without any orientation on security issues. They can easily make costly blunders. Reviewing the questions one may be asked is helpful. Think through how you will relate and communicate with authorities. Some workers get to know the authorities well, so that if there is a problem, they have a friend who may help them. Others avoid officials like the plague, lest they ask questions they do not want to answer. In dealing with government officials and paperwork, answer all the questions honestly, but be concise. There is no need to attract undue attention. One plan that is being implemented in the Middle East involves introducing new tentmakers to one key, experienced, knowledgeable person who is outside the country for initial orientation. That person puts the new worker in touch with one key contact inside the country who handles further introductions as needed. These key contacts may be T-3, T-4, or T-5 experienced tentmakers. It is wise for tentmakers in every country to utilize a non-residential missionary (NRM) for this purpose. Individual workers do not need to know everyone, their story, and what is happening in other places. Should a person be arrested and questioned, the less one knows, the better. Having one person outside the country coordinating information about the various ministries happening inside the country greatly reduces the risk of security breaches. The NRM informs us of who we need to know, when, where, and why. By keeping this "information coordinator" informed, he can coordinate the affairs of all the teams and workers in the country. This NRM then hosts annual or bi-annual meetings of strategic leaders to discuss their work, problems, and future plans. Working together enhances our fruitfulness

(Ecclesiastes 4:12) and blesses the Creator and us (Psalm 133). In addition, this enables to focus on the main work of evangelism, discipleship and church planting.

Being discreet is necessary for continuity in the ministry. It takes years to win and disciple new believers. Continuity in the ministry is important if we are to disciple leaders to maturity in their faith. It is also wise to protect the local church. Churches have good reasons for adhering to government policies. Few like to make waves. Not associating with the local church may be the best way to protect local believers. I was at an international Christian conference in Korea. A pastor of one of the largest churches in our country heard I was from his country, so he looked me up. After a minute of introductions, he realized I was not a church worker. He wisely cut our discussion short saying, "Tell me no more. The less I know about you, the less I have to tell the authorities should they pressure me for information." In the Navy we learned, "Loose lips sink ships."

Our loose lips can harm many others besides ourselves. Though my family had to leave our first country, no one else on the team was indicted. Once I was taken into the police station for interrogation, I knew we were going to be deported. Rather than feign innocence, I acknowledged all "wrong doing," taking the blame for everything presented against me and for the allegations put forward about others. When they asked me, "Did you teach Mohammed to be a Christian?" I explained to them Jesus' role in the conversion process. Knowing they would not be satisfied with that answer, and that another person actually shared the gospel with Mohammed, I honestly replied, "Yes, I prayed for him often, and though you may not understand how Christian prayers work, I believe my prayers prompted Mohammed to pick up the Bible and read it. In reading the Bible, Mohammed met Jesus." In responding this way, I took "responsibility" for Mohammed's conversion. I did not mention any other names or imply others were involved. As a result, I was able to shield my teammates from further questioning. Throughout the interview, I kept reminding Jesus of His promise to give me His words to speak (Matthew 10:19). When the officials asked me if others were involved in evangelizing Muslims, I sensed the presence of God and honestly answered, "Yes, Jesus was: He is alive and with me." When they pushed for names of other workers I answered truthfully, "All believers are to share their faith. Do you expect me to tell you the names of every Christian in this city? I expect they have all shared with Mohammed. And if I may ask, if you were me, would you inform on your friends for their obedience to their God?"

When threatened, we need to take the offensive. We should share Scripture with those interrogating us about how blessed are the persecuted (Matthew 5:10), how we are commanded to lay down our lives for our friends (John 15:13), and remind them that martyrs get front row seats in heaven (Revelations 6:9). Like Paul, appeal to Caesar; take the issue to a higher level. Let the authorities know their arresting or harming you or your family could lead to wider repercussions. Tell them bluntly, "You may jail me, but understand that CNN, Time, and Newsweek will love this story. Do your leaders want that kind of press?" Speak with humility and a quiet voice. Let them know that you fear God more than them. Sharing these points in humility, without anger and frustration, greatly discourages interrogators.

Often, we do not know where the government draws the lines on evangelism, so we need to test the lines. If we have a viable job, rarely are we deported for our first offense. But that offense tells us how far we can push and what we can openly do. In many countries, the law grants religious freedom. Nonetheless, understand that it is the local religious leaders who have the hearts of the people and thus their votes. In this way, religious leaders may manipulate officials to do their bidding and override the law. Where the laws are vague, discretionary powers will be extensive. Again, though laws may be restrictive, if relationships with the religious and government leaders are good, they will not bother us or at least they will warn us before they are pressured to take action against us.

The communication between security departments of different countries varies. More communication happens between fundamentalist groups in various areas who are outside the control of the governments than between governments themselves. Even within a country, communication is often lacking between the various government departments. Just because the religious officials are unhappy with you does not mean the immigration officials are unhappy. Steve writes, "A government may be willing to put up with the nuisance of one's Christianity because of how they perceive the value of that person's contribution to the country. But the religious leaders do not care." Integrity and viability are important. If you are doing what you say you are doing, there should be fewer tensions. Anticipate questions; plan ahead the process of discipling new believers and the security issues both they and yourself may encounter. Think through your relationships with both local Christians (if there are any) and government officials. Know what outside threats authorities fear. In Beijing, street evangelism threatens authorities; in Guangdong it does not. In Indonesia, being a Communist threatens authorities more than being a missionary.

Answering Questions

One practical solution for dealing with authorities or snoopy neighbors is thinking through the questions you may be asked. Jesus was a master at answering questions, or should I say, at not answering questions. From the start of His ministry in Matthew 4 where He answers Satan on His terms, not Satan's, to the end of His earthly ministry in Acts 1:6–8, where he refocuses the disciples' self-centered perceptions, Jesus models the art of answering questions. One of the best ways to answer an unwanted question is to ask another question. In this way, Jesus reveals only what He wishes to reveal (Matthew 21:23–26). Jesus often responded to a question with a statement that redirected the focus of the discussion (John 8:5–7). At times, Jesus would also define the words used to question Him, allowing Him to either teach a point or answer the question as He wished (Matthew 12:2–8). We need to train one another in the strategies of answering questions with the wisdom of Jesus.

One of the tougher questions we face is, "Are you a missionary?" In replying to this question, I suggest two things depending upon whether or not the person is a close friend. If it is a friend, I always ask, "What do you mean?" Asking people to repeat questions gives me time to pray for His words to come to me. In addition, people answer familiar ideas quickly. Repeating the question or asking for clarification causes the questioner to think it may be a new topic or thought for me. When they then repeat the question, I reply, "You know how important the Bible is to me. In the Bible, it says we are all to be witnesses of our life and relationship with Jesus, and that includes loving all people. So I guess you could say all Christians are missionaries." That has never been a problem. Sometimes I add, "Of course, just like all Muslims are missionaries if they are true Muslims, all Christians are missionaries too."

For people who do not know my testimony and my life, I define the question. "Do you mean did I come here to force people to change their religion? No, I am not here to do that. I do love God and wish to serve Him, as I think you do. And I am very happy to talk to anyone about the joy I have in my relationship with Jesus. Is that okay?" I often ask their permission to do something. Once I have their permission, I can quote them to other people as having their "okay" to share.

Another common question is, "How can you afford to live at the level you do on the salary you receive?" People ask this because they believe you may be with the CIA, not Jesus Christ. Two simple replies are, "Due to some good investments, I have money in the bank in my home country that I can live off." You do not have to clarify that those investments are stored up in heaven (Matthew 6:20). I may also reply, "I made so much money in the past that I can supplement my income here with that." Randy adds, "I tell people I can afford to live on my local salary because my family at home subsidizes my income. As my parents, brothers, and sisters do financially support us, this is the truth. I simply do not mention the dozens of others who also support/subsidize my salary."

The following are frequently asked questions you should think through how to answer. If you need help with some answers, check www.opennetworkers.org for more ideas.

Why are you here?

Why are you learning the language?

How much are your course/school fees?

How did you find this course/job?

How can you afford to stay here and study without a job?

What is your job?

What is your company's name?

Where is your company located?

Who pays you?

How much do you get paid?

Are you a missionary?

Are you a tentmaker?

Where will you retire?

Are you paid by churches?

How much is your rent?

Why are you home all day?

Mistakes

There are some workers who have been deported due to stupid mistakes. Home churches can be among the biggest security risks. It is a challenge to educate the church back home concerning security, whether they give you financial support or not. Pastors, mission committee members, and friends need to be clearly informed of what they can write to you and where to send things. Churches should never post details about your life and work on their website, in a newsletter, or in their church directory. A letter should be sent to all prayer partners explaining what they may and may not share with others. Your full name, mission organization, and country of service should never be mentioned on the same page. Mail should be sent to a nearby secure country. Some tentmakers have only one person in their sending country who knows their mailing address. All mail is routed through that person who screens each piece of mail.

Many ministries enjoy the benefits and recruiting opportunities short-term workers offer; however, they are a big security risk as well. Short termers must be thoroughly briefed on what they may and may not say to their friends back home. Pictures need to be closely edited so as not to give away information that could betray field workers. The wisest thing is to never allow your picture to be taken with Christian leaders or short termers. Avoid pictures with any Christian group. Many governments employ agencies to search all kinds of magazines for anything said about their country. The printed page is watched very carefully and thus, is the most dangerous security leak.

While overseas, prepaid hand (cell) phones are the securest. Do not use real names of team members on telephone lists, speed dials, or in notes and e-mails; use abbreviations or symbols for names. Several countries record conversations on expatriate phone lines. The officials are not listening to the conversations; they are simply taping them. However, should the worker get into trouble, the officials then go and listen to past conversations, resulting in trouble for others too. We may get around this by having a national friend apply for a telephone line for us and having his name, not ours, listed in the phonebook.

Be careful how you handle or give Christian literature. Literature is very traceable. Authorities can follow the evidence back to its original source. One of the first questions MBBs are asked is, "Who gave you the Bible?" We find the best way to solve this problem is to never give a Bible to anyone. There are two ways that we get the Scriptures out. One, we encourage short-term workers to give Bibles to our local friends. We give the Bibles to short-term worker Al, who gives them to short-term worker Bee, who gives them to short-term worker Che, who gives them to our local friend. In this way, if Che is asked, "Where did you get this Bible?" He can honestly answer "from Bee." Normally we have short termers give away Bibles on their last day in the country. Another way to get around this is to meet your local friend in some public place, like a restaurant. When you get up to leave, place the Bible or literature on a chair from which the friend can then pick it up if he or she so desires. In this way, you can honestly tell officials you did not "give" them the literature, but you left it behind and when you returned for it later, it was gone. Return a few hours later and ask the manager if anyone has turned in your book. When the officials approach you, be sure to thank them for finding your Bible, and ask them to return it to you.

Within the team, keep one another informed of your activities. For example, "I may go to a meeting in Cyprus for four days. While there, I may also do some shopping, swimming, and sightseeing." So I may tell my friends I am going there for a business seminar, while a team member may say I am going on a vacation. When new team members arrive, it is important for the entire team to review together how the team first contacted them and how they came to work with us. Initial introductions can be embarrassing. Though the whole team knows the new worker, our local office staff do not. Thus, the first time the new worker (short termers included) comes to the office, she is introduced to everyone, both team members and non-team members, as if she knew nobody. There is no lie. We would never say to Joe team member, "Joe have you met Sally (short termer) before?" This would force him to lie or say "Yes," causing Joe to explain why he already knows Sally. We simply take Sally around to all the staff and say, "This is Sally, the Cambridge University student who is apprenticing with us this summer." At the office, all team members know never to talk about team ministries in any way, shape, or form. Though everything is ministry, we separate business and team matters.

Security needs will vary from country to country, even person to person. If you do not worry about security, you must still respect the security concerns of others. The Word of God says, "Do not cause anyone to stumble, whether Jews, Greeks or the church of God—even as I try to please everybody in every way. For I am not seeking my own good but the good of many" (1 Corinthians 10:32–33). Mature believers will be sensitive to the needs or fears of others. Whether we believe those needs or fears to be real or imaginary, we should treat others as we would wish them to treat us (Matthew 7:12). When in doubt, remember the words of Solomon, "Discretion will protect you, and understanding will guard you."[86]

We need to take every precaution with our computers. All computers should be password protected with a screen saver set to lock after a few minutes of inactivity. It is too easy to forget to shut down a file that we do not want others reading, when we step out for a cup of coffee. Never send ministry-related e-mail through a friend's computer. Avoid internet cafes, but if you must use one, be sure to shut down all programs and files before leaving. Remember to brief your children on your job. If you are a non-native English speaker, do not teach your children English words like "missionary" or "tentmaker."

E-mail / The Internet

The internet is easily the greatest threat to a tentmaker's security. Information flows freely on the internet. Anyone can find out almost anything about another person. Workers from several countries have been "discovered" for being clandestine missionaries as a result of local friends simply typing their names into "Google." Thus, it is imperative that you cannot be readily found by a general web search. The best way to prevent this is to do periodic web searches on yourself and your teammates on several comprehensive internet search sites. Should something come up, write to the offending site owner or designer immediately and request the removal of the compromising information.

There are a few simple measures that can keep our PCs more secure. Periodically, run an antivirus program and keep it up to date. Run Windows updates and change the passwords annually. Use non-obvious passwords. Back up your files quarterly. Be sure you have at least one adequate firewall. When you e-mail, send everything blind copy; this makes it harder for hackers to know the e-mail addresses of those you are communicating with.

All computers should utilize an encryption system to log on. This prevents anyone from turning on your computer and browsing through your files without knowing the password. E-mail should be encrypted as well. Sooner or later, one of your messages will leave the safety of your e-mail server. Many countries have the software to open and read e-mails. In 2003, there was the well-known incident of the Singaporean government scanning every computer in the country searching for illegal activities. Do not believe that deleting files alone will solve your problems. We may wipe a hard drive clean but investigators may still find information in the PC's recycle bin.

Contingency Plans

There is a need for a contingency plan whenever we take risks. It is never wise to devise a plan after the fact, based on emergencies or problems. "A prudent person foresees the danger ahead and takes precautions; the simpleton goes blindly on and suffers the consequences."[87] A good leader always has a plan A and a plan B. We should determine our values and plan from there. Thus, we need to think through the actions we should take if things go wrong. Exodus chapter one tells us the story of Shiprah and Puah, the Hebrew midwives. Pharaoh ordered them to kill all newborn boys, but fearing God, Shiprah and Puah developed a contingency plan; they simply arrived late to some of the births, so they could not kill the children. God commends these women. I would never advocate lying to anyone about anything, yet God is not upset with the midwives; in fact, He blesses them. Shiprah and Puah implemented their contingency plan which enabled them to obey God.

Contingency plans should be outlined for the team, local believers, and the NGO or business. A smoke alarm is not fail proof. Knowing a fire exists does not mean we are prepared to put it out. Each team should determine a strategy of what to say and do in the event of an emergency. Team members need to know how to contact one another quickly. Identify places that can be used as temporary meeting places both inside and outside the country. Set up a calling tree where each team member calls one or two other team members, who in turn call another one or two people, and so on down the line.

For the business, what steps need to be taken in case of an emergency? Is there a trusted national who can run things while you are away? Every effective disaster recovery program begins with a simple step; recognize that the employees are your most valuable asset. The next step is to prepare employees. Once a plan is designed, host a seminar for employees on how to prepare themselves and their family for potential disasters.

The most important step in surviving any kind of emergency is to make it a "rehearsed event." Create a plan, and then practice it until everyone knows what is expected of them.

GOVERNMENT RELATIONS

Each worker needs to think through in advance a strategy for relating to the authorities. Developing a close relationship with officials could be a blessing should you get into trouble with the religious leaders. However, should the political party you have good relationships with be ousted from power, you could find yourself on your way back to your homeland. As one worker told me, "I put all my chips on Mr. X (the political leader). I met him when he was a state official and watched him rise within the system for nine years to a seat in the prime minister's cabinet. Mr. X kept my visa alive, despite allegations from religious leaders that I was not a good influence on the students, as I would share my beliefs with them. But when Mr. X fell out of favor, it was just a few months later that my visa was revoked." Our team has chosen to work closely with the authorities. We have found them helpful in processing visas. We go out of our way to show them honor, even inviting them to special business functions.

Others take the route of avoiding the government authorities. The benefit of this is if you are in a city with many foreigners, you may slip by undetected. Also, the less time you spend with officials, the fewer the questions they can ask. Nonetheless, in areas where you are likely to stand out and be noticed, I recommend making some effort to befriend officials. A direct approach is less likely to be suspicious or draw attention to unusual activities, like attending meetings with other believers. If you are working for a local firm or international company, you might not need to interact with the government at all. But if tendered the opportunity to meet with officials, it would probably be a good idea to do so.

In a country where the party in power changes frequently, it is important to be politically non-aligned. Remaining nonpolitical sometimes takes great discipline. Even when a government is corrupt and evil, our top priority is to win hearts for the eternal kingdom and not reform a temporal one. Taking sides against the party in power or the government in general risks both our longevity in the country and our friendships with nationals. Locals may fear our ideas and positions could get them into trouble. Going to jail for Jesus is one thing, but it is another thing to be imprisoned for our political positions. More than one worker has been denied reentry into his country because of negative statements he made about the government in his prayer letter.

In dealing with the government, understand it takes much longer than promised to process papers and get approvals. Four months means eight. No matter how many jobs your business creates in the community, the officials will probably not care whether or not you are there. Realize officials are smarter about foreign business than you think. However, politics is politics, and sometimes against their own interests they will be forced to take on the role of adversary. Also, when working with officials and other business people, be clear about your business objectives. Do not assume their motivations are the same as yours. In meeting with officials, remember they need Jesus too. Seek to understand before sharing your plans. Ask about their political and personal agenda, struggles and dreams. Help to see the benefits your NGO or business may bring to the community and their personal constituency.

DUAL IDENTITY

Mark was not the type of person who could switch rapidly from one kind of activity to another, but he was diligent. While attending Bible school, Mark felt the Master leading him to the XYZ people of sub-Sahara Africa. At his church's encouragement, he studied missiology for one year at a nearby seminary. He was then commissioned by the church and sent out as a missionary with WMD mission. At the mission's encouragement, he did another masters program in English. Then he completed one year of language study at a mission-run language institute in a nearby country. Finally, his mission helped him find a job at a locally owned language center in a large African city among the XYZ people. There were other missionaries in the city working with an established church, but Mark was focused on serving among an unreached Muslim people group. He slept on a mission owned bed and studied at a mission owned table. As Mark began his teaching duties, he was bombarded by a number of upsetting questions, "Are you CIA? Are you a missionary?" Though Mark felt comfortable with most of his answers, the "missionary" question often kept him awake at night. He battled with the concern, "Am I lying?" After just a few months serving in the city he had prepared for years to live in, Mark had a nervous breakdown and was sent home.

Workers need to understand that having two identities is not just a sense of identity, it is who we are. Each of us needs assurance in the Spirit that our inner integrity in answering questions is honestly based within our public identity. As one worker in Africa points out, "Be prepared for schizophrenia." Withstanding the external pressures of language and culture is much easier if the tentmaker's conscience is not also producing accusations.

We need to decide if the vocation and ministry are really part of God's calling for us. Living a double life can be exhausting—mentally, emotionally, and spiritually. It is important to prayerfully reflect on whether we and those we are recruiting will be able to withstand the incredible pressures of living a double life. Many tentmakers will immediately respond by saying, "I have never lived a double life!" But I question how honest they are being with themselves. Most of us, those who have formal theological training, tell only part of our story to our close local friends. For example, on a job application we omit our years at Bible college and/or seminary. The time serving on staff with our churches back home is also tactically redefined. When we attend missionary meetings outside of our place of service, we tell others we are going on a holiday. In each of these cases we are not lying; we are simply not filling in all the blanks. However, some brothers and sisters feel they are lying if they know the answer but do not provide it. Though we may be under stress due to ministry struggles, the pastor and a close friend resigning in anger back at our home church, or our team is battling some financial issue, we cannot share any of these things with our best friends who are devout Muslims. In addition, we cannot share with our close friends back home about our visits inside the mosque, our practicing Muslim prayer forms, and the struggles we have in choosing a school for the kids. Well, we may try, and we may get some sympathy and prayer, but ultimately we stop sharing those things with our former best friends as we know they do not understand. Thus, there is a feeling of living a double life. We have one life we reveal to friends overseas and another life we reveal to friends back home. As one mother remarked to me in tears, "It's not that nobody understands me; it's that nobody can possibly understand me." Living a life of "half truths" increases one's stress level. Though having a dual identity rarely sidelines a worker, it is a real issue which wears on us.

As tentmakers, we need to honestly ask ourselves, "Where does my identity come from?" If your role in life (doctor, business person, social worker, missionary) is important to whom you are you will have struggles with your dual identity. In addition, does your primary sense of identity originate locally or in your home country? You are more likely to "feel" like a missionary if you have your identity based in your sending church or mission organization. It is essential that before going overseas, you settle that your identity is in Christ and in Him alone. If we receive support through a mission agency and this is bothersome, we need to think through other options of getting funds. If we feel we are being "sneaky," we may be headed for trouble. If we see ourselves as giving the good news of Jesus to people and making disciples in their context, there is less of a need to feel we are "undercover." In addition, there is the burden of our spouse and children carrying separate identities. People who know us on both sides of the ocean must be screened carefully and appropriately warned of the need to keep our identities separate and to themselves.

THE ETHICS OF TENTMAKING

Jerry White, former director of the Navigators, writes, "Ethics to the government is law. Ethics to the philosopher is a concept. Ethics to religion is morality. But ethics to God is obedience."[88] Integrity and faithfulness are cornerstones of any Christian business person's success. Many a godly successful businessman, as well as Christian leaders, have fallen by the wayside due to a lack of these building blocks in their lives. To succeed, tentmakers dare not be naive about the moral challenges we face. We must prepare for these challenges and plan to overcome them. We must show good judgment and the ability to make wise decisions when in dire circumstances, for this is the purpose for which Christ has called us to the marketplace. We must know how to live in the marketplace community without being influenced by its value system. We need to know how to shine His light without drawing attention to ourselves. We need to be able to share in its struggles without succumbing to its temptations. It is imperative that we are constantly aware of the fact that God in His sovereignty has placed us in this dilemma to demonstrate His character to a people in desperate need of a model.

Nik Mustapha, assistant director-general of the Institute of Islamic Understanding, writes,

> "We need ethics. This is because in the absence of ethics elaborate specification of details and enforcement costs will take a big bite out of the potential benefits of the transaction. Thus contract and law without ethics cannot protect the interests of those who lack information. In Islamic teachings, ethical practices in all aspects of human-related activities including business are aimed at realising the spirit of justice and fairness in human relationship. This holy objective can lead to social harmony and equilibrium, which eventually can contribute to social progress."[89]

Buddhists, Hindus, Muslims are religious beings and they know their own hearts. When we act in ways unbecoming of Jesus' name they know, they are watching us. Christlikeness requires us to constantly, minute by minute throughout each day, be subsumed in an intimate communion with Jesus.

Deception

While working as a regular missionary, I would meet missionaries in non-Christian surroundings. Since they did not know me nor I them, invariably I would ask, "What do you do?" The majority of the time the person would reply, "I am a teacher," or "I am a dentist," or "I am a manager." When they asked me in return, I would reply, "I am a missionary." To which they would excitedly reply, "Oh, really? Actually, I am too!" Why is it that regular missionaries consider tentmakers to be deceptive, yet they do not identify themselves as missionaries either? Some will point out that to identify yourself as a "missionary" may turn someone off, closing the door to an opportunity to witness later. I have heard several regular missionaries say they do not want to spoil a witnessing opportunity because the word "missionary" is sometimes offensive. This may be true. Yet, is it not a double standard for them to call us deceitful for not disclosing our full identity, when they practice the same thing?

Job serves as a model for us. Though he was in the midst of great suffering, he proclaimed, "As long as I have life within me, the breath of God in my nostrils, my lips will not speak wickedness, and my tongue will utter no deceit . . . till I die, I will not deny my integrity."[90] Some workers believe deception is a necessity, while others totally disagree. The Bible is clear that we must strive for a clear conscience in all we do (Acts 24:16). But understand, God has given some people stronger and others weaker consciences. In putting others first (Philippians 2:3), we need to be sensitive to these differences. We need not judge our brothers and sisters, but accept them, allowing God to deal with the motives of their hearts (1 Corinthians 4:4–5).

Deception can cause embarrassing moments and harm our testimony. A lot of energy may be wasted and risks incurred in the process of deceiving others. For example, our team holds an annual retreat at a nice hotel in a neighboring country. The first year, the five of us working in the office told our national employees we were all taking off at the same time, going to the same country, but we all gave different reasons! Nobody lied, but we each stressed different aspects of our time away: a vacation, a spiritual retreat, a seminar, visit friends, time with God. It creates suspicion if I tell someone my co-worker is traveling on business, and he tells them he is going on vacation.

What is deception? Some workers will defend outright lying. If the Nazis came to your door and you were hiding Jews, some would say it would be okay to lie. Abraham pretended to be Sarah's brother, twice (Genesis 12:13; 26:7). Moses deceived Pharoah in stating the reason the people needed to go into the desert was to hold a festival to God, which was true, but the implication was that the Israelites would return, and Moses knew they would not (Exodus 5:1). Moses also deceived the people by pretending to have a shining face long after the glow had faded (2 Corinthians 3:13). The Hebrew midwives (Exodus 1:19) and Rahab (Joshua 2:4) deceived people and were blessed by God. God commanded Joshua to deceive his enemies (Joshua 8:2). Gideon was timid and in hiding, yet God's messenger addressed him as "mighty warrior" (Judges 6:12). Samuel was given a second motive by God Himself for anointing David king (1 Samuel 16:2), and David feigned being crazy (1 Samuel 21:13). Several of these actions were ordered by God or his angel. Every one of these people was blessed by God, and not one was rebuked for their lack of full disclosure or deceitful words. In the New Testament, both John the Baptist (John 1:21–23) and Jesus (Matthew 21:23) side stepped direct questions, not sharing all they knew to be true. Was this deceit?

The necessity of disobeying human authority in order to obey God has been discussed many times in various articles. The biblical justification for disobedience toward oppressive authorities is most commonly found in Peter's example of refusing to obey the authorities in Acts 5. Nonetheless, it is arguable whether or not we may disobey human laws when they keep us from obeying God's law. In an increasingly duplicitous society, Gary Taylor asks, "Is our use of covert means to spread the gospel a biblically defensible method or mere opportunism?"

One tentmaker raises the point, "God has directed deception in the past, and He may be directing some to use it today in the face of extreme opposition." Should deception be used to enable missionaries to share the gospel in CANs? As in all of life, we need to seek the guidance of the Master so as to discern His specific will for our lives and ministries. It is important for all tentmakers to do a Bible study on the ethics of deceit so as to come to our own conclusions and convictions, so we will know how we should act. Surely, God has led different workers to different conclusions. Why, I do not know. But as with doctrinal controversies, we should respect one another's leading and allow for different standards of ethics among different workers and ministries.

Training

"Ethics must be in the training. Among a group of tentmakers once in a RAN, [restricted access nation] one couple felt much guilt about their situation after they were in the country. They actually went to government officials and 'confessed their sins'—and the sins of their fellow tentmakers."[91]

In preparing His disciples for their short-term missionary experience, Jesus teaches them to be shrewd (Matthew 10:16). In the parable of the shrewd manager (Luke 16:1–9), Jesus uses the same word in a positive way to describe the actions of an unfaithful manager who squanders his master's wealth and then deals dishonestly with his master's creditors so that they would owe him a favor after he was fired. If tentmakers are to survive and thrive as "sheep in the midst of wolves," we must apply Jesus' words and be shrewd. However, as Jesus points out, "the people of this world are more shrewd in dealing with their own kind than are the people of the light" (Luke 16:8). Due to our lack of shrewdness, it is imperative that tentmakers receive training in what it means to be like a dove, a sheep, and a snake, while living amongst a pack of wolves. Workers need to be able to live at peace with themselves. This requires understanding our own limits and our own consciences so that we know where to draw the line for ourselves in dealing with others. The challenges and temptations are often overwhelming. Satan literally destroys workers who have sensitive and fearful consciences over these issues. We need to study and discuss biblical lying, deceit, shrewdness, and practical applications for our daily lives and work. For all but those people who are black and white on issues, these are not easy decisions.

Mike McLoughlin hits the nail on the head when he writes,

"Shrewdness is a virtue in business decision making. The Concise Oxford Dictionary defines the word 'shrewd' to mean 'sagacious, sensible, discriminating, astute, judicious.' However, many unethical business practices are considered to be shrewd business dealing, such as bribery, cutting corners or cheating to achieve the end result—success. Although the sage in Proverbs does not approve of the practice he acknowledges its effectiveness. 'A bribe is a charm to the one who gives it; wherever he turns, he succeeds' (Proverbs 17:8). If one is not 'shrewd' in these matters it is commonly believed that one will not succeed or stay competitive in business. Absolute ethics would restrict this form of shrewdness in business decisions. Thus a Christian's adherence to an absolute standard of morality is not only seen as 'religious fanaticism' it is also viewed as business suicide. Faced with this hostile environment, how is a Christian in the marketplace able to be faithful to God and coexist with a value system that is contrary to their core beliefs? How can they relate to fellow managers or business people who would consider them naive for not acting shrewdly? How can they survive, let alone succeed in business? Jesus' answer: Be Shrewd."[92]

Realize different cultures will view lying, deception, and shrewdness differently. We need training to learn our culture's perspective on these issues and then evaluate what is acceptable in the light of Scripture.

Where can we find a seminary course on shrewdness? Specifically, we need training in the ethical areas of legitimacy, confidentiality, professional responsibilities, favors, bribes, loyalty, and mission versus business and family issues. We need to walk through in advance the questions both local friends and authorities may ask. It should be required for tentmakers to review business/NGO case studies of questionable conduct so as to consider biblical responses. We must learn that when faced with a moral dilemma, we must pray, seek God's mind, and talk it over with our mentors and trusted friends, both locals and expatriates. We should press on, praying and seeking advice; then act.

We must always take care to act in accordance with the Bible. God rarely gives us specific methods and strategies for solving problems. Rather, He provides His principles and guidelines for making decisions and clear directives and exhortations. Decision making is one of the hardest assignments we are given. It is surprising the small number of workers who know where and how to get help. Tentmakers need channels for expressing ideas and experienced workers to bounce ideas around with. For the younger generation who favor peer mentoring, there is a need for training in mentoring. Workers need to understand the practical benefits of having advisors in our lives and how best to utilize them. (Proverbs 11:14).

Bribes

There is a Turkish proverb which says, "Both the giver and receiver of a bribe are sinners." The Bible is also clear on accepting bribes, "Do not accept a bribe, for a bribe blinds those who see and twists the words of the righteous."[93] Paul could have bribed his way out of jail, but choose not to do so (Acts 24:26). However, the giver of a bribe is not chastised. "A gift given in secret soothes anger, and a bribe concealed in the cloak pacifies great wrath."[94] Yet, we know it is wrong to cause others to sin (Matthew 18:6–9).

A worker in Narnia writes, "Before I came here, I thought I understood the concept of bribery and held a standard evangelical position on it. But since living here, I've had to discern the difference between a bribe, extortion, and tipping. . . . In Narnia the lines between bribery, extortion, and tipping are unintelligibly fuzzy. One body language definition of bribery is to wink one eye while saying 'tip.' Our accountant lists our government-related expenses in two categories: those with receipts and those without. Is the receipt-less money he must give the tax clerk to process our papers a tip or extortion? Getting a driver's license, a car inspected, the trash men to come, a phone installed, a package out of the post office, even getting our child registered in a public school requires receipt-less money. Bribery? Extortion? A tip?"

In Asia and Africa, bribes and kickbacks are a common feature of doing business. If you work for a national firm, realize that it is relatively common for local employers to ask employees to do things westerners would consider fraudulent. Paying bribes, falsifying documents, bait and switch tactics, infringing on copyrights, false advertising, and cheating on taxes are the normal way of doing business. If you work for someone else, you need to know the culture and your conscience's boundaries.

If you own your own business, it is important to establish from day one your values on bribes, kickbacks, extortion, gifts, favors, and tips. Make a plan to disseminate your value system throughout the company. If you manage or own the business, there are other options for "getting things done." You may offer rewards for fast service or discounts for bulk and repeat business. Another worker suggests trading services. You help me, and I will help you. You can also enlist help from the community. One worker brings in a sports ministry team every year which blesses the children of the community, endearing his business to parents in a way that makes it hard for those parents who are in positions of authority to press him for favors. If you have a local partner, ensure he or she is in agreement with you, lest people learn to work around you. Don, in Central Asia, favors giving officials gifts. He writes, "I suggest proactively offering reward systems, which counteract greed and build back into the community. Government officials therefore gain face in their community by supporting your business project."

Gifts are a regular feature of doing business in many parts of the world. Your office needs to have a plan for giving gifts. Some cultures give more expensive gifts, and some have certain types for certain occasions. Interact with the national employees to learn the local culture of gift giving, and then seek to learn with them whether this practice honors the Lord.

Another option commonly used is to hire an intermediary for dealing with the government. We retain a lawyer for this purpose, but an accountant or some other cultural "go between" could suffice. The advantage of using an intermediary is that she will already have established relationships with the authorities and know how the system works. By paying them a small fee for their services, much time can be saved.

Many years ago Dwight Nordstrom, serving in China, taught me his "*lust* rule" for doing business. When I encounter a questionable situation, I follow the *lust* rule to see if I am "lusting" after this deal. I ask myself the following four questions. If I answer "Yes" to any one question, then I do not follow through on the deal or requested action.

1. Does the proposed action violate any *laws* under which the jurisdiction of this act occurs (local and international)?
2. Do co-workers, employees, or I have any *uncomfortable* feelings or a check in our spirit about the proposed action?
3. Does the proposed action violate anything in *Scripture*?
4. Is the proposed action being done in secret? Is anything being hidden from anyone and not *transparent* to everyone who is associated with the action?

Providing favors for people to process government papers or close a deal is also a natural part of life. Each situation should be evaluated separately. Consideration should be given to the *lust* rules, as well as the person's value and relationship to the business. Over the years, I have been asked for a variety of favors: a trip to the home office in America, a Rolex watch, writing a recommendation letter to a school in America, a discount on our services and the use of our company van for a family outing. If you give a favor, as I did with loaning out the van, as expected, many others have since asked (and been given) the same favor. If the favor, as with the Rolex watch, fails the *lust* test, I politely point out to the person that to my God, or in my culture or business, this favor would be wrong. I go on to say that I know they would not wish for me to offend my God or violate my conscience. This explanation is usually acceptable.

Be wary of granting favors for an individual. Granting a favor normally sets a precedent. Others who know about the favor may request it for themselves. Therefore, give out favors equally or not at all. Be aware that if you do favors without expecting a return, you cannot expect that to be reciprocated. Be wise in that if a local business person or government leader is unusually nice, they probably want something. Westerners often fall prey to unconsciously accepting a favor. When you do, in time, you can expect to be asked for a repayment. For example, a professor was invited out by a student to a nice restaurant for an expensive meal. After the meal, there was a request for assistance for a better grade. Do not be naive!

TIME COMMITMENT

My interviews with seventy workers serving in the 10/40 Window reveal that organizations are loosening their requirements and allowing workers to make shorter time commitments. Yet, those groups which are asking for four and five-year commitments are not seeing a decrease in new workers. Recruiters need to emphasize to new workers that the most difficult period of service is generally between the eighth and eighteenth month.[95] Culture shock is at its peak during this period. Kohls is more specific, stating that workers will have two low periods during their first two years overseas, the third to sixth month and the tenth to fourteenth month.[96] When workers become frustrated with the language and culture and experience the other common adjustment problems that all workers face, they need help to persevere. However, if we are just a few months away from going home, we can just hang on; we go through the daily motions and wait out our time to go home. Rather than deal with the pain and learn the lessons the Lord might wish for us to experience, we develop a strategy to cope with the pain, knowing that once we board the plane home we will be fine. It takes experience, which requires time more than anything else, for us to gain a clear perspective on our life, work, and ministry overseas. Over time, it becomes clear how the Lord would weave all our experiences together.

A worker's effectiveness increases with his or her length of time on the field. This may be due to the fact that those who make long-term commitments are forced by their time commitment into facing their problems and dealing with their issues. This results in their settling into the culture and staying even longer than initially planned. The point is that mission agencies and churches need to encourage people to make longer-term commitments. New workers and short-term workers who are struggling with their job, the culture, or ministry are usually self-focused. Short-term workers need to be guided into opportunities with time frames that will provide them an optimal emotional and spiritual experience so as to get beyond themselves. In this way, they discover both the needs of the field they are visiting, as well as the possibilities God has for them.

ENTRY STRATEGIES

There are numerous entry strategies being employed by tentmakers around the 10/40 Window. Much preparation and prayer can go into choosing the right strategy. In thinking and praying through the options, keep your focus on Jesus and not success. Success, in time, will flow out of focusing on Him.

In planning our entry strategy, we need to work backward from our goal. What is the ultimate objective? As my pastor says, "You do not fish in a park fountain as there aren't any fish there." Choose a strategy that will place you among or nearby those you are led to reach. Will the NGO or teaching position create chances for ministry? Will working fifty hours a week for a multi-national corporation open doors for accomplishing your evangelistic goals? With every job opportunity, we must answer the question, "Will this job open opportunities to share the gospel in both word and deed?" In planning an entry strategy, start with the ministry you feel led to do and then search for or start a business which will enable you to fulfill God's desires for you. Evaluate each job according to visa, longevity, access to the people, ministry opportunities, family needs, your skills and training, financial benefits, etc.

Tentmakers hold many types of jobs throughout the 10/40 Window. The research reveals business positions (marketing, finance, management) and medical/health care jobs are slightly more effective. However, in poorer areas, an NGO model is often the best strategy. The key is finding work that provides natural access to the people. Tentmakers who hold positions which are counter productive to ministry goals may succeed in doing business, but will prove less effective in ministry. Our jobs and projects should enhance our ministries.

Longevity and Boldness

Stuart Briscoe, senior pastor of Elmbrook Church in Milwaukee Wisconsin, said, "I can tell you who the pioneers are; they are the ones walking around with the arrows in their backs." In striving to reach the unreached, invariably there will be risks—big steps of faith—required of us. One of the tensest periods for all workers are the months preceding the renewal of our visas. We need to count the cost concerning security, involvement with the local church, employing nationals, etc. However, in choosing an entry strategy, it is important to plan ahead and think long term. Your children's education, the period you rent your home, and many other things will be based on the approval of your visa, and that visa may limit your options.

In selecting a job, determine beforehand how long you wish to reside in that location. Then ask our provider to reveal and provide a job or new strategy that will enable you to remain in the country for that precise period of time. Realize that many jobs provide a visa for only a year or two. Though many are renewable, not all are.

Choosing a witnessing strategy can also be a major source of tension. We are here to be witnesses. We wish for our light to shine forth and not be placed under a basket. Nonetheless, if we are arrested and deported, this would greatly hinder our ability to witness or disciple believers. Wise workers think through how bold we wish to be in sharing the good news. Learn what others have done. Get input on entry strategies from both expatriates and locals, government officials, Christians and non-Christians. Be open to new ideas. "Smart men are open to new ideas. In fact, they look for them."[97]

HEALTH

There are many health concerns for people working overseas. As with our material needs, we ought to commit our physical well being to Jehovah Rophe, our God who heals. As our bodies are the temple of God, all workers need to know their own bodies and treat them with respect. Whatever good habits we maintained before going overseas should be maintained once we are there. Know your own sleeping habits and exercise needs. If certain foods make you physically ill, it is okay to inform the host. We should also be responsible to get regular check ups. Martin Luther said, "A person should work in such a way that he remains well and does no injury to his body. We should not break our heads at work and injure our bodies." Jesus served people even when it was inconvenient; nonetheless, He persevered until He found time for the other serious disciplines of life, such as solitude. Times alone with the Father were Jesus' times of refreshing (Luke 5:16). Spending time lingering in the presence of God is an antidote for burnout. Whether it be through exercise, worship, reading, or solitude, we need to ensure we regularly refresh ourselves.

Stress-Burnout

Cultures are designed to protect us from problems, yet different cultures prioritize problems differently. It is natural to feel alone, unprotected, and vulnerable after settling into a new culture. Culture shock, a lack of a support team, poor communication with your spouse or leaders, changing values, and high expectations are a few of the issues that can cause us to crash and burn. Even though it is not realistic, many T-3 and T-4 tentmakers who receive support from churches feel they must produce in their ministry like regular missionaries. Whatever your role, living cross-culturally is stressful. Total immersion into a new culture, language, and ministry usually creates feelings within us we have never experienced. When the stress mounts and we feel like we are going to burst, we need to follow the example of Jesus and take a break and de-pressurize.

The best way to detour pressure is to stop, look, and listen. *Stop*; take a break—one day, five days, whatever is needed. Jesus' times alone varied in length with some lasting over a week. *Look* back on your life. Recall God's working in your past, His leading, and His purposes for your life. *Listen* to God. Make time to meditate on His word. Worship, pray, and read the Bible. Give yourself, your plans, things, and dreams to God again. Then wait; sit back and see what He does.

Bob in the Middle East shares, "My biggest problem is the constant distraction. I am constantly thinking about succeeding. My ego cares, my family cares, the culture and the government cares, not to mention the employees to whom I'm trying to provide a decent living and a testimony." Jeff confesses, "There is so much stress, so much to do, but as I think about it, most of the pressure is self generated." Though no empirical study has been done to validate this, the burnout factor appears to be higher among tentmakers than regular missionaries. Both have to deal with the heat, the bugs, and the disparity of culture. But missionaries often have their compound or mission community to retreat into. Tentmakers, on the other hand, especially those not associated with a mission organization, do not have the established networks of support and encouragement to which we can retreat for fellowship, refreshment, safety, and inner security.

Crisis intervention research reveals that when stressors outweigh their support systems, people are in crisis. Dr. Tim Lowenstein's "Life Stress Test" lists forty-two life factors, which if altered increase our susceptibility to have an emotional break down. Seventeen of these factors are altered just by moving overseas into an unfamiliar, cross-cultural setting! Ministering cross-culturally overseas is a high stress assignment. Peter reminds us, "Dear friends, do not be surprised at the painful trial you are suffering, as though something strange were happening to you."[98] Just as the Father prepared the Son through suffering so He will also prepare the Bride of the Son—us. The Father has brought us into this ministry to transform us into His image. Therefore, we should expect His transformation process, including reaching the unreached, to be difficult. Nonetheless, we take comfort in the fact that He will never push us beyond what we can bear (1 Corinthians 10:13).

Tentmakers need a supportive team that is on-site or makes regular visits. This support team stimulates, encourages. and prays with the field team. We each need to ensure we have a broad enough network to sustain us. Our network should touch the key areas of our lives, sharpening and widening our knowledge and skills, even taking us beyond our comfort zones. Our networks should be based on relationships. In times of change, stress, or confusion, our networks should serve as pillars of support. Within our networks, we should find people who are the answers to the questions; Who do you go to for. . . . Friendship? Encouragement? Recreation? Advice? Spiritual mentoring? Business mentoring? Ministry mentoring? Character mentoring? Marriage and family mentoring? New ideas? Inspiration? Help?

REASONS WORKERS QUIT

Bill has an interesting insight concerning worker attrition in the 21st century. "A holy and wrathful God is very unfashionable. It seems there is new God theology which stresses us over God. God sent His Son to live and die for us. Christ still dies for our sins, but there's no suffering on our part, and there is no guilt and no wrath. The problem of going overseas with such a perspective of God is that life is not as well ordered in other cultures, so things will not work out as easily as they seem to at home. The mission field causes us to face both God and ourselves in new ways. There are many excuses people give for leaving the field, but should the truth be spoken, the primary cause may be the inability of people to deal with their own failings." "Success," said IBM founder, T.J. Watson, "is on the far side of failure."

We need to remember that God is more concerned about the worker than the work. We too readily follow the patterns of the world, focusing our attention on activities and busyness, popularity and success. Being in the world, we need to remember not to step into the world's traps. Jesus warns that He is sending us out like sheep among wolves (Matthew 10:16). God's priority is to develop and purify who and what we are, so that He may live and minister through us. Though there are many reasons workers quit and go home before completing their assignment, there are seven which need mentioning here.

1. Marriage problems. Rarely is this highlighted as a cause for deciding to return home. Few admit this to their mission or church, but I believe it to be the number one root issue. Husbands and wives need training in what it means to submit to one another out of reverence for Christ (Ephesians 5:21–27). Sexual sins and frustrations contribute to marriage breakdowns too.

2. Poor leadership. Good leaders set the standards, keep people on track, and make hard decisions. Among the top qualities of poor leaders are: indecisiveness, lack of focus, limited vision, unwillingness to sacrifice for their people, mistrust of workers, failure to train up others, and pride. When culture shock strikes, it is common for the affected workers to lash out at their leader. The position of leader does not bring with it a mantle of perfection. Godly, gifted leaders are also sinners saved by grace. Leaders sin; leaders make mistakes; leaders fail.

3. Unrealistic expectations. New workers need help lowering their expectations. Encourage them to set goals and then counsel them to lower them a notch or two.

4. Lack of teamwork. There has been much improvement the past twenty years, but we still have a way to go. It is common for interpersonal conflicts to flare up and not be resolved. Tentmakers who have proved the reality of God's grace in their lives are in limited supply. Every team needs to review the principles of biblical peacemaking and reconciliation. We must be quick to forgive others who sin against us, and quicker to repent with brokenness for our own sins.

5. Sexual sins. Pornography on the internet is causing major damage to our field workers. We need to humble ourselves and share our tempta-

tions and failures, including specific questions about areas we are tempted in. We need to be transparent with one another, recognizing we too are sinners.

6. Inadequate funding. Financial pressures are still a huge issue for many workers, especially those from Latin America and Africa. Be encouraged; some new tentmaking models show promise for supplying needed support to third world workers.

7. Satan. I save the worst for last.

SUMMARY

Finding or creating a viable job is a great stress reducer and adds to the worker's longevity on the field. Select a position based on the people's view of the work to be done, not your own preconceived ideas. Time and our use of it can be a major tension. Plan ahead. When starting out, do not be afraid to put in the necessary hours in order to build up the business or NGO. This will result in greater freedom later. Choose jobs which place you deep into the culture and relationships. Learn the language before starting your job. Do not fool yourself into making the most common missionary mistake: "I will build my business and then learn the language." There are no easy answers for dealing with bribes and other ethical issues. A strong relationship with Jesus is key to overcoming the obstacles we encounter.

ACTION STEPS

- What are two weaknesses of the T-5 (faker) approach?
- What are some advantages and disadvantages of building close relationships with government officials?
- What questions do you need to think through, in case you are questioned by authorities?
- Do you have an emergency contingency plan for your team, your family?
- What are some advantages of working with an NRM?
- What steps do you need to take to make your computer secure? Do you have two or more firewalls? An encryption system? Talk with a computer friend this month about upgrading your computer's security systems.
- Search for your name and teammate's names on several internet search engines to ensure nothing compromising can be found.

- Is your identity firmly in Jesus, or is your church or job title important to you? If needed, seek out a mentor to disciple you in your identity in Christ.
- Read the articles on deceit and shrewdness on www.opennetworkers.net.
- Think through your long-term objectives and then consider what entry strategies will facilitate accomplishing those objectives.
- Do you have someone in your life who you can go to for. . . . Encouragement? Spiritual mentoring? Business mentoring? Ministry mentoring? Character mentoring? Marriage and family mentoring? New ideas and inspiration?
- Review the seven reasons workers quit. Which ones might cause you to fail? Find a mentor and develop a plan to strengthen these areas in your life.

"Paul is remembered for being an apostle, not a tentmaker."

Our work place is our evangelistic platform and our office is our pulpit.

Call to me and I will answer you and tell you great and unsearchable things you do not know.

chapter 17
TENTMAKING CONFLICTS

In 1987, when I was a regular missionary contemplating moving into the 10/40 Window, my supervisor came to me and said, "You cannot be a tentmaker! It is unethical!" That night I struggled over the issues of having dual motives for moving into the Muslim world. I prayed, "Lord, is it wrong to open a business when my primary objective is to plant churches?" The next morning I was reading in 1 Samuel 16. God tells Samuel to go to Bethlehem and anoint a son of Jesse as the new king over Israel. Realizing the dangerous consequences of appointing a new king when the old king is still in power, Samuel questions God, "How can I go? When Saul hears about it, he will kill me."[99] As a prophet, Samuel was well known. In Samuel's days, people did not venture far from home without a good reason. Samuel lived in Ramah, a couple of days walk from Bethlehem. While traveling he would be questioned, and in Bethlehem, he would stand out like a ham at a bar mitzvah. Certainly the authorities would report his movements to King Saul. In other words, Bethlehem was a restricted access area for Samuel.

God, understanding Samuel's dilemma, provided Samuel with another reason for going to Bethlehem. "The LORD said, 'Take a heifer with you and say, 'I have come to sacrifice to the LORD.' Invite Jesse to the sacrifice, and I will show you what to do.'"[100]

Sacrificing the heifer was a real assignment for Samuel, one he took seriously and performed with all the skill his job as a prophet required. The sacrifice not only gave Samuel a legitimate reason for going to Bethlehem, it also provided the context for Samuel to meet the sons of Jesse and perform his other job.

Therefore, God in His wisdom gave Samuel two assignments, yet he was to tell the authorities of only one. Both jobs were important and to be done unto God's glory, but the first job of anointing David as king was Samuel's primary job. Understand, Samuel knew where to go and what to do, but he did not know with whom he was going to do it; God would reveal that information later. The Lord only supplied what Samuel needed to get started. God provided Samuel with a plan that served as both a legitimate reason for being in the land, as well as a platform for performing His task. That morning, God showed me that tentmaking was His heifer for me.

It is important for missiologists and mission leaders to do their homework. It is said that "theoreticians do not mind living dangerously." The reason is obvious. Theoreticians are not responsible to make things happen. They only live dangerously on the conceptual level. Much of the criticism against tentmaking has been put forward by those who have never attempted it. Rather than building bridges, walls are being built. When John saw a man who was not one of the disciples driving out demons, he tried to stop him. But Jesus told him, "Do not stop him, for whoever is not against you is for you."[101]

ATTITUDES—THE SECULAR VERSUS THE SACRED

The division between church workers and the laity is as old as the church itself. Paul, a tentmaker, had to defend himself against those who saw his life and work as secondary to others (1 Corinthians 9). Though we are commanded to humble ourselves (1 Peter 5:5–6) and reproduce our lives (2 Timothy 2:2), as "full-time" Christian workers we often cling to the power, prestige, and positions which give us a sense of purpose. Though we would never teach or even encourage the separation of our religious lives and business lives, in all honesty, we model just that. Our emphasis on sharing the gospel in words alone proves that our faith is not integrated. Though people spend at least one quarter of the week at their work place, how often do you hear prayer requests shared for problems church members encounter in the office? Do people feel free to publicly pray for a raise so they can pay for their child's school tuition? Can we ask for our business to profit so that we do not have to lay off a father whose family is dependent on him for food? Though pastors preach that church is not just for Sunday, it is easy for those sitting in the pews to get the impression there are two lines in heaven: one for full-time Christian workers and one for everyone else.

Several times I have heard preachers state, "Business is preparation for ministry." If we are to reconcile everything to Christ (Colossians 1:20), then whatever job we have IS ministry. Business is not preparation, it is the real deal. Jesus worked in business fifteen years or more before He started His ministry. Could it be that His Father knew He needed that time to learn the heartbeat of the world and understand how to better relate to people? It appears as if pastors, seminary professors, and other professional Christians have a mental block against seeing business as an essential service provider in the world. Churchmen, academics, and others not dependent on the discipline of serving customers in order to eat or meet a payroll will naturally have a different perspective. The Spanish proverb applies: "Talking about bulls is not the same as facing them in the ring." Frank Payne, an American Baptist pastor, told me, "I confess, most pastors are afraid of businessmen." Churches provide care, not services. When you care for others, people like you. When you serve others, people barely notice you. People go to church; it is a place people go to worship. Thus, church can become like a club; you go, join, and pay dues. Church is just one part of our lives. For most tentmakers, our job is our church, and the work place is our place of worship. All Christians need to grasp the fact that business is a medium of pleasure to God and a tool of doing His good.

"However, for the tentmaking movement, the separation between regular marketplace Christians and the professional missionary persists because tentmakers are considered a specialized class of professional missionaries rather than being considered as marketplace missionaries. They are considered to be 'bi-vocational,' that is they have two vocations, one in business and the other in ministry. During the working week, they earn an income and in the evenings and on the weekend they plant churches. Stevens makes an excellent point about the confusion that exists in the missions movement concerning tentmakers. The frequent use of the term bi-vocational missionary when describing a tentmaker is misleading and incorrect. There is one calling or vocation, not two. Paul says that all Christians are called (Ephesians 4:1) and that the call of God is all-embracing: it includes Church, family, and society (Ephesians 4:1–6:20). The idea of vocation is quite different from what is involved in an occupation or profession, both of which are chosen by the person. To be a called person is to live one's life in response to the summons of Christ to discipleship, service, and holiness. There is no hierarchy of calls within the people of God; there are only different expressions of the general calling to all, according to gift, talent, and temperament of the individuals."[102]

Larry in Africa writes, "I used to explain what I did by saying, 'I have one foot in the ministry and one foot in business.' Over the years the Lord has graciously corrected me. I found out that I have both feet in ministry and my ministry happens to be business." Who would you pick to build an airplane? A godly pastor who can really pray, or a woman who has a Ph.D. in Aeronautical Engineering and has built her own airplane? The aeronautical engineer glorifies God by understanding and applying God's principles of aerodynamics.

In Christ, both the process and the result must bring glory to the Father. Thus, the means do not justify the end. The end result is embedded in the process and work of serving needs, which are both spiritual and practical. Returning to Paul's description, "There are many parts, but one body" (1 Corinthians 12:20). To divide our spiritual life from our roles in life is like separating the brain from the heart, meaning life would cease. There are many "parts" which make up who I am: husband, father, brother, business owner, missiologist, author, coach, elder, etc. But Christ is not just a part of me, He is all of me. He is not just integrated into these areas of my life; He oversees them, and He rules them. So whatever part I am playing at any point in time, He is involved. He is my Master.

People need to gain God's perspective when they consider mission work. When Jesus in me goes into the office, He is in the process of redeeming both me and the office. His atoning work on the cross was not just for me or for people. It is Jesus' desire to "reconcile to himself *all things*, whether things on earth or things in heaven" (Colossians 1:20, emphasis mine). I emphasize "all things" in that business, teaching, development work, etc., are all things which need to be reconciled to Jesus. To work in a business is not a means to an end; it is a holistic process, and this process is as important as any end that we may seek to attain. Whether Hudson Taylor preached the gospel in words or through practicing medicine, he was seeking to reconcile people to Jesus. In the same way, a businessman working in the marketplace is seeking to glorify God by seeking to reconcile the marketplace to Jesus.

A worker in Asia writes, "The 'traditional western worldview' is deeply flawed, particularly as we interface with more traditional cultures, as we have completely isolated the spiritual realm from the physical. When we talk 'spiritual' we can talk about God, Allah, conversion, Christian witness, preaching, our message, and CP [church planting]. But the physical realm—the realm governed by science and technology—is where things really get done, and this is where all development work is seen to belong. This worldview is not consistent with that of the majority of those we are trying to reach. Unfortunately, the influence of the West has meant that those who have 'benefited' from a higher level of education are more likely to have been influenced to see things 'our way'. Fortunately, the biblical worldview, which does not recognize this dichotomy but rather sees a continuum, is closer to that understood by those we are interfacing with."

Consider the missionary selection process. More often than not, we select missionaries because "there is nothing wrong with them." Once that is determined, we look for a place for workers to serve. Never in the process do we ask, "What does the church ultimately want the worker to accomplish?" Goals are set by the worker, not the church. The church supports the worker in his or her ministry, as if the church exists for the worker. Or to use Paul's terminology, the body exists for its parts. Yet shouldn't it be the worker who is supporting the church in its ministry?

To fight a battle we must interact with the enemy; we must see, hear, feel, and experience what our foe is like. When that happens, we are changed, along with the enemy. It seems that Christians do not wish to engage the enemy head on. I do not think we fear the battle, as we know we are going to win. Rather, I think we fear the changes that a battle brings. We fail to grasp that each battle is His plan to redeem the world through us AND transform us a bit more into His image. This is the problem in Iraq. Everyone wants a stable and peaceful government in Iraq, but few wish to have their comfortable life changed to see that become a reality. One of the West's mistakes is to work with corrupt governments. Good governments should encourage good business practices and in turn work with good business people. We cannot expect corrupt and greedy government leaders to reform a country. In the same, way we cannot expect corrupt and greedy business people to change the marketplace. Thus, there is a need for tentmakers. Transformed individuals will transform others. As tentmakers, we strive to step into the battle and seek to reconcile our part of the world to Jesus. Tentmakers do not serve so as to compare, compete, or consume; we serve so that Jesus might redeem the world to Himself.

Integration

Integrity by definition includes wholeness and honesty. If we have split personalities, we cannot live with integrity before the people we serve. Too many Christians are crippled in that they struggle to mix science and the Spirit, business and the Bible. Despite anti-science and anti-business attitudes among some believers, I am confident God mixes science, business, and His Word together just fine. The separation of the church and the world, the sacred and the secular is a human, sinful problem. An alternative to separation is integration. Integration is the act of bringing various parts into equal participation, whereby the parts become one whole. John Calvin wrote, "No task will be so sordid and base, provided you obey your calling in it, that it will not shine and be reckoned very precious in God's sight."[103] Clearly, in whatever job God leads us to do, He will provide opportunities to bring Him glory.

Church Versus Business Terminology

"Off the record, I find that workers with a traditional missionary mentality are really afraid of tentmakers. They are so used to cutting corners, being secretive, and saving money, they just don't understand us. I have learned to stop explaining myself, press ahead, and in time, the results speak for themselves," said a tentmaker in India.

The business and the mission worlds have different cultures, languages, and methods. Whereas the business culture exists to make a "profit" and is comfortable with the word "money," the mission culture is "not for profit." Money is something you may ask God or others for, but not something you normally work for. At times, the two cultures are as alien to one another as oil is to water. Bishop Stephen Neill expresses common, contemporary church thinking when he writes, "A mission which becomes a commercial concern, may end by ceasing to be a mission." With all due respect to Bishop Neill, are there not many churches that by altering the basic truths of God's Word ceased to be a biblical church? Do we stop planting churches lest the churches we plant fail? Business is one of God's systems. It teaches us to serve Him; it is a tool He uses to transform us. Our failure to redeem the marketplace is dishonoring to God.

Incompetence on the job and a strong witness for Christ are incompatible. Though the business versus church cultures are in agreement on that point, they tend to understand the intent of the point differently. A tentmaker in China reminded me recently of the standard business teaching, "Go with your strengths." The thinking is that if you strive to become proficient in a weak area, it will take too much time and effort away from working in the areas in which you are most productive and profitable. In other words, if you work to be good at everything, you will be great at nothing. Peter Drucker, the management guru, agrees, "Don't focus on building up your weaknesses. Understand your strengths and place yourself in a position where these strengths count. Your strengths are what will carry you through to success . . ."[104] It sounds like solid advice, but there is one problem. In seeking to redeem our corner of world, we (those in business) are not only fighting the battle in the marketplace, we are also doing battle in the heavenlies. And in fighting the Evil One, we understand that he does not fight fair. Rarely does he attack our strengths. Normally, he attacks our weaknesses. Thus, as tentmakers, we need to build on our strengths while fortifying our weaknesses, for it is our weaknesses that will knock us off the field.

Consider our training. Compare how you get a MBA versus a MDIV. Obtaining a MBA requires statistics and market surveys, while a MDIV involves seminary research and ministry preparation. The church gets ideas from the past, looking at what has been done. The business world anticipates the future and acts accordingly. Each works out of a very different mindset.

In seeking to serve God, churches tend to look backward instead of forward for direction. We look backward at what has already been accomplished and limit the opportunities for God to work based on what He has done in the past. He has worked in one way in the past, so we ignorantly believe He will work in that same way again. Consider how many churches earnestly seek God's face for His program for their growth, outreach, and transformation. Instead, church after church finds that unusual church that has sought God's face and had some success, and then tries to copy what they do. For example, every two years there is a new "must read" book, such as, *Experiencing God*, *The Prayer of Jabez*, or *The Purpose Driven Life*. All of these are fine materials, but using others' tools is not the answer to transformational ministry. The solution comes in the seeking. Many times God saved the Israelites from the hands of their enemies. Yet, did He ever do it the same way twice? Jesus reminds us not to pour new wine into old wineskins (Matthew 9:17). As the church cannot reproduce what it is not, the workers they send out also seek out tools and tricks to win the lost. Too many missions expect that the tribal Fulani of Senegal will be converted in the same ways as the tribal Datak of Indonesia. Many believe if we study what worked to win thousands of Bengali Muslims, this too, will work among the Baluch Muslims of Pakistan. We need to grasp that the real issue is not the methods but our hearts. Each model has its good points. The problem is not our tools, but whose hands the tools are in. Stan Guthrie informs us,

"Sometimes it seems our current strategizing and promotion tend to put people, rather than God, at the center of the missions process. We call people 'resistant' or 'receptive' to the gospel as if God has no say over the human will, as if it is our job alone to 'soften them up' so that the Spirit can work. . . . Or we latch onto evangelistic strategies that seem to be working as if the power of regenerating the human heart lies in the method rather than in the God who orchestrates all the conditions that contribute to making people 'open' or 'closed' to the gospel."[105]

As we consider crossing the globe to learn another language and culture, we may first need to learn and overcome the cultural challenge of the mission world. Twice I have met regular missionaries who wished to broaden their ministry—one through a small business and the other through an NGO model. They each needed additional funds to help grow their ministry and business. Knowing a few businessmen who wished to invest in missions, I offered to introduce them to these missionaries. The relationships seemed like a good fit, a natural win-win situation. The workers needed money to expand their businesses/ministries, and the businessmen wanted to financially help someone working in the 10/40 Window who was using a holistic ministry approach. Nonetheless, in both instances, I sat there dumbfounded as I watched both parties miscommunicate and offend each other. In most of what they were saying, they were unable to communicate. From my "bi-cultural" (secular and sacred) perspective, both parties were saying the same thing. However, their insistence on using their own words led to no agreement.

In making a presentation to businessmen, we must recognize that there are different values and usage of terms. Appendix E provides a translation of values and terms intended to assist communication between church and business cultures. These terms clarify some of the differences between the secular and sacred approach to ministry and work.

"Amaziah asked the man of God, 'But what about the hundred talents I paid for these Israelite troops?' The man of God replied, 'The LORD can give you much more than that.'"[106] Amaziah was very concerned about his money. To lose money is never pleasant or easy. Like Amaziah, when it comes to forfeiting money, even for godly reasons, our flesh struggles and is hesitant to make the sacrifice. We can always think of needs and wants and justify using our money in that way. For many, it is not easy to view finances in the light of faith. In the 21st century church, the doctrine of "we live" has usurped "we live by faith" (2 Corinthians 5:7). Jehovah Jireh is God, "Our Provider." We need to constantly be aware of our motives in business. It is extremely important for those who have access to worldly wealth to keep our focus on God and the ways He is working in and through us.

Agur, a former worker in the Middle East, writes, "Give me neither poverty nor riches, but give me only my daily bread. Otherwise, I may have too much and disown you and say, 'Who is the LORD?' Or I may become poor and steal, and so dishonor the name of my God."[107] Wealth and how we use our money is a tension for everyone, including tentmakers. Seventy-eight percent of the workers surveyed indicate they have sufficient income. The total income for the majority of workers is between $1,400 and $2,800 (U.S. dollars) per month. However, the worker's monthly income has little bearing on effectiveness. Workers who say that "my family's personal monthly salary from all sources in United States dollars is under $700 a month" are less effective than workers who earn more. However, those who earn the highest salaries are no more effective in evangelism, discipleship, and church planting than others.

Money is not a dirty commodity; it is a tool. As a tool, it can be used for good or evil. John Wesley had the right philosophy about money. He said, "Make all you can. Save all you can. Give away all you can." And that is what he did. In the first year of his ministry, his income was thirty pounds. He kept twenty-eight and gave away two. The next year his income increased to sixty pounds. He kept twenty-eight and gave away thirty-two. The third year it was 120 pounds. He lived on twenty-eight and gave the rest away. Throughout his entire life, he purposely limited his income.

Some day, we will each give an accounting of how we used the gifts God gave us. Even as we seek to hold every thought captive to Christ

(2 Corinthians 10:5), we need to seek to hold every dollar we spend captive to Him as well. Therefore, we need not be preoccupied with our income nor make comparisons with the lifestyle of others. When Peter questioned Jesus about His plans for John, Jesus responded, "What is that to you? You follow me" (John 21:22). We need not judge one another's lifestyle or motives; we are to follow Jesus. Jesus says,

> "No one can serve two masters. Either he will hate the one and love the other, or he will be devoted to the one and despise the other. You cannot serve both God and Money. Therefore I tell you, do not worry about your life, what you will eat or drink; or about your body, what you will wear. Is not life more important than food, and the body more important than clothes? Look at the birds of the air; they do not sow or reap or store away in barns, and yet your heavenly Father feeds them. Are you not much more valuable than they?"[108]

Paul learned the lesson of being content in all things (Philippians 4:11). When we compare ourselves to others or display jealousy of another worker's lifestyle, it reveals a sinful root issue within us.

In each of these passages, as in life, the issue is not us; it is Jesus. It takes just as much faith to trust God to supply our needs via church support as it does to trust Him to meet our needs by completing a business transaction or bringing students into a school. Some regular missionaries have boasted about their living by faith, yet in their newsletters they make bold appeals for funds. All God's children are to live by faith, no matter where we live or what our occupation or status is in the world. As tentmakers, we have to trust God to make a deal or provide customers so that we have the monies to provide for our family. In the exact same way, regular missionaries have to trust God to move people to give directly to them. We all must live by faith.

We must hold our monies and material things with open hands, enabling the Lord to both give and to take. This is especially true of our businesses. Most new businesses operate at a loss for the initial two years and once profitable, there are debts to be paid. But as soon as the company turns a significant profit, beware, for the greed factor kicks in. We need to plan ahead. We should write into our business or ministry plan what we will do with our profits, so we are held accountable for using His provision for His purposes.

Paul writes, "I know what it is to be in need, and I know what it is to have plenty" (Philippians 4:12). Many of us know "what it is to be in need," but few of us have learned "what it is to have plenty." Tentmakers are more likely to stumble over prosperity than adversity. It is a dangerous thing to be prosperous. Dr. D., my pastor, put it this way, "The crucible of adversity is a less severe trial to the Christian than the refining pot of prosperity." Money is a tool, and if God prospers our businesses, He expects us to reinvest that money in people and projects that return glory to Himself (Matthew 19:12–27).

> "Being rich is not intrinsically evil as long as it does not lead to selfishness (2 Timothy 6:17–19). The rich and the poor alike both have to give offerings, even to the point of self-sacrifice (Romans 12:1). Although nobody automatically has to sell everything, the sharing of all necessary resources is always available as a temporary option, as demonstrated so clearly by the early church (Acts 2:45). Giving without love and compassion is of no value to the giver himself (1 Corinthians 13:3); everything that we give in faith according to what we understand as the will of God is given to God; and He will reward all in His time (Revelations 22:12). Tentmaking does not negate this principle, which itself may serve as a powerful model of unselfishness and of Christian generosity."[109]

Islamic world leader, Mahathir Mohamad, writes, "As for poverty, Islam takes a serious view of it, to the extent of regarding it as close to ungodliness."[110] As Christians, we should never feel a need to apologize for God's grace and provision in our lives. Worldly wealth should be used to bring others to Jesus (Luke 16:9). If the church can use bingo, child care, carnivals, Vacation Bible Schools, contemporary music, dance classes, and bake sales (need I go on?) as tools to attract non-believers to the gospel, surely we can use "worldly wealth." Why has Coca Cola gotten to the ends of the earth in less than one hundred years, but the gospel has not gotten there in two thousand years? The world welcomes economic wealth. As both physical and spiritual beings, we need to address people's needs in both areas. Many people believe that Jesus ministered primarily to the poor. The poor in spirit, yes, but not poor in material wealth. James' and John's family had servants (Mark 1:20). As they were partners with Peter and Andrew, it is likely, they too were well off (Luke 5:10). Nicodemus and Matthew were wealthy, as were some of the women who followed Jesus (Luke 8:3). We need to focus on those things which are eternal: God's Word and people. Money is a tool, which when placed in Christ's hands, is sanctified for His purposes.

SUMMARY

The discrepancies between the secular and the sacred are often based on differing views of money. Money is a tool for accomplishing God's purposes. The Lord asked Moses, "What is in your hand?" Moses replied, "A staff"(Exodus 4:2). The Lord then turns that staff into a snake. God works many miracles through that staff. The staff becomes a symbol of God's power and comfort to Moses. God expects us to use what is in our hands for His glory. What is in your hand? Computer skills, an English degree, social work, or business experience? Let it be used by and for Jesus.

Tentmakers need the encouragement and support of the church. Both regular Christian workers and tentmakers need to work at improving their communication and upholding one another. We need to learn to integrate our various works in ways that will effectively uproot the strongholds of the enemy. We desire to reconcile all things to Jesus.

Wealth can be a blessing and a curse. Throughout this research it is apparent that within tentmaking mission work, money is a two-edged sword. On the one hand, money helps and enhances, while on the other hand, it hinders and hurts. Money helps missions through the support of effective workers doing church planting in unreached areas. Money enhances our partnerships with developing national churches and facilitates the training of nationals along with developing materials which strengthen the local ministries. Money hinders missions by distracting us from evangelism, and keeping us from relying on Jesus to meet our needs. Among nationals, money can create an unhealthy dependence on foreigners. Money hurts missions by allowing foreigners to control national churches which should be self-supporting and self-governing. Money also hurts missions as it encourages national workers to serve God for ungodly motives, creating jealousy between those receiving and not receiving financial support. The research stresses it is of comparatively small importance how a missionary receives his income. It is also of comparatively small importance how the finances of the churches are arranged. However, the identity of a worker does have a bearing on a worker's effectiveness. This tells us that what is of supreme importance is how financial arrangements may affect the attitudes of the people toward us, and so promote or hinder the spread of the gospel.

ACTION STEPS

- What can you do to encourage a friend to bring worship into his or her work place?
- Explain to one friend why tentmaking is not "bi-vocational."
- What needs to be changed about the missionary selection process? How can you help your church understand this?
- How might you become bi-cultural in the sacred and secular spheres? Study the concepts in Appendix E.
- Do you agree that money is a tool? Defend your answer to two friends who have read this chapter.
- Where does your identity come from? Your job, ministry, education, lifestyle, relationship with Jesus? Ask three friends if they agree with your conclusion.

"You may be disappointed if you fail, but you are doomed if you don't try."

BEVERLY SILLS

"Opportunities are usually disguised as hard work, so most people don't recognize them."

ANN LANDERS

Do not follow where the path may lead, go instead where there is no path and leave a trail.

INDIAN PROVERB

"When evening comes, you say, 'It will be fair weather, for the sky is red,' and in the morning, 'Today it will be stormy, for the sky is red and overcast.' You know how to interpret the appearance of the sky, but you cannot interpret the signs of the times."

JESUS

chapter 18
WE GOT NEXT!

In various sports, while two opponents are playing, there will be others waiting to compete. When facilities are limited, it is common for the next person or team in line to tell those who arrive after them, "We got next." This means when the current match is finished, the ring or court is ours.

I just got off the phone with Timothy. He is twenty-three, single, zealous, full of ideas; he is young. He represents a generation wanting to glorify the name of Jesus. He is looking for someone to mentor him in missions and business and wants to know if he can come and work for me for two years. What do I say? It seems like a no brainer—a talented young college kid, enthusiastic, wanting to reach a Muslim people group. Who would not want this guy? But then he told me where he believes God is leading him. I know the place well, having been there several times. I had many friends there. All were rudely thrown out of the city, and the handful of believers they were working with were tortured. I cannot convey in words the hurt I felt at that time for what my dear friends suffered. How do you train someone to jump into a bonfire? How do you help people count the cost and then ensure they have added correctly?

The doors to most Muslim, Hindu, and Buddhist countries are closed to regular missionaries, and some are locked. However, tentmakers have a key. No mission strategy offers greater hope for getting in these closed doors than tentmaking. Adequately equipped tentmakers can unlock doors. Opportunities exist for those who are equipped, accountable, and care little for their livelihood and lifestyle—their very selves. It is encouraging to see the next generation stepping into the ring and lacing up their gloves, ready to go the next round with the forces of darkness.

John Beckett talks about the evolution of power through the centuries. He points out,

"Before 500 BC the nations with the biggest militaries ruled. From 500 BC to AD 1500 the nations were ruled by religion. Religious leaders influenced military leaders or kings. Examples of this are Islam, Confucianism, and the Crusades. During AD 1500—AD 1950 Governments (city, states, politicians) ruled, influencing the military and setting limits on religious practices. Since AD 1950 business has become the major influencer of political leaders, who in turn oversee the military and religious leaders."[111]

Missions need to grasp the heartbeat of the marketplace while maintaining our biblical values and church planting goals. The minds of people seek prosperity, and the marketplace is where they find it. The heart of the marketplace is commerce; that is where people are. It is where they learn their values and gain their satisfaction. As we enter the 21st century, it is crucial that we meet people where they are in life with godly values and satisfaction. People need someone in whom the life of Jesus is incarnated to come alongside them, so they may see for themselves the way, the truth, and the life.

Tentmakers are God's people who are determined to find ways to present the gospel to the unreached peoples of the world, peoples who are beyond the reach of regular missionary work. Many of these people, in both open and closed countries have erected their own barriers. Many are hostile toward Christians and westerners. But we know if the church is to see "every tribe and language and people and nation" represented before the throne (Revelations 7:9), it must break new ground. Business as usual won't do, and that is the point. We need to attempt some mighty unusual business.

Today's tentmakers, like Timothy, are taking on the challenge in a global business world. Though we have been misunderstood and criticized, we have stood the tests. We are finding His place for us in His church, as His witnesses to the unreached world. Though there are some disadvantages to tentmaking, the advantages when working among the unreached outweigh them. Future tentmakers need to count all the costs of making tents. We acknowledge there will be wear and tear on our families, our bodies, even our own hearts. We strive for a persevering, godly character, for evangelistic zeal, and for clear objectives to which we are held accountable. We seek to serve with a team of like-minded others. We are committed to learning the language and culture well. Our motives are none other than the glory of God and to have His transforming power work in and through us.

Regular missionaries dominated the playing field of missions for centuries. Their Christ-like service has penetrated 75 percent of the world. However, the remaining 25 percent is mostly beyond the reach of traditional strategies, methods, and missionaries. Without the entry of tentmakers, there is little hope for these hidden people. The need for us to move into the darkness has never been greater. The opportunities for tentmakers to shine His light in the darkest places have never been better. It is time for organizations and churches to recognize, "We got next!"

GLOSSARY

10/40 Window: The area of the globe extending from 10 degrees to 40 degrees north of the equator; it stretches from the Atlantic Ocean across North Africa, Central Asia, and China to the Pacific Ocean, plus the Indonesian archipelago. The 10/40 Window contains the largest population of non-Christians in the world and contains the heartlands of Buddhism, Islam, and Hinduism.

Bi-Vocational Worker: A cross-cultural missionary who utilizes his or her "secular" skills as a means to gain entry/residence to serve in an area where "missionary" visas are restricted or not issued. The bi-vocational individual (also referred to as a "tentmaker") has two vocations (one being a missionary, the other being a job in a business or NGO, teaching, etc.). This individual prepares for and is accountable to both vocations.

Christian Background Believer (CBB): A believer who grew up in a Christian home (nominal, evangelical, or Catholic).

Creative Access Nations (CAN): A country where the government does not issue residence or work visas to expatriates for officially recognized missionary activity, requiring "creative" methods for accessing the country long term. (Also referred to as a RAN.)

Focus People Group (Focus People): A people group, or group of people having unique characteristics (such as language, religion, culture, caste), which you or your team is concentrating on reaching with the gospel. (Formerly referred to as "target people.")

Home Ministry Assignment (HMA) or **Home Assignment**: A period of time that a missionary returns to his/her sending churches to report on the ministry he/she has been doing overseas. (Formerly referred to as "furlough.")

Muslim Background Believer (MBB): A believer of Jesus Christ who has converted from Islam.

Missionary Kid (MK): A child who has lived overseas and whose parents are missionaries.

Non-Residential Missionary (NRM): See Strategic Coordinator.

People Group: A significantly large grouping of individuals who perceive themselves to have a common affinity for one another. From an anthropological viewpoint of evangelization, this is the largest possible group within which the gospel can spread without encountering barriers of understanding or acceptance.

Restricted Access Nation (RAN): A country where the government "restricts" missionary activity and does not issue residence or work visas to expatriates for officially recognized missionary activity. (See CAN.)

Strategic Coordinator (SC): A person who is called to a focus people group that is not easily accessible to missionaries. He or she lives "outside" that nation (thus, non-residential), focusing on mobilizing others to reach that country or people group, serving as a "clearing house" of information and intercession. The SC may regularly engage the focus people in specific ministries.

Third Culture Kid (TCK): A child that is raised in a country different from the home country of his/her parents. Thus, the child learns parts of his/her parents' culture, and the culture he/she was raised in; not feeling comfortable in either one, generates his/her own culture, a third culture.

Unreached People Group (UPG): A people group among whom there is no indigenous community of believing Christians with adequate numbers and resources to evangelize their own group without requiring outside (cross-cultural) assistance.

APPENDIX A

SHORT-TERM WORKER QUESTIONS

One of the primary reasons that short and long-term missionaries have unsuccessful overseas experiences is because their expectations are not met. It is essential that short termers have realistic expectations of what their conditions will be like and of what they will learn and accomplish. If you are going overseas to discern His will for you, there are eight questions you should answer before committing to a short-term ministry. I recommend you get these answers from a field worker you will be working with and not from someone in the home office.

1) Role:

What role or duties will you perform?

How essential are these duties to the ministry or team?

Will you be able to use your _____ (business, teaching, nursing, Bible, etc.) skills?

Is this a real or artificial tentmaking/mission experience? (Would this ministry take place if you did not go and do it?)

Will you be able to fail and embarrass yourself? (Most long-term workers fail frequently. To this end, will your experience protect, pamper, or posture your time so that you have a "good" experience, or a real experience? You want an experience that is as real as possible. You want to test yourself so that you will know if serving overseas is something the Lord would have you do long term. I have met many long-term workers who have said, "This is nothing like my short-term experience." Is it any wonder these long-term workers quit and go home? A good short-term experience will expose you to both the local people, the missionaries and teach you new things about yourself.)

2) Missionary Relationships:

   Will you spend time with long-term workers? (Rubbing shoulders with effective long-term missionaries and their families is an explosive phenomenon that has changed the direction of many a life.)

   Will you be able to live with a missionary family?

   How much time and mentoring will you get with the more mature workers?

3) Ministry:

   Will you be exposed to many different types of ministry? What kinds? How? Though you may spend most of your time doing one job, what other skills, jobs or ministries can you expect to be exposed to?

   Will you spend time with locals? What will you do? How will you meet locals?

   Will you be able to do evangelism? What kind? (Some varieties of ministries to consider are church planting, tentmaking, evangelism, teaching, discipleship, or job skills, such as: computers, teaching English, or NGO work (healing the sick, feeding the hungry, etc.). The context may also vary among rich and poor, educated and illiterate. In discerning His will, it is good to be exposed to as many types of missions work as reasonably possible. You wish to discern where you find His pleasure working through you.)

4) Training:

   Will you be given on-the-job training and field education?

   Will there be some formal discipleship or teaching times as part of your training?

   What will the training include?

   Will you have a mentor/supervisor? How often will he/she meet with you?

   May you contact your field supervisor before making a commitment? (By contacting the field mentor directly via e-mail, you can ensure that you understand his/her expectations for your short-term ministry and he/she yours.)

5) Language and Culture:

Will you be given language assignments which will test your ability to learn the language?

How much of the language can you expect to learn? (Learning the basics of the language will also enable you to establish relationships with the local people.)

Will there be opportunities to meet people, eat their food, and wear their clothes?

May you live with a local family for a time?

6) Local Friends:

Will you have opportunities to make local friends?

How much of your day will be spent with nationals?

What will your average day look like? (Remember friends are not animals in a petting zoo. If your objective is to meet with God and discern His will, leave the camera at home, it will enable you to focus on Him and His priorities.)

7) Debriefing:

Will there be a debriefing session at the end of your experience? (The intention of the debriefing session is to help you to see how to integrate your short-term experience into your everyday life back home and to tie things together concerning God's leading for your future. This should help you to be a better steward of your experience, especially in regards to sharing your experiences effectively with others.)

8) Expectations:

What expectations or objectives does the field leader have for you during and after the short-term service? (Share your expectations to ensure you have a good understanding of one another's goals. Ask the workers for a brief history of their ministry. As they ask for your testimony, do not hesitate to ask for theirs.

What books, articles, or websites you should read in preparation for going?

What should you wear? Bring or not bring?

Pioneer Church Planting Phases

by Dick Scoggins and James Rockford

Phase I: FORMING, PREPARING AND LAUNCHING THE TEAM

This phase begins when someone is confirmed to form and lead a new church planting (CP) team. This phase is comprised of all of the vital pre-launch activities aimed at forming the team and preparing for its effectiveness.

CRESTPOINT: Phase I ends and Phase II begins when the first team members (TMs) join the team leader (TL) on the field (though others may follow later).

SUGGESTED ACTIVITIES:
1. The TL prepares a Vision & Strategy Paper.
2. The TL and TMs obtain approval from their sending church(es).
3. TL is appointed from sending organization.
4. Research best information available on language, history and culture of country and people group. Learn to see the people as God sees them.
5. Research work roles and residency. Lay the groundwork for residency and identity (one's visa, as well as being able to answer, "Why are you here?").
6. Research practical life issues (e.g. housing, schooling, banking).
7. Set up secure communications, including secure email.

8. Research existing church planting efforts currently underway, if any, and begin communications with other workers.

9. Prepare family and prospective TMs for the transition to the field.

10. Resolve conflicts within the family that may arise from your calling and moving overseas.

11. Recruit the team. Plan the kind of TMs and team you want. Whether you are starting on the field or from your home country, begin working with sending offices to identify candidates and initiate contact.

12. Develop a Memorandum of Understanding (MOU). Anticipate issues of life and ministry together; pro-actively communicate about them. TL and TMs discuss mutual expectations. Ensure each TM has a copy of and understands the policy on "recourse".

13. Clarify the role of the TL wife.

14. Each member/family budgets for one-time outgoing needs and monthly needs. Raise sufficient financial support.

15. Develop a strong home prayer team.

16. Identify pre-field training needs, and see that this is carried out (e.g. in the people group's religion, evangelism, culture, contextualization).

17. In particular, plan and get training for creating an excellent team language-learning program.

18. Get the team to own the vision and strategy for CP, adjusting it as appropriate. Build your team unity and identity together.

19. Line up a ministry coach, as well as a business/NGO coach where appropriate.

Phase II: LEARNING THE LANGUAGE AND CULTURE

The CP team is now on-site and laboring to reach a level of proficiency in the language sufficient to effectively plant churches, which also involves an ever-deepening understanding of the culture. While the level of fluency aimed at may vary from person to person, depending on envisioned ministry roles, most will need to be in a mode of concerted language learning (LL) for 2–3 years. The workers develop a growing identity as belongers among their host people.

CRESTPOINT: Phase II ends and Phase III begins when most of the CP team have reached their appropriate level of fluency, and now are ready to spend most of their ministry time in disciple-making rather than language learning. Whereas evangelism probably took place before this point, it now begins in earnest.

SUGGESTED ACTIVITIES:

1. Members "land" and secure suitable housing. Learn how to function and enjoy life in your new environment. Adapt and renew your devotional life. Enable family to do the same. Make a plan for regular rest and a day off; develop a sustainable pace.

2. Continue to develop your role in society (i.e. job, business, humanitarian project, etc.). However, because being fulltime in language learning (or nearly so) is so important during this phase, job expectations should be kept as minimal as possible.

3. Address conflicts arising in the home.

4. Work through the Peacemaking manual together as a team. Address conflicts arising in the team.

5. Develop your team life, in relationships, communications, accountability, and mutual support. Develop a spiritual team life that sustains members. Team meetings should include prayer, time in the Word, and strategic planning.

6. Appoint a Team Language Coordinator, who receives intensive training and creates a strong team LL program, including training and accountability. Link up with a language learning coach and other essential resources.

7. All work hard at learning the language. Husbands and wives work out respective strategies for appropriate goals.

8. Begin developing spiritual components of your language, such as learning special vocabulary and memorizing Scripture.

9. Clarify roles for team women and men. Work through differing expectations (e.g. regarding mothers of young children, business facilitators, etc.).

10. Develop relationships of varying depths with many local people, especially those who do NOT speak YOUR language. Enable family members to do the same.

11. Bring redemptive elements into your relationships. Look for those who already know the Lord or are spiritually sensitive.

12. Learn local forms of hospitality and become hospitable in that culture.

13. Seek opportunities to demonstrate God's love for the people practically and culturally, standing alongside those in need in appropriate ways.

14. Grow in character through the stresses of adapting to your new life, not only personally, but also as a family and as a team. Develop the mindset when stressed by new things: "It's not right. It's not wrong. It's just different."

15. Collect evangelistic tools available in your new language.

16. Form links with any others in your area who are engaged in ministry to your intended people group.

17. Before too long, bring in a coach—preferably a couple—to help in all of the above.

18. If not done already, seek to enter a relationship with a mentor who can eagerly support your vision and give appropriate help.

Phase III: PREACHING THE GOSPEL TO GROUPS AND INDIVIDUALS

As most of the team has now reached a good level of fluency, they spend most of their ministry time seeking to share the gospel and persuade people to become followers of Christ. Some may share mostly with individuals, while others may seek to evangelize whole groups of naturally connected people. All team members will be engaged in "friendship evangelism" Most teams will also begin experimenting with different kinds of "apostolic evangelism." It is also common that teams discover one or more who already know the Lord, with whom close relationships are formed for the sake of fellowship, discipling and moving forward in CP. The team develops a tentative approach for how new believers can identify themselves in their faith to their broader community.

CRESTPOINT: The team is recognized as having moved to Phase IV when a member of the team is discipling a believer from the intended people group, who has a potential group of friends or relatives. However, members of the team do not stop sharing the gospel, for the sake of reaching more and more, breaking into new social networks, and being examples to the believers.

SUGGESTED ACTIVITIES:

1. If one's ministry time in Phase II was perhaps 80 percent language-

learning and 20 percent evangelism, it shifts to 80/20 the other way in Phase III. Develop a revised LL plan for the reduced but ongoing pace.

2. Every day tell God you are available and ask Him to direct you to those in whose hearts He is working.

3. Cultivate faith to believe God will lead friends to Himself.

4. Model Christ's life before your friends and in your relationships, especially when difficulties arise.

5. If necessary, strengthen and adjust your role in society in terms of work, residency and viability.

6. Grow in your understanding on what are people's felt needs, as well as their spiritual obstacles and opportunities.

7. Train together in effective ways to communicate the Good News and in vital apologetics.

8. Learn to share key Biblical truths and promises in the language. Memorize key Scripture verses, and possibly some verses from their holy book as well.

9. Share Jesus with many, and see an openness to the gospel develop in friendships.

10. Evaluate team members' abilities and gifting in light of CP. Regardless of team members' gifts, all can use their gifts evangelistically and contribute to the team's overall outreach. Where helpful, two or three team members can work together, combining complementary skills (e.g. relationship-building with hospitality). Discern who from the team should be involved in which social networks.

11. Develop a strategy for reaching receptive people's social and work-related networks.

12. Develop outreach tools and materials, bearing in mind different audiences (socially, men/women, children).

13. Start a Bible Study with a friend and see it grow into his or her social network.

14. Regularly pray in Jesus' name for those who are sick or have urgent needs.

15. Lead someone into following Jesus, preferably with others in their social network.

16. Learn what are the marks of a "man or woman of peace" (M/WOP), or "respected person" in the culture.

17. Prayerfully evaluate your friend as a respected person in society (i.e. M/WOP) or as an avenue to such.

18. Identify one or more potential respected persons.

19. Begin to discern what is the good news for this social network and the respected persons in it.

20. Somehow introduce "Jesus" into the conversation within 30 minutes of every new person you meet.

21. Follow up any leads regarding existing believers.

22. Plan and begin to implement some kinds of "Apostolic Evangelism".

23. Every team member should develop multiple ways of meeting new people (e.g. clubs, sports, etc.).

24. Implement a systematic way within the team to stay focused and motivated in the invaluable job of sowing many seeds.

25. As you lead people to Christ, or you form relationships with existing believers, invite faithful ones to a deeper discipling relationship.

26. CPer baptizes the believer(s).

Phase IV: DISCIPLING BELIEVERS AND WORKING TOWARD GATHERING

Discipling one or more believers, especially working with them to win their social network to the Lord. From the earliest days with new believers, CPers teach that truly following Christ is in community, and that Christ wants to form a new group of His followers, committed to one another and, indeed, committed to growing and reproducing. As people come to faith and grow in Christ, the CPers seek to form individuals and existing groups together as the Body of Christ. Progress toward gathering will likely involve a variety of pre-gathering activities (e.g one-off get-togethers, building bridges between believers, etc.).

CRESTPOINT: Discipling never stops. But the team moves to Phase V once there is a fellowship group of 3 or more believers of the people group regularly meeting together.

SUGGESTED ACTIVITIES:

1. Use a plan of Bible study for the believer's personal growth and development.

2. The believer(s) learn Bible stories that will impact life practices.

3. Come to understand the place of suffering in the Christian life (such as we see in I Peter).

4. Respond to sin by repentance and developing new patterns of life.

5. Live out Christ's life in the extended family (e.g. Matthew 5–7).

6. Develop godly patterns in husband-wife relations including: godly submission and loving leadership, resolving conflict, forgiveness and reconciliation.

7. Develop godly patterns of child raising.

8. Develop a regular habit of turning to Scripture and prayer.

9. The believer(s) shares the good news with family and friends and God's plan for Kingdom communities.

10. CPer(s) helps new believers break any occult involvement.

11. Believers who are already baptized baptize new believers.

12. Where appropriate introduce local believers to each other with the aim of fostering trust and fellowship. Host one-off events (e.g. birthday parties) as a "safe" venue for trust relationships to form over time.

13. The CPers decide which believers should be gathered together in fellowship, and which should be developed as starting points for separate fellowships.

14. Continually teach believers the New Testament concepts of fellowship and community, so that they will own the conviction of being linked with other believers in ekklesia . Help them obey Christ's teaching about relationships with other believers, conceptually and in practice. A fellowship group is formed.

15. Begin to identify believers' gifts and calling in the Kingdom.

16. Implement godly patterns of conflict resolution with you, the church-planter, and with others.

17. Become familiar with God's plan for the extension of the Kingdom from the book of Acts.

18. Men disciple men and women disciple women.

19. Help the believer(s) develop how to present their identity in Jesus to family and friends.

Phase V: DEVELOPING THE BODY OF BELIEVERS

Working with the new community of faith—and especially with emerging leaders—in order for them to grow numerically, in personal and corporate koinonia maturity. This crucial phase includes them developing a group identity and mutual commitment to one another as the Body of Christ, and also grasping a vision for leading others to Christ and forming new fellowships, locally or in neighboring places. Generally speaking, the team is either working with a single fellowship at this point that they hope will grow to medium or large size, or else they are aiming at a network of small house fellowships. In the case of house fellowships, the numbers below are evaluated collectively, in total.

CRESTPOINT: Phase V ends and Phase VI begins when the fellowship reaches these criteria of size and depth ("critical mass"):

GROUP COMMITMENT: The local believers have committed to one another and see their assembling together as an expression of being a local church (using whatever word is most suitable for ekklesia reality).

SIZE: Around 10 or more believers of the people group regularly involved, including older believing children. This does not necessarily mean that meetings average 10 or more, just that there is regular involvement of the 10+.

BREADTH: 3 or more married men (heads of households), and 2 or more mature women, of local believers regularly involved (whether or not their spouses are believers).

LEADERSHIP: At least 2 key believers who seem to be "elders in the making", who are assuming more and more shepherding and overseeing, and whom the others recognize as leaders .

STRENGTH: Not all hidden believers with hidden faith. Some believers are baptized and have already faced serious threats and persevered, maintaining their faith and their "confession of Christ before men" (Mt.10:32). Believers regularly share their faith; prayer and planning have begun for starting a sister fellowship.

SUGGESTED ACTIVITIES:

1. The community is meeting together regularly for worship, fellowship, instruction, and prayer. Passages such as Acts 2:42–47 are studied as an example to follow.

2. It is not uncommon for CPers to do substantial teaching and leading

in the group early on, depending on the maturity of the believers and the group.

3. Local believers develop their identity together as a community of faith (e.g. through covenanting). ⬚

4. The group develops their sense of spiritual identity to those outside as well.

5. Older believers determine appropriate way for membership in the community.

6. Older believers understand and model Biblical "one anothers" which define community.

7. Believers learn to break previous or active occult involvement of new members. (See Acts 19:11–20)

8. The community celebrates the Lord's Supper, with older believers presiding.

9. The believers are doing the work of evangelism with their family and friends.

10. Older believers have baptized new believers.

11. Older believers disciple new believers.

12. Older women believers disciple newer women in Titus 2 skills and other needs.

13. Believers learn to support each other through persecution, interrogation and hard times.

14. Believers develop an attitude of sacrificial generosity towards the poor and needy, particularly to other believers in need. They begin to seek opportunities to demonstrate in practical ways Christ's love for those in need.

15. Community meetings are organized by believers. Older believers trained to lead community meetings (various components). Certain mature or gifted believers given opportunities to teach the Word.

16. Appropriate male/female roles in public meetings determined and practiced.

17. Mature believers are emerging and begin functioning as shepherds.

18. Growth in godliness in the home of emerging leaders sets the pace for the community.

19. Multitude of gifts encouraged and developed for edification of the community.

20. Peacemaking skills exercised by the community. Believers forgive

and forbear as normal hurts occur.

21. Past family hurts explored and forgiven.
22. Believers adequately contribute to the support of their extended family.
23. Confronting, exhorting, reproving of erring members.
24. Shunning and disfellowshipping those persisting in sin.

Phase VI: EMPOWERING AND INSTALLING LEADERS, AND THE BEGINNINGS OF REPRODUCTION

A continuation in the growth of body life and Kingdom commitment in the new ekklesia, with the CPers now focusing primarily on developing multiple leaders, especially potential elders. The CPers intentionally take a lower profile in the fellowship. They are also looking to recognize those believers with possible evangelistic gifts who are keen to share the gospel and initiate CP ministry in other locations.

CRESTPOINT: The appointment of 2 or more elders from the people group over the church (or network of house churches) . And the church has embraced a Great Commission vision.

SUGGESTED ACTIVITIES:

1. Some or most CPers withdraw from believers meetings and focus on starting new fellowships. One or more CPer(s) remain involved, but adopt lower profile. Leaders-in-training spend time with the CPers in all sorts of contexts—not just teaching or worship settings—so that CPers' behavior can be modeled in every setting.
2. If not already in place, the church commits to times of corporate prayer, acknowledging their full dependency on Christ as His Body.
3. Older believers exercise deliverance ministries in the community.
4. Gifts encouraged and developed for edification.
5. Married believers are specifically helped in their marriage relationship and character issues by older believers or CPers.
6. Church life and leadership concepts are taught and implemented. Believers determine ways to develop healthy biblical community life.
7. If there are other churches around, begin to network emerging leaders with leaders of other groups as appropriate.

8. Intense teaching on reproducing communities. Community embraces goal of reproducing and networking.

9. Local believers and expat CPers look for new men and women of influence around whom to start new fellowships.

10. Older, more mature believers trained to take leadership of community gatherings. Believers take responsibility for Biblical instruction. Several given chance to "try out" leading meetings, teaching the Word, and leading the body in worship.

11. Respective avenues for men's and women's leadership identified and promoted.

12. Mature believers preside at the Lord's table.

13. If there is one strong leader, he or she is taught and implored with the biblical necessity of plural leadership in the church and enlisted to make that a reality. Their broader ministry should be encouraged in multiple fellowships.

14. Erring members are confronted, exhorted, reproved and helped. Those persisting in sin receive church discipline according to the NT.

15. Discerning the will of the Lord by leaders and community taught and practiced.

16. The body continues to discuss and refine their identity vis. society around them. They decide whether to be an underground church or an open, perhaps registered church.

17. There are special activities, parties or retreats outside regular meetings for outreach and fellowship.

18. Leaders' place in conflict and peacemaking in the community taught and practiced.

19. Ephesians 4:11–12 giftings recognized and appropriate forums established for developing these gifts. CPers encourage believers with possible evangelistic gifts to share the gospel boldly and start ministries in other locations, with substantial prayer backing from the body.

20. CPers select elder candidates in consultation with the believers. Those who agree to undertake this process are introduced to the church as "elder candidates", and the Body is urged to help.

21. Elder candidates begin special process of character growth, examination of motives, and intensive learning about ekklesia and shepherding.

22. Meetings of leaders begin with CPer present. Team spirit develops

amongst leadership. [Men and women leaders may meet separately or together, as appropriate.]

23. Conflicts about leadership appointment dealt with. Those not selected may need special encouragement.

24. Leaders look for new ones to develop as leaders and begin to mentor them (e.g. prospective deacons).

25. CPer often absent from fellowship meetings. New leaders lead.

26. CPer sometimes absent from leadership meetings.

27. CPers appoint some or all of the elder candidates (if there are two or more; preferably three or more). Elders formally ordained.

Phase VII: REPRODUCTION & MOVEMENT

The church or churches are now somewhat mature and are under the leadership of local elders from the people group. The CPers now labor for a wider spread of the gospel, with emphasis on church reproduction and a CP movement. There are two primary avenues for the CPers to make this happen:

A. Working with the newly planted church or churches to help them reproduce and work toward a CP movement. AND/OR

B. Mobilizing, training, facilitating and possibly overseeing local CPers. This option may eventually mean creating a national sending structure.

CRESTPOINT: In a sense, this phase never ends, as the ministry has hopefully ignited a spreading of the gospel and multiplication of churches that becomes a movement. CPers may exit after the completion of Phase VI (appointing elders). Some, however, may stay on for varying lengths of time in order to strategically catalyze church planting reproduction and/or mobilization of local CPers.

SUGGESTED ACTIVITIES:

1. The local elders fully assume shepherding and feeding responsibilities in the church, including protecting the faith and doctrine of the community (Titus 1:9).

2. Deacons are appointed, as needed, to help the elders.

3. Vision developed for planting new churches in the local area.

4. Role of expatriate CPers determined (see 'A' and 'B' primary avenues and Crestpoint above). Responsibilities between CPers and local elders defined for the new community.

5. CPer(s) redefines relationship to leaders as coach, attending leadership meetings only when invited.

6. Great Commission vision includes recognizing, training and sending local evangelists and church planters to other cities, and even to other countries.

7. Vision given by leaders to congregation.

8. Evangelists guided to go out to other cities, towns or villages.

9. Indigenous CP teams sent out by themselves or with expat team.

10. New gatherings started.

11. Ephesians 4:11–13 gifted believers regularly visit other churches and emerging fellowships.

12. Elders and Ephesians 4 ministers take responsibility to develop new leaders and new Ephesians 4 ministers.

13. Leaders begin to network with emerging leaders of new gatherings including taking some responsibility for their training.

14. Communities concerned for each other and resources shared (especially Ephesians 4 equippers).

15. Peacemaking skills are practiced among leaders.

16. Leaders formally recognize newer emerging leaders (e.g. new elders or deacons).

17. Expat CPer(s) commends old community to God and leaves community meetings, but may visit on occasion.

18. Elders (with church planter(s)) lay hands on new elders in the newer community.

19. Relationship between different communities and leaders worked out and formalized.

20. Peacemaking skills between communities and leaders communities exercised.

21. Especially with model 'B' above, some means developed to mobilize gifted and proven national CPers (e.g. bivocational roles, administration, etc.).

See www.churchplantingphases.com for related papers.

APPENDIX C

M.O.U.
(MEMO OF UNDERSTANDING)

SUGGESTIONS FOR WHAT TO INCLUDE
IN A TEAM MOU.

INTRODUCTION

Team mandate/calling

Provide an overview of team life, work, and ministry.

Provide an overview of the people group you are focusing on. (Be as specific or as broad as you wish, covering social status, religion, geographic location, ages, races, etc.)

STRATEGY AND GOALS

Mission statement

Vision statement

Strategy and Goals

How will evangelism be done?

When there are believers, how will they be discipled?

Which church planting strategy, if any, will you implement?

Additional objectives?

FIELD PRIORITIES—MINISTRY NON-NEGOTIABLES

Where and how may the language be learned? To what level?

If two languages must be learned, which will be learned first? To what level?

How will the culture be learned?

Which contextualization strategy, if any, will the team use?

Which bonding strategy will the team utilize?

Which church planting strategy will the team emphasize?

What entry strategies (NGO, businesses, teaching, etc.) are available and recommended for team members?

Which lifestyle/standard of living strategies will you favor?

Will work and ministry be closely related?

Frequency of communication and relationship of team members with their sending church(es)?

What security guidelines are there for doing ministry and business and interacting with other workers in the area?

What security guidelines are there for interacting with friends and churches at home?

WORK PRIORITIES

Will each team member be responsible for finding their own job and visa?

Must a team member's job have direct access to the focus people group?

If a team member loses their job, what happens?

Discuss strategies of how work and ministry may be integrated.

TEAM RELATIONSHIPS

What is a team? Define a team.

Will you be a community? Define community.

How will team members be nurtured: spiritually, mentally, emotionally, and physically?

How will the team interact? (volleyball, soccer, athletic team style)

How often will you meet as a team? As individuals?

What is required to join the team?

What will be the leadership style of the team?

How will team members be trained and mentored?

How will accountability work within the team?

If there are conflicts within the team or with outsiders, how will they be resolved?

If there are conflicts with the team leader, how will they be resolved?

Are locals allowed to join the ministry team? How will they be supported?

Any policies on house-hold help? Vacations? Home ministry assignments? Children's education?

TRAINING AND PREPARATION

What pre-field training is required?

Will potential team members be required to visit the field first?

Must the team member be sent out by a local church?

TIME COMMITMENT

Are short termers welcome?

How long are team members expected to initially commit to the team?

DOCTRINE

State your mission's doctrinal position.

State any other team doctrinal preferences.

FINANCES

How will business profits/income be utilized?

How much support is needed?

What percentage of financial support may come via the business?

If a team member is under-supported, what happens?

Provide a sample budget. Include monthly salary and one-time moving and set-up expenses.

APPENDIX D

QUESTIONS TO ASK BEFORE JOINING A MISSION ORGANIZATION OR TEAM

Though good advice lies deep within a person's heart, the wise will draw it out.

PROVERBS 20:5 LB

The following questions should be asked of those you will be working with on the field. There are no right or wrong answers, but in asking, there is understanding. For example, if you are being led to Timbuktu, you should not expect to find good "health care" there, but you should know what options are available. Many questions may be irrelevant to your situation, but asking ensures you understand the situation so as to make wiser decisions.

Be sure to follow up each question with a "Why?" or "How?" so as to draw out understanding.

TEAM Questions

What is the mission or team's vision?

What is the mission or team's mission statement?

What are the mission or team's values?

What is required to join the team?

What is required to join the mission organization?

Are all team members from one organization?

Are all team members from one home country?

Are there national team members?

Describe the team. (volleyball, soccer, athletic team)

How often does the team meet?

What does the team do during team meetings?

How often do team members meet together as individuals? What do they do during these times?

Do their local friends associate with other team members? Or does each worker basically have their own friends and ministry?

What distinctives does the team have?

How does the team involve nationals in both the work place and ministry?

What is the leader's leadership style?

What is the history of the team?

How often would I meet with the team leader?

How are team decisions made?

How are conflicts resolved?

How does the team apply biblical peacemaking?

How does the team practice reconciliation (rebuke, correct, train)?

What accountability structures does the team have?

Who holds the team/field leader accountable?

Who would hold me accountable?

Will I have a specific mentor?

How often would we meet?

What will we do?

What training can I expect? (in language, culture, business, outreach)

In what areas of life and ministry are team members held accountable? How does the accountability process work?

Do I need to raise support? How much?

Do team members live near one another?

Do team members socialize with one another?

Are there any lifestyle requirements? (do not eat pork, women, veil, etc.)

How does the team measure the progress it is making in accomplishing its task? How often does the team evaluate its progress?

Does the team have an exit strategy?

Does the team have a contingency plan for emergencies?

How do team members involve their sending churches in their ministries?

How often do team members communicate with supporters and prayer partners?

Are team members growing in prayer? The Word? Evangelistic skills?

Are team members encouraged to attend seminars to learn new skills?

Are team members thankful? Do they esteem one another? Do they serve one another?

Do team members joyfully submit to one another and the leader?

How well do team members know the language?

Observe: Are the team members at home in the culture and language when interacting with local friends?

Are the marriages growing and good?

Are team members generous toward one another?

Do the team members seem flexible? Teachable?

How do team members have fun together?

How do team members solve problems, separately or together?

Do team members set and review goals?

Ask for examples of how team members shared the gospel this week.

What is the team's church planting strategy?

What is the team's plan for discipling new believers?

Ask team members:
    What is most enjoyable about the ministry? About living overseas?
    What is most difficult about the ministry? About living overseas?

MINISTRY Questions

Which people group does the team minister with?

What is the geographical area the people group lives in?

What contextualized approach does the team favor? (C-1 to C-5)

Does the team minister primarily with Christians or non-Christians?

Would I be working with an unreached people group?

How many churches exist in this people group?

How many believers exist in this people group?

How many workers from other organizations are reaching this people group?

What are the difficulties/barriers to reaching this people group?

What would my ministry be? (evangelism, discipleship, teaching, etc.)

What church planting phase is the team currently in?

What experience does the leadership team have in ministry? In leading a team?

Does the team share funds in any way?

How do team members befriend locals?

How would I learn the language? How long will I need to study full time?

What level of language proficiency is required? How and where is the language learned?

What would be my visa? My identity in the community?

WORK/BUSINESS/JOB Questions

What business/NGO does the team/mission operate?

What is the vision of the business/NGO?

Is the business/NGO perceived as Christian?

What jobs to team members do? How many hours a week do they work?

Is the job I would do working with the local unreached people, with Christians, or with team members?

Do team members all work for one business?

How are visas obtained?

Could I use my _____ training/background?

Do team members work with one another?

How are profits used?

TEAM LEADER or SUPERVISOR Questions

How much does he or she pray?

Does he or she study the Word regularly?

Does the leader . . .

 Get regular spiritual input?

 Demonstrate the fruits of the Spirit?

 Reflect transparency about sins and weaknesses?

 Have victory over sin?

 Manage his/her household well?

 Readily forgive others?

 Submit to authority?

 Have one or more mentors active in his/her life?

 Serve those she/he leads?

 Accept correction?

 Persevere in trials?

 Discern God's guidance through the Word and prayer?

 Communicate regularly with team members and those in authority?

 Mentor team members well?

 Listen with understanding?

 Give wise counsel?

 Provide or enable adequate shepherding?

 Provide or enable real accountability?

 Ensure team members are growing in the Lord?

 Manage his time well?

Is the leader . . .

Sent out by a church?

Under the authority of a field leader?

Able to recruit others to his/her vision?

Able to articulate his/her vision well?

Able to raise necessary funds?

Able to train or find adequate training for team members?

Sensitive to local culture?

Able to anticipate and solve problems?

Able to guide team members in using their gifts and skills?

What experience has the leader had in leading teams?

PERSONAL Questions

Who do I feel God is leading me to minister to?

Rich or poor? Educated or uneducated? Reached or unreached?

Which is more important in God's plan for me? Team? Location? Team Leader? People Group? Country? Type of ministry?

Do I expect to be able to use my education? Training?

What amount of access to the local people do I expect my job to create for me?

With which social class do I hope to identify?

How often may I return home?

How often may I receive outside visitors?

What is the vacation policy?

Do I need insurance?

Do I need any vaccinations?

What health care is available?

FOR FAMILIES

What are the options for my children's education? And language learning?

What role(s) will my wife have with in the team? The community? In ministry?

FOR SINGLES

Do I have the gift of singleness?

Is there a dating policy? Among team members? Among nationals?

What are my living options? (alone, with other team members, with nationals)

Who decides who I may live with?

For single women, who will I be accountable to? The team leader? The leader's wife? Another woman?

SECULAR versus SACRED TERMINOLOGY

Many tentmakers are uncomfortable being called "missionaries." Thus, many missionaries are uncomfortable with tentmakers.

Organizations today are fond of using words like empowerment, process re-engineering, networking, strategic alliances, shared values, shared corporate culture, strategic intent, etc.; become familiar with these words and their meanings.

OLD PARADIGM	NEW PARADIGM
Sacred vs. Secular	All is sacred
Clergy vs. Laity	One body: different but equal callings
Full-time clergy vs. part-time Christian	Interdependence
Special calling for clergy	All are called
Pastors/ministers run the church	Christ runs the church; pastors equip
Congregations observe pastor	Pastor observes congregation
Laity pay and pray	Congregation ministers
Test of faith: church attendance	Test of faith: being salt and light to the world
Work is a necessary evil	Work is worship
Fulfillment only possible for clergy	Fulfillment found in using your gifts
Feelings of unimportance	Feelings of destiny
Evangelism: bringing people to church	Evangelism: taking God to people
Discipleship: a good idea few do	Discipleship: normal lifestyle
Kingdom of God: God's rule via church	Kingdom of God: God's rule in daily life
Missions requires a special calling to go	Missions requires a special calling to stay
Missions is for called	Missions is for all
Worship is singing	Worship is whatever pleases God

Traditional Missionaries
    Bible college/seminary
    Viewed with suspicion
    Expensive
	Tentmaker Missionaries
	    Discipled on the job
	    Viewed as normal people
	    Much cheaper

MISSION	BUSINESS
Counts lives	Counts minutes
Values people	Values production
Time is a gift; God will guide	Time is precious, to be managed, bought or sold
Contentment comes from knowing God	Contentment comes from what is earned
Failure is a step in God's process	Failure is final
Focus on events	Focus on day-to-day operations
Participants are adversaries	Participants are friends
The goal is agreement	The goal is victory
Make concessions to cultivate relationship	Demand concessions as a condition of relationship
Be soft on people	Be direct with the people
Trust others	Distrust others
Disclose your bottom line	Mislead as to your bottom line
Search for a single answer: one they will accept	Search for a single answer: one you will accept
Insist on agreement	Insist on position
Yield to pressure	Apply pressure
Majority decides	Boss decides
Influenced by sentiment	Influenced by facts
Focus on big things	Focus on details, day to day
Conviction based on relationship	Conviction based on profit
Exposition to entertainment	Exposition to results
Want instant info, but slow to decide	Want instant info, but quick to decide

MISSION	BUSINESS
Decisions open for discussion	Decisions final
Need to know to predict and control	Need to know to decide
Grace oriented	Production oriented
Religion is private	Business is public
Religion is not in office	Best workers take work home
Religion is compartmentalized	Business affects entire life
Mistakes yield forgiveness	Mistakes yield "you're fired"
Tardiness for church tolerated	Tardiness for work forbidden
Majority makes decisions	Boss decides
People focus on big things	Bosses want details
Conviction to sentiment	Conviction to profits and feasibility
Activity provides meaning	Activity provides benefits
Deliberate over decisions	Make decisions instantly
Decisions based on past experience	Decisions based on future projections
Seminary is knowledge oriented	MBA is practically oriented
Give	Build wealth
Faithfulness	Compromise
Serve	Compete
Pursue God	Pursue profit
Humility	Success
Meet needs	Make profit

NOTES

CHAPTER ONE

[1] Robert J. Kriegel and Louis Patler, *If It Ain't Broke Break It!: And Other Unconventional Wisdom for a Changing Business World* (New York: Warner Books, 1991), p. xviii.

[2] Matthew 4:19.

[3] Hebrews 13:8.

[4] Matthew 6:24–25.

[5] George MacLeod, *Only One Way Left* (Glasgow: The Iona Community, 1956), p. 38.

CHAPTER TWO

[6] Colossians 3:17.

[7] 1 Corinthians 9:16.

[8] Jonathan Lewis, editor. *Working Your Way to the Nations: A Guide to Effective Tentmaking* (WEF: Pasadena, 1993), p. ii.

CHAPTER THREE

[9] Mahathir Mohamad, *The Challenge* (Malaysia: Pelanduk, 1997), p. 13–14.

[10] Galatians 6:10.

[11] Colossians 3:23.

[12] Gary Taylor, editor, *Trailside Companion*, David Morris, "What I Learned in 12 Years of Business Tentmaking" (unpublished), p. 16.

[13] Ephesians 4:28.

[14] Acts 20:35.

CHAPTER FOUR

[15] Herbert Kane, class notes, Trinity Evangelical Divinity School, 1980.

[16] Proverbs 15:22.

CHAPTER FIVE

[17] Proverbs 14:12.

[18] Luke 9:23–25.

[19] *Crucified in weakness and living by the power of God*, Working Document on "Lessons Learned in Church Planting," Presenters: H. N. (OM), Steve Cochrane (YWAM), Lanny Arensen (AIM), Richard Hibbert (WEC), Pat and Mary Ann Cate (Christar). p. 2.

[20] *Crucified in weakness and living by the power of God*. Working Document on "Lessons Learned in Church Planting." Presenters: H. N. (OM), Steve Cochrane (YWAM), Lanny Arensen (AIM), Richard Hibbert (WEC), Pat and Mary Ann Cate (Christar), p. 1.

[21] 1 Thessalonians 2:8.

[22] Proverbs 10:9.

[23] 1 John 3:18.

[24] 2 Thessalonians 3:10.

[25] John Stott, *New Issues Facing Christians* (London: Marshall & Pickering, 1999), p. 18.

[26] Daryl Anderson, *Understanding Missionary Support* (www.efca.org/international/media/gv-understandingmissionarysupport.pdf), p.1.

[27] Rick Warren, *The Purpose Driven Life* (Grand Rapids: Zondervan, 2002), p. 67.

[28] Jeremiah 33:3.

[29] 1 Corinthians 11:1.

[30] Matthew 8:20.

[31] Romans 10:1.

[32] Romans 1:14.

[33] John 14:15.

[34] Romans 15:20–21.

[35] 2 Corinthians 5:14.

[36] John 12:32.

CHAPTER SIX

[37] 2 Timothy 2:15.

[38] Paul G. Hiebert, R. Daniel Shaw, and Tite Tienou, *Understanding Folk Religion* (Grand Rapids: Baker, 1999), p. 26.

[39] Bridgeman, Johnson, and McAlpine, *Short-Term Mission Handbook* (Ontario: Student Mission Advance, 1986), p. 9.

[40] Tetsunao Yamamori, *God's New Envoys: A Bold Strategy for Penetrating* "Closed Countries" (Portland: Multnomah, 1987), p.77–78.

[41] Jim Collins, *Good To Great* (New York: Harper Business, 2001), p. 41–42.

CHAPTER SEVEN

[42] Matthew 18:3.

[43] Alison Thomas, *Voyager* March/April, 2002 ,"Language & Business," p. 47.

[44] Stephen Covey, *The Seven Habits of Highly Effective People* (New York: Simon & Schuster, 1989), p. 235.

[45] *Crucified in weakness and living by the power of God.* Working Document on "Lessons Learned in Church Planting," Presenters: H. N. (OM), Steve Cochrane (YWAM), Lanny Arensen (AIM), Richard Hibbert (WEC), Pat and Mary Ann Cate (Christar), p. 1.

[46] 1 Corinthians 9:19–22.

[47] Greg Livingstone, "Tentmaking Among Muslim Peoples" (unpublished in-house article).

CHAPTER EIGHT

[48] Romans 1:16.

[49] 2 Timothy 4:2.

[50] John 14:14.

[51] John 13:35.

[52] Proverbs 24:27 Living Bible.

[53] Exodus 20:12.

[54] Matthew 7:12.

[55] John Travis, "Must all Muslims leave Islam to Follow Jesus?" *EMQ* October, 1998, 34:3.

[56] 1 Peter 4:12–13.

[57] Wang Ming-dao, Dowsett 2001, p. 162.

[58] Lareau Lindquist, "Pastoral Encouragement: Seven Letters to Christian Workers,"

in *Doing Member Care Well: Perspectives and Practices from around the World* (Globalization of Missions Series), ed. Kelly O'Donnell (William Carey Library, 2002), p. 177–192.

CHAPTER NINE
[59] Mark 1:35.
[60] Colin Powell with Joseph E. Persico, *My American Journey—Colin Powell* (New York: Random House, 1995), p. 52.
[61] John A Byrne, *Jack Welch, Straight From The Gut* (New York: Warner Books, 2001), p. 385.
[62] Rick Love, "Leader to Leader" January 2003 (#21) "Leaders are Team Players" in house e-mail newsletter.
[63] Brian O'Reilly, "What It Takes To Start a Start Up," *FORTUNE*, June 7, 1999, Volume 139, Number 11, p. 136.
[64] Personal in-house e-mail.
[65] Harold, A Reply to "Tentmaking as a Means to Doing Apostolic Mission among Muslim People," June 1987.
[66] Proverbs 15:22.

CHAPTER TEN
[67] Gary Taylor, Editor, *Trailside Companion*, David Morris, "What I Learned in 12 Years of Business Tentmaking." p. 16.
[68] Proverbs 25:13 New Living Translation.
[69] Greg Livingstone, "Tentmaking Among Muslim Peoples" (in-house paper).
[70] Gary Taylor, "Rips in the Goatskins" (personal newsletter) p. 3.

CHAPTER ELEVEN
[71] Proverbs 3:21–23 Living Bible.
[72] Job 27:3–6.
[73] Paul G. Hiebert, R. Daniel Shaw, and Tite Tienou, *Understanding Folk Religion* (Grand Rapids: Baker, 1999), p. 27.
[74] Proverbs 16:20 Living Bible.
[75] Chris Sandlund, "Quality Time." *Solutions For Growing Businesses—Entrepreneur* (New York, July 2002), p. 67.
[76] Matthew 6:19, 21.

CHAPTER TWELVE
[77] Randy Alcorn, *Money Possessions & Eternity*, "Choosing a God-Honoring Lifestyle," *http://www.thegoodsteward.com/article.php3?articleID=1400*, p. 5.
[78] 1 Corinthians 9:25.
[79] Luke 16:10.
[80] Anita Barany, "What Imaginary Door Is Blocking Our Progress" (unpublished article).
[81] *USA Today*, March 2, 2000.

CHAPTER FOURTEEN
[82] Proverbs 22:6.

[83] Luke 9:62.

[84] Luke 14:26.

CHAPTER FIFTEEN

[85] Marjorie Foyle, *Overcoming Missionary Stress* (Wheaton: EMIS, 1987), p. 130–135.

CHAPTER SIXTEEN

[86] Proverbs 2:11.

[87] Proverbs 22:3 Living Bible.

[88] Jerry White, "Five Commands for Business Ethics," *Discipleship Journal*, Issue 5, September 1981.

[89] Nik Mustapha Nik Hassan, "Shared Values Key to Better Productivity" (paper for the Institute of Islamic Understanding).

[90] Job 27:3–5.

[91] James A. Tebbe, "For Tentmakers: A Matter of Integrity," *EMQ*. January 1989, p. 48, 50.

[92] Mike McLoughlin, "The Ethics of Shrewdness: Term Paper for Marketplace Ethics Course." Regent College, Vancouver, BC, August, 1997, p. 2.

[93] Exodus 23:8.

[94] Proverbs 21:14.

[95] Myron Loss, *Culture Shock* (Indiana: Light and Life, 1983), p. 53.

[96] Robert L. Kohls, *Survival Kit For Overseas Living* (Chicago: Intercultural Press, 1979), p. 68.

[97] Proverbs 18:15 The Children's Bible.

[98] 1 Peter 4:12.

CHAPTER SEVENTEEN

[99] 1 Samuel 16:2.

[100] 1 Samuel 16:2.

[101] Luke 9:50.

[102] Robert Banks, and R. Stevens, Cit Article on the "Theology of Tentmaking."

[103] John Calvin, *The Institutes of the Christian Religion, Book III*. sec. 10, para. 6.

[104] Robert J. Kriegel, and Louis Patler, *If It Ain't Broke Break It!: And Other Unconventional Wisdom for A Changing Business World* (New York: Warner Books, 1991), p. 218.

[105] Stan Guthrie, *Missions In The Third Millennium* (UK: Paternoster, 2000), p. 26.

[106] 2 Chronicles 25:9.

[107] Proverbs 30:8–9.

[108] Matthew 6:24–26.

[109] J. Bonk, *Missions and Money: Affluence as a western Missionary Problem*, 2nd printing (Maryknoll: Orbis Books, 1991), p. 112.

[110] Mahathir Mohamad, *The Challenge* (Malaysia: Pelanduk, 1997), p. 15.

CHAPTER EIGHTEEN

[111] John Beckett, "Taking Faith To Work," an address given at the Kingdom Business Forum, Atlanta, GA, October 4, 2002.